sticks, seeds, pods & leaves

a cook's guide to culinary spices and herbs

To David + Vera,
Enjoy this fresh look at herbs, spices!

sticks, seeds, pods & leaves

a cook's guide to culinary spices and herbs

Includes more than 150 recipes

With Best Wishes

Ian Hemphill

Ian & Elizabeth Hemphill

with Philippa Sandall

Photography by Greg Elms

Hardie Grant Books

Published in 2007
by Hardie Grant Books
85 High Street
Prahran, Victoria 3181, Australia
www.hardiegrant.com.au

Sticks, Seeds, Pods & Leaves was previously published as Herbaceous and Spicery
in 2003 and 2004 respectively.

National Library of Australia Cataloguing-in-Publication Data:

Hemphill, Ian R. (Ian Rupert), 1949– .
    Sticks, seeds, pods & leaves : a cook's guide to culinary
    spices and herbs.

    Includes index.
    ISBN 978 1 74066 557 5 (pbk.).

    1. Spices. 2. Herbs. 3. Cookery (Spices).
    4. Cookery (Herbs). I. Hemphill, Elizabeth. II. Title.

641.338

Co-written with Philippa Sandall
Photography by Greg Elms
Styling by Celia Dowzer
Design by Ellie Exarchos
Typesetting by Megan Ellis
Index by Fay Donlevy
Photographs on pages 73, 132 and 140 by Joe Ashton;
    photograph on page 309 courtesy of istockphoto.com
Printed and bound in China by SNP Leefung

Every effort has been made to incorporate up-to-date information. The publishers regret any
errors and omissions and invite readers to contribute additional relevant information to
Hardie Grant Books.

10 9 8 7 6 5 4 3 2 1

To Rosemary Hemphill, who started it all.

contents

herbs

introduction

IAN: My earliest memories are of plants and fragrances. My parents, John and Rosemary Hemphill, owned a citrus orchard that metamorphosed into a plant nursery and ultimately became a pioneering herb and spice business known as Somerset Cottage. My mother was the first Australian to have a book published on herbs in 1959, and since that first title *Fragrance and Flavour* she and my father went on to write several more books on herbs and spices which were published in Australia and overseas. Numerous school holidays and weekends were spent helping Dad propagate cuttings, and picking lavender, lemon verbena, rose petals and scented geraniums for pot-pourri. After leaving school the lights of the theatre beckoned me and I enrolled at NIDA. Although I was not destined for a career on the stage, Liz cast me in her graduation play, love blossomed and we married at the ripe old age of twenty.

We worked in the family business for fifteen years, and while our three daughters were growing up Liz ran the shop at Dural on Saturdays, wrote a delightful children's book called *Your First Book of Herb Gardening* and made fragrant sleep pillows filled with herbs picked from the family garden at Dural. During this time I took thousands of visitors around the herb garden, gave lectures and answered myriad questions, a background that prepared me for writing it all down one day.

By the mid-1990s, our daughters had left home to pursue their careers and while walking on the beach one holiday Liz and I hatched the idea of opening a specialty spice shop in Sydney. Liz had become increasingly aware of the difficulty in finding many spices in cuisines that were becoming popular such as Moroccan, Middle Eastern and Indian, so why not have a shop that not only sells these, and also every culinary herb and spice imaginable?

So the seed for starting Herbie's Spices was planted. Herbie had been my nickname since school days; after exhausting a list of trendy names that never seemed right, we set on Herbie's. Liz is a natural family cook who always manages to make interesting meals taste delicious with the judicious use of herbs and spices. It seems that I am destined to be in a household where recipes are always under development. Liz now does what my mother did, constantly experimenting and creating recipes for our books, newsletters and spice packs.

In *Sticks, Seeds, Pods & Leaves* Liz and I demystify the world of herbs and spices in an accessible and approachable manner. We talk about the growing of herbs for keen gardeners, unlock some of the mysteries of the ancient spice trade and the way the unique flavours of spices develop after harvesting. It's a journey of discovery. We offer advice on buying and storing and show how herbs and spices can be used in everyday cooking.

ELIZABETH: When I met and fell in love with a young acting student in 1969, I didn't know that I would be marrying into Australia's herb and spice aristocracy. The ensuing 38 years have been both an apprenticeship with masters, and a love affair with herbs and spices.

I grew up in a household where the use of herbs was restricted to parsley in scrambled eggs and the white sauce for corned beef, and sage in the chicken stuffing – perfectly appropriate, if restricted, uses for herbs. My dad was addicted to black pepper and used it with such abandon that his dinner plate was invariably a uniform black all over. The discovery of the wonderful flavours and culinary excitement offered by all the other herbs and spices, not familiar in my childhood, has been an ongoing delight since I became a part of the Hemphill family.

My mother-in-law Rosemary Hemphill was an inspiration to me, as she was to so many Australian cooks and gardeners. So when it appeared that all of her books would soon be out of print, we decided, along with our colleague Philippa Sandall, to re-present all that valuable and valid information in an updated form, and *Herbaceous* was born. *Spicery* followed as naturally as night follows day and spice follows herb. We are delighted to see the two combined into *Sticks, Seeds, Pods & Leaves*.

Ian and I started Herbie's Spices in 1997. Many caring friends feared for our future at that time, but we have been amazingly lucky to have a business where we can indulge our passion and talk food all day with our customers! We feel deeply privileged that we are able to communicate our knowledge and experience through our shop, our annual spice discovery tours to India, and our books.

Ian & Elizabeth Hemphill

cook's notes

We believe cooking involves a certain amount of instinct and 'feel'. It's also a pursuit involving unreliable ingredients; for instance, do you have a big, juicy, hydroponic tomato, or are you using a drought-affected, not-too-juicy, but very tasty one? We all know that the behaviour of flour can change from one harvest to the next. The only totally consistent foods are those that have been highly processed.

Please don't feel too stressed about exact quantities for the recipes. If you find that you've emptied your flour bin and you're still 10 grams short, it doesn't matter. A medium-sized egg, or a large one? It doesn't matter. Perhaps you use one of those nifty metric cup measures, or perhaps you still use the breakfast cup that your grandmother always used. It doesn't matter. Should you put ten capers in the pasta sauce or sixteen? It doesn't matter!

The main thing is to enjoy discovering new uses for your herbs and spices, and to enjoy the flavours as much as we've enjoyed compiling these recipes for you.

*Note: All recipes include Australian tablespoon measurements (1 tablespoon = 20 ml).

equivalents for ingredients

capsicum — bell pepper
caster sugar — superfine sugar
coriander (leaves) — cilantro
cornflour — cornstarch
eggplant — aubergine
plain flour — all-purpose flour
prawn — shrimp
rocket — arugula
spring onion — scallion
zucchini — courgette

*Note: The term 'spring onion' is used to describe the non-bulbus fresh green onion (also known as a shallot).

conversion tables

oven temperatures	
°C	°F
140	275
150	300
160	320
170	340
180	350
190	375
200	400
210	410
220	430

Oven temperatures are expressed in Celsius (°C). If using a fan-forced oven, as a guide, reduce the temperature by 20°C.

volume

Metric	Imperial
50–60 ml	2 fl oz
75 ml	2½ fl oz
100 ml	3½ fl oz
120 ml	4 fl oz
150 ml	5 fl oz
170 ml	6 fl oz
200 ml	7 fl oz
225 ml	8 fl oz
250 ml	8½ fl oz
300 ml	10 fl oz
400 ml	13 fl oz
500 ml	17 fl oz
600 ml	20 fl oz
750 ml	25 fl oz
1 litre	34 fl oz

weight

Metric	Imperial
10–15 g	½ oz
20 g	¾ oz
30 g	1 oz
40 g	1½ oz
50–60 g	2 oz
75 g	2½ oz
80 g	3 oz
100 g	3½ oz
125 g	4 oz
150 g	5 oz
175 g	6 oz
200 g	7 oz
225 g	8 oz
250 g	9 oz
275 g	10 oz
300 g	10½ oz
350 g	12 oz
400 g	14 oz
450 g	1 lb
500 g	1 lb 2 oz
600 g	1 lb 5 oz
650 g	1 lb 7 oz
750 g	1 lb 10 oz
900 g	2 lb
1 kg	2 lb 3 oz

length

Metric	Imperial
5 mm	¼ in
1 cm	½ in
2 cm	¾ in
2.5 cm	1 in
5 cm	2 in
7.5 cm	3 in
10 cm	4 in
15 cm	6 in
20 cm	8 in
30 cm	12 in

ces

spice essentials

In spices, we are lucky enough to have a hobby that is also our passion, our business, and our livelihood ... and it's something that other people also find interesting. While green, leafy herbs are reassuring and familiar, there is an edginess about spices, a rawness, an element of danger that fascinates and lures.

Our friend Alan Saunders once commented that the difference between herbs and spices is this: herbs you can grow at home in your garden and on your window sill; spices you have to go out for. And the ancient traders went out for them in spades. They went out to the East Indies all the way from Holland, Portugal, England and Spain, out to the West Indies, out to China and India – out to fascinating, dangerous, foreign, exotic lands.

Two thousand years ago, most known spices were a luxury only the wealthy could afford. As new spices such as cinnamon were discovered, their origins were surrounded in mystery and fantasy by spice traders, who were keen to maintain their exclusivity and high prices. The spice trade was extremely lucrative, with single voyages yielding profits ten times the original investment, fostering a breed of swashbuckling adventurers who went on intrepid journeys of discovery to bring home these precious commodities. But had it not been for the fact that spices store well once dried, and can be readily transported and traded, there may never have been a spice trade at all.

The 15th and 16th century explorers Bartholomeu Dias, Vasco da Gama and Ferdinand Magellan were searching for faster and safer routes to the sources of spices when they went on their voyages of discovery. Christopher Columbus was sailing west to find a shorter way to the Indonesian archipelago when he bumped into the Americas and discovered allspice,

chillies and vanilla (as well as chocolate, tomatoes and potatoes). The spice trade was so significant by the end of the 16th century that The British East India Company was founded in 1600, and by 1602 The United Dutch East India Company, the largest corporation in the world in those times, was formed.

So what is it about these ancient commodities that continues to captivate the imagination, thousands of years after humans discovered that nothing quite titillates the taste buds like spices? What would those traders have thought if they could have gazed into a crystal ball and seen that all these centuries later, we are still seeking out these highly desirable prizes? How amazing and fantastic it is that, although they have remained unchanged in their own attributes and characteristics for millennia, they still relate perfectly to our modern cuisines.

In the 21st century we are all exhorted by every second lifestyle magazine to 'Spice up our lives'. Every town that aspires to being a beacon on the culinary map, holds a 'Hot and Spicy' food festival. Star chefs base their success on an ability to amaze the taste buds with their spice craft. Spices have made their way into more and more items on the supermarket shelves – not only hiding in traditional products like pickles and Worcestershire Sauce, but in mustard-seeded mayonnaise, poppy seed and cracked pepper water biscuits, lime and chilli salad dressings, ginger-spiced marmalades … the list is endless, and growing all the time!

Arguably, the most misunderstood aspect of spices is the vast and varied range of tastes they present to us, and that is the most likely reason we continue to find them so irresistible. Thinking of spices only in terms of 'hot and spicy' would be like thinking of colour as only red, and ignoring the amazing spectrum of hues that we encounter every day. It would be like thinking of music as middle C with no other notes!

As you read about each spice, you will discover that their attributes and personalities are as varied as the colours of the rainbow. They have the ability to create as many different taste sensations as all the works of the great composers have done with music. What makes spices really exciting though, is that to appreciate them fully you don't have to be the culinary equivalent of Rembrandt or have the genius of Beethoven. Everyone can use spices in everyday cooking, and with more practice, one can only look forward to more satisfaction.

So what are spices and what makes them so different from herbs? Broadly speaking, herbs are the leafy parts of edible plants and spices are generally the buds, bark, roots, berries, aromatic seeds and any other edible part of a plant (except the leaves) that is used, mostly dried, to flavour food. All encompassing isn't it? There's certainly more to spices than what you can find at a chilli festival!

While many uses for herbs require them to be fresh, the majority of spices are dried. This is because drying activates naturally occurring enzymes in spices that ultimately create their flavours. Vanilla beans are tasteless and odourless when harvested, black peppercorns are green and cloves are devoid of pungency when picked.

Nearly all seed spices have dried naturally on the plant by the time they are gathered, and nothing

grains of paradise

sumac

allspice

enhances the incredible complexity of flavours in a chilli more effectively than simply drying it.

Until a couple of centuries ago, spices were used only by the affluent. Just think that a collection of ingredients, used relatively sparingly by a minority of privileged diners should spawn such an enduring industry.

Spices are now so much a part of our lives that it would be hard to imagine a world without them. And next time you hear someone say 'I don't like spicy food!' just ask them if they like cinnamon donuts or vanilla ice-cream, which are both flavoured with spices. We don't think anyone will make such a claim after using the recipes we've given you in this book.

There are some myths about spices that need to be dispelled, here and now.

myth 1: spices mask the taste of rotten food

This misconception probably developed because it has always been desirable to enhance the flavour of very bland foods or make meats with strong flavours more palatable. For example, an old joint of mutton with overpowering lanoline flavours, benefits greatly by slow-cooking in a selection of aromatic spices. But using spices to disguise rotting ingredients is a different thing altogether.

Our interpretation is that this myth arose because journalists (who reputedly never let the facts get in the way of a good story), began to refer to this use of spices in somewhat colourful terms, feeding to their readers images of yokels gnawing at rotting bones on picturesque hillsides. The fact is that anyone so poor as to try and survive on rotting food (which although it may be relished as a delicacy by our dog, will most likely kill people) would not be able to afford spices anyway. And food poisoning is food poisoning, regardless of how many spices are added between the pot and the plate.

myth 2: spices are preservatives

This second myth has a stronger basis in logic, as many spices do possess anti-microbial properties, however we have never encountered a herb or spice that has preservative qualities *per se*. The most common forms of food preservation in ancient times were by dehydration and using salt or acid (usually vinegar) to preserve wet products. As salt and vinegar have extremely pervasive tastes of their own, the addition of spices helped to make foods preserved with them more palatable. The anti-bacterial qualities in garlic and mustard seeds were a bonus in the preserving process and even today, many manufactured food products owe their stability to the use of spices in conjunction with established preserving techniques.

buying and storing

Spices are agricultural commodities, and like any other food that is grown, harvested, processed, traded, blended, packaged, stored, distributed, sold and ultimately consumed, huge variations in flavour and appearance will occur. Once you have tasted food prepared with the very best quality spices, you will never again be dismissive about the importance of quality in spices.

Over the years, we've spent many hours in many factories and warehouses in many parts of the world, seeing what factors determine quality. Our purpose here is to pass that experience and knowledge on to you, so that you can differentiate between good and bad when you are buying.

Growing is naturally where it all begins. Soil, climatic conditions, plant varieties and harvesting techniques will all contribute to the quality of a spice; the problem is, that as a consumer you have almost no way of identifying any of these factors. Spices are now grown in many tropical and temperate regions around the world, and while conventional wisdom may indicate that the best spice is one grown in its country of origin, these days that is not necessarily the case.

Pepper vines are native to the south of India, and Indian pepper has a distinctive flavour characteristic that many pepper lovers prefer. However, black pepper from Lampong in Indonesia has light, lemony notes that have their own attraction while pepper grown in North Queensland, Australia, has a pleasing mild fruitiness that others prefer. So just like wines, spices can give us distinct varietal differences. Where country of origin can make a significant difference to the flavour of a spice, the spice seller should make some reference to this on the label. For instance, sweet paprika from Hungary has a different flavour profile to mild paprika from Spain. Each is equally good in its appropriate cooking application, it is just that they are different, which is why it helps in some cases to know where the spice came from.

The importance of processing after harvest will vary depending upon the spice. For most seed spices the process is relatively simple, whereas with vanilla it is highly complex and if it's not done correctly it could render the final product useless. Processing usually involves some sort of grading and cleaning. With whole spices it is very easy to see if you are getting some extra pieces of sticks and stones, all charged at the same price as the spice!

The flavours and aromas of spices are contained in the volatile oils held in their cell structure. A cinnamon stick may not have much aroma when you smell it; however, when you break it, the cells are ruptured and they release these volatiles, filling the air with the sweet fragrance of warm, spicy oranges. Volatile oils are destroyed rapidly by heat, and even a slight

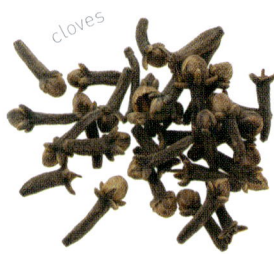
cloves

cinnamon

star anise

increase in the moisture content after drying will cause the oils in a spice to oxidise more quickly. So you can see that storage and transportation conditions also affect quality.

What has to be remembered is that all herbs and spices will deteriorate over time as the volatile oils gradually evaporate and the flavour and aroma dissipates. Don't be tempted to use twice the amount of a spice that is well past its 'best before' date, as this will only double the strength of the deep, base flavours and not compensate for the loss of fragrant, volatile top notes that have been lost.

The best advice when buying spices is to look for reputable brands that are packed in high-barrier packaging. This may be either clear laminate plastic with a re-sealable zip seal, or glass jars. When stocking your pantry, try not to buy quantities that are too large. You should definitely try to use a spice by the 'use by' or 'best before' date on the pack – don't keep it any longer, even if there is a little left.

Never buy cardboard or cellophane packs, although the lower price might be tempting. They allow the volatile oils to escape and oxygen to get into

the product, so it is already deteriorating by the time you take it home. It's false economy. Some people like the romantic notion of scooping out their spices from bulk bins, however these spices have been exposed to a considerable amount of air, insects and possible contamination from other ingredients stored in close proximity. Sadly, the result is an inferior flavour and shorter shelf life, so take home a photo of the charming shop full of open sacks, but buy your spices somewhere else.

For those who like to have herbs and spices on display in a spice rack, make sure they are positioned out of direct sunlight, and use the rack for either whole spices or your favourites, which are used frequently. When you spring-clean, don't hesitate to throw away any herbs and spices that have passed their 'use by' date. It's simply not worth it to add to a meal something with hardly any flavour left. When you work out the cost of herbs and spices and the small amount used in a recipe, they are really very economical.

We are often asked if spices should be stored in the fridge or freezer. Spices do not store well for long periods in the freezer. Also, when the spice is removed from the cold environment, condensation will form on the pack and that introduces moisture, something that accelerates deterioration. Therefore, if you want to keep a spice for a long time before you use it, the best option is to store it away from extremes of heat, light and humidity.

Another tip to make sure your spices last well is to avoid shaking or pouring the contents over a steaming saucepan. The steam will condense around the inside of the pack, and the moisture will make the spice go hard, or worse still, it may go mouldy.

When you're wondering whether your spices are still good to use, simply smell them and if you can detect some aroma and pungency in your ground spices, they should be alright. Have a little sniff of any spice you are adding (be careful if it's chilli), each time you cook with it. You will become very familiar with the aroma, and this helps you get a feel for what flavour is best to add and at the same time you will develop an understanding of good and poor quality.

If you want to check the freshness of whole spices, you will need to either break the piece (say for cinnamon sticks or cloves) or for a spice like nutmeg, scrape it with a knife or grater to release the aroma.

using whole or ground spices

Whether spices are used in their whole form, or ground to a powder, depends on the cooking method and the most effective way to get the best flavour out of them. A cinnamon stick may be added to fruit during stewing, so the flavour is infused and the liquid remains clear. If ground cinnamon were used, the liquid would be muddy-looking. However, when making a curry, mixing spices with flour for cakes and biscuits or rubbing spices onto meats before cooking, ground spices are always used so they mix readily with other ingredients, or impart their flavours more rapidly, having been crushed.

Some cooks say that you should always buy spices whole and grind them yourself. This is not a bad idea if you're not sure of the quality and freshness of ground spices. And if you're an infrequent user, whole spices have a longer shelf life than ground ones. On average, whole spices, when stored as suggested above, will last for three years while ground spices will start losing flavour after twelve to eighteen months. Good-quality, freshly ground spices are as flavoursome as those you have ground yourself, so if you use a lot of ground spice, don't be put off the convenience of ready ground.

Grinding spices yourself can be extremely rewarding, especially if you do them in a pestle and mortar, (the pestle is the bit you pound with and the mortar is the bowl), so the aromas waft up as you pound away. We are often asked if there are any good spice grinders as an alternative to a pestle and mortar. Sadly, spices vary so much in size, hardness, texture and oil content that it is nigh on impossible to find a domestic grinder that will handle them all. Seed spices, like pepper, can be ground in a normal pepper mill. Then again, you can use a coffee grinder, but electric grinders can generate excessive heat that can destroy some of the lighter volatiles, so don't over-grind. And if you don't want your coffee tasting of cumin and fenugreek, the easiest way to clean any grinder is to grind a tablespoon of rice in it. Rice flour is gritty and cleans the contact surfaces effectively while absorbing residual oils, leaving the mechanism quite clean. So when it comes to all those other spices, take heed of the trendy television chefs, and use the trusty pestle and mortar that has been a cook's most useful implement of choice for thousands of years.

roasting spices

Some cooks may tell you that roasting spices brings out the flavour. Wrong! Roasting spices *changes* the flavour. So in the same way that a slice of toast tastes different from a slice of bread, so a roasted spice tastes different from an unroasted one. Spices are roasted to create greater depth of flavour and robustness, often when used with red meats. The majority of Indian curries are enhanced when roasted spices are used; however, one would never roast cinnamon, allspice, nutmeg and ginger before adding them to a cake. We also prefer to use unroasted spices in fish and vegetable dishes as the more delicate, fresh-tasting top notes are still recognisable and complement these foods better than robust, roasted flavours.

Spices may be dry-roasted when they are whole or ground. Heat a heavy-based pan on the top of the stove until it is almost too hot to touch. (If it is too hot the spices may burn, turning them bitter.) Then put your spices into the hot pan and keep them moving so they don't stick or burn. When fumes begin to emanate and the colour starts to darken, they are sufficiently roasted and should be tipped out of the pan ready for use within a day or two. We do not recommend storing roasted spices for more than a few days, as after roasting the flavours deteriorate quite rapidly. Many cooks like to roast them whole for the same reason as buying spices whole. Similarly, good-quality, freshly ground spices will roast perfectly well.

spices found in popular cuisines

Countless books have been written on the nuances of many cuisines and the extraordinary variety of ingredients that contribute to their character. So it may seem a gross over-simplification to identify a combination of herbs and spices that represents the flavours perceived as dominant in a particular cuisine. However, the fact remains that for the majority of popular foods from different cultures there are certain herbs and spices, which, with the readily available ingredients of those regions, contribute to their unique character.

Therefore when the following herbs and spices are incorporated into even the most basic of meals (stir-fries, grills and curries) a flavour will be imparted that is reminiscent of that cuisine. The spices are shown in descending order, so the first ingredient is used in greatest quantity.

INDIAN: Coriander seed, turmeric, cinnamon, cumin, fenugreek seed and leaf, ginger, pepper, chilli, cloves, tamarind, cardamom and saffron.

MOROCCAN: Coriander seed, turmeric, paprika, cumin, cinnamon, ginger, cloves, pepper and chilli.

AFRICAN: Coriander seed, cumin, allspice, ginger, pepper and fenugreek seed.

MIDDLE EASTERN: Paprika, pepper, cumin, coriander seed, sumac, thyme, cassia, cloves and cardamom.

INDONESIAN: Coriander seed, cumin, fennel seed, cassia, turmeric, lemongrass, galangal, ginger, pepper (black, cubeb and long), cloves and chilli.

galangal

ajowan

bush tomato

MALAYSIAN: Coriander seed, cumin, fennel seed, cinnamon, turmeric, pepper, chilli, ginger and galangal.

THAI: Coriander leaf, kaffir lime leaf, lemongrass, green chilli, garlic, galangal and ginger.

CHINESE: Star anise, fennel seed, cassia, Sichuan pepper, cloves and ginger.

JAPANESE: Sansho (Sichuan pepper leaves), black sesame, mustard seed, salt, wasabe and various types of dried seaweed.

MEXICAN: Paprika, cumin, oregano, chilli and coriander leaf.

spice blending

There is enormous pleasure to be had by combining individual flavour characteristics to create completely different tastes. Spice blends are convenient and effective, and making your own combinations is simple with just a basic understanding.

Spice blending is an art as much as a science and every spice blender will have an individual approach to making a blend. The way of achieving a blend may vary considerably depending upon the user's requirements. A multinational food company wanting a spice blend to

use in fast food outlets will be concerned about cost, a flavour profile that does not offend anyone and uses readily available, consistent quality ingredients. In the mid-20th century, the majority of these blends were high in salt, sugar and monosodium glutamate. By the 1990s things had changed. Still high in salt, wheat flour as a filler kept the weight up and the price down, and free flow agents stopped the powdered blends going hard if kept for too long. Starches are still often used in spice blends, so consumers, especially those with gluten intolerence should always read the ingredients list on the label.

Like the people in your neighbourhood, spices all have different characteristics. Some are strong and could be even described as unpleasant when tasted in isolation. Others (like one of our favourites, cinnamon), are a delight to experience even on their own. In making a spice blend, we seek to create a different taste that can only be achieved by putting a particular combination of spices together. Sometimes a spice blend bears little resemblance to any of the individual spices used, in other cases a few characteristic spice flavours may dominate; for example, in mixed spice where cinnamon and cloves are often the first aromas one might detect. Although the following guidelines will help you make your own spice blends, there are really no rules as such and you can use your own creativity and instinct to create a range of different tastes.

The art of making a good spice blend is to bring a range of different tastes and textures together so they create an ideal balance that tantalises the taste buds. Just as when cooking a meal we balance the sweet, salty, sour and bitter taste elements, when combining spices we balance their different attributes. For this purpose, the spices are grouped into five basic categories: sweet, pungent, tangy, hot and amalgamating.

Sweet spices are those that have varying degrees of inherent sweetness and are associated mostly with sweet foods such as puddings, cakes and pastries. It is worth remembering, though, that these sweet spices have a role to play in balancing savoury foods as well. Sweet spices include cinnamon, allspice, nutmeg and vanilla.

Pungent spices are unmistakeable as they have very strong aromas that may be camphor-like and astringent. Spices such as cloves, star anise and the cardamoms fall into this category. Australian native herbs and spices such as bush tomato (akudjura) and wattleseed would be grouped here as well. The pungent spices are valuable because even in small proportions they contribute a freshness of flavour to food that may otherwise be lacking. Use all pungent spices sparingly; the chart at the end of this section indicates the proportions in which each of these spices should be used. This is an approximate guide only, as even within the pungent group, ground star anise for example is stronger than ground caraway seed.

However grouping still helps one gain an instinct for the relative strengths of different spices.

Tangy spices make an important contribution to the balance of spice blends in the same way that sourness is important in balancing meals. The astringency of tamarind is usually added at the cooking stage, as it is a messy spice to handle and would not blend readily with dry spices. However sumac with its fruity lemon-like freshness makes an excellent tangy addition to a dry spice blend, as does amchur (green mango) powder.

Hot spices, when added judiciously, can make or break a dish. This collection of relatively few spices is essentially responsible for the overused reference people make to 'spicy' food. Hot spices such as pepper and chilli stimulate the palate, causing the release of endorphins, those chemicals produced by the body that give us a sense of well-being. Spicy heat in food makes it appetising and often only needs to be used in tiny amounts to have the desired effect.

Amalgamating spices are often unsung heroes. They make a very important contribution to spice blends, which is often underestimated. There are only a few regularly used amalgamating spices, however they are found in the majority of spice blends. For example, with coriander seed it is almost impossible to use too much. Sweet paprika is similar in the amount you can use. Strangely sweet paprika is a member of the chilli family but it has no heat, and is used with gay abandon in the famous casserole Hungarian Goulash (see page 125).

The following chart on page 11 is a basic guide showing the most commonly used spices in the five groups just mentioned. The quantity in teaspoons at the bottom of each row gives an approximate indication of the proportion (by volume) that you would find in a typical blend. For example, a tasty meat seasoning to sprinkle on steak before grilling may contain:

2 teaspoons ground cinnamon
½ teaspoon ground ginger
1 teaspoon amchur powder
½ teaspoon ground black pepper
¼ teaspoon ground chilli
5 teaspoons ground sweet paprika
salt to taste

Note that although pepper and chilli are both hot spices, the relative differences in their flavour and heat strength makes some variation in quantity appropriate.

Simply remember that these proportions can be varied as you experiment and become familiar with the spices. The following suggested quantities are a good starting point, so keep this little table handy to help avoid disaster!

Don't panic if the spice mix or curry you made today answers to 'harsh' when you were hoping for 'mellow'. Spice blends round out and become better balanced after about 24 hours. So tomorrow the complexities will have amalgamated, smoothing off the rough edges ... providing, of course, all the proportions of sweet, pungent, tangy, hot and amalgamating spices were balanced in the first place.

Have fun with the many different blends throughout the book. We hope spices bring you as much enjoyment as they have brought us.

spices and their five basic flavour categories

SWEET

Allspice, Cassia, Cinnamon, Nutmeg, Vanilla bean

2 teaspoons

PUNGENT

Ajowan, Asafoetida, Bush tomato, Caraway seed, Cardamom, Cloves, Cumin seed, Fenugreek seed, Galangal, Ginger, Juniper, Licorice, Mace, Nigella, Star anise, Wattleseed

½ teaspoon

TANGY

Amchur, Sumac, Tamarind

1 teaspoon

HOT

Chilli, Mustard, Pepper

¼ teaspoon

AMALGAMATING

Coriander seed, Fennel seed, Paprika, Poppy seed, Sesame seed, Turmeric

5 teaspoons

hot chilli

ajowan

Trachyspermum ammi

An alphabetical listing of spices should surely start with a zing, and although little mouse-brown ajowan seeds may look rather uninspiring and don't make the front pages, just wait until you taste them! The flavour hit is surprisingly herbaceous, with a pungent thyme-like tang and a breath-freshening hint of camphor.

This is a spice that is more at home in the chorus line than under the spotlight. Ajowan hides amongst its more outgoing cousins, coriander, cumin, dill, fennel and caraway, which all belong to the same Apiaceae family (formerly Umbelliferae).

The plant itself resembles wild parsley, but the leaves aren't used for cooking – it's the small grey-to-light-brown seeds that pack the punch and are a commercial commodity. Native to India's northern areas, it also grows prolifically in Iran, Egypt and Afghanistan. In days gone by it was prized for its essential oil, thymol, used in mouthwashes, toothpaste and herbal medicines.

choosing and using

Because they are small, (about the size of a flea), ajowan seeds are usually available whole. If you want to grind them, do it only when you are ready to use the powder so that the flavour is the freshest it can be. But be careful – a light touch is needed with this peppery, fragrant spice so that it doesn't overpower the dish.

Store whole seeds in an airtight container, preferably away from the light. Light bruising just before using will release the oils and increase the flavour.

In India, ajowan adds a kick to savoury pastries and batters for bhajis and perks up pakoras and snacks such as bhujia mix, potato balls and breads including parathas and na'an.

These seeds have a strong affinity for starchy carbohydrates. A family favourite is a cheesy biscuit with ajowan seeds. Add the seeds to breads as well – a useful rule of thumb is no more than a teaspoon of whole seeds for every cup of flour.

As longer cooking mellows the flavour somewhat, you can add ajowan seeds with a more liberal hand to chutneys and pickles, and being small and chewable when cooked, you rarely need to grind them.

Try adding a few to a homemade whole grain mustard. If you want to spice up vegetables with this sassy seed, toss green beans, cabbage, pumpkin and just about all root vegetables in a little butter and ajowan, allowing about $1/4$ teaspoon whole seeds per cup.

- When you want the flavour of thyme with a slight peppery spiciness, add 1 teaspoon of whole seeds per 500 g meat in slow-cooked dishes.
- In savoury biscuits and pastries, simply add a few whole seeds after you have combined the butter (or margarine) and flour; or add 1 teaspoon ajowan seeds per 100 g butter to pastry when making meat, chicken or fish pies.
- If you're a dhal-fancier, stir in a few ajowan seeds, some cracked pepper and fresh chopped chilli halfway through the cooking time. In fact, add a little to recipes using beans, peas or lentils for that matter.

Ajowan combines well with chilli, coriander seed, cumin seed, mustard, paprika and most herbs and gives the Ethiopian spice blend known as berbere its distinctive flavour.

berbere spice mix

Berbere, an essential ingredient in the traditional stew called 'wat', can be somewhat explosive if you overdo the chilli. Try using it like a curry powder to make a tangy casserole with chicken, tomatoes and roasted capsicum strips. Or, sprinkle over beef, lamb or chicken when grilling or barbecuing.

2 teaspoons cumin seeds

2 teaspoons coriander seeds

1 teaspoon ajowan seeds

1 teaspoon whole black peppercorns

¾ teaspoon fenugreek seeds

½ teaspoon allspice berries

1 teaspoon ground ginger

½ teaspoon ground cloves

½ teaspoon ground nutmeg

½–1 teaspoon hot chilli powder (depending
    on your heat tolerance)

3 teaspoons salt

Lightly roast the cumin, coriander and ajowan seeds, the peppercorns, fenugreek seeds and allspice berries and then grind them coarsely in a pestle and mortar. Add the ground ginger, cloves, nutmeg and chilli (to taste) and blend thoroughly. Store in an airtight container and use within 3–4 weeks.

Makes about ¼ cup

sweet potato and ajowan loaf

Inspired by the delicious loaf in Anneka Manning's Good Taste Collection – *Baking* (Text, 1999).

400 g orange sweet potato,
    peeled and cut into 1.5 cm pieces

100 g butter at room temperature, cubed

450 g self-raising flour

pinch of salt

½ cup chopped continental parsley

2 teaspoons ajowan seeds

¾ cup buttermilk

1 egg, lightly whisked

extra flour for dusting

Preheat the oven to 200°C and lightly oil a baking tray. Combine the sweet potato with half the butter in a medium saucepan. Cover and cook over medium-low heat, stirring frequently, for 20–25 minutes until the potato starts to break up, the butter is absorbed and all the liquid evaporates. Mash until smooth. Set aside.

Combine the flour and salt in a mixing bowl and rub in the remaining butter until the mixture resembles fine breadcrumbs. Add the parsley and ajowan seeds and stir to combine. Stir in the buttermilk and egg then the mashed sweet potato. Add to the flour mixture and mix with a round-bladed knife using a cutting action until almost combined. Use your hands to bring the mixture together. Turn the dough onto a lightly floured surface and knead lightly for 1–2 minutes until smooth. Shape into a 20 cm round, about 3 cm thick and place on the baking tray. Use a sharp knife than has been dipped in flour to make 5 mm deep slits to mark into 8 wedges. Bake for 40 minutes until the loaf is cooked through and sounds hollow when you tap the base. Stand for 5 minutes before serving warm or transferring to a wire rack to cool.

Makes 1 loaf, and serves 4–8, depending on how hungry everyone is

african berbere paste

For more oomph than tomato paste, add a tablespoon or more of this paste with its hearty, spicy flavour to stews and casseroles. It will keep in the refrigerator for up to six months.

3 teaspoons Berbere Spice Mix (see page 14)
1 onion, chopped
2 garlic cloves, chopped
2 teaspoons salt
3 tablespoons red wine
200 g sweet paprika
1 teaspoon cayenne (or more to taste)
1¼ cups water

Roast the Berbere Spice Mix in a hot, dry pan for 1 minute, then process to a paste with the onion, garlic, salt and wine. Stir in the paprika, cayenne pepper and cold water.

Simmer gently over low to moderate heat, stirring constantly, for 15–20 minutes, until the onion is cooked. Taste and add more salt or cayenne if required. Cool, then spoon paste into a screw-top jar and cover with a film of oil.

Makes about 3 cups

roasted mushrooms with ajowan

This recipe is ideal for when those big flat field mushrooms are in season.

½–1 teaspoon chilli powder, depending
    how hot you like it
3 tablespoons olive oil
8 large field mushrooms, stems removed
2 cloves garlic, crushed
2 teaspoons butter, divided into 8 pieces
1 teaspoon ajowan seeds
sea salt
4 handfuls wild rocket
cracked pepper to taste

Preheat the oven to 150°C and lightly oil a baking tray or shallow ovenproof dish large enough to hold 8 mushrooms. Mix chilli with olive oil and set aside to allow the flavour to develop while you prepare the mushrooms.

Place a little crushed garlic and a piece of butter in the centre of each mushroom, then sprinkle each with just a pinch of ajowan and a little salt. Arrange the mushrooms face up on the baking tray and bake for 15 minutes or until heated through.

Rinse the rocket well under running water; drain, gently pat dry and toss with the chilli oil. Place a mound of rocket on each plate, and serve with two mushrooms and cracked pepper.

Serves 4 as a starter

allspice

Pimenta dioica

This unique berry causes all sorts of confusion. Firstly, Christopher Columbus named it *pimienta* (anglicised as pimento) because he thought it was a kind of peppercorn. Secondly, although the French name for allspice is *tout-épice*, there are those who insist on calling it *quatre épices*, despite the fact that this term is already used for two other spice blends. As if that wasn't confusion enough, there's also the 'bay rum' issue. Contrary to general belief, the fragrant oil used in 'bay rum' toiletries, does not come from *P. dioica* at all, but is distilled from the leaves of another member of the myrtle family, *P. racemosa*.

Also called Jamaica pepper, pimenta,
pimento, clove pepper, bay rum berry
Flavour and aroma pungent and
sweetly aromatic with hints of cloves
Flavour group sweet

It's easy to believe that there are several ingredients in allspice. Its tantalising aroma offers you delicious hints of cloves ... no, it might be a whiff of nutmeg ... but yet, it could be cinnamon ... or even a tiny dash of pepper? So, what more logical name for this chameleon berry than allspice?

The matte, reddish-brown berries are usually a little larger than a peppercorn. On the base are the remains of a small calyx, which looks a bit like a slightly frilled round scar. Berries are harvested before they ripen, as the ripe berries do not have the aroma.

From the same family as the clove tree (Myrtaceae), allspice was prized by buccaneers who kept bunches of the glossy, dark leaves on board ship in case of toothache on the high seas. Like the clove oil your dentist uses, allspice leaves contain eugenol, a numbing oil that can help to relieve toothache.

The tropical evergreen tree that produces allspice berries is native to the rainforests of Central and South America. The allspice we buy today, however, comes from plantations (called 'walks') in Mexico, Honduras and in Jamaica – the main exporter, where a happy marriage of climate and soil combines to produce the very finest berries.

The trees have smooth, silvery-grey trunks and an attractive spreading habit reaching an average height of 7–10 m. Driving over the green, fragrant hillsides above St Anne's Bay, Jamaica, you can see the walks of allspice trees, laden with berries, awaiting harvest. Because the trees are planted about 10 m apart to allow for the full canopy of fruit-bearing branches, there are no rigid plantation lines. Trees just seem to be growing where they please (or where the birds dropped the seeds) on a carpet of soft, lush grass.

At harvest time, the berries are cut from the tree rather than torn, as careless harvesting can damage trees and result in poor crops for years. Mechanised picking is very difficult because of the height and spread of the trees, so handpicking is common. Methods vary depending on the age of the picker. The young, small and agile climb up into the tree and cut the berry-bearing clusters, dropping them down to those waiting below. Older pickers use a blade on a long stick.

There are no culinary uses for freshly picked berries. The fresh berries are spread out to a depth of about 5 cm to dry on a black painted concrete platform about the size of a tennis court called a 'barbecue'. After a day in the sunshine, the farmers rake up the berries and lock them in a shed overnight to protect their precious harvest. This routine continues for up to two weeks until the berries are dried and the seeds inside rattle when you shake them.

choosing and using

Whole dried allspice will keep for three years or even longer when stored away from heat, light and humidity in airtight containers.

The flavour and aroma of allspice is most pungent when the berry has been ground to a powder. You can grind it in a spice mill, an electric coffee grinder, or a mortar and pestle as you need to use it. The freshly ground spice will be rich and dark brown and will keep for up to 12 months in perfect storage conditions.

The warm sweet flavour of allspice lends itself to a wide variety of foods from spiced tea mixes, cakes, and pies to mulled wine, benedictine and chartreuse. Today, most of the world's production finds its way into commercial products such as ketchup, pickles, meat pies and sausages.

Allspice's Spanish/Jamaican heritage is apparent in the fiery jerk pastes commonly used to marinate chicken, meat or dish before cooking. Jerk paste is made mostly of onions and chilli, but it derives its characteristic pungency from allspice.

Its sweet-yet-peppery flavour combines well with meat and can be found in Spain's escabeches and other preserving liquids, in moles in Mexico, and in fish casseroles in northern Europe. It is an essential ingredient in Scandinavia's pickled herrings and fish marinades, and in Germany is added to sauerkraut. Allspice is a popular seasoning for meat and rice dishes throughout the Middle East, and in North Africa's tagines.

The English also took readily to allspice, adding it to pickles, chutneys, soups, game dishes and corned beef, as well as stewed fruit, fruit cakes, pies and puddings. And an American pumpkin pie without it? Unheard of!

- For an aromatic peppermill mix, combine about a teaspoon of whole berries with black, white and green peppercorns.
- Spice up meatloaf or hamburgers with about ½ teaspoon ground allspice per 500 g ground beef.
- Add a few whole cracked berries to hearty soups (especially those with beans, root vegetables or tomatoes), a pot roast or a rich, winter-warming, beefy casserole.
- Delicious in fruit compotes – just add half a dozen lightly bruised berries to the syrup.

Stronger than cinnamon, darker in flavour than nutmeg, with more aromatic complexity than cloves, allspice makes an excellent ingredient in a mixed spice blend, along with other sweet spices like nutmeg, cloves, cinnamon, cassia and coriander seed.

And although the French might sometimes call allspice *quatre épices*, the actual sweet spice blend of that name combines ground allspice with smaller quantities of nutmeg, ginger and cloves.

The Maroons, Jamaican slaves who had escaped from the British in the 17th century, hunted wild boar, which they preserved by marinating and slow cooking. This technique became known as 'jerking' and is a Jamaican tradition still used for seasoning meat.

jerk seasoning

To season meat (ideally pork) blend the following 'Jamaican Jerk' spices together, with just enough dark rum to moisten. Coat the meat with the seasoning mix and set it aside in the refrigerator for about an hour to let the flavours develop before pan-frying, grilling, roasting or barbecuing.

4 teaspoons ground allspice

2 teaspoons medium-heat chilli flakes

1½ teaspoons ground ginger

1 teaspoon ground black pepper

1 teaspoon dried thyme leaves

Makes about ⅓ cup

tsire powder

Tsire powder is a West African blend of crushed, roasted peanuts seasoned with spices and salt and varying degrees of chilli powder. A traditional use for tsire is to dip meat into oil or beaten egg before coating with the nut and spice blend, and then cooking. We use it most with chicken, which is the traditional family-sized readily available meat source in the average West African village.

¼ teaspoon ground cloves

½ teaspoon ground allspice

1 teaspoon ground cinnamon sticks

1 teaspoon medium-heat chilli flakes

½ teaspoon ground ginger

½ teaspoon ground nutmeg

1 teaspoon salt

100 g crushed roasted unsalted peanuts

Combine all the ingredients in a mortar or food processor. Be careful not to process for too long or the peanuts will turn to mush.

Makes about 1 cup

classic rich spiced christmas cake

125 g glace cherries

125 g sultanas

125 g raisins

125 g crystallised pineapple

125 g glacé figs

125 g crystallised paw paw

125 g shelled almonds

100 g mixed peel

260 g plain flour

40 g self-raising flour

1 teaspoon salt

1 teaspoon ground cinnamon

1 teaspoon ground cloves

1 teaspoon ground allspice

1 teaspoon ground nutmeg

250 g butter

100 g raw sugar

125 ml good honey

5 eggs

juice and grated rind of 1 lemon

1/2 cup rum

Preheat the oven to 150ºC and prepare a 20 cm cake pan by lining with two thicknesses of brown paper (the inner layer oiled with butter). Prepare the fruit, halving the nuts and cherries and chopping the bigger fruit into smaller pieces.

Sift the flours and spices together, and mix a small portion of this with the fruit – just a tablespoon or two is enough, the fruit needs to be coated so that the pieces stay separate.

Cream the butter and sugar, add the honey, the eggs one at a time, the lemon juice and the grated rind. Fold in the sifted spiced flour, then the fruit, and lastly the rum. Pour the mixture into the prepared cake pan and bake for 3–4 hours or until the top of the cake springs back when touched in the middle.

Makes about a 2 kg cake

mulled wine

And for serious Christmas spirit, here's the mulled wine to serve with the cake!

3 cups red wine (cask wine will do)

150 g soft brown sugar

1 orange, skin left on, sliced

1 lime or lemon, skin left on, sliced

6 allspice berries

1 cassia stick, about 9 cm long

1 teaspoon sliced ginger

peel from half an orange

1 cinnamon stick, about 10 cm long

4 cloves

Place the wine, sugar, and fruit in a saucepan. Combine the whole spices on a chopping board and bruise with a rolling pin, being careful not to lose them off the edge of the board. Add the spices to the wine and heat (medium heat) until almost simmering. Reduce heat so that it does not boil and keep at this heat for 20 minutes for the flavours to infuse. Strain before serving.

Makes about 750 ml

borscht

This is a must-have when beetroot (beets) are in season. It's very satisfying to make this delicious soup from scratch by preparing your own stock if you have a rainy Saturday afternoon to fill. However, as we don't always have that luxury, there is a shorter alternative; that is, a litre of a good-quality beef stock. We know little boys who love this soup because they can pretend to be Dracula and tuck into what they like to call 'blood soup'!

Stock

1 tablespoon cooking oil

2 onions, sliced

1 clove garlic, sliced

2 pork spare ribs

4 cups water

2 teaspoons salt

1 teaspoon black peppercorns

1 bay leaf

6 allspice berries, lightly crushed

Soup

1 tablespoon cooking oil or butter

2 carrots, halved lengthwise and
    cut into 1 cm slices

1 potato, cut to similar size pieces as the carrots

120 g cabbage, shredded

60 ml tomato paste

2 teaspoons ground allspice

1 cup water

4 cups stock

3 large fresh beetroot, peeled

250 ml sour cream

2 tablespoons fresh dill tips, chopped

To make the stock, heat oil in a large saucepan and add onions, garlic and ribs. Brown for 2–3 minutes, then add the rest of the ingredients. Simmer for 1½ hours or until meat is tender. Strain and reserve stock.

To make the soup, heat oil or butter in a large saucepan and add carrots and potato, stir for 2 minutes over medium heat. Add cabbage, tomato paste, allspice and water, stirring to combine. Cover and simmer for 10 minutes, then add 1 litre stock and bring to a simmer. Grate the beetroot while stock is heating, then add beetroot. (It might look too dry, but the grated beetroot will soften and give up moisture as it cooks.)

Cook a further 10 minutes, and add more water if you feel it is too thick. Stir in the sour cream, reheat and serve garnished with dill tips. For a more elegant version, allow to cool a little, then purée before adding the sour cream.

Serves 6–8

amchur

Mangifera indica

Green mangoes are widely used as a souring agent in Indian and South-East Asian cooking. Amchur is a fine, off-white to pale grey, tart-tasting powder made from dried, sliced green mangoes. The colour can vary depending on quality and seasonality, as with many agricultural products. Its name simply means mango powder – *am* is Hindi for mango and *choor* powder. Spelling is variable, which is not surprising, as the original Hindi doesn't use Roman letters!

Also called green mango powder, aamchur, amchoor
Flavour and aroma fruity, acidic and lemony
Flavour group tangy

Early in the mango season in India, unripe green mangoes are picked and used fresh to add a tang to curries, and to have a supply for later. The surplus mangoes are peeled and sliced. The slices are sun-dried and sometimes dusted with turmeric to protect them from insects. You can sometimes buy dried slices in markets but most of the crop is ground to make amchur powder.

choosing and using

Sometimes amchur powder can be lumpy, but don't worry, just break the lumps up before you use it. From our experience, a fine pale powder has a fresher, livelier aroma and flavour than the darker ones. Stored in the dark, in airtight containers, amchur powder will keep its flavour for about 12 months. It has a fruity acidity reminiscent of lemon juice. To give you an idea of its tartness, 1 teaspoon of amchur has the equivalent acidity of about 3 tablespoons of lemon juice.

Amchur adds piquancy to curries, soups, dhals, pickles and chutneys (where you'll sometimes find whole slices), potato pakoras, samosa fillings and marinades for meat and fish, where it also shows off its tenderising qualities like lemon and lime juice. If you find yourself without a lemon, a pinch of amchur can be used even in Middle Eastern or Moroccan dishes to achieve a tangy freshness.

A good pinch gives a lift to stir-fried vegetables, prawns or chicken and to pulse dishes, and it can be sprinkled over fried Indian snacks in the same way that a lemon is squeezed over fish and chips.

Amchur complements fish and even adds a delicious tang to red meats when rubbed on with a little freshly ground black pepper before barbecuing, grilling or roasting. The powder adds a delicious lemony tang to spice blends and is a far more pleasant ingredient than citric acid, which is now much overused in many commercial spice mixes. One of our favourite uses for amchur is in chaat masala, a quintessentially Indian combination of salt and spices that we somewhat cheekily refer to as an Indian 'all purpose sprinkle'.

chaat masala

Chaat masala is a salty, tangy seasoning used in popular Indian snacks such as bhel puri, tossed though dry snack mixes and sprinkled on vegetables and fruit. Although the aroma of this blend is a little off-putting, cooking smoothes the edges and the result is delicious. Toss potato wedges in chaat masala before cooking for a tasty snack. When we make an Indian curry, we use a tablespoon or so of chaat masala instead of salt. It makes the flavour very authentic.

8 teaspoons ground cumin seed

3 teaspoons sea salt

3 teaspoons black salt

2½ teaspoons ground fennel seed

2 teaspoons amchur powder

2 teaspoons garam masala

1 pinch asafoetida

1 pinch medium-heat chilli powder

Combine all the ingredients and store in an airtight container.

Makes about ½ cup

pan-seared ocean trout on a bed of spinach and potatoes

A really good piece of fish doesn't need to be heavily spiced – save that for the shark (see Kuwaiti Fish Stew, page 43). We love the simplicity of this dish, which is so quick and easy at the end of a busy day.

2 pontiac potatoes, scrubbed

100 g silverbeet or English spinach, shredded

2 x 200 g pieces ocean trout (single serve chunks)

½ teaspoon amchur

freshly ground black pepper to taste

sea salt

1 tablespoon olive oil

Boil the whole potatoes in salted water until tender. Drain and set aside. Steam the greens until just wilted – add salt to taste and keep warm.

Dust both sides of the fish with the combined amchur, pepper and salt. Heat oil in a pan and fry fish for about 3 minutes on each side.

Cut the potatoes in 1 cm slices and place on the centre of two plates. Top with greens, then arrange fish on top. Serve immediately.

Serves 2

Roasted Mushrooms with Ajowan (recipe page 15)

Pan-seared Ocean Trout on a Bed of Spinach and Potatoes (recipe page 24)

tuna croquettes with curry leaf pesto

Carol Selva Rajah's croquettes are delicious as a main meal and ideal as finger food for parties. You can make them with canned tuna (in springwater) for the family and save the fresh tuna version for a special occasion. For more bite, add another green chilli to the pesto!

500 g tuna gently poached until the flesh flakes
4 medium potatoes, peeled and cooked
1 medium Spanish onion, very finely chopped
75 g finely diced spring onions
¼ cup roughly chopped curry leaves
2 teaspoons amchur powder
½ teaspoon chilli powder
½ teaspoon turmeric powder
2 teaspoons dry-roasted then pounded cumin seed
salt and pepper to taste
3 x 60 g eggs, lightly beaten
egg wash, made with 1 egg and 1 tablespoon milk
⅓ cup dry breadcrumbs for coating the croquettes
½ cup vegetable oil for frying

Curry Leaf Pesto
1 cup curry leaves, tightly packed
2 shallots, finely sliced
2 cloves garlic, chopped
3 tablespoons desiccated coconut
1 green chilli, seeded and finely chopped
⅓ cup lime juice
salt to taste (optional)

To make the croquettes, mash the tuna and the potatoes separately, then mix together thoroughly with the onion and spring onion. Add the spices and season with salt and pepper to taste. Add the lightly beaten eggs mixing well with fingers until mixture leaves sides of bowl.

Divide the mixture into about 16 equal portions and mould into croquettes about 5 cm long and 2.5 cm wide. Place the breadcrumbs in a shallow bowl then dip the croquettes into the egg wash and then into the breadcrumbs to coat each one thoroughly. Cover the croquettes with cling film and refrigerate for about an hour so that they will stay firm when you cook them.

Heat the oil in a heavy-based pan and fry the croquettes a few at a time until golden brown. Drain on paper towel before serving with the curry leaf pesto.

To make the pesto, place all the ingredients in a blender or food processor and process on high until the pesto has a thick, creamy consistency. Add more lime juice if required.

Serves 4 as a main meal or 8 as an entrée

asafoetida

Ferula asafoetida

Named because of its fetid aroma, asafoetida is
a resin that comes from a 3 m high plant rather like
giant parsley. When it is 'resin-ready', the stems
are scored close to the root, and the milky sap
that flows out quickly sets into a solid resinous
mass that dries into very hard, dark lumps about
the size of a cherry. These lumps are collected then
finely ground and blended with wheat flour to make
the spice easier to use. This process is repeated
time and again over a couple of months, by which
time each plant has
yielded up to around
a kilo of resin and the
root has dried up.

Asafoetida's smell is not very pleasant – after all, 'fetid' is part of its name, and whoever coined the nickname 'devil's dung' did so for a reason! But when it's added in very, very small quantities to food, it acts like a natural MSG and lifts the flavours of everything with it, while adding a tasty, earthy flavour reminiscent of onion and garlic.

Because of its resinous quality, the gum is almost impossible to grind, so it's usually blended with some form of starch to make it manageable. The natural colour of ground asafoetida blended with wheat flour is a neutral kind of brown, and it usually has a fairly grainy texture. Yellow asafoetida, which has a little turmeric added (making the flavour a little milder) as well as the wheat starch, is more finely ground and is often more popular with cooks because it amalgamates into the food more easily.

choosing and using

Asafoetida is most commonly sold as a powder as described previously. This can be added directly to the cooking pot in small quantities.

It is also sold in lumps about the size of a small walnut, and in this form, the image of devil's dung is never far away! To stop your entire kitchen smelling of asafoetida, consider placing your screw-top jar of whole asafoetida inside another screw-top jar. (Then bury it in the garden.) Often, an Indian housewife will press a whole piece of asafoetida resin onto the inside of her saucepan lid, where the aroma will contribute to the dish, then she'll remove it without ever actually adding it to the food.

This powerful spice lasts well over a year stored properly away from heat, light and air. Keep very well sealed to prevent the sulphurous flavour contaminating other ingredients in the pantry.

The first and most important point to make is that asafoetida should be used in **absolutely minute** quantities. A pea-sized amount is plenty for a large pot. Add it directly to cooking liquid.

Asafoetida is used mostly in Indian vegetarian meals, especially those traditional foods for Brahmin and Jain castes where onions and garlic are prohibited. The fetid flavour dissipates on cooking and adds a garlic-like flavour with onion overtones that enhances many dishes. Just as a little dried amchur is handy when you are out of lemons, so a hint of asafoetida will tide you over when the garlic bowl is empty.

The magic attribute of this pungent spice is its calming influence on the digestive system, so it's no coincidence that it's used in many bean, pea or lentil dishes. Indian sambar, vegetarian soups, pickles and chutneys, and seafood dishes rely on the subtle flavour of asafoetida, and it's almost essential as a seasoning for pappadums and naan bread.

Asafoetida combines well with spices like cardamom, chilli, cinnamon, coriander seed, fennel seed, ginger, mustard, pepper, tamarind and turmeric which makes it useful in curry blends and chaat masala.

sambar spice mix

Use this blend when you're cooking lentils. Make a slurry with oil and spice mix, cook for a minute, then add a couple of handfuls of chopped vegetables and water to cover. Once the vegetables are tender, add cooked lentils and you have a wonderful soupy-stewy concoction to serve over rice in a big soup bowl. The ultimate comfort food! More simply, you can just stir a tablespoon of the spice mix into a couple of cups of cooked lentils or split peas for a really delicious dhal.

9 teaspoons ground coriander seed

9 teaspoons besan flour (ground channa dhal)

3 teaspoons ground cumin seed

$1\frac{1}{2}$ teaspoons black peppercorns, coarsely ground

$\frac{3}{4}$ teaspoon salt

$\frac{3}{4}$ teaspoon ground fenugreek seed

$\frac{3}{4}$ teaspoon amchur powder

$\frac{3}{4}$ teaspoon brown mustard seeds

$\frac{3}{4}$ teaspoon mild chilli powder

$\frac{1}{2}$ teaspoon ground cinnamon

$\frac{1}{2}$ teaspoon Alleppey turmeric powder

8 curry leaves, dried and chopped*

$\frac{1}{4}$ teaspoon asafoetida powder (yellow or brown)

Combine all the ingredients and store in a screw-top jar.

Makes about 1 cup

*Note: Fresh curry leaves may be used if the sambar is to be made straightaway. Otherwise use dried curry leaves, as you can then store your sambar mix for up to 12 months.

delhi dhal

This dhal is unusual in that the main ingredient is red kidney beans rather than peas or lentils. You can spend hours of your precious time soaking and cooking the beans from scratch, or whip this cheat's 'can-do' version up in half an hour. Thanks to the asafoetida, you can have this for lunch with rice or Indian bread and spend all afternoon with your boss or your mother-in-law without any embarrassing moments!

2 x 420 g cans red kidney beans, undrained

1½ teaspoons Madras turmeric powder, or 1 teaspoon
    Alleppey turmeric powder

½ teaspoon chilli powder

½ teaspoon asafoetida powder

1 medium onion, grated or puréed

2 cloves garlic, crushed or puréed

1 tablespoon peeled and finely grated ginger

½ teaspoon chilli flakes

1 tablespoon ghee or butter

1½ teaspoons whole cumin seeds

1 teaspoon whole brown mustard seeds

1 x 420 g can chopped tomatoes

2 teaspoons ground coriander seeds

1 teaspoon ground cumin

1 teaspoon garam masala

2 tablespoons plain yoghurt

salt

a handful fresh coriander leaves

Combine undrained beans, turmeric, chilli powder and asafoetida in a saucepan. Heat to simmering, remove from heat, cover and stand to allow flavours to marry. Combine onion, garlic, ginger and chilli flakes in a bowl. Drain the beans, reserving 1 cup of the liquid.

Heat ghee, add whole cumin and mustard seeds and allow to pop for a minute. Then add in order, onion purée, tomatoes, ground coriander, cumin and garam masala, the yoghurt, the beans and the reserved liquid, stirring well after each addition. Add salt to taste and simmer, covered, for 10 minutes, stirring occasionally.

Garnish with a generous amount of fresh coriander leaves and serve with rice or Indian bread.

Serves 4–6

bush tomato (akudjura)

Solanum centrale

The Australian native spice suffers from an identity crisis. While the whole berries are known as 'bush tomato', once ground to a rough powder, the name reverts to the indigenous name of 'akudjura'. It's the ground form that is mostly used in cooking.

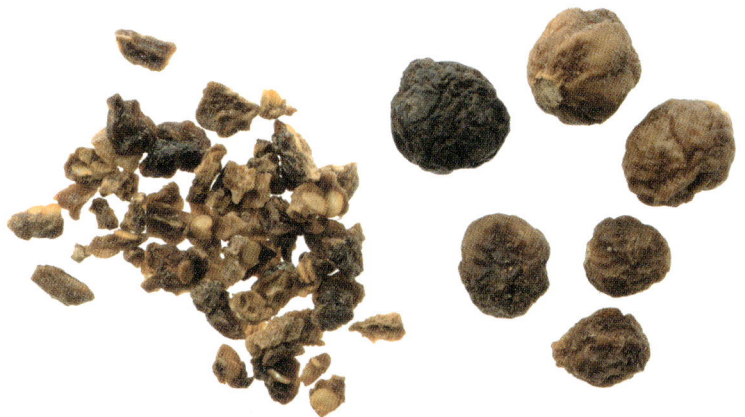

Also called desert raisin, akatyerre, ground bush tomato and akudjura in its ground form
Flavour and aroma intensely flavoured with an initial caramel and somewhat sweet taste followed by a lingering acidity
Flavour group pungent

Imagine a hot, dry afternoon in Central Australia – the sky is huge and deep blue, the landscape is mulga and scrubby sandhills, the earth is a searing paprika red. We are in the company of a small group of Aboriginal women ('the girls' in spite of their age), on Napperby Station, and they are collecting bush tomatoes from scrappy, almost-dead-looking small plants of the potato family.

They warn us not to eat the green fruit – they are left on the bush until they are shrivelled and almost completely dried, though a little sticky in the middle. We feel as though we have stepped back into an earlier millennium, in spite of the bright flowered dresses of our companions.

For Central Australia's Aboriginals, bush tomatoes have long been a staple. The women gather the ripe fruit in the wild, mash them with water to make a thick paste which they shape into large balls and leave in the forks of mulga trees or store on the roof of a humpy to eat later. But today they are more often than not hand-picking the fruit for Australia's growing Bush Food industry. The current annual crop is around 10 tonnes, which may not sound like a lot, but again it's one of those spices where a little goes a long way.

The edible bush tomato (probably better known in its ground form as akudjura) is a relative of the tomato and potato. This tough little perennial with its woody stems and sharp spikes at 5–8 cm intervals looks unlovable, yet it has a gentle side, with soft down-covered, greyish-green leaves. The violet coloured flowers, in the shape of a five-pointed star, with brilliant yellow stamens, are similar to tomato, potato or borage flowers. The unripe green fruit (around 2 cm in diameter) shrinks as it ripens, darkening to a reddish chocolate brown and developing a chewy raisin-like consistency.

Like many Australian plants, these members of the Solanaceae family thrive after bushfires, and in an area that has been ravaged by fire you can see the raisin-sized fruits everywhere, sprouting defiantly out of hard red soil in that prickly landscape.

However, don't head off to Central Australia to forage without an expert alongside. Like mushrooms, you have to know exactly what you are looking at! Kitty, our guide, pointed to what seemed like an absolutely identical plant to our eyes (*S. quadriloclatum*) and described it as, 'Cheeky! Emu and kangaroo eat' meaning it is extremely poisonous and should be avoided.

choosing and using

Bush tomatoes are pale tan to dark brown and have a fruity, caramel-like flavour and slightly tangy acidity. Another name for bush tomato is desert raisin, which gives you some idea of the tangy, acid, yet sweetly caramel flavour of this unique berry. Don't get too hung-up on exactly what colour it should be – like so many agricultural crops, each harvest can be a little different from the last one, depending upon weather conditions.

Because of the semi-moist consistency of a bush tomato, when it is ground, it tends to clump together a little bit. It's not a big problem, but just make sure that it is well broken up when you are stirring it through other ingredients.

Bush tomatoes are strong-flavoured and hardy. Although you may not wish to store yours in the fork of a tree in the garden, the general rule of airtight containers is not so very important for this Australian spice. However, once it is ground, airtight is good.

Use in small quantities to enjoy its unique flavour – too much will cause the bitter sharp notes to dominate and mask the fruity sweet caramel flavours.

The whole fruit (try just four or five to start) flavours stews and casseroles while the akudjura powder gives a baked taste to sweet biscuits and fruit crumbles. We have added 2 teaspoons of akudjura to an Anzac biscuit recipe with great success – and it makes them even more Aussie than ever!

- In a pestle and mortar, make a tangy spice mix including akudjura, black and white peppercorns, mustard seeds and salt to sprinkle over tomato sandwiches.
- For a different and delicious potato salad, toss cooked kipfler potatoes in a blend of mayonnaise made up as follows: to 250 ml mayonnaise add 1 teaspoon minced garlic, 2 teaspoons akudjura, 1 tablespoon well-chopped fresh parsley, and a good grind of pepper. Add a little prepared mustard if you want to, but make sure it doesn't drown the flavour of the akudjura.
- Roughly chop a few bush tomatoes and add them to a tomato-based pasta sauce or cook homemade tomato soup with 5 bush tomatoes per kilo of fresh tomatoes. Purée or strain the soup before serving.

Akudjura brings a tang and piquancy to many spice blends. For example, you can make a rub of ground akudjura powder, coriander seed, wattleseed and a little salt to dry-marinate red and white meats and full-flavoured fish such as salmon and tuna before grilling or barbecuing.

We first made the Egyptian spice blend, dukkah, about five years ago. Then we got to thinking, there's a possibility for a play on words with the good old Aussie word, 'ocker'. So we now have Ockkah, the Aussie dukkah. Besides the pistachios, hazels and sesame seeds, which are the body of the blend, there are akudjura, ground native pepperberries, and wattleseed to give a finished product with a fantastic nutty flavour and surprising sweetness from the native spices.

ockkah

3½ tablespoons hazelnuts
3 tablespoons pistachio nuts
9 teaspoons white sesame seeds
6 teaspoons whole coriander seeds
4 teaspoons akudjura
1 teaspoon wattleseed, roasted and ground
pinch ground native pepperberry
salt to taste

Roast the hazelnuts and pistachio nuts, then chop them into small dice in a food processor.

Toast the sesame seeds in a dry pan until golden brown. The coriander seeds may be roasted whole and then ground, however we find the flavour is lighter when plain ground coriander seeds are used.

Blend all the ingredients together and store in an airtight container (if you don't eat it all at the next sitting).

Makes about 1 cup

fresh oysters with bush tomato dressing

This wonderful recipe from Raymond and Jennice Kersch was first published in *Edna's Table* (Hodder Headline Australia).

1 long cucumber
½ cup dry white wine
2 tablespoons akudjura
1 tablespoon oil
250 ml good-quality light mayonnaise
24 fresh oysters
salt and pepper to taste

Roughly chop three-quarters of the cucumber and place in a saucepan with the white wine. Cook at a strong simmer until the wine has almost evaporated, leaving the cucumber softened and very moist. Purée the cucumber in a blender.

Fry the ground bush tomato in the oil until lightly browned to enhance the flavour.

Blend the puréed cucumber with the ground bush tomato and mayonnaise, then stir through the remaining cucumber, diced into 1 cm cubes.

Season to taste and serve in little ramekins with the oysters.

Serves 4 as an entrée, if you can stop at 6 oysters each

tasty pumpkin bites

Serve with drinks, at a picnic, or as a luncheon vegetable dish. Queensland blue pumpkin is ideal for these tasty bites, but butternut is fine.

500 g pumpkin, peeled and seeds removed
1 cup Ockkah (see page 32)
olive oil (spray is easier)

Preheat oven to 180°C. Cut the pumpkin into pieces approximately 3 cm square. Pour the Ockkah into a bowl and roll the pumpkin squares in it, one at a time.

Lightly oil an oven tray, place the pumpkin squares on the tray and lightly spray with a little more oil. Bake for 15 minutes, or until pumpkin is just tender but not falling apart. Leave to cool a little before serving as finger food.

Serves 2–3 as a vegetable accompaniment, 4–6 as party nibbles

caraway seed

Carum carvi

The first time we saw caraway growing in any
quantity was at the Spices Research Board farm
outside Ahmedabad in the Indian state of Gujerat.
This farm specialised in seed spices such as
fennel, fenugreek, ajowan, dill and caraway, and the
fields of these plants in bloom, with a sea of
delicate, hazy white and yellow flowers,
was as pretty as any
English country garden.

Also called caraway fruit, Persian caraway, Roman cumin, wild cumin
Flavour and aroma sweetly pungent, with hints of anise and an initial mintiness; warm and very individual, not to everyone's taste
Flavour group pungent

Over a concrete floor, a low shade-providing roof had been constructed from chicken wire and straw from previous seed harvests, and from this roof hung many bunches of caraway, flowers down, so the seeds could fall onto the concrete floor and be swept up. Nearby, in the lukewarm breeze created by an old electric fan, which somehow looked strangely modern in this pastoral setting, two young women winnowed the seeds from one basket to another to remove sticks and chaff.

Although we call them seeds, those crescent caraway shapes are actually the fruit of the plant. Each 'seed' is half the fruit and at first glance even the most experienced foodie can confuse caraway with its cousin cumin, unless the seeds are side by side. Both are slightly curved, with ridges or grooves running lengthwise, although caraway is a much darker shade of brown.

choosing and using

It is best to buy whole caraway seeds, because once they're ground, the flavour will begin to diminish. Having said this, it must be remembered that caraway has a strong and distinctive flavour, and the loss of these characteristics, once the seeds have been ground, would be pretty slow. Caraway seeds should be dark and clean, and should be kept away from direct light in an airtight container.

Back in Shakespeare's day caraway was a common seasoning for food and an essential ingredient in potions to prevent lovers from straying! The proof was apparently in the pudding – well, at least in the bread. Pigeon fanciers used a bread heavily textured with caraway to ensure their pigeons came home to roost.

With its warm, fresh fennel and anise notes, caraway seed can be an acquired taste on its own, but its culinary versatility is unquestioned and it even transforms cabbage (a vegetable that begs for transformation). Throughout Europe it provides the characteristic flavour in rye breads, seed cakes, goulash, sauerkraut and coleslaw for example. It is an appropriate addition to many potato dishes and root vegetables and is added to some cheeses such as Munster, where fresh anise and fennel notes help to balance the fatty richness and robust flavours, especially those of smoked cheeses. Try blending a little caraway into cream cheese or add a (very) few seeds to a cheese and onion flan.

Fruit with cores, such as apples, pears and quinces, marry well with caraway. Try sprinkling a little ground caraway over while they're baking, or add to a crumble mix for the topping.

Always bear in mind the pungency of caraway, and use a light hand. Many people have been turned off it for life after encountering a seed cake too heavily flavoured with caraway. If in doubt, grind the seeds so that the flavour is less direct and more gently distributed through the dish.

The seeds provide an aromatic essential oil, which is an ingredient in gin, schnapps, kummel and aquavit. Don't be misled here – *kummel* is German for cumin, but it is caraway that flavours the liqueur kummel.

Used judiciously, caraway is something of a secret success factor in many spice blends combining well with allspice, cardamom, cinnamon, coriander seed, cumin seed, fennel seed, ginger, paprika and turmeric. It's an important addition to that fiery Tunisian paste, harissa, and its pungency adds subtle depth to the best blends of India's garam masala. You will also find it in tandoori spice blends, satay spices and that Moroccan specialty, ras el hanout, where in an ingredient listing of 22 different spices, no one flavour dominates.

In experimenting and developing our own blends at Herbies, we have used it to great effect in a special East–West fusion blend we call 'Balmain & Rozelle Spice' (known overseas as Sydney Spice) which we originally developed for a bit of fun a few years ago to reflect the character of our local area.

As Balmain was originally a working class 'blue-singlet' area, it was essential to have an earthy base to the blend, and this was provided by a combination of turmeric, cumin and caraway. Australian lemon myrtle, once prolific in the area, was a must, and we built the top notes of the blend from the Asian and Moroccan flavours so well employed by the trendy sidewalk cafés of Balmain and Rozelle.

This tongue-in-cheek blend was an instant success, and it adds a delicious taste to chicken, fish and lamb when sprinkled on to the meat about 10 minutes before cooking, whether grilling, barbecuing or baking. Sprinkle a little into stir-fried vegetables while cooking and then add a little coconut milk, or simply toss new potatoes in butter and Balmain and Rozelle Spice – it's a true all-rounder.

growing

This delicate plant with lacy, frond-like foliage, has summer-blooming flowers that appear in the second year. The flowers themselves are so tiny that the flower umbel almost looks like the skeleton of a flower head even when in full bloom. When the flowers die, they are followed by fruit or capsules that explode when ripe, scattering the dark brown, crescent-shaped, aromatic, versatile seeds.

This self-seeding annual can grow to 60 cm in a sunny, sheltered position in the garden. If you want to grow caraway, take yourself off to the local nursery and buy seedlings, as the germination failure rate is very high with seeds. Plant seedlings in late spring in medium-textured, well-drained soil about 20 cm apart. Fertilise for best results. If you are determined to start from scratch, sow seeds in early spring in the garden, again about 20 cm apart. Caraway seedlings do not like being moved, so there's no need to start them in seed boxes. However, they are perfectly happy in a pot as long as it's in a sunny, sheltered spot, but please remember to provide water. And to fertilise. Whether in a pot or garden bed, caraway's decorative tiny white flowers tend to attract beneficial insects.

This is one plant that you want to go to seed. Let the minute, white, umbrella-like flower heads fade and the petals fall, so that the tiny aromatic fruit or capsules that hold the seeds will form.

Caraway Coleslaw (recipe page 38)

Kuwaiti Fish Stew (recipe page 43)

drying

In autumn, cut the heavy flower heads off before they drop. Caraway needs to be harvested in the very early morning while the dew is still condensed on the fragile umbels; once dry, the seeds will scatter all over the garden as you try to collect them.

Spread the flowers out to dry on sheets of paper in a warm, well-ventilated area with some direct sunlight. The seeds are ready to store when the fruit falls away easily from the shrivelled flower heads if given a light shake. Sieve out any pieces of stalk and pack the seeds into airtight containers.

balmain and rozelle spice

Use fresh kaffir lime leaves and coriander if you are using the blend immediately. Otherwise use dried.

6 teaspoons finely chopped fresh kaffir lime leaves (or
    1 tablespoon dried)
3 teaspoons finely chopped fresh coriander leaves
6 teaspoons turmeric powder
7 teaspoons ground cumin
6 teaspoons dried lemon myrtle leaves, ground
5 teaspoons ground ginger
2 teaspoons medium-heat chilli flakes
1 teaspoon ground galangal
1 teaspoon ground caraway
2 cloves garlic, crushed
salt to taste

Combine all ingredients and store in an airtight container if you are not using immediately.

Makes about 1 cup

tunisian tabil-style condiment

We keep a jar of this in the fridge and slather it over barbecued meats and baguettes with cold roast lamb. You can put all the ingredients in the blender for a smoother paste, but we prefer the chunkiness of the hand-pounded mortar and pestle version. This will keep in the fridge, covered, for a couple of weeks.

1 large sweet red capsicum, peeled
1 fresh red chilli about 10 cm long
3–4 cloves garlic, peeled
1½ teaspoons ground caraway seed
3 teaspoons chopped coriander leaves
½ teaspoon mild paprika
½ teaspoon salt
a good grind of pepper

Peel the capsicum by holding over a flame until the skin burns and blisters, or soak it in very hot water for a few minutes until the skin loosens. Cut the chilli into lengths, remove seeds, then drag a sharp knife across the flesh to remove it from the tough skin.

Finely chop the peeled garlic, capsicum and chilli, then mash vigorously with all the other ingredients in a pestle and mortar.

Makes about 1 cup

caraway coleslaw

Lighter and brighter than the original coleslaw, this crispy salad leaves a wonderful refreshing tang.

120 g tightly packed, very finely shredded cabbage, outer leaves discarded and spine removed

1/2 red capsicum, seeds removed and finely chopped

3–4 cm long red chilli, finely chopped (more or less to taste)

1 small clove garlic, crushed

3 teaspoons white wine vinegar

salt and pepper to taste

1 teaspoon caster sugar

1/2 teaspoon sweet smoked paprika

1/2 teaspoon ground caraway

1/4 teaspoon whole caraway seeds

Dressing

1 tablespoon sesame oil

1 tablespoon sour cream

Combine the shredded cabbage, chopped capsicum and chilli in a bowl. In a small jug, mix the garlic, vinegar, salt, pepper, sugar, paprika and caraway. Stir into the coleslaw and leave to stand for at least 15 minutes.

To make the dressing, whisk the sesame oil and sour cream together and fold through the salad just before serving. The oil and cream may tend to curdle, but the flavour is worth it!

Serves 2 as a side salad

root vegetable tagine

Finely slice the vegetables into rounds and serve this tangy tagine over couscous.

1 tablespoon mild paprika

1 tablespoon ground coriander seed

1 teaspoon cinnamon

salt and pepper to taste

1 or 2 caraway roots, peeled and sliced

1 swede or turnip, peeled and sliced

2 parsnips, peeled and sliced

3 carrots, peeled and sliced

1 tablespoon virgin oil

1 x 400 g can tomatoes

2 cups vegetable stock

Combine the spices with the salt and pepper and toss through the root vegetables. Heat the oil in a heavy-based pan or casserole, add the root vegetables and cook gently for 5 minutes. Add the tomatoes and enough stock to cover, stir, then cover with a lid and simmer for 30 minutes or until the vegetables are tender (this will depend on how finely you have sliced them).

Serves 4

cardamom

green cardamom *Elettaria cardamomum*

brown cardamom *Cardamomum amomum*

Cardamom has a eucalyptus-like aroma that adds a delicacy and freshness to curries like no other spice, and complements sweets and fruits as well. In southern India, pepper is the King of Spices, and cardamom is the Queen.

There is a completely different variety of cardamom, brown cardamom (*Cardamomum amomum*) that you may come across, and it should never be used as a substitute for the green cardamom we are referring to here.

Native to the tropical forests of the western ghats of southern India and Sri Lanka, cardamom absolutely thrives in warm humid areas at altitudes ranging from around 900–1370 m. During one of our Spice Tours, we visited Kerala's gentle Cardamom King, Mr Jose, in what are called the 'Cardamom Hills' just inland from Cochin. His plantation looks like a dense jungle as the forests aren't cleared – perennial cardamom prefers the canopy's shade. The locals boast that it's the only truly environment-friendly crop! Cardamom plants look rather like tall clumps of ginger, but what makes them different is that the flower stems grow out from the base and the pods form on these stems, literally only centimetres above the ground.

The green pods are picked before fully ripe (ripe pods tend to split) and kiln dried. On Mr Jose's farm, there was a huge wood-fired furnace manned by an energetic, wiry-framed octogenarian. Upstairs from the furnace room was a drying area with a slatted floor covered with wire mesh, and drying frames with wire mesh bases. This allowed the hot air to rise and circulate around the trays of cardamom pods, which dried within 24 hours. Down the hallway, we heard a rhythmic sound, like gentle waves breaking on pebbles, and discovered about a dozen women sitting and winnowing the dried pods in slightly elliptical wicker trays to remove any remaining stems or pods that had burned or split during drying. This timeless image has never left us.

Cardamom is an expensive spice, and thus a valuable crop. Today there are cardamom plantations in Guatemala, El Salvador, Costa Rica, Tanzania, Sri Lanka, Indo China and Papua New Guinea, but it's generally accepted that the best comes from Guatemala and India. However, virtually all of India's production is sold to its domestic market. As with all agricultural products, it's a risky business and the 'best producer' award can vary from season to season depending on all those conditions that combine to produce bumper harvests one year, and crop failures the next.

choosing and using

It is generally accepted that cardamom pods with a bright green colour are superior, so it's hard to believe that only a generation ago, it was considered desirable to soak the pods in hydrogen peroxide or sulphur dioxide to make them white. Perhaps it was so that the pods would not discolour as they aged, so that consumers could not guess how old they were. Green pods will fade to yellow and eventually to pale brown as they age, especially if exposed to light.

Choose even-coloured, lime green cardamom pods, and keep them in a cupboard unless you want to see them fade very quickly. Inside the tough, papery shell are about a dozen hard, slightly sticky, black seeds. These are the real essence of the cardamom pod, as the skin has no flavour at all. It is possible to buy seeds already removed from the pods, and these will keep their flavour for a couple of years if stored in a good airtight container.

Powdered cardamom is often the whole pod, shell and all, ground to a powder. Better quality ground cardamom is purely ground seeds, and this will have a hint of pinkness throughout the blackish powder. Buy this in small quantities as you require it, or grind your own.

You can lightly dry-roast the cardamom pods over a medium heat before you remove the seeds from the pods, although it's not essential. Be careful not to include the membrane when you take seeds for grinding. An electric mill will do a fast job for you, although the heat generated will steal a little of the flavour as payment for the convenience. Using a pestle and mortar will be satisfying, and you can pound just the amount you need.

The strong camphor-like flavour earns cardamom a position among the pungent spices and it is therefore used in small quantities. Many recipes require a bruised cardamom pod – you can achieve this with a gentle thump with a rolling pin, or pressing down firmly with the flat side of a knife to burst some of the volatile oil-containing cells. This just allows the flavour to amalgamate more readily with the other ingredients. You can leave the whole pods in when you serve your curries – those who love cardamom will merrily crunch them up, and those less excessive will leave them on the side of the plate.

The pods, seeds and ground seeds are used extensively in all sorts of Indian food, both sweet and savoury, although we stayed in one international hotel in India where the chef said management had decreed that no cardamom was to be used because it was too expensive. Cardamom is also widely used in Egypt, and it was the Egyptian preference for green pods for their coffee that changed the commercial habit of bleaching the pods.

As the name Queen of Spices suggests, cardamom, especially in its ground form, goes particularly well with desserts and fruits. It is traditional in Danish pastries, and popular in Scandinavia (see Margaret Fulton's Sour Cream and Cardamom Cake on page 42). All it takes is a few pods to transform something simple into something special. Include a bruised pod or two in the syrup when poaching apples, pears or stone fruits. Or sprinkle a little sugar and ground cardamom over a halved grapefruit for breakfast or dessert.

- In desserts and baking, add a little ground cardamom to custards, junkets and ice-cream, or in a pastry mixture just before adding the liquid; use it in gingerbread, in coffee cake, in fruit dishes and in rice pudding.
- Add ground cardamom seeds to a curry for a 'high' fresh note to balance with the deep spicy flavours and the chilli heat. And always put a few bruised pods in the rice when you are cooking rice to accompany a curry or a North African stew.
- Make a spiced coffee by adding one or two bruised pods to the plunger before pouring the water over.

Cardamom combines well with allspice, caraway seed, chilli, cinnamon, coriander seed, cumin seed, fennel seed, ginger, paprika, pepper, star anise and turmeric. It is an absolutely essential component of spice mixes such as baharat, garam masala, ras el hanout, tagine spice blends, Indian curry powder blends, and in many other forms of Indian cooking from rice dishes to desserts and confectionary.

persian spice blend

This is an exotic and aromatic blend of ground spices, which can be used directly on seafood or meat before cooking, or blended with flour as a base for casseroles and stews. We like to coat pieces of swordfish with the spice mix and pan-fry them with a little olive oil, to serve with vegetables.

2 teaspoons black peppercorns, lightly ground

2 teaspoons ground cumin

2 teaspoons turmeric powder

1 teaspoon ground green cardamom seeds

1 teaspoon amchur powder

salt to taste

Combine all ingredients and, if not using immediately, store in an airtight container away from direct light.

Makes about 2 tablespoons

margaret fulton's sour cream and cardamom cake

From one of Australia's national living treasures, a recipe from Finland. Moist and richly flavoured, this cake can be made easily using a simple mixing bowl and wooden spoon. You can freeze this cake – and it microwaves back to life perfectly!

2 eggs, lightly beaten

500 g sour cream

330 g caster sugar, plus extra for dusting

3 drops almond extract

450 g plain flour

1 teaspoon bicarbonate of soda

1 teaspoon ground cinnamon

1 teaspoon ground cardamom seeds

$1/2$ teaspoon salt

Sour Cream Icing

160 g caster sugar

1 tablespoon sour cream

Preheat oven to 180°C and grease and sugar-dust a 23 cm kugelhopf, bundt or deep cake tin.

Place eggs, sour cream, sugar and almond extract in a large bowl and, using a wooden spoon, stir until well combined. Sift together flour, bicarbonate of soda, spices and salt, then stir into egg mixture until just smooth. Pour cake batter into prepared cake tin and bake for $1\frac{1}{4}$ hours, or until a cake tester withdraws clean. Stand cake in tin for 10 minutes before turning out onto a wire rack to cool.

Meanwhile, sift icing sugar into a bowl, then stir in sour cream to form a thick icing. Spoon a little icing over the top of cake, allowing it to drip down the sides.

Serves 6–10, depending on the size of slices

kuwaiti fish stew

This easy recipe, given to us by friends from Kuwait, uses black limes. These dried limes are actually light tan to dark brown in colour and have the most wonderful citrus-like fermented flavour, which complements fish and chicken dishes. Make a few holes in the skin of the black lime with a skewer or fork and leave in the pot during cooking. Try using one in the cavity of poultry while it is roasting.

6 tablespoons vegetable oil

2 medium onions, chopped

3 teaspoons crushed garlic

1 large green chilli, seeded and chopped

1 bunch fresh dill, leaves roughly chopped

1 bunch fresh coriander leaves, roughly chopped

3 tomatoes, chopped

2–3 tablespoons tomato paste

2 whole black limes, pierced with a skewer in a few places

2 tablespoons Persian Spice Blend (see page 42)

1 teaspoon salt

2–3 cups water

4 fillets fish (choose a firm white-fleshed fish)

2 tablespoons plain flour

Heat 3 tablespoons of the vegetable oil in a large saucepan and sauté the onions until cooked but not browned. Mix in the garlic, chilli, dill, coriander, tomatoes, tomato paste, black limes, 2 teaspoons of the Persian Spice Mix and the salt. Add 2 cups water, stir, cover and keep warm while preparing fish.

Sprinkle the remaining spice mixture over both sides of fish and dust with flour. Heat the remaining 3 tablespoons of oil in a large pan and fry the fish lightly on both sides.

Transfer fish to the saucepan. Add more water if needed to cover fish. Simmer gently for 15–20 minutes until fish is cooked. Serve with rice.

Serves 4

brown cardamom is no substitute for green

Don't be confused when following your Asian and Indian cookbooks – a reference to cardamom pods will always mean green unless the writer specifically asks for brown. Never substitute brown for green! Brown cardamom (also called bastard cardamom, black cardamom, elaichi, and winged cardamom) is quite different from green, and gives a delicious smoky taste to marinades for tandoori-style cooking. It goes well in butter chicken. The pods are dark brown, oval and about 2.5 cm long. When the whole pod has been cooking for some time, the skin tends to lift a little and can look a bit like wings. This is why it's not a bad idea to remove brown cardamom pods before serving the meal so that your guests don't think you've cooked a cockroach!

chilli

mild *Capsicum annum*

hot *C. frutescens*

fruity *C. baccatum*

extra hot *C. chinense*

hairy leaved *C. pubecens*

Although there are five main species, there are hundreds of varieties as chilli plants are constantly hybridising. But all of them descend from the original ones discovered by the Spanish when they found the Americas.

Around 90 per cent of chillis belong to a species called *Capsicum annum*. We know now that what seems very hot to the uninitiated is seen as quite mild to the chilli addict, so one can only imagine the burning lips and streaming eyes of the Conquistadors when they first tasted chilli! It's lucky that they had time to learn to appreciate it so that they happily carried the first seeds back to Europe.

Birds snacked on the ripe fruits and did a wonderful job of carrying the seeds far and wide. The warming bite and delicious capsicum taste was eventually enthusiastically embraced by nearly every nation on earth, which is why you'll find some form of capsicum or chilli in nearly every cuisine. As they spread, climatic differences led to changes in the size, flavour and shape of the fruits, so that now a chilli from Mexico is quite different to one from India or Spain.

We prefer not to use the term chilli pepper, as it tends to cause confusion and, indeed, muddy the water somewhat. In Spanish, pimento means pepper, however, because they mistook allspice berries for actual peppercorns, the Spanish explorers called these berries pimento. So now we have:

- allspice = pimento = Jamaica pepper
- chilli = pimento = chilli pepper
- capsicum = pimento = bell pepper
- peppercorns = piper = pepper.

Chillies belong to the Solanaceae family, the same as tomatoes (and if you are growing them they like similar conditions). They are green until they ripen, turning to wonderful vibrant reds, oranges, yellows, browns, purples and sometimes almost black.

During our visit to Gujerat in 1991, we took our group to the town of Unja, a thriving market town totally dedicated to chillies, turmeric and garlic (think of it as Spice Heaven). It's a trading town, and the roads and alleyways are lined with warehouses brimming with hessian bags bursting at their seams as if the chillies are trying to escape. You certainly can't escape the aroma of chilli and its hot sinus-clearing, throat-searing substance called capsaicin. Not only did most of our travellers retreat, coughing and spluttering, to the bus, with eyes and nostrils streaming, but the bus driver had to close all the doors and windows and drive a few blocks away! It's not a place for anyone with sensitive lungs or upper respiratory disorders; but it's a breathtaking reminder that the heat of chilli affects more than just the taste buds.

Chillies may have originated in South America, but today they are grown worldwide from North Africa, to India, to Asia, to America, to Europe, where they flourished in gardens and were dried by cooks so that there was a year-round supply.

If you want to grow your own chillies, keep in mind that they like a warm climate with plenty of sunshine (at least half the day) and a well-drained soil with plenty of organic matter. Plant seeds or seedlings in spring in the right conditions, and you should be picking your own chillies about three and a half months later. Of course, you can pick them at any stage, but keep in mind the riper the fruitier. When chillies are happy in their garden spot, they will grow like weeds.

choosing and using

Chillies are available fresh virtually year-round from vegetable suppliers. Fresh chillies have a lighter, fresher flavour than dried, and there are appropriate uses for both. What is a Thai or Malaysian stir-fry without slices of fresh chilli? And what use is a Singapore chilli crab without lots of whole, dried red chillies? Can you imagine guacamole without a nice hot chilli powder? And those wonderfully mild and fruity whole dried Mexican chillies, soaked in warm water then chopped into sauces and stews, that bring much joy to the consumer! We are particularly partial to dried chilli flakes, which give a lovely fruity flavour to curries and Italian pasta sauces as well as heat. Our opinion is that a truly well-stocked kitchen should have powder, flakes, whole dried and fresh chillies to meet every requirement.

Dried chillies are rather prone to bugs. No matter how clean the product is when it is packed, these little creatures with their cast-iron stomachs manifest themselves over time, in much the same way that beautifully fine, triple-sifted flour can become infested with webs and moths if stored for too long. If a pack lasts a long time in your kitchen, seal it well and keep it in a cool, dark place to prevent the wildlife from hatching!

When it comes to fresh chillies, you can tell if they are fresh by how firm they are. Ripe fresh chillies should be smooth in appearance. Use them within a day or two of buying them to take best advantage of the freshness. Wrinkling of the skins means that they have started to dry or may not have ripened on the bush.

A good way to reduce heat is to remove the seeds, because it's actually that creamy flesh holding the seeds to the walls of the chilli that bears most heat.

This is why generally the smaller the chilli the hotter, as it has a higher ratio of seeds and thus capsaicin. Be careful to wash your hands immediately after chopping chillies (or wear rubber gloves), as they can cause an irritation to the skin and eyes. If you're suffering from a mouthful of hot chillies, don't drink water as it makes it worse. The best way to ease the burning sensation is to have some cucumber and yoghurt or a glass of milk. A few grains of sugar, or a piece of candy, will also take the burn away.

Dried chillies have a very different flavour to fresh ones. The curing or slow-drying process concentrates the colour and helps develop the flavour as the sugars caramelise, creating a delicious, robust taste not found in fresh chillies, in much the same way a sun-dried tomato has a more complex flavour profile than a fresh one. Many Indian recipes will use dried chillies in preference to fresh for this reason.

Not only does the flavour change with drying, but sometimes there's a name change too, as with Mexican chillies, for example:

* fresh jalapeno chillies become chipotle when they are dried and smoked;
* fresh poblano chillies become ancho when they are dried if they are red, and mulato when they are dried if they are blackish; and
* fresh chilaca chillies become pasilla when they are dried.

Mexican chillies as a rule are sweeter and fruitier than the chillies of India and Asia. Especially once they are dried, they offer a delicious, richly flavourful heat.

Soaking dried chillies in a bowl of water for an hour before chopping brings them to the consistency of a roasted capsicum, perfect for chopping, and the water can be used as a kind of mild chilli stock or a booster for chicken stock.

It's difficult to recommend quantities for chilli use, because everyone's taste and heat tolerance is so different. The best rule of thumb is to start with a small amount, taste, then add more if you want to. Remember, you can put more in, but you can't take it out if you've made it too hot.

Chilli flakes are the 'not-too-heavy, not-too-light' part of the chilli story. You can sprinkle them onto a pizza if you find biting on a piece of chilli is more fun than a dusting of chilli powder. You can put them in a curry when you want to ingest a little with each mouthful rather than leaving the whole chilli on the side of your plate. They soften quickly enough to be added to an omelette, where they add flashes of brightness, whereas chilli powder can make the colour of an omelette a little murky.

The **Aleppo pepper** referred to often in Middle Eastern cookbooks is a small reddish-brown chilli grown in those areas, and it is usually ground into powder or sold as dried flakes. It's quite hot, with a sharp fruitiness.

Chilli powder may be a mixture of dried ground chillies, aromatic seeds, spices and herbs, or it may be the ground chillies unmixed; the flavour differs with the manufacturers' formulas, and varies from mildly hot to very hot. At first it is better to use a little less rather than too much. The best and hottest chilli powder comes from small bright red chillies known as birdseye – the aroma is fiercely peppery, the colour a rust red and the flavour hot and glowing. Not only is it traditionally used in chilli con carne, but it has also become indispensable in fiery Asian dishes, certain sauces such as peri peri and some hot curry powders.

Cayenne pepper is actually a blend of hot chillies that are mixed to give a consistent-heat chilli powder, with a heat level of about 8 out of 10. Use with care whenever a really hot chilli bite is required! Be careful when you're using English recipe books – it seems that the cayenne pepper there is milder than we are used to in Australia. Cayenne is an excellent culinary spice, and also has digestive properties.

Paprika and smoked paprika (see pages 121–5) are made from the paprika fruit, which is similar to a capsicum.

Chillies aren't just a great way to burn the roof of your mouth and make your eyes water; they are used regularly in Indian, African, Asian and Mexican cooking because of the flavour they contribute as well as the heat. You might hear people making nod-nod-wink-wink suggestions that chillies act as an aphrodisiac. Are they right? Possibly. It's all to do with the endorphins that our bodies release in response to the chilli burn – they create an uplifted feeling and increase the metabolic rate. So dieters, eat up your chillies to burn off your fat!

When the Spaniards introduced it to Europe, chilli provided an alternative to highly expensive pepper, providing even the most humble householder with an easy-to-grow, very cheap, very effective flavouring. Now it is a traditional ingredient in goulash, paella, tagine, curry, snack foods, chilli con carne ... in fact, you can find it almost everywhere in the world.

Fresh chillies are common in stir-fries, salads and as a garnish, whereas dried chillies are good to use whole in curries and in any other liquid that is slow-cooking.

Ground chillies, like all ground spices, are particularly convenient when they are to be blended, as in curry powder and dozens of spice mixes. As an ingredient, chilli powder is taken for granted in a wide range of curries, sauces, pickles, chutneys and pastes.

There is no such fruit as a white chilli, but you might come across 'white chillies' occasionally. These may be pale yellow chillies, or most commonly are red chillies that have been marinated in yoghurt and salt prior to drying. The heat level can vary depending on just what chillies are used. They are excellent in seafood dishes and may be fried in a little oil and eaten as an appetiser with drinks.

In one form or another chilli is essential in:

- paella, a Spanish rice dish
- cajun, a hot and spicy blend from the southern states of America
- chermoula, a North African spice blend used to season chicken, lamb and even pumpkin!
- curry, a great vehicle for chillies. As a very general observation, Thai curries use fresh chillies, while Indian, Malay and Indonesian use dried
- sambal, a paste of fresh chillies and salt, much enjoyed in Indonesia, Malaysia and Singapore
- Hungarian goulash
- harissa, a fiery Tunisian paste, made predominantly from red-hot chillies and used as an accompaniment to a wide variety of foods.

Here are some easy meal ideas to spice up with a touch of chilli.

- For an easy, different meal, soak a chipotle chilli in a cup of hot water for 30 minutes. Lift the chilli out, remove the stem and seeds, and chop the flesh roughly. Use the soaking water with a good chicken stock base to make a cup of stock, then purée the chilli and stock together with a can of tomatoes and some oregano. Chop a few onions, slice and cook until transparent, then cover the base of a shallow ovenproof dish with them. Lay chicken breast or thigh pieces on the onion, pour the chilli/tomato stock over. Bake at moderate heat for about 45 minutes, until chicken is cooked.
- Add a teaspoon or two of fresh or dried chilli flakes to your favourite pasta sauce.
- Drop a dried Mexican chilli into your next pot of vegetable soup. It will soften during cooking, and you can lift the whole thing out at the end. For mild chilli flavour, discard the cooked chilli. For medium heat, lift the chilli out, purée the soup, then return the whole chilli. For maximum heat, purée the chilli with the soup.
- Combine a couple of dried chillies with a cupful of dry sherry. Store and add a few drops to soup at serving time.
- Make chilli sambal when fresh chillies are plentiful. Cook them in boiling water for about 5 minutes, then drain and chop in a food processor. Add 1 teaspoon salt for each 200 g of chillies, and store in an airtight container in the fridge. Serve in little side dishes as a condiment.
- Shred dried Mexican chillies (ancho, mulato, poblano) into the finest juliennes you can manage, and serve ice-cream with a small crown of chilli shreds on top.

Chilli combines well with all spices, as that extra tantalising bite gives another dimension to food, while the unique fruity notes of dried chillies are highly complementary. Chilli is particularly good with allspice, amchur, cardamom, cloves, coriander leaf and seed, cumin seed, fenugreek leaves and seeds, ginger, kaffir lime leaves, mustard seeds, paprika, pepper, star anise, turmeric and wattleseed.

harissa

Delicious with North African rice and couscous dishes, on cold meat sandwiches instead of mustard and with hommos on crusty bread. Fiery food lovers adore harissa sprinkled onto meats as a dry marinade before cooking. Harissa paste is made with dried chillies, as their complex taste is more suitable than using fresh chillies.

10 teaspoons dried chilli flakes, soaked in the same
      amount of hot water for 15 minutes
3 teaspoons freshly crushed garlic
3 teaspoons sweet paprika
2 teaspoons each of caraway seeds and coriander seeds
1 teaspoon cumin seeds, roasted
1 teaspoon salt
6 fresh spearmint leaves finely chopped

To make harissa paste, blend the ingredients then crush them in a pestle and mortar until a thick paste is formed. Store in the refrigerator and use within 4 weeks.

Makes about 1 cup

avial (mixed vegetable curry)

500 g mixed vegetables (brinjal, pumpkin,
      cucumber, string beans, eggplant, yam,
      potato, drumstick, snake gourd etc as available)
      cut into long thick slices
1 small onion, sliced into big pieces
4 green chillies, split lengthwise
6–10 curry leaves
1/2 cup water
1/2 teaspoon turmeric powder
salt to taste
1/2 teaspoon whole cumin seeds
3 cloves garlic
2 cups fresh coconut grated (or 2 cups desiccated
      coconut soaked in water for 5 minutes then
      squeezed to remove water)
125 ml plain yoghurt
1 tablespoon coconut oil

Place the vegetables, onion, chillies and curry leaves in a saucepan with the water, turmeric and salt. Steam gently over low heat until vegetables are almost cooked.

Purée the cumin, garlic and coconut in a blender to a rough paste, then add yoghurt.

Add the coconut-yoghurt paste to the vegetables and continue to cook until the vegetables are tender. Add the coconut oil before serving for additional flavour.

Serves 4–6 as part of a meal

chicken with mexican flavours

2 tablespoons butter

3 tablespoons vegetable oil

6 chicken breast fillets, skinned

salt and pepper to taste

¾ cup tequila

4 pasilla or ancho chillies, seeded and chopped

1 tablespoon onion, chopped

1 clove garlic, chopped

500 ml chicken stock

1 teaspoon soft brown sugar

1 tablespoon cornflour,
     dissolved in 60 ml water

Heat butter and 1 tablespoon of the oil in a frying pan. Add the chicken and cook for about 20 minutes over low heat until done, turning once. Do not allow to brown. Add salt and pepper to taste.

Remove chicken from the pan and set the pan aside, reserving the fat. Place the chicken in a large saucepan, add the tequila, and ignite. Allow the flames to finish, then set aside.

Reheat the fat in the frying pan and sauté the chillies, onion and garlic over medium heat for a few minutes, stirring occasionally. Put the mixture in a food processor along with half the stock and process in two or three short bursts. The result should still be a little chunky.

Heat the remaining 2 tablespoons of oil in the pan and add the chilli mixture. Cook over medium heat for 3 minutes. Add the chicken, sugar, remaining stock and the cornflour mixture. Lower the heat and simmer until the sauce thickens, approximately 10 minutes.

Serves 6

polenta with mulato chilli and crème fraîche

1 whole dried mulato chilli

2 cups boiling water

4 cups chicken stock

2 cups slow-cook polenta

2 tablespoons freshly grated parmesan cheese

1 teaspoon salt

10 black olives

1 tablespoon olive oil

250 ml crème fraîche

½ cup coriander leaves

Soak the chilli in the boiling water until soft. Remove the chilli and reserve. Bring the soaking water and stock to the boil, slowly pour in polenta and reduce the heat. Keep stirring until cooked (30–40 mins). If mixture dries out before it is cooked, add a little more water. Add parmesan cheese and salt and stir well.

Wash the seeds out of the mulato chilli and discard them. Chop the chilli roughly and blend with olives and olive oil until a near paste. Add three-quarters of the paste to the polenta and stir through. Stir the remaining paste through the crème fraîche.

The polenta can be served warm and soft straight from the pan. Alternatively, spread the polenta out on a shallow dish and refrigerate until set. Cut into wedges and grill until warmed through. Either way, serve with a dollop of crème fraîche and a sprinkling of coriander leaves.

Serves 6–8

cinnamon

Cinnamomum zeylanicum

and cassia

C. cassia

One of the world's most popular and well-known spices, cinnamon can easily be confused with cassia – a spice that's just as popular. This confusion runs right through the supply chain from consumers, to traders, processors and even the growers themselves.

CINNAMON *Cinnamomum zeylanicum*
Also called cinnamon bark, cinnamon quill,
cinnamon stick
Flavour and aroma mildly sweet and fragrant;
warm and delicate
Flavour group sweet

CASSIA *Cinnamomum cassia*
Also called baker's cinnamon, bastard
cinnamon, Dutch cinnamon
Flavour and aroma sweet and fragrant,
with intense warmth
Flavour group sweet

So, what's the difference between cinnamon and cassia and does it matter? Firstly, although they are both members of the Lauraceae family (which also includes the bay laurel, camphor laurel and the avocado), they are very different trees. Secondly, the aroma of cinnamon is delicate, sweet and subtle, and it's virtually impossible to use too much in your cooking. Cassia, on the other hand, is quite hot if you chew on a piece of bark, and its sweet fragrance is more aromatic and more immediate in its effect – use too much and there is a distinctly hot, slightly unpleasant, overtone. Thirdly, the best cinnamon is a very thin under-layer of bark from a quite young piece of branch, while cassia is the complete thickness of bark from the fully grown tree.

Cinnamon is an evergreen tree with light brown smooth and mottled bark, native to Sri Lanka and the neighbouring Malabar coast of India. Its leaves, twigs and bark are all highly aromatic, and all have their uses. Today, cultivated plantations grow the trees as small bushes no higher than about 3 m as the stems are continually cut back to produce new stems for

bark. The best cinnamon grows along the coast south of Colombo.

The processing of cinnamon bark in Sri Lanka is possibly one of the most amazing skills demonstrated by spice workers in the traditional spice trade today that we have ever seen – and naturally, it's all done by hand. The very thin underneath layer of bark is carefully peeled off cut branches and then tightly rolled in concentric layers by cinnamon peelers into metre-long sticks like a giant cigar. These long sticks are dried and then cut into the familiar shorter sticks.

Cinnamon and cassia leaves both have a distinctive rather clove-like aroma and taste and are used, fresh or dried, in Indian and Asian cooking in dishes such as curries and slow-cooked pot meals. You might see them referred to as Indonesian or Indian bay leaves (more usually *C. burmannii*) or tejpat (more usually *C. tamala*). If you have a cinnamon tree, select mature leaves, preferably last year's growth, snip them with secateurs and use them fresh from the tree. If you don't have any, don't be tempted to use a traditional European bay leaf instead – the flavour is quite different. A good substitute is just one clove.

It is easy to see how people get confused about these two spices, because when we visited the cassia forests in the north-west of Vietnam we found that even the growers there referred to cassia as cinnamon. *C. cassia* is native to southern China and Burma but today most of the commercial growing is in Vietnam, Indonesia and China. The finest quality cassia in fact comes from Vietnam where the trees are harvested when they are just under eight years old (for tax reasons), by which time they stand at about 12 m. The tree is basically ring-barked to remove large curls of bark about the length and diameter of an adult forearm. The tree is then felled, and every branch and twig is stripped of its bark.

Because the entire tree is harvested, (the timber is used for building), the seeds are collected from the forest floor for germinating and replanting. As with allspice, seeds that have passed through the intestines of birds are preferred as they ensure a more successful germination rate. Cassia growing is a profitable business and the bark from three trees will earn a grower enough to build a house in the village.

choosing and using

So, which to buy for what and how can you tell them apart?

In some countries it is illegal to sell cassia as cinnamon, but there's very little policing, so this regulation hardly has any effect. In the United States, true cinnamon is almost unheard of, so anything called cinnamon is bound to be cassia, unless it's called Mexican cinnamon. We have had customers who believe there is a cinnamon growing industry in Mexico because they've heard of Mexican cinnamon, but the truth is that Mexico buys so much true cinnamon from Sri Lanka that the traders there have a grade called 'Mexican'!

You can tell cassia sticks from cinnamon just by looking at them. Cinnamon sticks are made up of many paper-thin pieces of bark, layered together before they're rolled, so that they look something like a Flake chocolate bar. On the other hand, cassia bark is quite chunky, and a stick is just one solid piece. It's a little harder with the powder, because the colours vary, but really good-quality cinnamon powder is quite pale, like a very creamy milk chocolate. Really cheap, poor quality cinnamon is very dark and grainy because it's

made from the whole bark from a mature tree. Ground cassia is between the two, being a richer brown than ground cinnamon, with a slight reddish tinge, and it's as fine as talcum powder.

Cinnamon sticks have an aromatic fragrance and can be put into stewed compotes of fruit, used to flavour curries, spicy rice dishes or even mulled wine, where the flavour gently infuses. A centimetre broken up and put into a coffee plunger with the grounds imparts a delicately spiced flavour.

Ground cinnamon bark from mature trees is most likely to be used in savoury applications. It has some cinnamon aroma, but lacks fragrance and has a rather harsh flat taste, certainly not the delicate sweetness you would want for cakes and puddings.

Cassia sticks or flat pieces of bark can be used in the same way as cinnamon sticks. It's worth bearing in mind that if you have an Asian recipe calling for a cinnamon stick, it is probably cassia.

When it is ground, cassia has a highly fragrant cinnamon aroma which makes it the baker's choice for things like cinnamon donuts, spiced fruit buns and sweet breads, hence other names for cassia such as Saigon cinnamon and baker's cinnamon. If you buy cinnamon sugar from the supermarket, you have a 50–50 chance of getting cassia sugar instead!

Be careful to use moderation with cassia – just a touch too much will introduce a hot, rather bitter back note that will spoil your dish. What often works well is a combination of cassia and cinnamon for a fragrant but still warm and gentle influence.

Whole spices stay fresher than ground ones and in this case whole sticks will last quite a few years, and ground cinnamon and cassia about a year.

In our shop, we have an entire bale of cinnamon, which stands about a metre high with a diameter of 60 cm. The sticks are literally as they are when they leave the farm in Sri Lanka, ungraded and tied with hemp rope. The long sticks have surprisingly little aroma, but once they are broken or bruised, all the wonderful fragrance floods out, evoking images of oranges warmed by the sun.

Keep cinnamon sticks in an airtight container away from heat to preserve the flavour. Ground cinnamon has a more immediate flavour; however, it can lose its aroma quickly, so needs to be stored in an airtight container.

Cinnamon and cassia have similar uses and are almost interchangeable:

- Both add a cosy warmth and sweetness to Middle Eastern and North African dishes such as lamb tagines and spiced eggplant.
- They are used in curry powder and garam masala.
- Whole sticks are used in biriyani and pilau dishes.
- They are essential in fruit cakes and puddings.
- They make a great addition to milkshakes, cakes and they spice up vegies, such as pumpkin and zucchini.

Cinnamon and cassia are great flavours to spice up the start of the day, for instance:

- Toast — mix about ½ teaspoon ground cinnamon sticks or cassia with 1 tablespoon sugar and sprinkle over hot buttered toast.
- Pears or stone fruits — poach with a cinnamon stick in the syrup.

- Blend about ½ teaspoon ground cinnamon sticks or cassia with 1 tablespoon sugar and sprinkle over hot pancakes with a squeeze of lemon.
- Whip cassia with butter to serve with flapjacks.
- Stir ground cinnamon sticks and currants into porridge before cooking.

When we think of sweet spice blends, cinnamon and cassia come readily to mind, however they also play an important role in savoury spice blends like curry powders and tagine spices.

When to use either cinnamon or cassia in a spice blend is very much a matter of choice. We tend to use cinnamon in dishes that do not have robust flavours or in recipes from India and Sri Lanka. Cassia is more appropriate in Asian cooking and it adds an extra dimension to North African and Middle Eastern foods. Cassia also works well when there are a lot of other spices, such as in a Moroccan tagine. (Strictly speaking, a tagine is the pottery, conical-lidded cooking pot that is traditionally used for making Moroccan casseroles. The use of the name has broadened to encompass many North African casseroles, which are loosely referred to as tagines.) The flavours in a typical tagine spice mix go particularly well with lamb, especially if it has a strong, almost gamey taste, which these spices help to neutralise.

Cinnamon and cassia will go with most spices, however they are particularly compatible with allspice, caraway seed, cardamom, chilli, cloves, coriander seed, cumin, ginger, licorice, nutmeg, pepper, star anise, tamarind and turmeric. Any premixed mixed spice blend will probably contain cinnamon, cassia or both.

Mixed spice is the popular sweet spice blend that is often confused with the individual spice, allspice. Mixed spice has its origins in European cooking and is the most popular way to flavour fruit cakes, shortbread, sweet pies and all kinds of delectable pastries. To impart a delicious sweet spice flavour to cakes, biscuits and pastries, add 2 teaspoons of mixed spice per cup of flour to the dry ingredients. Fruit cakes, mince pies and rich or sweet foods require more, up to twice the amount if a distinct spiciness is desired.

mixed spice

You may be surprised to see the quantity of ground coriander seed in this recipe, however as an amalgamating spice it brings the sweet and pungent spices together with a fragrant delicacy that would not otherwise be achieved. We have also taken the liberty of using both ground cinnamon sticks and ground cassia, as these two spices happen to balance each other beautifully. If you like that extra flavour hit in cassia, blending it in equal parts with cinnamon is a safe way to enjoy the best of both spices.

4 teaspoons ground coriander seed

2 teaspoons ground cinnamon

2 teaspoons ground cassia

$1/2$ teaspoon ground nutmeg

$1/2$ teaspoon ground allspice

$1/2$ teaspoon ground ginger

$1/4$ teaspoon ground cloves

$1/4$ teaspoon ground green cardamom seed

Blend ground spices and store in an airtight container.

Makes about $1/3$ cup

tagine spice mix

5 teaspoons mild paprika

$2^{1}/2$ teaspoons ground coriander seed

1 teaspoon ground cassia

1 teaspoon medium-heat chilli powder

$1/2$ teaspoon ground allspice

$1/4$ teaspoon ground cloves

$1/4$ teaspoon ground green cardamom seed

Blend ground spices and store in an airtight container.

Makes enough spice mix for a tagine for 4–6 people

The recipes we have chosen illustrate cassia's 'out-there' outgoing nature and cinnamon's 'in-there' subtlety. Try interchanging them and notice the difference!

strawberries with a cinnamon–rose glaze

1 cup water

100 g caster sugar

2 cinnamon sticks, broken in half and lightly bruised

1 teaspoon rosewater

250 g strawberries at room temperature

Combine the water, sugar, cinnamon and rosewater in a saucepan and bring to the boil.

Add a few strawberries at a time, lifting out with a slotted spoon after about 5 seconds. Continue the process until all strawberries have been braised and set aside in a bowl.

Continue to simmer the syrup until it is reduced by more than half, and it thickens to coat the back of a spoon. Remove from heat and pour through a strainer into a small jug and allow to cool.

Serve the strawberries with a creamy vanilla ice-cream and the syrup spooned over them.

Serves 2

lamb shanks tagine

The best way to experience how well this unusual spice blend complements lamb, is in this recipe. We have allowed two shanks per person. If the shanks are very big, one per person is probably plenty, even for a main course.

8 small or 4 large lamb shanks

3 tablespoons Tagine Spice Mix (see page 55)

2 tablespoons olive oil

2 parsnips, peeled and cubed

4 carrots, chopped

3 onions, chopped finely

1 x 400 g can peeled tomatoes

6 prunes

2 tablespoons tomato paste

2 tablespoons garlic purée

3–4 peppercorns, crushed

2 cups orange juice

4 cups water

salt

Preheat the oven to 180°C. Coat the lamb shanks with the spice mixture and seal lightly in hot oil. Place the shanks in a large ovenproof pot with the vegetables, prunes, tomato paste, garlic purée and peppercorns. Add any remaining spice mixture and the orange juice and water. Cover with lid or foil and gently bake for 1½–2 hours, or until the meat is very tender. Add salt to taste.

Serve with couscous.

Serves 4, allowing 2 shanks each

banana cassia muffins

600 g self-raising flour

225 g soft brown sugar

2 teaspoons ground cassia

2 eggs

1½ cups semi-skimmed milk

3 very ripe bananas, mashed

1 cup vegetable oil

Preheat oven to 200ºC. Sift flour into large bowl, add sugar and cassia and mix together. Make a well in the centre. In another bowl mix together the eggs, milk and bananas. Pour egg mixture and oil into the well and stir, gradually incorporating the dry ingredients until you have a thick batter consistency.

Pour into a greased muffin tray and bake on top shelf for 15 minutes or until muffins are cooked through.

Makes 12–15 muffins, depending on size

growing

Cinnamon is not a tree for a small garden, eventually growing to around 9 m. Cinnamon trees thrive in tropical or subtropical conditions with plenty of rain. They do best in full sun or dappled shade in well-drained soil. Select your spot and propagate from cuttings in autumn or choose a small tree — hard to find but worth the effort if you succeed. Harvesting the bark to make sticks is an exercise of immense skill, and best left to the experts. However, once your tree is over five years old, you may cut off a small branch here and there and peel some bark with a sharp knife, as you would peel a carrot. (Don't cut your fingers!) Buying cinnamon sticks is easier but not as personally interactive and satisfying.

clove

Eugenia caryophyllata

Who would have thought that nations would fight over dried flower buds? A tropical evergreen tree, native to a handful of tiny islands in eastern Indonesia, produces such flower buds, and they are known as cloves.

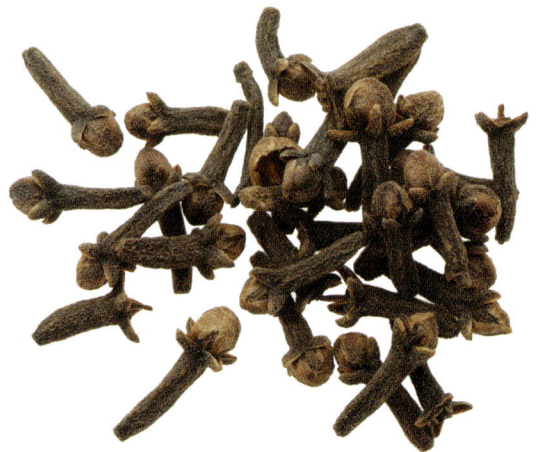

Also called nelkin, ting-hiang
Flavour and aroma warm, pungent and numbing,
faintly peppery with camphor-like aroma
Flavour group pungent

Cloves were one of the major spices, along with nutmeg, that were right in the middle of that ruthless business we rather romantically call 'the spice trade' when a handful of cloves was worth a handful of silver!

How's this for a swashbuckling movie scenario? It is the year 1522. The sultan of a small island called Ternate gives a plot of land to the Portuguese, who are thrilled to have found cloves and nutmeg in the area. They install a governor and proceed to rape, torture and generally make mischief between themselves and the Spanish on a neighbouring island, Tidore. After about seven years of squabbling, they agree that if the Spanish keep the Philippines, Portugal will keep both Ternate and Tidore.

Everything runs fairly smoothly for about 20 years, until another Spaniard, Francis Xavier (later Saint Francis Xavier), arrives and becomes chummy with the sultan, but still manages to throw him in gaol for refusing to surrender his lands. When all else fails, the sultan is murdered, which leads to five furious years of retribution on the part of his orphaned son. Eventually the Portuguese are also forced to leave.

Free of foreigners, Ternate lives in peace and harmony for a decade or so, until the English adventurer Francis Drake arrives and quickly becomes such good mates with Sultan Baab that he gladly places himself and his possessions in English hands. His vessel loaded to the gunwales with precious spices, Drake hotfoots it (if one can across oceans) home.

Now the English and Dutch spice traders are allies (in theory) against the Roman Catholic Iberian nations, but base commerce has no conscience, and eventually the traders of the Dutch East India Company find a reason to seize, torture and execute their British counterparts in the Moluccas (now Maluku). The British are not amused, and are also effectively out of the game.

Ruthlessly, the Dutch spice traders set about destroying any clove and nutmeg trees not on Dutch-owned plantations, and put to death anyone growing or trading in cloves. Loss of trade leads to poverty and decay for these regions, and the once-splendid sultanates fade into obscurity. A Frenchman called Pierre Poivre makes himself famous by smuggling clove seedlings to Isle de France (later Mauritius) but in 1810, the British get control for a few years, and take the opportunity to legally send clove seedlings to places like Zanzibar, Pemba and Mauritius.

Cut to today. Nature triumphs! High on the slopes of Api Gamalama volcano on an island in northern Maluku, a tree that's almost 400 years old has survived Dutch ecological vandalism and is still producing around 600 kilograms of cloves in a bumper year. The saga of the Dutch clove and nutmeg monopoly is over. Roll credits.

Although Indonesia is currently the world's biggest producer of cloves, it's also the world's biggest importer, because huge amounts of ground cloves go up in smoke in over 100 million kretek cigarettes a day.

An uncle of ours visited Zanzibar many years ago, and has told us that he could smell the richness of the cloves from a mile out to sea as the boat approached. This sounded wonderful to us, and we felt we had to go and experience it. Unfortunately, by the time we made our trip, the socialist revolution had endowed all the farms to 'the people' and farming methods were less than efficient. Visits to spice farms are a major tourist attraction there, but although it is still a major exporter on the world stage, as a clove-producing area, Zanzibar's finest days seem to be done.

Clove trees don't start producing until they are about six to eight years old and even then they usually only deliver a bumper crop every four years or so. Harvesting is painstaking, as rough handling may diminish subsequent yields. When the flower buds are full size, the clove clusters are hand-picked. The buds are then removed from the flower stems by twisting the cluster against the palm of the hand and spread out on woven mats to dry in the sun.

Now and again, you will see a flutter of yellow amongst the darkening cloves, when a bud has burst into flower just at picking time. During drying, the flavour develops thanks to the enzymatic reaction that forms eugenol, a volatile oil used in germicides, perfumes and mouthwashes and for many of us an all too pungent reminder of the dentist's chair.

choosing and using

Unless you're making a clove pomander for your linen cupboard, you'll probably use cloves in very modest quantities, so buy small amounts and store them well.

Good-quality cloves should be intact, uniform in size and shape, dark brown with a lighter brown top to the bud and have no pieces of stem. Whole cloves will last for at least three years.

Ground cloves are commonly adulterated with clove stem, which does not have such high oil levels and has more fibre and less flavour than the buds. Because it is such a pungent spice, the flavour loss of the ground spice will be very gradual.

If you want to grind your own with a pestle and mortar, keep the elbow grease handy, or vandalise the cloves by taking the bud out – they are softer and will crush more easily. For grinding whole cloves, an electric coffee grinder makes the job easier.

Surprisingly for a spice so strong in aroma and pungent in taste, cloves can actually add lightness and freshness when used judiciously. They bring flavour to many foods, particularly meats and bakery products, but probably most famously, apples. In Europe and the USA the spice is a characteristic flavouring in traditional Christmas holiday fare, such as wassail and mincemeat.

Strawberries with Cinnamon–Rose Glaze (recipe page 56)

Pork Fillet in Orange Sauce (recipe page 66)

Whole cloves are frequently used to flavour cooking liquids for simmering fish, poultry, game and meat. By pushing the tapered end into the meat like a nail, (the German name for cloves, *nelkin*, means *little nail*), whole cloves are often used to stud hams or pork before baking.

Although the consumer is generally not aware of it, cloves hide away in many kinds of pickles and preserves, Worcestershire Sauce, mulled wines, stewed fruits, meat dishes, stocks and soups.

Being native to Indonesia, it's not surprising to find cloves in curry mixes and rich Chinese spice blends. In India, the Middle East and North Africa they are used with rice dishes, while the Europeans favour flavouring breads and cheeses with them.

- Stud an onion with a few cloves and simmer in soups or stews. Remove before serving. Or, add just one clove to a beef or lamb stew – it will not be overtly noticeable, but the meat will be tastier.
- Drop a clove into the hollowed-out centre of a cooking apple, pack with butter and brown sugar, and bake in a 180°C moderate oven until tender, about 25 minutes, depending on the size of the apple.
- Drop one or two cloves into your coffee plunger with the coffee grounds to have a spicy wake-up call.
- Beat a small amount of ground cloves into cream or mascarpone (about ¼ teaspoon to 250 ml and serve with steamed puddings.

- And, if you have a toothache, bite down on a clove to release the numbing oil that may relieve your pain until you see your dentist.

When one smells the pungency of cloves it is easy to understand how they need to be used sparingly with other spices. Life is full of surprises though, and an unexpected benefit of using cloves moderately with various spices, is that they actually introduce a light breath of freshness that would otherwise be missing.

All the pungent spices, like cloves, actually perform a very important role in spice blends, for without them many a curry, mixed spice, ras el hanout, tagine, garam masala or even Chinese five-spice would be dull and lifeless. For all their strength, cloves blend well with allspice, cardamom, chilli, coriander seed, cumin seed, ginger, licorice, nutmeg, star anise, tamarind and turmeric.

The French have a spice blend that causes a little confusion, and this is because it comes in both sweet and savoury versions. The blend of four spices is creatively called *Quatre Epices* (see page 119) and in its savoury form is comprised mostly of white pepper that is balanced with cinnamon, nutmeg and cloves. The sweet version substitutes ground white pepper with ground allspice, and hey presto, you have a strong sweet spice mix that is ideal for rich fruit cakes, puddings and spicy shortbread biscuits.

spiced tea (chai)

There are two ways to make chai – the traditional Indian way with milk and sugar, or the black tea way, which is preferable to many Westerners. Here are both versions.

Indian Chai

2 cups milk

2 teaspoons tea leaves

1 tablespoon sugar (more or less to taste)

10 cloves

1 cinnamon stick, about 10 cm, broken

6 green cardamom pods

Place all ingredients in a saucepan and bring to the boil, stirring occasionally to help sugar dissolve. Allow to cool slightly then pour the tea through a strainer into two cups. Serve immediately.

Makes 2 cups

Western Chai

2 cups boiling water

2 teaspoons tea leaves

10 cloves

1 cinnamon stick, about 10 cm, broken

6 green cardamom pods

Place all the dry ingredients into a teapot or coffee plunger. Pour the boiling water over and allow to stand for 2–3 minutes. Strain when pouring and serve immediately.

Makes 2 cups

pain d'épices (gingerbread)

225 g self-raising flour

3 teaspoons ground ginger

1/2 teaspoon sweet *quatre épices* (see page 119)

100 g raw sugar

100 g butter

100 g treacle

175 g golden syrup

1 egg white

1/2 cup milk

Preheat the oven to 180ºC and butter a loaf pan. Sift the flour and spices into a large bowl. Melt the sugar, butter, treacle and golden syrup until sugar is dissolved. Beat the egg white with milk for 1 minute, then combine all ingredients to make a smooth batter. Pour into the prepared tin.

Bake for 45 minutes or until cooked. Cool on a rack. Once completely cooled, store in an airtight container.

Serves 10

coriander seed

Coriandrum sativum

Where would today's 'fusion' food be without coriander? Whether it's the unique flavour of the leaves with that clean, appetising taste most often associated with Thai and other Asian cooking, or the seeds with their mild, lemony taste that complements both sweet and savoury dishes, it's not surprising to learn that coriander is valued on every continent.

Also called Chinese parsley, cilantro
Flavour and aroma sweet, aromatic, warm, mild
Flavour group amalgamating

If you are looking for a value-for-money herb/spice, you can't go past coriander because you can eat the whole thing – leaves, stems, seeds and taproot. It's a thoroughly modern herb/spice.

The spice, coriander seed, goes way back and seems to have originated in the Mediterranean. Early datings place it in Egyptian tombs some 3000 years ago, and it is even mentioned in Exodus (16:31), where manna is described as 'small round and white like coriander seed'. (We have to make allowances for the translation — coriander seed is actually a creamy-beige colour.)

One could equate coriander seed to a very good personal assistant — discreet, efficient, and indispensable. It is the quiet achiever in the spice blends business, gently holding more assertive ingredients together, smoothing the edges, creating harmony. But in spite of its behind-the-scenes subtlety, it's a fantastic spice that deserves its own grinder. Move over, pepper, and make way for freshly ground coriander seed over the dinner plate!

choosing and using

Coriander seeds are available both whole and ground. The commercially ground powder is quite fine, suitable for mixing into spice blends or combining with flour. Because the dry seed is fairly brittle, it's rather fun to pound your own in a mortar, where you have the control to leave it at whatever texture you prefer.

Most of the coriander seeds available in Australia are Australian-grown, with a creamy-golden husk and a delicious nutty flavour. Indian coriander seeds are ovoid (sort of egg-shaped) rather than round, the colour is pale yellowy-green and they have a fresh, lemony flavour that makes them perfect for use with chicken and fish.

Whole seeds keep indefinitely. Their flavour may be enhanced by a light roasting before use, but remember, once a spice is roasted, it should be used within 24 hours because the oils will begin to oxidise and the flavour will deteriorate. Ground coriander, like all ground spices, will lose its flavour and aroma unless it is stored in an airtight container away from heat and direct light.

The most common use of coriander seed is in curry powders, where it is the bulkiest constituent, often rough ground in India to give a crunchy texture. Because we use no starches or fillers, we find ground coriander seed the perfect bulky base on which to build many of our blends.

It enhances fish dishes and, with other spices, may form a delicious coating for spiced fish or chicken, rubbed into the scored flesh and grilled. Try frying a few seeds with sausages to add an unexpected flavour.

Roasting or frying of coriander is much practised in India and Sri Lanka, as well as by modern chefs worldwide, to enrich the flavour – think of toast having a richer flavour than bread. The seeds are not only for curries; they can be used just as happily in stews and soups. They blend well with smoked meats and game, and feature in traditional English black pudding recipes and Italian mortadella sausage.

The ground seed is included in sweet mixed spice preparations used in cakes, breads and other baked foods.

Coriander is a characteristic of Arab cookery, being common with lamb, kid and meat stuffings. Taklia, a popular Arab spice mixture, is coriander and garlic crushed and fried. In some parts of Africa, the ground seed is measured into food by the cupful rather than the spoonful.

Coriander with cumin is a common combination and features in falafel, as well as in the Egyptian appetiser dukkah, which consists of those spices plus sesame seeds, hazelnuts, salt and pepper, roasted and crushed (see page 151). Because coriander seeds are usually cheaper than cumin seeds, it's a fairly common practice to cut pure ground cumin with coriander to reduce the price, so watch out for ground cumin that looks brown rather than khaki.

Latin American cuisine also makes much use of the seeds, having taken coriander to its heart after it was introduced by the Europeans. The fruit has even been used to flavour cigarette tobacco.

And just to top off the versatility and range of this fantastic spice, it is also used to flavour gin, pickles and sausages, and is a component of cosmetics and perfumes!

Coriander seed complements every spice, so when making spice blends its amalgamating properties make it one of the most useful spices there is. No respectable sweet mixed spice blend, curry powder, fiery Tunisian harissa blend or Ethiopian berbere would be complete without it.

When we were faced with the prospect of making a tantalising blend using Australian native herbs and spices, we turned to coriander seed for assistance. Spices like bush tomato, wattleseed and native pepperberry have quite pungent flavours, which can dominate even quite strongly flavoured foods. However, when these spices are blended with a generous amount of ground coriander seeds and a little lemon myrtle leaf, the result is balanced and tasty.

See also pages 231–4 for coriander leaf.

aussie fish seasoning blend

This Aussie Fish Seasoning Blend is a perfect dry marinade for all types of fish, whether pan-fried, barbecued or grilled. For strongly flavoured fish such as salmon and tuna, use a more liberal coating before cooking.

5 teaspoons ground coriander seed

1 teaspoon ground lemon myrtle leaf

1/2 teaspoon ground native pepperberry

1/4 teaspoon roasted and ground wattleseed

2 teaspoons salt, or less to taste

Combine all ingredients and store in an airtight container.

Makes about 2 tablespoons

pork fillet in orange sauce

1 x 250 g pork fillet

2 tablespoons olive oil

1/3 cup dry sherry

Marinade

1 tablespoon olive oil

juice and zest of 1 orange

1 tablespoon soy sauce

1 tablespoon white vinegar

1/2 teaspoon salt

1 tablespoon ground coriander seed

Caramelised Onion

2 onions, sliced thinly

2 tablespoons caster sugar

2 tablespoons olive oil

Combine all the marinade ingredients in a shallow bowl and place the pork fillet in it. Allow to stand for at least 1 hour.

Cook onions, caster sugar and oil in a pan over low heat. Stir occasionally, until golden and caramelised – about 15 minutes. Remove to a bowl and keep warm.

Remove pork from the marinade and drain. Heat oil in a pan and cook over moderate heat until browned on all surfaces and cooked to your liking (about 5–8 minutes). Remove the pork to a plate and keep warm.

Add the marinade to the pan and boil for about 10 minutes to reduce. Add the sherry, return to the boil and stir well. Add any juices from the plate holding the cooked fillet. Pour sauce into a gravy boat. Slice the pork fillet diagonally and divide between two plates. Serve with the caramelised onion and the sauce poured over.

Serves 2

cumin seed

Cuminum cyminum

black cumin *Bunium persicum*

If there's a single spice that makes one think of curry, it has to be cumin. But cumin plants in fact grow wild around the Mediterranean, in the Sudan and across Central Asia spreading from there to just about everywhere – including India, where it now seems so at home.

Also called jeera, white cumin
Flavour and aroma pungent, earthy, slightly bitter, warming, lingering
Flavour group pungent

The incredible popularity of cumin is nothing new. Way, way back in 5000 BC, cumin was used along with anise and marjoram to mummify royal cadavers. Cumin was well known to the Ancient Greeks, who considered it a symbol of greed. (Was this because it made food so delicious? We can only guess that it might have been.) Poor old Marcus Aurelius of Rome will never live down being greedy, because his nickname was Cumin!

Today, from South America to North Africa, Europe and all over Asia, cumin is one of the world's most widely used spices. The main growing areas are Iran, India, Turkey and Morocco, and as an indication of how much the world consumes annually in foods, beverages, liquors, medicines, toiletries and perfumery, India can produce up to 167,000 tonnes a year! Cumin is a small, rather delicate looking annual from the parsley family that likes hot, sunny climes and grows up to about 60 cm. Its small white or pink flowers produce the 'fruits' which we call cumin seeds. These are boat-shaped, about 4–5 mm long, have nine ridges and are pale brown to khaki in colour.

As with many spice crops, harvesting is very labour intensive as the seeds are usually collected and threshed by hand, since the small, tender plants are difficult to harvest mechanically. Each seed has a little hair-like 'tail' coming from one end, and this needs to be removed. In Gujerat, we noticed teams of women rubbing the seeds across the palms of their hands to remove this tail, letting handfuls fall past a giant old rattle-trap electric fan that blew the fine particles away as the seeds fell to the ground.

choosing and using

The story is the same for all seed spices. Whole seeds will retain their flavour quite well for at least two years, however when ground be sure to store them carefully in a well-sealed container.

Good-quality ground cumin seeds should be khaki in colour, and the powder should have an 'oily' feel. It's not uncommon to find cumin with a duller brown colour, and this will have been blended with cheaper coriander seed to reduce the cost. Naturally enough, it also reduces the flavour impact, so why bother? Due to the relatively high oil content of pure ground cumin, it can be dry-roasted in a pan quite easily and without burning.

Black cumin seeds are thinner and more fragile-looking than standard cumin, darker in colour yet not entirely black – rather like those infuriatingly adhesive seeds from the weed known as farmer's friend or cobbler's pegs. If the seeds you are offered are small, irregular-shaped and very black, they will be nigella seeds or kolonji, which are often wrongly called black cumin seeds. Black cumin seeds are usually left whole, and are dry-roasted before using.

Cumin is one of those seeds that cooks often like to grind themselves for maximum flavour, and more than likely it's because they've encountered the adulterated ground cumin. If you have good-quality ground cumin, save yourself some time and use it. We often like to use a combination of both, so that we have the well-dispersed flavour of the powder plus the pleasure of biting on the whole seed.

Dry-roasting is particularly applicable to cumin, partly, as mentioned before, because of the high oil content. Just heat a heavy-based pan until it is warm but still able to be touched with a fingertip. Add the seeds and move them around with your fingers or a wooden spoon to allow them to gently toast until the wonderful aroma swirls around your head. Once the seeds are roasted, use them within a day or two, but preferably cook with them straightaway.

What would an Indian curry be without cumin? Sadly lacking, that's what! Whatever other spices may be added or subtracted, cumin is the essential curry flavour that is intrinsic. The same goes for South-East Asian curries too.

Being native to the Mediterranean regions, cumin is also a natural addition to food from all those regions: Gulf States, Iran and Iraq, Lebanon, Syria, Palestine, Egypt and northern Africa. It's found in rice pilaff, fish and lamb stews, meatballs, savoury pastries and vegetable stews.

In Germany, where it's known as *kummel*, cumin finds its way into sauerkraut, rye bread, and cheese, as well as pickles and chutneys. In most cases, the whole seed is used. Not just in Germany, but all over northern Europe and Britain, cumin crops up in everything from sausages, stuffings and beans to liqueurs.

Cumin is a very important part of Central American and South American cuisines, along with other spices like chilli (called peppers in that region) and cinnamon.

Mexican chilli powder is a blend of chilli, paprika, sometimes oregano, and cumin.

- Mash whole seeds into cottage cheese with a little lemon juice for a spread or dip.
- Stir 1 teaspoon whole seeds and 1 teaspoon ground seed into 250 ml hummus.
- Coat lamb backstraps all over with ground cumin, then cook on a barbecue. Cool, slice, and serve with store-bought tahini liberally enhanced with ground cumin.
- Add a generous amount of ground cumin (say, 1 tablespoon to 500 g meat) to minced beef when making Mexican burritos or tacos.
- Toss in some whole cumin seeds when cooking lentils or pea soup. It's a great marriage!
- Mix 1 tablespoon Chermoula Spice Mix (see recipe page 71) with 250 ml of plain yoghurt. Spread over both sides of 4 tuna steaks and bake or grill.
- Cumin goes particularly well with pumpkin. Add one or two teaspoons to pumpkin soup, and sprinkle over pumpkin pieces while they're roasting. Chermoula Spice Mix can be used the same way.

Cumin is referred to so often as 'the curry spice' that it is often tempting to dismiss it as such and fail to appreciate its true virtues as a valuable flavour in many other spice blends. The taste of cumin need not dominate a dish, and with even the subtlest application, it has the ability to be surprisingly effective in balancing and rounding-out the bouquet of other spices.

This talent of cumin's was borne out quite dramatically when we were developing a blend to season a stuffing mix for a roast chicken producer. We had all the basic elements one would expect to go with the breadcrumbs, such as onion, garlic, thyme, sage, marjoram, parsley, oregano, bay leaves and sweet paprika. However when we cooked it, the result still seemed a little sharp and lifeless ... until we added a pinch of cumin. This small addition, so small that very few people would recognise that cumin had been added, transformed the stuffing so that it was beautifully balanced and full-bodied.

tasty stuffing mix

This is an excellent example of dried herbs being better than fresh. The spice blend makes about ¼ cup.

Spice Blend

5 teaspoons sweet paprika

2 teaspoons ground coriander seed

1 teaspoon dried sage

1 teaspoon dried thyme

½ teaspoon ground cumin seed

½ teaspoon dried oregano

¼ teaspoon ground black pepper

salt to taste

1 onion, finely chopped

1 tablespoon finely chopped fresh parsley

1 cup fresh breadcrumbs

a generous knob of butter

Combine all the spice blend ingredients.

To make the stuffing mix, stir the spice blend into the onion and parsley.

Rub the breadcrumbs with the butter and then mix in the spiced onion mixture to make the stuffing. The consistency may be a bit crumbly, but will be fine as long as it is contained.

Makes enough to stuff a large chicken

chermoula spice mix

Chermoula combines the robust flavours of cumin, paprika and turmeric with the freshness of onion, parsley and coriander leaves plus a hint of garlic and cayenne pepper. Use Chermoula Spice Mix as a rub for meats and poultry before roasting or barbecuing or use to marinate a firm-fleshed fish like tuna for about 20 minutes before cooking.

You can also change the proportions and make it more like a salsa with the onion and fresh herbs forming the bulk of the mixture, which you then lightly spice.

1/2 onion, finely chopped

1 teaspoon finely chopped fresh coriander leaves

2 teaspoons finely chopped fresh parsley

1 clove garlic, crushed

3 teaspoons ground cumin seed

2 teaspoons mild paprika

1 teaspoon turmeric powder

pinch cayenne

salt to taste

ground black pepper to taste

Makes about 1/3 cup

Some more ideas for chermoula:

- Rub chermoula generously over a butterflied leg of lamb. Allow to stand for 30 minutes then cook on the barbecue. Add a squeeze of lemon from time to time as it cooks.
- Add chermoula to lamb patties for that Moroccan influence. Serve on a bed of cooked spinach or silverbeet tossed with finely chopped preserved lemon peel.
- Add chermoula to a damper recipe and serve with salad and hummus to make a meal of it.

moroccan cocktail scones

These are always a big hit at our Spice Appreciation Classes. Flour can vary enormously from one batch to another. You may need to adjust the quantity of milk.

300 g self-raising flour

125 g salted butter

1 tablespoon Chermoula Spice Mix (see this page)

1/2–2/3 cup full-cream milk or pouring cream

Preheat the oven to 200°C. Place flour and butter in a food processor and process in bursts until mixture resembles breadcrumbs. Stir in the chermoula then add most of the milk, stirring gently. Use your hands to lightly combine, adding more milk if necessary, until the mixture holds together in a ball. Do not knead – the lighter the touch, the lighter the scone.

Gently press the mixture out to about 2 cm thick (do not roll) then cut into small, cocktail-sized squares or diamonds. Cook on a floured baking tray for about 10 minutes or until the scones have risen and browned on top.

Break into halves while still warm and serve with either hummus with ground cumin stirred in, or eggplant and garlic purée with a little chilli powder added.

Serves 10–12

white beans with tahini

This seriously wonderful recipe was created by Sophia Young and first published in *Australian Gourmet Traveller* (April 2003).

350 g cooked white beans (canned are fine)

3 tablespoons tahini

1 clove garlic, finely chopped

$1/3$ cup lemon juice

2 teaspoons cumin seeds, dry-roasted

2 tablespoons verjuice

salt and pepper

2 teaspoons sweet paprika

$1/3$ cup extra-virgin olive oil

2 tablespoons flat-leaf parsley, chopped

$1/2$ cup pine nuts, roasted

Prepare beans (warm them if they are canned) and set aside. Place tahini, garlic, lemon juice, cumin seeds and verjuice in a bowl, season to taste with salt and pepper and whisk to combine well. Place beans in a large bowl and, while still warm, add tahini mixture and mix gently. Cover and stand at room temperature for 1 hour for flavours to develop.

Whisk paprika into olive oil in a small bowl and stand for 30 minutes or until paprika settles in base of bowl, then carefully spoon off oil. Stir parsley and $3/4$ of the pine nuts into beans, then drizzle with paprika oil and scatter with remaining nuts.

Serves 4

bruschetta with purée of artichokes

Purée heaven ... use it as a dip or part of a mezze plate.

1 x 420 g can artichoke hearts, drained

1 small tomato

1–2 tablespoons olive oil, plus extra for brushing bread

6 black olives, pitted and chopped

1 teaspoon chilli powder or to taste

2 teaspoons ground cumin seed

1 small clove garlic, finely chopped

salt and pepper to taste

a squeeze of lemon juice (about 2 teaspoons), or to taste

4 thick slices French bread

Chop the drained artichoke hearts finely, and peel, seed and finely chop the tomato.

Heat the oil in a pan, add the artichokes, olives, tomato, chilli, cumin, garlic and salt and pepper. Stir to combine and heat through, adding a little water if necessary to combine the ingredients. When the tomato is softened, add a squeeze of lemon juice and process the mixture to a fairly chunky purée.

Brush the slices of bread with olive oil and toast both sides under a grill. Top each slice with artichoke mixture and serve immediately.

Serves 2

Moroccan Cocktail Scones (recipe page 71)

Master Stock Spices
(recipe page 96)

Pickling Spice (recipe page 109)

Ras el Hanout
(recipe page 142)

Mulling Spice

Madras Curry Powder
(recipe page 74)

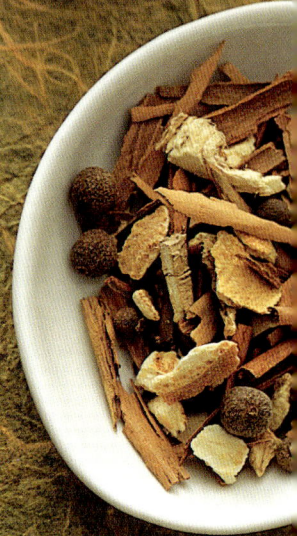

Za'atar
(recipe page 162)

Dukkah
(recipe page 151)

curry

spice mix

Of course we can't let cumin off the hook without using it to make a curry. One of our most memorable curry experiences was in 1986 when we were living in Singapore and revelling in the delights of the spice trade there. We took a couple of friends to lunch at a basic, white-tiled hawker stall in Keppel Road with the appropriate name of 'Glutton's Corner'.

In the traditional manner, the dhoti-clad Indian waiter put banana leaves in front of us and spooned out a couple of cupfuls of light, fluffy rice from a dodgy-looking ex-kerosine tin. Next we pointed to the spice-clad delights on display including tandoori prawns, lamb curry, dhal, samosas and steaming naan fresh from the tandoor. These were accompanied by an array of pickles and hot chilli pastes, doled out of a serving arrangement made from five tomato soup cans wired together and held by a fencing-wire handle.

The pre-tasting aromas were so mouth-watering that we found it almost impossible to draw breath between mouthfuls and before the hour was out we were all clutching distended bellies, thankful that we had exhausted the gambit of all offerings available and did not have to try any more dishes. When we got home all we could do was lie down and attempt to digest our inordinately tasty repast. Although we try to be a little more moderate these days, we will never forget that memorable lunch at Glutton's Corner.

Now there are many kinds of curry, and the sheer joy to be had from experimenting with various combinations has to be shared. We are sharing our basic principles of curry making with you and adding some suggestions for your own variations.

A good curry begins with a well-balanced curry powder. You can make one by grinding your own spices, or using good-quality ground spices from a reputable spice merchant. This blend is a basic 'Madras' style of curry powder, which is pleasantly balanced, is quite fragrant and reasonably 'punchy' without being too hot. For more heat, just add more chilli powder or for less heat, substitute some or all of the chilli powder with a mild paprika. This blend may be used immediately, or stored in an airtight container for up to 12 months.

madras curry powder

For a robust flavour, which is most appropriate with red meats, these spices may be dry-roasted whole and then ground. Be careful though not to burn them, as they will become intensely bitter. A roasted blend should be used within the next few days, as once roasted the spice oils will oxidise and degenerate over the following weeks. For more details on blending and roasting spices see pages 8, 9, 10.

5 teaspoons ground coriander seed
2 teaspoons ground cumin seed
1 teaspoons turmeric powder
3/4 teaspoon ground ginger
1/2 teaspoon ground black pepper
1/3 teaspoon ground yellow mustard seed
1/3 teaspoon ground fenugreek seed
1/3 teaspoon ground cinnamon sticks
pinch teaspoon ground cloves
pinch teaspoon ground green cardamom seed
pinch teaspoon chilli powder (more or less to taste)

Makes about 1/3 cup

curry

This curry uses the Madras Curry Powder (see page 74) in its unroasted form. The blend itself is then dry-roasted before being made into a curry paste.

6 teaspoons Madras Curry Powder (see page 74)

2 tablespoons oil

3 teaspoons Panch Phora (see page 113)

1 onion, finely chopped

500 g beef, lamb or chicken cut into 2 cm cubes

2 teaspoons lemon juice

400 g can whole peeled tomatoes

1–2 cups water (depending on desired consistency)

2 teaspoons garam masala (see page 79)

2 teaspoons chaat masala (see page 24)

2 tablespoons freshly sliced garlic

2 tablespoons tomato paste

8 curry leaves (fresh or dry)

1 teaspoon methi (dried fenugreek leaves)

Preheat the oven to 125°C. Heat a heavy-based, ovenproof pan on the stove, add the Madras Curry Powder and dry-roast, stirring continuously with a wooden spoon for around 2 minutes, being careful not to let the mixture burn. Add oil and make into a paste. Add panch phora and stir until the seeds start popping. Add onion and stir for 2 minutes, taking care not to overcook. (See page 76 for instructions on making pastes.)

Add the meat, about 6 pieces at a time, making sure each piece is browned and coated with spices. To avoid burning and to prevent the meat from sticking to the base of the pan, add a few teaspoons of water as you stir. This also helps to form the spices into a smoother 'curry gravy'.

Add lemon juice and tomatoes and water, roughly chopping tomatoes while stirring. Sprinkle garam masala and chaat masala over surface and drop in slices of garlic. Add tomato paste, curry leaves and methi, stir and turn off the heat.

Cover the pan with a lid and cook in the oven for 2 hours. Remove curry from oven, allow it to cool and store in the refrigerator to heat and serve the next day.

Serves 4

Here are some ideas for different curry spice blends.

- For a Sri Lankan (Ceylonese) curry use more cumin, ground cinnamon, cloves and cardamom while reducing the ginger, mustard and fenugreek.
- For a Korma curry (which gets its creaminess from yoghurt or dairy cream) increase the coriander seed, ginger, cinnamon and cardamom; add some ground almonds and leave out the mustard and fenugreek seeds altogether.
- For a sharp, hot curry, increase the chilli, ginger and black pepper. Substitute the cinnamon with cassia and use 1–2 teaspoons of amchur powder instead of lemon juice.

Variations

You may vary the spice combinations above to create your own special curries which will no doubt impress your friends greatly, and maybe also lead to some long afternoon naps to sleep off the result!

curry pastes

There is no need to get stressed about the notion of using curry pastes; you can make your own so easily. What makes something wet? Water! To quote the famous Pat Chapman of the Curry Club, 'Mix the spices with water to make a paste. Add the paste ...'

Many people have become used to the idea of curry pastes, which they can buy in jars and feel they are getting something very convenient. But dry spice mixes can be used in just the same way.

If you particularly want a curry paste, use this method: lightly fry some finely chopped onion and garlic in oil, add the curry powder of your choice and add water to make a paste. You can also add some tomato paste to make it richer and more brightly coloured. For an extra fresh flavour, add chopped fresh coriander or curry leaves, and use a little tamarind water, which is made by soaking a piece of tamarind in water and straining it off. Keep refrigerated.

fennel seed

Foeniculum vulgare dulce

Poor old fennel is somewhat in the 'always the bridesmaid, never the bride' category. Although stronger in flavour than coriander, fennel seed is one of the amalgamating spices, having that highly sought after ability to bring other flavours together while imparting its own delicious fresh anise notes. But while this seed makes a worthy flavour contribution in many spice mixes, it is mostly listed as an also-ran rather than a winner.

Also called common fennel, Florence fennel, sweet fennel, finnochio. Another member of the fennel family is Lucknow fennel

Flavour and aroma warm, spicy-but-not-hot, breath-freshening flavour with a wheat-like faint anise freshness. Lucknow fennel: very sweet with licorice flavour

Flavour group seeds amalgamating

Native to southern Europe and the Mediterranean, this ubiquitous plant has made itself useful around the world as a spice, a vegetable, a herb and an aid to digestion. When the plump, crisp, pale fennel bulbs appear at the greengrocer, they are nearly always labelled as aniseed, which of course they're not. It's another case of fennel's attributes being overlooked.

If you visit a gourmet delicatessen or a good spice shop, you may well find there are at least three different fennel seeds on offer. The plain, all-purpose ones are fairly large golden-coloured sweet seeds with a distinctive anise/licorice flavour. Sometimes they are larger than at other times, and this is because there are two crops in a season. The first crop is larger and more succulent, while the second crop after a dry season yields smaller seeds.

Sugar-coated fennel seeds are exactly the same seeds coated with candy – they are traditionally served like this after a meal because, like cousins dill and caraway, they play an important role in aiding digestion. At Herbies we decided that candy-coated fennel seeds are like a larger version of the familiar 'hundreds and thousands' with which every Australian family makes 'fairy bread'. So we named them 'lakhs and crores' in our shop. (In India, a lakh is 100,000 and a crore is 10,000,000 – that's inflation for you!)

The third fennel seed is known as Lucknow fennel. It is about half the size of a standard fennel seed and much greener in colour and sweeter in flavour. In fact it is so sweet and flavoursome that you could close your eyes and imagine you were eating licorice candy. It is served after dinner like the sugar-coated ones, but it doesn't need candy to embellish it. Often you'll find it in a traditional paan mixture, which the Indians like to wrap in a betel leaf and chew in lieu of coffee to round off a meal.

choosing and using

Fennel seeds should be pale yellow to green and have a characteristic 'anise' flavour. Make sure that the seeds are clean and not contaminated with any tiny pebbles that might break a tooth. Store in airtight containers, and once the seeds are ground, keep them in an airtight container away from direct light.

In Indian and Asian cooking the seeds are often lightly roasted before being added to curries and satay sauces. It is the sweet, light flavour of fennel that helps to differentiate Asian curries from Indian ones – it is used in greater proportions in Asia.

The seeds, whole or ground, can be added to soup, breads, spicy sausages, pasta, tomato dishes, sauerkraut and salads. Watch out for Italian specialties such as taralini (savoury biscuits) showing anise as an ingredient – in fact it's fennel.

- Add whole fennel seeds to a pork and veal mince to make a sophisticated meat loaf or terrine.
- Enhance a rich chutney with fennel seeds and serve with cheese.
- Add a teaspoon of ground seeds to batter or breadcrumbs for frying fish fillets.
- Use fennel seeds (alone or mixed with cumin, mustard and nigella) in bread dough, scones or savoury biscuits. Try them in dumplings!

Fennel seeds, with their light anise notes, blend well with most spices and have amalgamating properties similar to coriander seeds. They should be used a little more sparingly than coriander seed though, so their anise flavour does not dominate.

Fennel seeds combine with allspice, cardamom, chilli, cinnamon, cloves, coriander seed, cumin seed, fenugreek seed, galangal, ginger, mustard, paprika and turmeric. They are an essential ingredient in garam masala and should always be used in Chinese five-spice, Cajun spice blends, panch phora and Malay curries.

See also pages 247–50 for fennel leaf.

garam masala

Garam masala is a traditional Indian blend of spices that's added to all sorts of dishes including curries and butter chicken. It's so convenient to use that it's often added instead of the individual spices. The blend we have created is a balanced, almost sweet blend, with just a hint of a peppery bite. It doesn't have the characteristic 'curry' notes of cumin, coriander and turmeric, which makes it a very handy spicing agent across a wide range of dishes.

4 teaspoons ground fennel seeds
2¹/₂ teaspoons ground cinnamon sticks
2¹/₂ teaspoons ground caraway seed
¹/₂ teaspoon ground black pepper
¹/₂ teaspoon ground cloves
¹/₂ teaspoon ground green cardamom seeds

Blend the ground spices and store in an airtight container.

Makes about 2 tablespoons

satay spice blend

This spice blend may be made up and kept in an airtight container until you need it to make satay sauce.

5 teaspoons ground coriander seed

4 teaspoons ground fennel seeds

1½ teaspoons turmeric powder

1 teaspoon ground ginger

¾ teaspoon ground cassia

½ teaspoon ground black pepper

¼ teaspoon ground cloves

¼ teaspoon ground green cardamom seeds

¼ teaspoon chilli powder (more or less to taste)

Makes about ½ cup

satay sauce

A homemade satay sauce is particularly satisfying because it does not require the large amount of vinegar used in commercial sauces to achieve preservation.

3 tablespoons Satay Spice Blend (see this page)

½ tablespoon peanut oil

½ tablespoon dark palm sugar
   or soft brown sugar

6 tablespoons crunchy peanut butter

Dry-roast the spice blend in a saucepan until the aroma wafts up to your nostrils and the colour darkens slightly. Be careful not to over-roast as this will make the spice mixture bitter.

Add the peanut oil and gula melaka, stirring constantly for 1–2 minutes. If the paste starts to stick to the base of the saucepan, add a little water (1 or 2 teaspoons at a time) while stirring.

Add peanut butter and keep stirring until all ingredients are blended together and the sauce is heated through. This sauce may be used straightaway or kept in the refrigerator for 2 or 3 days.

Makes enough for 500 g meat

franz's regal peshawari naan

Our customer and friend Franz Scheurer was inspired to create this version of naan bread after he discovered Lucknow fennel in our shop.

300 g plain flour

1 teaspoon gluten powder

1 teaspoon baking powder

1 teaspoon salt

1 teaspoon sugar

2 teaspoons poppy seeds

1 tablespoon Lucknow fennel seeds

1 teaspoon sesame seeds

1 teaspoon ground green cardamom seeds

4 tablespoons currants

1 tablespoon coarsely crushed pistachio nuts

1 tablespoon pine nuts

2 teaspoons active brewer's yeast

$2/3$ cup milk, lukewarm

160 ml country style yoghurt

1 tablespoon rosewater

1 egg, beaten

Put the flour, gluten powder, baking powder, salt and sugar into a bowl with the seeds and currants. Lightly roast the pistachio nuts and pine nuts and once they have completely cooled, add to the flour.

Crumble the yeast and mix it with a little of the lukewarm milk. Beat the yoghurt into the remaining milk, add the rosewater and heat this mixture until lukewarm. Stir in the yeast paste. Gradually add this mixture to the flour and mix to a dough. Knead well, then add the beaten egg and knead thoroughly again.

Cover the dough with a damp towel and leave in a warm place to rise until it doubles in size. This will take about 90 minutes.

Preheat the oven to 230°C. Break the dough into 8 pieces, roll into balls then flatten with your hands. Place on baking sheets and bake for about 12 minutes or until the bread is puffed and blistered. Serve hot.

Makes 8 pieces

fenugreek seed

Trigonella foenum-graecum

Tasting fenugreek on its own, one has to wonder why it was ever adopted as a food, as it has a very bitter flavour, with a lingering suggestion on the breath of old cooked cabbage. Originally, fenugreek was used as fodder (the word means 'Greek hay') until some bright spark found that, in the right proportions, it could be blended with hot and amalgamating spices to make a curry.

Also called bird's foot, cow's horn, goat's horn, Greek hayseed, hilbeh
Flavour and aroma sharp, slightly spicy aroma, and bitter
Flavour group seeds pungent

This member of the bean and pea family has earned common names like 'goat's horn' and 'cow's horn' thanks to its pod that looks rather like a miniature curved broad bean and contains 10–20 hard yellow-brown seeds with a strong, spicy-yet-sweet scent that reminds you of green peas. The seeds are a vital ingredient, whole or ground, in curry mixes and the blend, panch phora.

Somewhat surprisingly, the seeds are also used to make artificial maple syrup – think of this next time you smell them, and you'll detect that sweet, maple-syrup aroma beyond the initial spiciness.

choosing and using

Fenugreek seeds vary little in quality; however, check carefully before grinding your seeds, as it's possible to find tiny stones in the pack if they haven't been properly cleaned.

Buy ground seeds in small quantities as a little usually goes a long way. The ground seeds retain their flavour fairly well for at least a year, and if you like to make your own curry powder from scratch, it is much easier to use the powder!

A little caution is necessary on the quantity front – too much definitely spoils the flavour.

Curry spices are sometimes dry-roasted before grinding, but be especially careful with fenugreek, as overcooking at this stage will make them far too bitter.

Fenugreek seeds are one of the hardest spices – it's not only in looks that they resemble little pieces of gravel! We once encountered a recipe which suggested that the seeds should be ground using the back of a spoon, and immediately we concluded that the writer had never tested the recipe! If you are making a wet curry paste, soak the fenugreek seeds overnight and they will swell and soften. Then they can easily be mixed with other ingredients to make your paste.

The sharpness of fenugreek seed sprouts combines well with the mild grassiness of alfalfa, and you can grow them easily. Just put some seeds into a glass jar and cover the top with a piece of gauze or old stocking, held in place with a rubber band. Run some water into the jar, swill it around to wet the seeds, then drain it off, placing the jar on its side. Do this twice a day as the seeds sprout. Add them to sandwiches and salad with a little oil and lemon dressing.

Fenugreek seeds are team players. Their main role in the kitchen is as an ingredient in curry powder, especially curries with bite, such as vindaloo and Sri Lankan curries. We make one curry blend with no fenugreek at all, and customers love its soft, rounded aroma and flavour. It is interesting to smell that blend and then immediately smell a more traditional blend containing fenugreek – the sharpness of the fenugreek is very obvious.

North African food often features quite heavy doses of fenugreek, which must be an acquired taste, as those recipes we've tried have seemed far too strong. Soaking ground fenugreek in water produces a hummus-like texture, indicating the very efficient thickening properties of this spice.

In India the roasted ground seeds have sometimes been infused for a coffee substitute or adulterant, their bitter edge mimicking the bitterness of some coffee – but you'd have to be desperate! Like all seed spices, fenugreek seeds can be infused to make a tea – once again, only for the desperate or taste-bud-deficient.

- Use fenugreek seeds sparingly in curries, African stews and obscure Yemeni condiments.
- Fresh fenugreek sprouts make a spicy addition to salads, sandwiches and omelettes.
- Leaves, fresh or dried, complement vegetable curries and stews.

The sharp, appetising flavour of fenugreek seeds is used extensively in curry powders (see page 74) and is an important ingredient in sambar (see page 28), as the beany notes complement dhal deliciously. Fenugreek combines well with cinnamon and cassia, cloves, coriander seeds and leaves, cumin, curry leaves, fennel seed, ginger, mustard, nigella, black pepper and turmeric. With the exception of panch phora, where fenugreek is a major ingredient, we would recommend using no more than 5 per cent of fenugreek seeds in any spice blend, including curry powders.

When a spice blend calls for roasting some of the ingredients before mixing, roast the fenugreek quickly and separately from the other spices. This will avoid over-heating, a cause of intense bitterness.

The smoky notes created from burning charcoal when cooking in the tandoor contribute to tandoori cooking's distinctive flavour, and a good tandoori spice blend provides a convenient way to emulate this famous taste. An important point to note is that tandoori dishes do not have to be bright red. Sadly, too many restaurants and paste manufacturers resort to using tartrazine (colour additive E102) and Sunset Yellow (colour additive E110), both potentially allergic dyes for some people.

Rub the following Tandoori Spice Blend into any meat (lamb, pork, chicken pieces or wings and fish) or tofu, and allow to dry-marinate for about an hour before cooking. It does not contain salt so it doesn't draw out the succulence. Simply add some salt to taste just before cooking or after if required.

See also pages 251–4 for fenugreek leaves.

tandoori spice blend

This blend is easily made using the ground spices listed below. For those who like it hot, the quantities of ginger, black pepper and chilli may be increased by 50 per cent or more. The quantity of spice blend used in a dish will depend on the surface area of the meat being marinated. For chicken wings, allow about 2 teaspoons of spice blend per 500 g and for a roast leg of lamb, use 1 teaspoon for 500 g.

5 teaspoons sweet paprika

1 teaspoon ground cumin

1 teaspoon ground coriander seeds

$1/2$ teaspoon turmeric powder

$1/2$ teaspoon ground ginger

$1/2$ teaspoon ground cinnamon

$1/2$ teaspoon ground fenugreek seeds

$1/2$ teaspoon ground black pepper

$1/3$ teaspoon medium-heat chilli powder

$1/4$ teaspoon ground caraway seeds

$1/3$ teaspoon ground green cardamom seeds

1 brown (Indian) cardamom pod, ground

$1/2$ teaspoon dried mint (do not grind)

Mix all ingredients thoroughly and store in an airtight container, protected from light and heat, for up to 12 months.

Makes about $1/2$ cup

hilbeh (yemenite dip)

We have changed this very traditional dip just a little, to make it more acceptable to Western palates. The fenugreek bite is quite overt, which has a stimulating effect on the taste buds – think of Campari and Angostura bitters. If you'd like to taste it in a more authentic version, leave out the coriander seeds, tomato paste and water.

2 teaspoons ground fenugreek seeds,
    soaked in $1/2$ cup water for at least 3 hours

$1/4$ teaspoon grains of paradise

$1/4$ teaspoon caraway seeds

1 teaspoon ground coriander seeds

1 fresh, ripe tomato, peeled and chopped

1 teaspoon salt

1 heaped tablespoon fresh chopped
    coriander leaves

1 red chilli, about 10 cm long, chopped

1 clove garlic, peeled and chopped

1 tablespoon tomato paste

$1/2$ cup water

Make sure that the fenugreek seeds soak for the longest time possible as this modifies the bitterness.

Grind the grains of paradise, caraway and coriander seeds using a pestle and mortar.

Combine all the ingredients in a blender and process until smooth. Transfer the purée to a small saucepan, bring to the boil and simmer for 3 minutes, removing any scum that appears on the surface. Cool and store, covered, in the fridge.

Serve as a dip with pita bread, or treat as a Yemeni alternative to chutney.

Makes about $1^1/2$ cups

galangal

greater galangal *Alpinia galanga*

lesser galangal *Alpinia officinarum*

kencur *Kaempferia galanga*

There is a family of culinary rhizomes, which includes ginger, turmeric, galangal, kencur, orris root and zedoary. They all bear a family resemblance without duplicating each other, although the latter three have been rather overtaken by the preceding three.

GREATER GALANGAL *Alpinia galanga*
Also called Java root, galanga, Laos
powder, lengkuas, Thai ginger, kha
Flavour and aroma pungent, acidic,
tangy, a little horseradishy
Flavour group pungent

LESSER GALANGAL *Alpinia officinarum*
Also called China root, Chinese ginger,
colic root, East Indian catarrh root, san bai
Flavour and aroma ... milder than greater
galangal, mostly used medicinally

KENCUR *Kaempferia galanga*
Also called kenchur, kentjur
Flavour and aroma slightly chalky,
mild, lightly acidic, camphor notes
Flavour group pungent

The word that comes to mind with galangal rhizomes is 'sleek' – while cousins turmeric and ginger twist and turn like tortured arthritic joints, galangal's shape is more serene. Many people first knowingly strike (literally) galangal as those fibrous, woody slices in tom yum soup. In fact this is a spice that's seldom eaten on its own and is more normally grated or pounded up with ingredients like garlic, lemongrass, chilli and onions to add its incredible perfume and pungency to South-East Asian fare. Thai cooks like it fresh and add it in copious quantities to soups, stir-fries and red and green curries – though never combined with ginger; in Thai tradition, you use one or the other.

Although we think of this very much as an Asian spice, in medieval times Europeans used it in great quantities for both cooking and medicinal purposes and you can find references to it in some surprising places like Chaucer's *Canterbury Tales*:

> A Cook they hadde with hem for the nones
> To boille the chiknes with the marybones,
> And poudre-marchant tart and galyngale.
> (Geoffrey Chaucer, 'General Prologue',
> *The Canterbury Tales*, c. 1387)

The perky, pep-up properties of this aromatic root were also recognised by the Arabs who found it handy to ginger up their horses, by the Tartars who took it in their tea and throughout the Orient where powdered galangal was taken as a snuff.

The galangals are members of the tropical ginger family. Greater galangal, with its sharp, sinus-penetrating perfume and hot clean taste, is the one widely used in cooking in Thailand, Indonesia and Malaysia.

Growing to a height of around 2 m, it has long, elegant, blade-like leaves and green and white flowers with red tips. Like ginger, the edible bit is the knobbly, orange-brown skinned rhizome. The pungent taste comes from the resins similar to those also found in ginger and grains of paradise. Galangal is used fresh and dried and is available in slices or as a powder. Fresh galangal has a distinct fragrance, while the dried galangal is spicier and sweetly aromatic, almost like a rather head-clearing version of cinnamon.

Kencur, a more unassuming cousin, has a milder flavour with a distinct chalkiness and gentle fragrance. Only growing to about 15 cm in height, it has small rhizomes looking rather like puny ginger. The bright green, lily-like leaves are eaten raw as a salad vegetable in Asia, while the rhizomes are pounded to a paste before adding to fish curries.

choosing and using

Galangal is available as fresh whole rhizomes and as dried slices or powder. The pure and refreshing aroma of the fresh spice will change to a more medicinal and sweet taste by drying.

Most Asian specialty food stores will stock the fresh rhizomes alongside the fresh ginger and turmeric rhizomes and it can be tricky to pick the right one. Galangal rhizomes look like ginger, have the characteristic circular stripes around them but are up to twice the size of ginger, and not as orange as fresh turmeric.

The dried slices can be bought from specialty spice shops and Asian stores and keep their flavour for around two to three years if stored properly, away from light and humidity. Don't even attempt to grind the dried slices yourself – if you want powder, buy powder. But remember, the powders lose their flavour faster, so buy in small quantities.

If you need to substitute, one slice of the root is equivalent to half a teaspoon of powder. Generally small quantities are specified in recipes, galangal being used in larger amounts than kencur.

Like ginger, its aroma merges well with garlic, and gives a fresh, lemony lift to a dish. A tip worth remembering is that a pinch of galangal powder helps level out the 'fishiness' of strongly flavoured fish.

The dried slices are, well, very dry. Soaking before use for 30 minutes helps to reconstitute them, but it's generally best to remove the slices before serving, as they are not chewable to any but the most hardy of diners. Generally use galangal slices in soups such as tom yum, where they will contribute to the sourness of the soup.

Use fresh rhizomes peeled, grated or chopped, and if fresh is not available, use the powder in sauces, soups, satays and sambals, chicken, meat and vegetable curries.

These rhizomes find themselves very much at home in the food of Singapore and Malaysia, such as Nonya laksas and sambals.

When thinking galangal and kencur, we tend to think orchestra rather than soloist, as both spices are usually found blended with others to make beautiful music together.

Galangal's pungency makes it an important ingredient in many Asian spice blends. Although it is advisable to use galangal sparingly, it often works best when combined with its cousin ginger. Galangal goes well with allspice, cardamom, chilli, cinnamon and cassia, cloves, coriander seed, cumin, fenugreek seed, ginger, mustard, paprika, tamarind and turmeric.

thai spice mix

This is a spicy, tangy, fresh-tasting blend of spices that gives a characteristic Thai flavour to dishes. Sprinkle over stir-fries while cooking and add to minced seafood when making fish cakes. You can add a teaspoon of this blend to a cup of boiling water to make the basis for an instant hot, sour soup. Then just add a little soy and fish sauce, some prawns and instant noodles, and hey presto! This blend can be made from dried ingredients and stored for up to 12 months in an airtight container. If made using the fresh ingredients (shown as optional) it will keep in the freezer for up to 3 months.

4 teaspoons dried and crushed kaffir lime leaves

   (or 6 teaspoons fresh)

4 teaspoons dried lemongrass

   (or 6 teaspoons finely chopped fresh)

2 teaspoons sea salt

2 teaspoons dried coriander leaves

   (or 3 teaspoons chopped fresh)

1 teaspoon dried jalapeno green chilli

   (or 1 teaspoon fresh green chilli, seeded and chopped)

1 teaspoon dried minced garlic

   (or 1 clove fresh garlic, crushed)

1 teaspoon ground galangal

1/2 teaspoon sugar

1/2 teaspoon ground ginger

Makes about 1/2 cup

To make Tom Yum Soup, add 1 teaspoon Thai Spice Mix with 1 teaspoon soy sauce and 1/2 teaspoon fish sauce to each 1 cup water. Add the desired amount of raw prawns and cooked noodles. Simmer until prawns are cooked and serve.

To make a Thai Green Curry, stir-fry 500 g of chicken and vegetables with 2 teaspoons Thai Spice Mix. Just before serving add enough coconut milk to achieve the desired consistency and serve with steamed rice.

nasi goreng spice mix

Add to fried rice for a nasi goreng flavour. To make a sambal paste, mix one measure of nasi goreng Spice Mix with an equal quantity of water. Add half a measure of oil and stir until blended. Keep refrigerated or use at once.

3 teaspoons medium-heat chilli powder

2 teaspoons garlic powder

2 teaspoons dried red chilli flakes

1 teaspoon sugar

1 teaspoon salt

1/2 teaspoon amchur powder

1/2 teaspoon ground galangal

1/4 teaspoon ground ginger

Makes about 1/3 cup

laksa spice mix

12 teaspoons Madras Curry Powder (see page 74)

3 teaspoons ground fennel seed

1$^1/_2$ teaspoons salt

1 teaspoon ground galangal

1 teaspoon medium-heal chilli flakes

1 teaspoon sugar

This spice mix may be blended and then stored in an airtight container for up to 12 months.

Makes about $^2/_3$ cup

laksa

1 tablespoon peanut oil

6 teaspoons Laksa Spice Mix (see this page)

$^1/_2$ chopped onion

2 cups chicken, fish or vegetable stock

$^1/_2$ teaspoon shrimp paste, optional

1$^1/_2$ cups coconut cream

250 g chicken, tofu or seafood (sliced)

100 g bean sprouts

200 g Asian noodles (cooked and drained)

$^1/_2$ tablespoon fresh Vietnamese mint leaves

$^1/_2$ tablespoon coriander leaves

Heat the oil in a large heavy-based pan. Add the Laksa Spice Mix and stir to a paste.

Add the onion and stir for 2 minutes. Add the stock (up to 3 cups for a less creamy soup) and shrimp paste and bring to boil. Add coconut cream and chicken, tofu, prawns or seafood and simmer gently for 10 minutes or until cooked.

When ready to serve, add bean sprouts, noodles, Vietnamese mint and coriander leaves, heat through and serve.

Serves 6

balinese duck curry

Our friend Asian chef Tony Tan, has shared this wonderfully aromatic recipe with us. The kencur adds a completely new dimension to the dish, which is also rather mild in comparison to other curries. We like to strip the duck meat from the bones before serving over rice in a big bowl, almost like laksa. If using a whole duck, cut into serving portions. It works very well with chicken too.

Spice Paste

1 medium onion, peeled and chopped

4 cloves garlic, peeled

2.5 cm fresh galangal

5 cm fresh ginger

2.5 cm fresh turmeric

2.5 cm fresh kencur or 1½ teaspoons
      dried kencur powder

4 fresh red long chillies, chopped

1 teaspoon coriander seeds, roasted

4 candlenuts

1 teaspoon shrimp paste

2 teaspoons black peppercorns

2 cloves

pinch nutmeg

⅓ cup tablespoons vegetable oil

1 whole duck or 4 duck marylands

2 litres thin coconut milk

2 salam leaves or kaffir lime leaves

2 lemongrass stalks, crushed

1 teaspoon dark palm sugar

salt to taste

fried shallots to garnish

To make the spice paste, blend the ingredients in a food processor until fine.

Heat the oil and fry the spice paste over medium heat until aromatic. Add the duck pieces and continue to fry for another 3 minutes. Add the coconut milk, salam or kaffir lime leaves, lemongrass and palm sugar. Simmer, uncovered, stirring now and then, until the duck is tender and the sauce is reduced, about 40 minutes. Add salt to taste. Serve garnished with fried shallots.

Serves 4

ginger

Zingiber officinale

Ginger. What a world of memories and aromas the word conjures up. Whole pieces in syrup in exotic blue and white ceramic jars. Crystallised, sugary morsels. Ginger ale. Ginger beer. Gingernuts. That speedy gingerbread man of nursery rhyme fame. Ginger Rogers, Spice Girl Ginger, Gilligan's Island Ginger. Glamour, excitement, and a hint of danger. This spice has really made its presence felt and entered the language – think 'ginger up', 'ginger group' …
but never gingerly!

Flavour and aroma warm to hot,
sweet but biting, pungent, appetising
Flavour group pungent

Ginger is valued the world over as a culinary herb, condiment, spice, and home remedy, with beneficial properties that have long been recognised and recorded. So it's a bit surprising that we don't know exactly where it originally came from, as it doesn't seem to grow anywhere in a wild state. It is believed to be a native of southern Asia, and we do know that it has been cultivated in both China and India for hundreds and hundreds of years.

If you added the kilometres up, this spicy rhizome would have to have more frequent flyer points than Superman. Thanks to Roman tax records, we know ginger reached Europe around two thousand years ago, you can also read about it in the Koran and 11th century Anglo-Saxon medicinal books, which suggests it arrived in England long before William the Conquerer. And before you could say 'potato', 'tomato' or 'corn', it was indelibly imprinted on European taste buds – by the 13th and 14th centuries it was second only to pepper in the polls. In fact it was so popular, no one left home without it. The Arabs took it from Asia to East Africa in the 13th century, and the Spanish established ginger plantations in Jamaica in the 16th century.

Ginger's success can be put down in part to its great taste, but also to the fact that it's a great grower. Those spicy rhizomes are readily transported live in pots and are amazingly adaptable, shooting forth vigorously in subtropical and even some temperate climes (it thrives in our garden on the New South Wales Central Coast).

Major commercial producers of ginger are found in nearly every tropical and subtropical country in the world: India, Jamaica, Nigeria, Sierra Leone, Brazil, China, Japan, Indonesia, Taiwan and Australia. Ginger root, or rhizome, is the knobbly part that grows and multiplies underground in tuberous joints. Rhizomes are essentially underground stems. The aroma and flavour can vary depending on the variety (and there are hundreds), the stage at which it is harvested and the region where it is grown.

We have often found when we visit India that people in the spice industry want to impress us with their modernity, but we were lucky enough to meet someone who was not afraid to let us see the old traditional ways of processing ginger. We had often seen go-downs stacked high with nose-tingling sacks of ginger, but we were curious about what happened between field and sack.

Our Indian contact took us some hours' drive into the countryside, where large, smooth sheets of rock covered much of a gently sloping hillside. It was government-owned land, leased at this time of year to a growers' co-operative. The rocks, warmed by months of sun, were spread widely with freshly dug hands of ginger, all the individual growers staking out their own little areas. Frames of wonky poles held strips of hessian, providing shade for workers, who sat with the handle of a reaping hook held between the soles of feet pressed firmly together. On the curving blade they scraped the ginger to remove dirt and some skin.

The partly cleaned pieces were tossed onto a tablecloth-sized sack which was picked up by two young men (one at each end) who shook and agitated the sacking while the bits of ginger rolled about in the middle. It looked like a game, but it was actually a very efficient abrasive cleaning method. Dried, cleaned and packed into sacks, the ginger then made its way to the city to be traded. Ginger dried whole like this is sold exclusively for grinding into ginger powder.

choosing and using

Ginger is an ingredient that comes in a variety of forms – fresh, pickled, dried, and crystallised among them. In each of its incarnations, however, ginger makes its simultaneously hot and refreshing presence known.

Ginger harvested early is less fibrous and has a sweeter taste than that which has been left in the ground long enough to become hot and coarse. Although ginger powder lacks the volatile fresh rhizome aroma, it retains that spicy fragrance and unmistakable taste.

Ginger root, or rhizomes, should be bursting with freshness. The younger they are, the better – rosy-cheeked and unblemished, so fresh that they will break with a clean, juice-releasing snap. This is the way to get ginger's big lively punch in its purest form. You can treat fresh ginger in lots of ways. Simply slice into discs to toss into marinades or julienne into the smallest of all possible strips for stir-fries. Peeled and finely grated is the best way to release the juices, which amalgamate so easily into food. Purpose-built ginger graters work well to make a fine pulp while leaving the long fibres attached to the part you're holding.

You can keep fresh ginger for up to a month in the refrigerator. Just cut off what you need, when you need it. The cut edge will dry and toughen, and can easily be trimmed when you want more.

Ginger slices are fresh rhizomes, which are either sliced and dried or sliced and pickled. Dried slices are handy in clear soups and marinades when the flavour is to be infused and the pieces removed before serving. Pickled slices are very popular in Japan where they add a refreshing tang to sushi.

Ginger powder, while not at home with fresh Asian applications, has a world of its own encompassing gingerbread, ginger pudding and innumerable cakes, biscuits, cookies and puddings.

Freeze-dried ginger powder retains the tang of freshly grated ginger and is ideal for using in uncooked dipping sauces and quickly prepared stir-fry dishes as a substitute for fresh ginger.

Crystallised or sugar-coated ginger cubes vary depending on how long they have matured in the ground before harvest. Ginger from Buderim in Queensland has earned a reputation for mildness and tenderness because it is harvested young. More mature ginger gives a tougher, stringier, hotter result. Store dried and powdered ginger in airtight containers.

If you're a cookies-in-the-oven type of guy, the word ginger will immediately bring to mind gingerbread men, biscuits and cookies, steamed pudding with ginger sauce, fruit cake, and all manner of sweet morsels. You'll also add it to your homemade curry powder, as well as the pickles and chutneys filling the shelves in your well-stocked pantry.

Or if you're a fresh-is-best kind of gal, you'll especially love the brightness and lightness that freshly grated ginger brings to Asian stir-fry and marinades. You'll add paper-thin, pink, pickled slices to sushi, and add a hint of fresh ginger juice to fruit salads. And, if you're lucky, you might find tender green nodules pushing forth from your fresh ginger root. These can be finely chopped and added to the most wonderful green salad you've ever made.

Then again, if you're an if-it's-beer-it's-okay kind of bloke, you can use either fresh or dried ginger to make ginger wine, ginger beer – or ginger tea for the ladies.

If you are an addicted ginger lover, you'll always be able to come up with one more use for this more-ish spice!

- Store peeled fresh ginger slices and a couple of whole fresh chillies in sherry. This infusion will improve with age – use in stir-fries or add a slurp to a bowl of soup.
- Ginger goes well with fish. Deep-fry juliennes of ginger and drain well for a crunchy garnish.
- Add ground ginger to shortbread and melting moment dough, and add a little ground ginger to icing for date loaf or carrot cake.
- Finely chop crystallised ginger and sprinkle on top of roasting pumpkin.

You may be surprised to learn that ginger powder is used in many spice blends, even those that may have no hint of gingery notes. This is partly due to the fact that ginger can be hot or mild, and also because it goes equally well with sweet and savoury foods. Ginger is found in many barbecue seasoning mixes, which benefit from its meat-tenderising attributes. North African berbere, Jamaican jerk seasoning, Asian red and green curries, Indian curry powders, tandoori spice blends, ras el hanout and sweet mixed spice all owe much of their character to this zingy rhizome.

Ginger combines well with allspice, cardamom, chilli, cinnamon and cassia, cloves, coriander (leaves and seeds), cumin seed, curry leaves, fennel seed, galangal (a close relative), kaffir lime leaves, lemongrass, lemon myrtle, paprika, star anise and turmeric (also a relative).

Although sliced dried ginger may be one of the least appetising-looking spices, it is an important ingredient in our Chinese master stock. When we make this master stock, fully intending to put it in the fridge for later use, we are often lured by its mouth-watering aroma while it boils to make something sinful with it straightaway, such as pork spare ribs.

A master stock is something like a sweet, thick, spicy soy sauce and we often use it in Asian cooking as a substitute for regular soy sauce. The secret is in the spices, which are all tied up in a muslin ball and infused with the soy sauce, sugar and water. This ball can be used more than once and in China, families will keep a master stock ball for many years, adding more spices to freshen-up the flavour until they end up with something the size of a soccer ball. We've even been told about families that have willed their master stock ball to the next generation! Being cautious Westerners though, we'd recommend using a master stock ball about three times and keeping it in the fridge in-between infusions.

master stock spices

This particular master stock spice blend is made from whole and chopped spices. We like to chop some of the spices as this helps them release their flavour more effectively.

6 teaspoons broken star anise
(broken into approximately 5 mm bits)

3 teaspoons chopped licorice root

3 teaspoons cumin seeds

3 teaspoons dried chopped ginger
(use secateurs to cut dried ginger
slices into 5 mm pieces)

2 teaspoons Sichuan pepper

2 teaspoons allspice berries

2 teaspoons fennel seeds

1 cassia stick, broken

1 teaspoon coriander seeds

1 teaspoon medium-heat chilli flakes (depending on how
spicy you like it, you could add more chilli flakes,
use whole birdseye chilli or add blistering
habanero chillies)

1 teaspoon dried orange or mandarin peel

Divide the mixture into two equal parts and wrap each in a muslin square to make infusion balls.

To make a master stock, dissolve 100 g sugar in 2 cups boiling water. Add 1/2 cup soy sauce and one infusion ball filled with spices. Leave to simmer for about 1 hour.

Makes approximately 2 1/2 cups stock

hot and sweet pork

1 tablespoon palm sugar

2 teaspoons ground ginger

juice and zest of 1/2 lime

2 medium-sized pork fillets

2 teaspoons black sesame seeds

1 tablespoon sesame oil

Combine the gula melaka, ginger and lime juice and zest in a pestle and mortar until it is a smooth paste. Coat the pork with the paste (we use one fillet to wipe out the last of the paste from the mortar), sprinkle with black sesame seeds and allow to stand for 30 minutes.

Meanwhile, preheat oven to 160°C and heat a baking tray for a few minutes.

Pour in the sesame oil and roll the pork to coat all over with oil. Bake for 15–20 minutes. (We usually put a few quartered potatoes in the tray 15 minutes before the pork, so that they are ready at the same time.)

Remove the pork from the oven and transfer to a plate. Leave to rest for a few minutes. Add 2 tablespoons of water to the baking tray over medium heat, add salt to taste and stir until pan juices and water have combined to make a caramel-coloured sauce. Drain any juices from the meat back into the sauce. Slice the pork diagonally into slices, and spoon liquid over. Serve with rice or vegetables.

Serves 2–3

Balinese Duck Curry (recipe page 91)

Kangaroo with Spiced Crust (recipe page 100)

christmas morning cocktail

This little summery heart-starter is part of our family's Christmas Day tradition! Call us old-fashioned, but the watermelons with seeds seem to have more flavour than the seedless variety. Sliced into 1–2 cm wafers, it's easy to flip the seeds out from each side.

2 tablespoons finely chopped fresh ginger, with its juice
½ cup ice cubes
2 cups seeded watermelon
½ cup blueberries
mint sprigs, for serving
1 tablespoon vodka (optional)*

Place the ginger, ice cubes, watermelon and blueberries in a blender and whiz until smooth. This can be served as a soft drink, garnished with a leaf of mint and extra ice cubes to taste.

Makes 4 cocktails or 2 long soft drinks

*Note: For an adult version, use around 1 tablespoon vodka to 2 tablespoons or more of juice. Serve in martini glasses with ice cubes and mint to garnish.

mango and ginger sorbet

2 cups water
100 g caster sugar
3 slices fresh ginger plus 1 heaped tablespoon
    grated fresh ginger
2 mangoes, flesh chopped into 1 cm dice
juice of 2 lemons (around 2 tablespoons)

Boil water, sugar and sliced ginger until sugar is dissolved. Reduce heat and simmer for 5 minutes. Allow to cool and remove ginger slices.

Place mango, grated ginger and lemon juice into a food processor and purée until smooth. Combine syrup with mango purée, mix well and pour into a freezer tray. When ice is beginning to form, stir with a fork and return to freezer. When ice forms again, stir again. Repeat process until the sorbet is completely frozen. Alternatively, use an ice-cream maker and follow manufacturer's instructions.

Serves 4

growing

Ginger is easy to grow if you live in a frost-free area. First you need a rhizome with some tender new nodules forming. Plant it into some good potting mix in a small pot and make a little hot-house by pulling a plastic bag down over it and securing it under the base of the pot. Keep it somewhere warm and watch for the first shoots, then remove the plastic bag. Let it establish a little more on your windowsill, then you can plant it out in the garden – ideally in a spot where there is rich, well-drained soil with filtered shade. Give it plenty of room, as it will grow into a sturdy clump with leaves up to 1 m tall.

Let it grow for a few months before attempting to harvest your first produce – ideally, harvesting time should be when the long, slender leaves die away in the autumn.

What you don't use immediately can be stored in the fridge or in a well-ventilated cupboard.

grains of paradise

Amomum melegueta

syn. *Aframomum melegueta*

If you think grains of paradise are virtually unobtainable, spare a thought for the spice merchant trying to track these precious seeds down for his ras el hanout blend. This elusive spice had been the subject of a seemingly endless quest since before we opened Herbie's back in 1997.

Also called Guinea grains, guinea pepper, ginny grains, melegueta pepper, atar, alligator pepper
Flavour and aroma aromatic, spicy, pungent with intense and lingering pepper heat, tasting of ginger and cardamom, with the piney aroma of juniper
Flavour group hot/pungent

Although we found packs of it in Paris spice shops, we were still unable to find our own supplier. Finally, in 2001, we located a source in Sierra Leone who promised reliability and the precious seeds winged their way to Australia some months after payment had been made. Of course there was more waiting at this end while the Australian Quarantine Inspection Service viewed the seeds with unease. To the suspicious mind, 'grains of paradise' must sound just a short step from 'ecstasy'!

All this makes it hard to believe that there was a lively and profitable trade of grains of paradise, cubeb and long peppers with West Africa even before the trade routes from Western Europe to the East Indies were established.

Originally transported across the Sahara by camel caravans, grains of paradise were popular in Europe from the time of Elizabeth I, who, it is said, was extremely partial to them. But in the 17th century with the spice trade to the East Indies flourishing, grains of paradise couldn't face the strong competition from black pepper, clove, mace and nutmeg. Their value and importance diminished and trade dwindled away to virtually nothing.

So where did the name come from? One theory has it that when it was traded in the Middle Ages as a pepper substitute, many people knew the little seeds came from somewhere far-away and exotic, but didn't know exactly where, so 'paradise' was as good a name as any for their place of origin.

Grains of paradise are native to the steamy forest areas of Africa's Gulf of Guinea coast, including Liberia, Ivory Coast, Togo, Nigeria and Cameroon. The tropical, reed-like plant is a close cousin of the ginger and cardamom family. Growing from a rhizome (the ginger connection) to about 1 m, the plant has narrow, bamboo-like leaves and a flower rather like a single pink lily at the base of the plant, followed by reddish-brown pear-shaped capsules that contain many red to brown angular seeds in a jelly-like pulp. Both the flowers and rhizomes have a gingery smell. Unlike cardamom, the seeds are removed from their pod before drying. They have a sharp peppery bite and refreshing astringency, rather like a combination of pepper and cardamom.

choosing and using

Not a mainstream spice by any means, you might find grains of paradise in specialty food stores. The seeds should be dark and dry, without any hint of mustiness. Because the seeds are so hard and pungent, they will keep for a few years in an airtight container.

If you have no grains of paradise, but need their input for a recipe, substitute the given quantity of grains of paradise with a mixture that is half black peppercorns, half green cardamom seeds.

Grains of paradise are often included in ras el hanout mixtures, as well as spice mixes for Tunisian and African cooking (see Hilbeh on page 85).

If you have a spare peppermill, fill it with grains of paradise. Grind, judiciously, over meats and salads. Grains of paradise also complement Tunisian stews, and are particularly appropriate with game and slow-cooked red meat dishes.

Like that other hot, peppery rarity, Tasmanian pepperberry, grains of paradise are not to be taken lightly. However, once discovered, they can become a true soulmate for the kind of palate that appreciates their particular bite and heat.

- Bruise or crack the grains and add to rice for a curry accompaniment.
- Sprinkle ground grains sparingly over fresh fruit and allow to marinate.
- Add a little ground grains to guacamole dip, and grind with gusto over avocado on toast.
- Include bruised grains when making stocks and soups.

This spice is so rare it is not widely used in blends. However, it has sometimes been included in North African ras el hanout and tagine spice blends.

strawberries and spice

Serve with a creamy accompaniment such as ice-cream, cream or crème fraîche.

250 g ripe strawberries
1/2 teaspoon grains of paradise
cream or ice-cream for serving

Hull and slice the strawberries into a shallow bowl. Grind the grains of paradise finely using a mortar and pestle and sprinkle over the strawberries (or place them in a peppermill and grind directly over the fruit). Allow to stand at room temperature for at least 2 hours, during which time the berries will give out some juice. Serve with cream or ice-cream.

Serves 2

kangaroo with spiced crust

1/2 teaspoon salt
1 teaspoon crushed grains of paradise
1 teaspoon akudjura
2 teaspoons ground coriander seed
1/4 cup packet breadcrumbs
30 g butter
2 x 250 g kangaroo steaks, about 3 cm thick
1/2 tablespoon oil

Combine the salt, spices and breadcrumbs in a bowl and rub the butter through with your fingers until the mixture is crumbly. Pressing the mixture together firmly, pack half onto each kangaroo steak, pressing it on hard so that it holds together. Allow to stand for 30 minutes.

Meanwhile, preheat oven to 175ºC. Brush the base of an ovenproof pan with the oil, then carefully add kangaroo steaks. Bake for 20–25 minutes, depending on how rare you like your meat. Remove from oven and rest for 5 minutes, then serve with vegetables or salad.

Serves 2

juniper

Juniperus communis

Juniper berries can sweep one away to far-off pine forests with one whiff of their clean, resinous aroma. You'll often find them in French and German kitchens lurking in casseroles, sauerkraut and coleslaw, as well as marrying their flavour with that of game meats such as duck, quail, rabbit and venison.

Also called juniper berries, juniper fruits
Flavour and aroma piney, fresh, pungent,
reminiscent of gin
Flavour group pungent

This popular and ornamental conifer from the cypress family has tiny blue-grey needle leaves. The colour of its miniature flowers will tell you the gender of the tree – yellowish for male and pale green for female. The female bears small fleshy green cones, known as berries, each of which contains three seeds. When the berries ripen they turn bright navy blue, slightly flushed with a faint bloom. If you have a tree in your garden, add a twig or two to the barbecue fire and share the elusive piney aroma with the meat, the fish and the whole neighbourhood.

choosing and using

Even when technically 'dried', juniper berries are at their best when they are still moist and soft to the touch, squashing relatively easily rather than dry crumbling.

Many people are unaware that the decorative juniper in their garden has edible berries. The real challenge, however, is getting to them through the needle-sharp leaves! The preferred Hemphill method involves sliding a baking tray under the tree until it touches the trunk, then, using chopsticks, plucking the berries and letting them drop into the tray. A less adventurous person might find it easier to buy a pack from the store, but where's the fun in that?

To us, one of the pleasures of winter is the aroma of lightly crushed juniper. Just give your berries a quick bash with the flat side of a knife, or the back of a spoon, to break up the cell structure a bit so that they release their delicious essences during cooking.

Store juniper berries like other spices, away from heat and light, in an airtight container.

As well as delivering its fresh pine-like flavour, juniper cuts the gaminess of game and the fatty effect of duck or pork. Just add about half a dozen (or more if you love the flavour) crushed berries to the breadcrumbs and herbs when you're making stuffing for any such meats. Berries can also be added to fish or lamb dishes.

Juniper berries blend well with other herbs and spices such as thyme, sage, oregano, marjoram, bay leaves, allspice and onions and garlic, in stuffings or casseroles. One of our favourites for a cold night is a simple chicken casserole moistened with a good slurp of red and spiced with all of the above – including a few juniper berries, of course!

If you're a gin drinker, you'll recognise the characteristic aroma of juniper in a good-quality product, as the berries are a key ingredient in gin. They also find themselves in some liqueurs, as well as a rather individual version of mulled wine.

There's no such thing as a quick juniper fix, unless you want to knock back a tipple of gin! Crush a couple of berries and add to your salad dressing, giving it time to rest and work its magic, or add a few berries to preserved citrus fruits, such as cumquats in brandy. You can never go wrong including juniper berries in stuffings for poultry or pork.

Although not commonly used in spice blends, the piney, rich food-balancing freshness of juniper combines well with allspice, bay leaves, marjoram, onion and garlic, oregano, paprika, peppercorns, rosemary, sage, tarragon and thyme. For those who are game to have a go, the following Game Spice Blend may be used as a more complex, yet highly complementary substitute for straight juniper berries.

game spice blend

We like to make this blend by placing all the whole ingredients in a pestle and mortar and then crushing them roughly so the oils from the juniper berries are absorbed by the other spices. The resulting coarse, moist powder bears a pleasant amalgamation of flavours that will complement a stuffing, a casserole or even a meat loaf. Use 1 teaspoon or more of game spice blend to 500 g of meat, or the same quantity that you would have used of juniper berries.

2 teaspoons juniper berries

1 teaspoon whole allspice

1 teaspoon black peppercorns

½ teaspoon coriander seeds

2 cloves

1 whole dried birdseye chilli

1 dried bay leaf

Makes about 2 tablespoons

gretta anna's chicken liver and juniper berry stuffing

This rich and delicious stuffing makes your everyday roast chook a masterpiece. The recipe is from *The Gretta Anna Cookbook*, one of our favourites since its publication in 1978.

1 large onion, very finely chopped

1 teaspoon oil

1 teaspoon butter

3 or 4 chicken livers

70 g cooked and salted rice

1½ tablespoons chopped blanched almonds

1 tablespoon juniper berries, crushed

chicken stock

salt and pepper to taste

Sauté the finely chopped onion in oil and butter until very brown. Remove from pan and set aside. Sauté the chicken livers in the same pan, (adding more oil and butter if necessary), until just cooked through so that they are not releasing blood, but are not dry and grainy. Remove and chop into pieces.

In a bowl, combine the onion and chicken livers with the cooked rice, almonds, juniper berries, and enough chicken stock to moisten. Season to taste.

This quantity is enough for a fairly large chicken – stuffings should never be tightly packed into poultry as they expand on cooking.

rabbit with juniper berries

This is a plan-ahead meal, as you have to marinate the rabbit for 3–4 hours beforehand. It is delicious on wintry weekends, served with heaps of mashed potatoes! For a change, try making it with 500 g chicken thigh pieces, or throw in some soya beans for a variation.

1 rabbit, jointed

1/3 cup olive oil

12 juniper berries

2 teaspoons dried thyme leaves

2 cloves garlic, chopped

8 rashers bacon

1 x 400 g can chopped tomatoes

Marinate the rabbit with the oil, berries, thyme and garlic for 3–4 hours.

Preheat oven to 180ºC. Remove rabbit pieces from marinade (reserving the mixture) and wrap each in a single bacon rasher to make a parcel. Pour the tomatoes into an ovenproof dish, arrange the parcels in a single layer on top and pour over the marinade. Roast in the oven for 45–60 minutes, basting once or twice.

Serves 4

growing

Juniper is easily cultivated in temperate areas in a sunny spot with well-drained soil. It grows to about 6 m but because it's a great spreader – up to 3–4.5 m, it's not really suitable for small gardens or containers. Be careful pruning, as old leafless wood rarely sprouts.

Propagate hardened tip cuttings in late spring (in mild zones) and autumn in colder climes. Press 10 cm cuttings into a pot of sand or potting mix and keep lightly watered. Roots normally form quite quickly. When your seedling or rooted cutting is large enough to handle, plant it out into a well-drained soil.

Juniper is really a tree for patient gardeners as it will be a good two or three years before the green berries turn blue-black and ripe for picking. Harvest time is when your chopstick skills come in handy! A less exciting but probably more efficient way to harvest the berries is to don very sturdy gardening gloves and make sure you have a pair of good, sharp secateurs. Thrust your hand into juniper's over-protective foliage and snip off the ripe berries. Let them dry out a little by spreading them on an airy rack then pack in airtight, labelled containers ready to use. They go darker as they dry and are still in a squashable, semi-moist condition when they are deemed dry.

mustard seed

black mustard *Brassica nigra*

brown or Indian mustard *B. juncea*

white or yellow mustard *B. alba, sinipas alba*

There is some degree of confusion about mustard because in English we use the same word for the plant, the seed, and prepared mustard, a condiment which itself comes with variety of taste sensations ranging from sinus-searing heat to a velvety smooth tang.

Also called rai, biji sawi, Chinese mustard,
Indian mustard, leaf mustard, mizuna mustard,
mustard greens
Flavour and aroma a sharp, fiery seed with
virtually no aroma
Flavour group hot

It's perfectly understandable that the condiment won the naming rights, as it claims to be the oldest prepared condiment in the history of food, the first known recipe dating from 1336. Mustard seeds only release their heat and pungency when you mix them with cold water, thanks to a zesty little enzyme called myrosinase. The original recipe seems to have been to add vinegar, but during the Middle Ages this was replaced by grape 'must', an unfermented wine, hence 'moutarde' (it's a French innovation) and 'mustard'.

If you enjoy the bite mustard adds to beef or find it absolutely indispensable in a vinaigrette or mayonnaise, you are not alone. People have enjoyed mustard's ability to turn the bland into the biting for thousands of years. The Romans are credited with taking this paste to France and other parts of Europe from where it migrated over the years via voyages of discovery, empire building and colonisation to the four corners of the globe.

We are often asked why some mustards are so fiercely hot they make your eyes water while others are mild, almost sweet, if they all come from basically the same seeds. Are English seeds hotter than American? Not at all. The different styles of prepared mustards essentially get their flavours from the way the seeds are processed.

Hot English mustard for instance does not use mustard seeds from England. It is achieved by soaking the yellow seeds in water prior to milling, thus creating the biting hotness. On the other hand, Dijon mustard is soaked in wine or verjuice, inhibiting the enzyme reaction that makes mustard hot and creating a milder mustard with definite white wine notes. The darker German and French mustards have also been made to have less heat, and the bitter background note of mustard is masked by pungent and sweet spices such as cloves and allspice.

Mustard is a member of that very extended Brassica family along with cruciferous cousins broccoli, cabbage, cauliflower, cress, rocket, radishes, turnips, a number of Asian greens (bok choy, Chinese cabbage and Chinese broccoli) and, of course, mustard greens. It's a very hardy annual with bright yellow spring flowers followed late in the summer by green pods heavy with seeds. The three types most often used for culinary purposes are white or yellow, black, and brown.

White or yellow mustard is the smallest plant and its seeds have the mildest flavour. It's the traditional ready-made mustard of the Western world. The seed is in fact not white at all but a rather creamy yellow, which is why we opt for 'yellow' rather than white to describe them.

Black mustard is a bigger plant with small seeds that pack a big punch. However, the seed pods are brittle and have to be hand gathered, which rather limits its commercial appeal.

More pungent than yellow, and less than black, brown mustard seeds (the rai of India) look almost identical to black seeds and can be used in its place. Usually, when a recipe calls for black seeds, brown are an acceptable alternative, and were possibly used in the original recipe anyway.

Because ripe mustard pods shatter easily, they are harvested when they are nearly fully developed but not ripe. After cutting, the mustard 'hay' is stacked in sheaves to dry then threshed to remove the seeds. Driving along a country road in Gujerat some years ago, we were entranced by a basic spice-processing operation happening by the roadside. A big heap of mustard hay had just received a thorough threshing by being driven over by a buffalo-drawn cart executing tight circles across it. A few young men had scooped some of the battered mustard stems from the ground into a wide sieve, which they swung between them while it rained a steady stream of brown mustard seeds around their ankles. An assistant piled more bundles of mutilated herbage and seed pods as the level in the sieve diminished. It may be a good thing that procedures are more mechanised and quality controlled now, but it's a great loss to Messrs Fuji and Kodak!

choosing and using

Black mustard seeds are seldom produced commercially, and any that you see in a market place are most likely wrongly labelled brown seeds. There is practically no difference to the naked eye, although the brown seeds have a slightly reddish glow.

Whole brown or yellow seeds should be clean and dry, without any clumping together of the individual seeds. They will keep for up to three years in a dry, airtight environment.

There are two kinds of mustard powder – one is simply ground yellow mustard seeds, complete with the finely ground bran-like husk. Use this one if you're making up your own curry powder. Because it has good emulsifying properties, you can add a little of the ground seed to a salad dressing to stop that annoying habit of the oil and vinegar separating the minute you stop stirring it.

Finely sieved mustard powder is made from ground yellow or brown mustard seed with the husk sieved out. This superfine powder is the one you mix with milk to make a smooth, biting yellow paste to have with your corned beef. When dry, it is as bland as cornstarch – but don't taste it to see if we're right, because as soon as it mixes with your saliva, your mouth will be burning!

You need a little science lesson to understand the ins and outs of mustard making. It's all to do with the enzymes and their reaction to different liquids. To get the enzyme and heat thing happening, any kind of liquid will do – water gives a hot sharp taste, vinegar a mild tangy flavour, wine a pungent spicy taste and an extremely hot flavour. Hot water will kill the enzyme, and vinegar will stop the reaction so that its full flavour will not develop. Once the enzyme bit has happened, then other ingredients can be added to enhance the taste: take your pick from grape juice, lemon or lime juice, vinegar, beer, cider or wine, salt and herbs. Even when water is used to make a hot mustard, you still need a dash of vinegar as a preservative.

Mustard greens and sprouts can be produced from all varieties, although the sharp, tangy flavour of black and brown mustards makes them the more popular choices. There are two important rules for sprouting:

- Don't let the seeds dry out.
- Don't drown them.

You can sprout mustard seeds in a glass jar with gauze, a piece of pantyhose or light fabric stretched across the top and held in place by a strong rubber band. Run some water into the jar, swill around to wet the seeds, then drain it off again, placing the jar on its side. Repeat this method three or four times a day as the seeds sprout, and when the jar is full of delicious, succulent, living morsels, empty it out and start again.

Mustard oil is a popular, mild cooking oil much favoured in Asia and India. It is sometimes blended with canola oils for use in salad dressings.

Prepared mustards are used as a universal condiment, and have chameleon qualities for pantry-deficient cooks who will find a glaze for roasts, a seasoning for steaks, a spread for a sandwich, a booster for gravy, and an emulsifier for salad dressing, all in one little jar. There are innumerable prepared mustards available throughout the world.

The French pride themselves on using only brown seeds in their famous Dijon mustard; the Americans have had a huge influence on mustard consumption by making it an essential part of the hot dog (yellow seeds, sugar, and turmeric for extra brightness of colour); the English make it hot and smooth, with yellow and brown seeds and extra turmeric; and the Germans have their own rather coarse and grainy style using brown seeds.

These jolly little seeds abound in many Indian dishes for flavour and appearance. Brown seeds, fried in a little oil, turn black and are the finishing touch in an enormous number of South Indian delicacies. The frying, or 'tempering' produces a pleasant nutty flavour without heat.

Mustard pickles contain ground mustard, and actually get colour from added turmeric, while pickled vegetables in clear liquid often have a variety of whole spices, including yellow mustard seeds.

Powdered mustard has a wonderful ability to act as an emulsifier in mayonnaise and salad dressings – a very useful tool to prevent separation of oil and acid. Brown and yellow seeds, whole or ground, are ingredients in curry powder.

Cooking with whole seeds is almost exclusively restricted to the Indian sub-continent. Most of the Western world is more likely to use a prepared mustard condiment as an ingredient, as in the recipe over the page.

- Brown mustard seeds are delicious in dishes as mundane as boiled cabbage.
- Add brown seeds to potato salad.
- Toss bread cubes in a pan with mustard seeds and hot oil to make croutons with pizzazz.
- Spice up a salad dressing by adding 2 teaspoons of pickling spice per 2 cups of oil and vinegar and allow to marinate.

In the majority of spice blends, mustard is used for its distinctive flavour rather than its bite, because in most cooking applications mustard's heat-producing enzymes are not activated. Mustard seeds combine with many spices and go particularly well with allspice, cardamom, chilli, cinnamon, cloves, coriander seed, cumin seed, fennel seed, fenugreek seed, ginger, nigella, paprika, pepper, tamarind and turmeric.

Little Onion Tarts (recipe page 114)

Asparagus and Pink Peppercorn Soup (recipe page 131)

pickling spice

This pickling spice blend is more versatile than it first appears, as it is actually a wonderful combination of whole and broken savoury spices, ideally suited to making infusions. When pickling vegetables or making most infusions, it is preferable to use whole or broken spices, as the flavours amalgamate during infusion, maintaining the liquid's clarity and avoiding the cloudy appearance that would result if ground spices were used. A traditional pickling spice like this one is a riotous collection of colours, textures and aromas and is made by blending together the following whole and broken ingredients.

3 teaspoons yellow mustard seeds

3 teaspoons brown mustard seeds

3 teaspoons black peppercorns

3 teaspoons dill seeds

3 teaspoons fennel seeds

2 teaspoons allspice berries

1½ teaspoons cloves

1½ teaspoons crushed bay leaves

1 teaspoon crushed cinnamon sticks

1 teaspoon birdseye chillies
   (more or less depending on how hot you like it)

Use approximately 1 tablespoon of pickling spice to every 1 kg of vegetables to be pickled. We like to have the spices floating around with the pickled ingredients, where the flavours continue to infuse and the myriad colours and textures add aesthetic appeal. Some cooks will tie the pickling spices into a muslin bag so all the pieces can be removed at the end of cooking.

Makes 1½ cups

pickled vegetables

Whenever we make pickles we think of the time when Mum and Dad (Hemphill) were given a quantity of pearly little white onions that were too small for the grower to send to market, so they pickled them with the pickling spice shown above to create crisp and spicy morsels. Here is how they pickled them:

Peel enough small onions (diced carrots, cucumbers and zucchini can also be used) to fill a 1 litre container. Sprinkle 30 g of salt over them and leave overnight.

Next day, boil 1 litre of cider vinegar with 1½ tablespoons of pickling spice for 10 minutes. Wash the salt off the vegetables, shake dry in a colander and add to the vinegar. Boil for 5 minutes. Remove the vegetables and pack into glass jars, then pour the vinegar onto them (making sure some spices go into each jar as well). Put the lids on the jars and allow to cool.

The flavours in pickling spice are similar to the American 'crab boil' spice mix and are highly complementary when added to the water when boiling crustaceans such as crab.

Makes around 4 cups of pickles

kangaroo fillets in mustard sauce

2 x 300 g kangaroo loin fillets

2–3 tablespoons whole grain prepared mustard

1 tablespoon vegetable or olive oil

2 tablespoons sliced mushrooms

160 ml cream

salt and pepper

Clean and trim the kangaroo fillets. Spread the mustard over all sides of the meat and allow to rest for 15 minutes. Heat oil in a heavy-based pan with a lid and add fillets. Fry over moderate heat, turning occasionally, until all sides are sealed.

Add the mushrooms, reduce heat, and cover. Cook, covered, for 3-4 minutes, depending on the thickness of the fillets. They should still be pink and moist in the middle. Remove meat to a separate plate.

Stir cream into the mushrooms and any residual mustard. Add salt and pepper to taste and tip any juices from the meat back into the sauce. Slice the kangaroo fillets diagonally, and serve on a bed of creamy mashed potato, with mushrooms and mustard cream poured over the top.

Serves 2

potatoes with mustard and curry leaves

4 medium-sized potatoes, scrubbed or peeled

1/2 teaspoon Madras turmeric powder

3 tablespoons olive oil

2 tablespoons brown mustard seeds

15 fresh curry leaves

Cut each potato into 4 or 6 pieces, each about the size of a small new potato, and boil or microwave with a little salt and turmeric until almost cooked. Drain well and pat dry between layers of paper towel to absorb excess moisture.

Heat 1 tablespoon of the oil in a pan and toss the mustard seeds and curry leaves in the hot oil for 30 seconds until they pop and crackle. Add the remaining oil and then the potatoes. Fry on a high heat, turning or tossing frequently until the potatoes are browned and well coated with the spices.

Serves 4–6

growing

Black mustard grows to about 2–3 m with branching stalks bearing smooth, bright green, pointed leaves with notched edges. Brown reaches about the same height, but its large oval leaves are not quite as pungent. Sow mustard seeds in spring, 30 cm apart in a sunny, open position. Mustard germinates quickly and has green shoots within a week of sowing. Plant a few crops throughout the year if you want leaves to pick year round. Mustard is planted for its alkaline properties, but continual planting depletes the soil, so move your crop around to rest the soil.

nigella seed

Nigella sativa

Let's get one thing straight from the beginning: nigella is not named in honour of any cooking show presenter! This misconception (and we do have a lot of customers who ask) is just the latest in a long history of mistaken identity.

Also called black caraway, kalonji, black onion seeds
Flavour and aroma pleasantly sharp, peppery
with little aroma
Flavour group pungent

Nigella is sometimes confused with black cumin (which is surprising, as it has quite a different taste and they don't even look alike) and occasionally wild onion and it's not that either. True onion seeds have little flavour and are usually only used for sprouting, so if you have a recipe calling for wild or black onion seeds, you can be pretty sure it's nigella you're after.

The culinary nigella plant is native to western Asia, the Middle East and southern Europe, but it's mostly grown in northern India, where the 45 cm high plants display a sea of misty, pale blue blooms. Plump seed pods succeed the flowers, and they are harvested and dried before being broken open to release tiny jet-black seeds with creamy-coloured centres. Nigella is a member of the buttercup family and a cousin of that pretty annual, love-in-the-mist (*N. damascena*), with its attractive blue flowers, feathery foliage and ornamental seed pods that are ideal for arrangements.

The lingering, peppery, slightly metallic flavour of nigella has never set the world on fire. There has never been rape, pillage, murder or any kind of colonial vandalism perpetrated in its name. In fact there's very little recorded history at all for this pleasantly sharp spice. But we do know that the Romans cultivated it and used it in their cooking and that early settlers took it to America where the seeds were used like pepper as a seasoning.

Just as we would probably have never heard of George Harrison had he not been one-fourth of The Beatles, so would nigella have fared without its association with the indispensable panch phora blend which comes from the northern areas of India.

choosing and using

Nigella seeds are best bought whole and will keep for up to three years if stored in an airtight container in a cool, dry place.

Lightly roasting or frying the seeds in a little oil before adding to recipes tends to bring out the nutty flavour and reduces some of the metallic sharpness. You can use seeds whole or ground, but whole is most common.

Nigella seeds are a sadly under-utilised ingredient in Indian cookery and are included mostly in chutneys, pickles, vegetable dishes and dhal. (While looking through a 300-odd page tome on curries recently, we found only six recipes listing nigella as an ingredient.) The seeds are used in Middle Eastern countries in sweet and savoury dishes (often mixed with sesame seeds), and are commonly sprinkled on Turkish bread and naan because the flavour complements carbohydrates so well.

- Add zest to vegetables such as cabbage or zucchini with a sprinkle of dry-roasted nigella seeds.
- Think potatoes, think nigella. It's a marriage made in heaven's kitchen.
- Include a teaspoon of nigella seeds when making savoury cheese straws.

Nigella seeds could be said to really come into their own when they are either used with carbohydrates or blended with other spices. Their distinctive, metallic flavour balances the stodginess of breads and potatoes and makes nigella a valuable component in the Indian seed blend called panch phora.

Nigella combines with allspice, cardamom (green and brown), chilli, cinnamon, cloves, coriander seed, cumin seed, fennel seed, fenugreek seed, galangal, ginger, mustard seed (yellow and brown), paprika, pepper and turmeric.

panch phora

The name comes from the Hindustani word for five, which is 'panch', and 'phora', which simply means seeds. However, this traditional five-seed blend is not to be confused with Chinese five-spice powder, something completely different with a flavour that is dominated by star anise. We fry a couple of teaspoons of panch phora with the onions when making a curry. Partially cooked chunks of potato, browned in a pan with lightly fried panch phora, make a tasty accompaniment to any style of curry or grill.

3 teaspoons brown mustard seeds
2$\frac{1}{2}$ teaspoons nigella seeds
2 teaspoons cumin seeds
1$\frac{1}{2}$ teaspoons fenugreek seeds
1 teaspoon fennel seeds

Combine all ingredients and use immediately or store in an airtight container.

Makes about 2 tablespoons

little onion tarts

Pastry

350 g prepared frozen shortcrust pastry,
   thawed to room temperature

2 teaspoons nigella seeds

Filling

1 tablespoon olive oil

1 tablespoon butter

2 large brown onions, sliced thinly

1 Ancho chilli, destemmed and seeded,
   sliced as thinly as possible

1 tablespoon soft brown sugar

1½ tablespoons balsamic vinegar

salt

½ cup ricotta

½ teaspoon chilli powder

Preheat oven to 180ºC. Roll the pastry out on a floured surface, until about 40 cm square. Sprinkle the nigella seeds evenly over the surface and roll again until about 50 cm square. (It may be easier to divide the pastry into halves and do two lots of 25 cm squares, depending on the size of the available work surface.)

Using a 7 cm round cutter, cut 24 circles from the pastry and place into greased patty pans. Allow to rest for 10 minutes.

Place pastry weights or a teaspoon of dried rice or lentils into each round, then bake in the oven for 10 minutes. Remove the weights from the bases and return bases to the oven for a further 5 minutes. Remove from oven and allow to cool.

Heat the oil and butter in a pan and add the finely sliced onion and chilli. Stir over medium heat for about 10 minutes until soft and lightly browned. Add sugar and vinegar and continue to stir over heat for a further 4 minutes. Remove from heat and allow to cool. Add salt to taste. Tilt pan so that excess oil drains away from the onion-chilli mixture.

In a bowl, combine the ricotta with the chilli powder. To serve, spoon a good ½ teaspoon of ricotta into each pastry case. Using a fork, place a walnut-sized bundle of the onion-chilli mixture on top. Serve immediately.

Makes 24

nutmeg and mace

Myristica fragrans

The nutmeg tree, which produces the fruit that gives us both mace and nutmeg, is a large evergreen native to the Banda Islands in the Moluccas (the Spice Islands) and today is grown in just about all of the world's tropical spice-producing countries.

Also called muskat, muskatnuss
Flavour and aroma nutty, warm, sweet, aromatic, pungent
Flavour group nutmeg sweet; mace pungent

The Dutch and English purpose-built ships for the spice trade had holds that could be filled with a king's ransom in fragrant nutmeg, mace, pepper and cloves for Europe, and huge fortunes were made from the proceeds.

Jealous of every valuable tree, the Dutch tried to sterilise the nutmegs so that they wouldn't germinate, however their efforts were thwarted by hungry birds stealing the unpicked fruit and dropping the seeds. For the whole greed-ridden story of the Spice Islands, see the chapter on cloves, page 59.

When you cut open a nutmeg fruit, the first thing you see is the bright red lacy layer of mace, called the aril, which surrounds the seed kernel (the nutmeg) inside. The aril is the placenta as it carries nourishment from the fruit to the seed kernel.

We were captivated when we saw a nutmeg fruit opened the first time. A South Indian farmer, Mr Peter, generously shared his time with us in 1997 and showed us around his 'spice garden'. Although it was a little early in the season, he picked a nutmeg fruit, almost identical to a ripe guava in size and colour. He cut the fruit open and the flash of wet, shining, blood red mace inside was simply breathtaking, and all the more special because it soon dulls once exposed to the air. Ever game, we tasted the pale creamy white flesh of the nutmeg fruit, and Mr Peter enjoyed some mirth as the bitterness showed itself in our pursed lips and squinting eyes. In parts of Asia the flesh is pickled in salt and sugar and used as a confection. However, you have to be quick as, like an apple, it begins to turn brown the instant you cut it.

When the fruit is harvested, (using a long stick with a loop or hook at the end), it is unceremoniously broken open and usually discarded. In Zanzibar, a farmer that we visited made good use of the fruits as mulch around his trees. The mace, wrapped like tightly gripping fingers around the seed, is lifted away and spread in a single layer, usually on a mat on the ground. Within a day of being placed in the sunshine, the mace will dry to the dull orange-red that we are familiar with. In this whole or roughly broken form it's usually called blade mace, which is quite fragile. If a recipe calls for a blade of mace, it would be a whole piece approximately 2 cm long and maybe 1/2 cm wide.

Once the mace is removed, the nutmeg in its shell is then left in the sun to dry for a few days. When it is dry enough, you can hear the nutmeg rattling inside the shell when you shake it. The dark brittle shell is then broken open, exposing the paler-brown nutmeg. Nutmeg is in fact one of the most oily spices and if you cut one in half you can see veins of dark brown oil cells.

Nutmeg trees are dioecious, which simply means that there are male and female plants, and not surprisingly you need both for fertilisation. However, no one can tell a tree's sex until it flowers and that takes around five years. This is important because the male trees have to be thinned out, leaving about one male tree for every ten females. Nutmeg trees become fully mature in 15 years and bear fruit for about 40–50 years. It's been estimated that a single mature tree produces up to 2000 nutmegs a year.

choosing and using

When buying nutmegs, be wary as the quality can vary enormously, and it's usually the case that you get what you've paid for. Whole nutmegs should be sound, firm and unbroken. When they have been stored too long, they dry out and often fall prey to insects that drill tiny holes through them. This reduces them to a grade we call in the trade 'BWP' meaning 'broken, wormy and punky'. Ground BWPs produce flavourless, pale nutmeg, and whole ones are useless for grating, as they crumble like old corks.

There are mills available specifically for grinding nutmeg, as, like pepper or coffee, the aroma of the freshly ground spice offers a glimpse of heaven. A nutmeg mill will shave fine pieces off the whole nutmeg and is generally safer for your fingers than using the finest part of your kitchen grater.

One whole nutmeg grated equals 2–3 teaspoons of ground nutmeg. Although it's absolutely fine to use up to a teaspoonful in something to be shared or eaten over the space of a few days (like a cake), don't overdo it with nutmeg. It contains a substance called myristicin, which is lethal if you make a meal of a couple of nutmegs at a sitting. In fact, it's the only spice prohibited in US jails!

Store both ground and whole nutmeg away from sunlight in airtight containers.

You may have noticed that mace is much more expensive than nutmeg. This stands to reason when you think that from one nutmeg fruit you get about a sixth of the amount of mace as you do nutmeg.

By the way, mace has no connection at all to mace spray, an irritant made from capsicum and so called because a mace is also a big stick used for personal protection – the queen of England is holding a sceptre and mace in her coronation photographs.

Nutmeg and mace have always been seen as having well-defined duties: nutmeg for sweet, mace for savoury. Like many rules, there's no good reason why this one can't be broken. Mace is traditionally used in savoury cooking and complements fish and shellfish, but nutmeg is delicious with red vegetables such as carrot and pumpkin and sweet potato, as well as with milkshakes, custards and, of course, nutmeg cake. Once you have discovered nutmeg with steamed silverbeet or spinach, you'll be hooked.

It is common to want to substitute nutmeg for mace, which is usually more expensive and more difficult to find, however this is not recommended as, rather surprisingly, the flavours are distinctly different.

With their active participation in the early spice trade, it's no surprise that nutmeg is still hugely popular with the Dutch. They use it for cabbage, potato and other vegetables, but also for meat, soups, stews and sauces.

Nutmeg whispers its pungent fragrance into vegetable or split pea soups, sausages such as mortadella and Scottish haggis. Use a light hand, or that whisper will become a raucous shout that will spoil your meal. Mace and nutmeg have both been used as ingredients in the Moroccan spice blend, ras el hanout, the exact contents of which can vary widely from one spice blender to another.

Nutmeg is used in many guises in the areas where it grows. In Indonesia, the pulp of the fruit is made into a tasty jam with a subtle nutmeg aroma, while in Malaysia, pickled or crystallised nutmeg fruit is popular as a snack. The famous Caribbean mix, Jamaican jerk seasoning, contains a zingy, exciting mixture of nutmeg, allspice, chilli and ginger.

- Steam your spinach with a pinch of nutmeg.
- Add a few blades of mace to the water when poaching whole or filleted fish.
- Stir ground nutmeg into softened, good-quality bought ice-cream, then refreeze.
- Sprinkle a few pinches of ground mace over meat before pan-frying or barbecuing.
- Sprinkle ground nutmeg over a baked custard for a classic touch.

While both nutmeg and mace will be found in savoury blends of spices, only nutmeg is sweet enough to be included in sweet spice mixes. Nutmeg is arguably the most pungent of the sweet spices, and should therefore be used sparingly. It combines well with allspice, cinnamon and cassia, cloves, coriander seed and ginger and is used in sweet mixed spice, *quatre épices*, baharat and berbere. Mace, on the other hand, is often blended with cloves, paprika, pepper and juniper and will be found in ras el hanout and pickling spice.

baharat

Baharat is a spice blend used widely in recipes from the Gulf States. The same combination of spices is often referred to as Lebanese seven spice, even though it may contain more or less than seven spices.

When we first made baharat we were pleasantly surprised by its aromatic, woody bouquet, cassia sweetness, deep pungency and apple-like fruitiness. It is a combination that, after smelling each ingredient individually, demonstrates the magical alchemy that occurs when many different spices collectively create a different profile than any one part on its own could suggest.

Baharat is the perfect dry marinade for red meats, whether they are being grilled, roasted or casseroled. Use approximately 1–2 teaspoons per 500 g of meat. It adds a depth of flavour to chicken and should only be used sparingly with seafood, however shellfish in rich, creamy sauces can take a little more. We have found these proportions to be the most pleasing:

4 teaspoons mild Spanish paprika

3 teaspoons ground black peppercorns

$2\frac{1}{2}$ teaspoons ground cumin

1 teaspoon ground coriander seed

1 teaspoon ground cassia

1 teaspoon ground cloves

$\frac{1}{4}$ teaspoon ground green cardamom seeds

$\frac{1}{4}$ teaspoon grated nutmeg

Stir the ground spices together until well combined. Store in an airtight jar.

Makes about $\frac{1}{2}$ cup

quatre épices

Quatre épices simply means four spices, however there are two versions – sweet and savoury. The sweet blend flavours cakes, biscuits, fruit cakes and desserts. In the savoury blend, used for meat for charcuterie, the nutmeg, ginger and cloves counteract the somewhat musty aroma of white pepper, and make *quatre épices* an interesting table alternative to ordinary ground black or white pepper.

Sweet *quatre épices*

7 teaspoons ground allspice

4 teaspoons grated nutmeg

$\frac{1}{2}$ teaspoon ground cloves

1 teaspoon ground cinnamon

Blend together and store in an airtight jar.

Makes about $\frac{1}{3}$ cup

Savoury *quatre épices*

7 teaspoons ground white pepper

4 teaspoons grated nutmeg

2 teaspoons ground ginger

$\frac{1}{2}$ teaspoon ground cloves

Blend together and store in an airtight jar.

Makes about $\frac{1}{3}$ cup

pumpkin and nutmeg risotto

4 cups chicken stock

$2\frac{1}{2}$ tablespoons olive oil

1 small onion, very finely chopped

2 cups Arborio rice

$2\frac{1}{2}$ tablespoons white wine

250 g pumpkin,
    peeled and cut into 1 cm dice

1 teaspoon ground nutmeg

3 tablespoons finely chopped parsley

100 g butter, cut into small cubes

1 tablespoon grated parmesan cheese

Have the chicken stock ready and simmering in a small saucepan.

Heat the oil and cook the onion, stirring constantly, until transparent. Add rice and stir to coat all grains with oil. Pour in the wine and stir while it evaporates. Ladle in enough stock to cover the rice with about 1 cm above the top of the rice. Stir almost constantly while the rice cooks and absorbs over medium heat, adding more stock as it is absorbed.

After about 10 minutes, add the pumpkin, nutmeg and parsley with the stock, keeping about $\frac{1}{2}$ cup stock in reserve. Continue to stir as it cooks. When the stock is absorbed, stir in the butter, parmesan and the remaining stock, and stir until butter and cheese have melted and the stock is absorbed. Remove from heat and stand, covered, for a minute or two. Serve immediately.

Serves 4–6

turkey timbale

This unexpected and aromatic dish finally releases turkey from the festive season and brings it into the real world.

1 full turkey breast, off the bone,
　skinned and cut into slices approx. 1–1½ cm thick
2 teaspoons ground mace
salt and freshly ground pepper
140 g cooked rice
1 teaspoon pink schinus peppercorns
1 tablespoon roasted pine nuts
200 g cooked spinach, chopped
1 egg yolk

Sauce
1 tablespoon butter
1 clove garlic, crushed
zest of 1 orange
1 cup chicken stock
salt and pepper
1 teaspoon cornflour

Preheat oven to 160ºC. Sprinkle the turkey slices on both sides with the mace, salt and pepper. Generously oil a deep casserole dish approximately 15 cm diameter, and cover the base with turkey slices, overlapping as little as possible, but making sure the entire base is covered.

Combine rice, pink peppercorns, pine nuts, chopped spinach and egg yolk in a bowl and mix well. If rice and spinach were not cooked with salt, add salt now. Spoon the rice mixture on top of the turkey, pressing down well. Place the remaining turkey fillets on the top, once again making sure that the top is completely covered with as little overlapping as possible. Cover the top with foil then cover with the lid. Place in the preheated oven and cook for 35 minutes.

To make the sauce, melt butter in a saucepan and add garlic – do not let it brown. Add orange zest, chicken stock and pepper to taste and simmer for 2 minutes. Mix the cornflour with a little cold water, then spoon some of the sauce into it, stirring thoroughly to make a smooth paste. Pour the cornflour mixture into the sauce, stirring constantly until smooth and thickened. Drain any pan juices into the sauce.

When the timbale is cooked, remove lid and foil, and run the blade of a knife around the sides of the dish to loosen. Place a serving plate upside-down on top of the casserole, then, holding both together, invert and shake to release the timbale. Pour a little sauce over the top for serving, and serve the remaining sauce in a jug.

Serves 4, cut into wedges

paprika

Capiscum annuum

Paprika is the name given to the sweet and slightly hot members of the Solanaceae family. They are larger and milder than chilli peppers and come in various shapes and sizes, from small and round like a mini sweet capsicum to long and thin like a giant chilli. But, while chillies are used mostly for their flavour and heat, dried and ground paprika is put on a pedestal for its vibrant red colour and agreeable, full-bodied flavour.

Also called hot paprika, Hungarian paprika, mild paprika, nyora paprika, smoked paprika, Spanish paprika, sweet paprika, sweet pepper
Flavour and aroma ranges from sweet and mild to pungent and fiery
Flavour group amalgamating, fruity, slightly hot, rather earthy

Like all members of the chilli-capsicum family, the paprika varieties are native to Central and South America. The fruits (yes, they are fruits, not vegetables) range in colour from bright to dark red and almost brown, and all are harvested when fully ripe. Their amazingly vivid colour is determined by the amount of capsanthin (a red pigment) and the lack of capsaisin (the hot stuff in chillies) present.

Originally a tropical plant, paprika capsicums happily adapt to prevailing conditions, changing character (like chameleons) to suit their environment. But wherever and however they grow, their strength of colour and warm, sweet depth of flavour endure.

In the same way that chillies gave the poor an accessible substitute for pricey pepper, paprika made it possible for everybody to enjoy a tasty, colourful condiment that would enhance almost any meal. The story of paprika as a spice is comparatively short and yes, good old Christopher Columbus played a part. The bright red fruits he brought back to Spain from the New World were immediately seized by enterprising 15th century Spanish foodies and milled to produce a deep red powder. The rest is history. Pimenton was an instant hit requiring no ad campaigns or brand management, and paprika has been cultivated and used in cooking in Spain since that time, spreading like wildfire around Europe, becoming especially popular in Hungary.

Hungary was ruled by the Turks in the 17th century, and *pimenton* was known as Turkish pepper. Growing it was prohibited on pain of death (the usual monopoly story), but the Hungarian farmers who had tasted its warmth and piquancy, planted their crops regardless. Their courage and determination, along with constant breeding ever since has given the world the milder, sweeter strains of a cooler climate paprika.

Each October in the Basque village of Espelette, there is a fiesta to celebrate their local capsicum, which they claim has a unique fruity sweetness. While the *Chevaliers de la Confrerie de Piment* (Knights of the Brotherhood of the Pepper) dress in traditional Basque costume, villagers and tourists mill around stalls decorated with ropes of freshly-strung smooth and tapering shining red sweet peppers.

choosing and using

With the exception of a few special varieties such as nyora, most paprika is sold in powdered form. The powder should be labelled to show whether it is Hungarian, Spanish or from some other source and at least state whether it's a mild, sweet or hot variety.

To make true smoked paprika, the ripe fruits are smoked over slow-burning oak wood, watched over closely to keep the temperature low, then milled to a fine powder. (Beware of so-called 'smoky' paprika, which is usually a mixture of paprika, smoke flavour and MSG.)

Paprika deteriorates quickly, so buy in small quantities and keep in airtight containers away from sunlight.

Fresh paprika fruits are processed into pickles and pastes, available in many delicatessens and specialty food stores. Both these products tend to be on the acidic side thanks to the vinegar needed for preserving, but the fresh paprikas can also be made into a delicious jam. In the famous markets in Istanbul, there are huge tubs of fresh paprika paste at many of the stalls – we wished we were staying somewhere with a kitchen, rather than at a hotel, so that we could have bought some. The paste can be used like tomato paste as a colour and flavour booster, or simply spread on a cracker with cheese.

Nyora paprika is a whole, dark red, intensely sweet-smelling bell-shaped paprika about 4 cm in diameter. These are picked when they are in their prime, and spread out to dry on tennis court-sized concrete slabs in the central south region of Spain. When the weather is doubtful, the farmers can take their crop to a central drying facility, but naturally this costs them more, so they only use it as a last resort. The flavour is uniquely sweet and warm, and it is an essential ingredient in Romesco Sauce, as well as a great addition to any kind of stew, soup or casserole.

Commercial food producers just love paprika. They use it in cheeses, processed meats, tomato sauces, soups, chilli powders, and all sorts of seasonings, especially for foods like barbecued chooks, where a healthy tanned look on nice crunchy skin is a definite plus. They love it also for its use as a natural colour.

Along with the ubiquitous parsley sprig, paprika is one of those garnishes that never fades away. Imagine cauliflower cheese or moussaka without a sprinkling of paprika over the creamy sauce ... impossible!

In home cooking sweet paprika gives goulash its characteristic colour and flavour, combining beautifully with the veal and cream. Paprika also enhances the flavour of pork and chicken and garnishes seafood including crayfish, prawns and crabmeat. It's important in Spanish dishes using the local cod. As for eggs, whether they be scrambled, poached, fried or hard-boiled or made into an omelette, they benefit from a judicious (and it's up to you to decide what's judicious) sprinkling of your favourite paprika.

Meal ideas are endless with this warm, amal-gamating spice. Here are a few of our favourites:

- A delicious chicken salad can be made by dusting chicken tenderloins with Baharat (see page 118). Pan-fry them until golden, slice and allow to cool. Place the sliced baharat chicken on a green salad and drizzle over a dressing made from 2 parts olive oil, 1 part pomegranate molasses and $1/2$ a part of toasted sesame seeds.
- Sprinkle your favourite paprika over melting cheese on toast.
- Add a couple of teaspoons of paprika to half a cup of tomato paste to boost the flavour of a stew, casserole, or savoury mince.
- Combine 2 teaspoons of smoked paprika with 3 tablespoons olive oil in a jar. Shake to mix, then stand for a couple of hours. The paprika will infuse with the oil, and then the solids will sink to the bottom. Carefully drizzle a little of the flavoured oil over hummus, dips or salads.
- Add a little smoked paprika to a salmon mousse to blush the colour and give a subtle smoky lift.

As an amalgamating spice, and one that has varieties that range from sweet, to sharp and bitter and even hot like chilli, paprika is the spice most used in commercial seasonings and spice blends. There is a very good reason for this, and it stems from paprika's ability to add appetising colour, a smooth agreeable flavour that complements proteins, and a knack of combining well with most other herbs and spices.

We prefer to use the sweet paprika (ideally the Hungarian Noble Sweet variety) in European dishes and blends made to season meats without a particular cuisine characteristic. However, when paprika is called for in Indian, North African or Cajun dishes we will always opt for the mild Spanish varieties. The Spanish paprikas have a slightly bitter background note and a more robust flavour, attributes that go well with the stronger spices used in these cuisines.

Paprika combines well with allspice, basil, caraway seed, cardamom, chilli, cinnamon and cassia, cloves, coriander seed, cumin, fennel seed, garlic, ginger, oregano, parsley, pepper, rosemary, sage, thyme and turmeric.

Paprika plays an important role in barbecue spice mixes, tandoori spice blends, baharat, Cajun spices, chermoula mixes, curry powders, harissa pastes, Mexican chilli powders, ras el hanout and tagine spice blends. Paprika is a very good substitute for chilli powder if you are making a recipe that calls for chilli and you want to tone it down a bit. By using paprika, you can reduce the heat, but still maintain the correct flavour balance, as the taste of paprika is almost identical to that of chilli.

When we opened Herbie's Spices, a number of customers asked for a versatile spice blend that could be used to crust meats for roasting, but they wanted something that was not too hot. The following blend of herbs and spices is a crusting mix, which can be rubbed onto chicken, a leg of lamb, rolled roast beef or a corner piece of topside.

crusting mix

Rub crusting mix all over meat to be roasted, grilled or barbecued and place, covered, in the refrigerator for about an hour (or overnight) to dry-marinate. Spray or brush oil over the surface before roasting. We usually roll potatoes and pumpkins in the crusting mix as well and when cooked, a sumptuous gravy can be made with the pan juices.

6 teaspoons ground coriander seed

4 teaspoons sweet paprika

3 teaspoons whole brown (black) mustard seeds

2 teaspoons sumac

1 teaspoon ground ginger

1 teaspoon caster sugar

1 teaspoon dried oregano leaves

¾ teaspoon coarsely ground black peppercorns

½ teaspoon ground allspice

1–2 teaspoons salt, more or less to taste

Blend all these ingredients together and store in an airtight container.

Makes about ⅔ cup

hungarian goulash (gulyás)

Classics like this can stand the test of time. We once tasted a gulyás made by a Hungarian woman who used five different types of paprika! Unfortunately it was not possible to get her recipe, but we are happy with this one. There are no hard and fast rules as to what you may or may not add – like paella in Spain, or meatloaf in Australia, every household contributes individual touches.

1 kg boneless veal, cut into 3 cm cubes

1½ tablespoons Hungarian sweet paprika

1 teaspoon hot paprika

1 teaspoon mild paprika

1 tablespoon cornflour

2 tablespoons vegetable oil

2 large Spanish onions, finely chopped

2 cloves garlic, finely chopped

½ teaspoon caraway seeds

1 bouquet garni ball, or 2 teaspoons bouquet garni herbs

1 x 400 g can chopped tomatoes

salt and pepper

500 g mushrooms, sliced

2 red capsicums, seeded and chopped

250 ml sour cream

Place cubed veal in a clean plastic bag with the paprikas and cornflour, and shake well to coat the meat.

Heat oil in a large heavy-based pot, add onions and garlic and cook until onion is transparent. Add the meat in 2 or 3 batches, and sauté until browned. If the pot becomes too dry, add a dash of water rather than more oil. Add the caraway seeds, bouquet garni and tomatoes, and stir to combine. Cover and simmer gently for 10 minutes.

Preheat oven to 120°C. Season to taste with salt and pepper. Gently stir in mushrooms and capsicum, replace the lid, and return to a simmer on the stove top. As soon as bubbles appear, transfer the covered pot to the oven and cook slowly for at least 2 hours, until very tender. To retain maximum moisture, place a sheet of greaseproof paper over the top of the pot before replacing the lid – steam can't cling to the paper, and all moisture returns to the food.

Stir in the sour cream just before serving.

Serves 6–8

pepper

vine pepper:

black pepper (including white, green and true pink) *Piper nigrum*

cubeb or tailed pepper *P. cubeba*

long pepper *P. longum* and *P. retrofractum*

Acknowledged as the 'King of Spices', the story of pepper is almost the story of the spice trade itself.

VINE PEPPER
BLACK PEPPER
(including white, green and true pink) *Piper nigrum*
CUBEB OR TAILED PEPPER *P. cubeba*
LONG PEPPER *P. longum* and *P. retrofractum*
Flavour and aroma biting and hot, cubeb has pine references, long pepper has eucalyptus hints, native pepper has a long, lingering heat
Flavour group hot

PINK SCHINUS
Schinus terebinthifolius
Flavour and aroma piney, sweet, mildly hot
Flavour group hot/sweet

PEPPER SICHUAN
Zanthoxylum piperitum
Also called Chinese pepper, fagara, Szechwan pepper, anise pepper
Flavour and aroma mildly hot, with lavender overtones and a fizzy aftertaste
Flavour group hot

It's been the world's most popular spice for thousands of years, and even today you can just about judge the importance of a restaurant by the size of the pepper mill tucked protectively under the arm of your waiter. A grind of pepper is the simplest way to transform the mundane into something better, and it's easy to see how the need for this spice has had far-reaching effects on commerce, voyages of discovery, cultures and cuisines.

The ancient Romans used to get their pepper from India, and some time during the Roman Empire, Hindu settlers carried plants to Indonesia. A procession of colonists and traders gradually introduced pepper to all parts of South-East Asia, which is now a major producing area.

All true pepper whether black, white, green or pink comes from the berries of a tropical evergreen vine. Imagine this vine with its wide heart-shaped leaves climbing up a coconut palm, or a timber frame in your tropical back garden. Twice a year, it has a flowering and fruiting season lasting two or three months, bearing little stems crusted with pepper fruits that begin green, gradually ripen through a soft yellow and finally become a rich pink when they're fully ripe. So you get your ladder and climb up to pick by hand the spikes of green peppercorns, dropping them into a cloth bag tied around your waist.

You rub the berries from their stems, then spread your harvest on a woven straw mat on the ground where it will get plenty of sun, and as the sun shines on them every day, you notice the skin darkening and puckering, until the basking enzymes in the skin have completely transformed green to black, and the sun has dried the berries down to just 12 per cent of its original moisture. Now you have black peppercorns, ready for the market, where everyone will swoon over that heady peppery aroma emanating from the skin, and love that flavour and bite when the black peppercorns are cracked open.

Suppose you also want some white peppercorns from your vine. You rein in your impatience and wait for the fruits to ripen until the berries are pink. Then up the ladder you go and collect the fully ripe berries. After removing them from the stem, you pack the ripe, dark pink produce into a sack, tie it tightly, and drop the whole bag into a nearby flowing stream of clean, clear water. The bag stays there for about a fortnight, then you retrieve it and find that the skins rub away very easily, leaving creamy-coloured peppercorns that are very full of water. Out they go into the sunshine to dry and bleach; then your white peppercorns are also ready for the market. Being skinless, the aroma has changed, and now all you can smell is a rather musty, fusty odour. But the flavour is white hot!

Somebody at the market wants green peppercorns! Scurry up the ladder again and gather all the stems of young green peppercorns. You look at your full sack and scratch your head. No good putting them in the sun – we know about those enzymes! So you boil up a big vat of water, throw in the green berries for 20 minutes to kill the enzymes, then quickly drain them. Now you have green peppercorns with a dead enzyme, and they can be dried in the air or in an oven and still keep their colour. These babies don't have a black pericarp to give them flavour and aroma, but they pack a hot punch with a lively, fresh bite.

Just before the season finishes, you realise you almost forgot to get any pink peppercorns! Luckily, since you harvested the ripe fruits to make your white peppercorns, more have ripened and you scoot up the ladder one last time to collect them. Now you have a problem ... if you try to dry the ripe, pink peppercorns in the sun, those pesky enzymes are going to do their thing and they'll all end up black. They're too soft and ripe for the boiling-water treatment. There has to be a way to arrest that enzyme, and it's done with a strong solution of brine. So you fill glass jars with your peppercorns and cover them completely with brine, lid them, and there are your pink peppercorns, held in their pink state and just needing a rinse to remove the salt before you enjoy their fruitiness and mature heat.

If you have ever wondered why ground black pepper is grey rather then black, here's the reason. If you carefully cut a black peppercorn in half, you'll see it's white in the middle, with a black outer shell. Now if you grind something that's mostly white, it can't make a black powder! Some people just love the flavour and aroma of that black pericarp, without the heat of the white inside bit, and sometimes you can buy it separately.

Cubeb pepper comes from a vine related to that vine in your back garden, but it's native to the Indonesian archipelago. The berries are about the same size as black peppercorns but they have a little spike or tail, hence the other name 'tailed pepper'. Used by the Arabs as early as the 10th century, they were quite commonly used in Europe for some centuries until unaccountably falling out of favour. Compared with black pepper, the flavour has an almost-juniper berry hint of pine forests as well as pepper heat.

Now out there in your backyard, far away from the tropical corner where your pepper vine flourishes, you have a lovely shade tree with softly drooping leaves. Native to South America, it's commonly called a pepper tree (not the tree prolific in Australian country areas), and in the summer clusters of bright pink seed pods hang from the branches. You gather these berries, light as rice bubbles, and dry them in the shade so that they retain their colour. If you had a neighbour with freeze-drying equipment in his shed, you could pop them in to him. They add a spark of colour to your peppermill blend, but because they're soft, too many will clog up the grinding mill. Their flavour, piney and sweet, combines surprisingly well with true peppercorns.

Yet another small vine related to true pepper and cubeb pepper grows through your back fence – it's long pepper. Instead of being round like a peppercorn, the fruits are about 1–2 cm long, with a peppery flavour, strong minty overtones and a slightly sweet almost floral aroma. While the fruits are still young and unripe, you can pick one to nibble on in lieu of cleaning your teeth! Otherwise, you pick them when they're ripe and dry them in the sun on the same mat you used for your black peppercorns.

Finally, in your garden, you grow a prickly ash tree. It's an attractive, deciduous tree about 3 m high, and the ruddy brown seed pods that remain after flowering are known as Sichuan pepper. It is not a true pepper at all, but the taste is hot like pepper, lingering and somewhat 'fizzy' on the tongue. Your Japanese and Chinese neighbours love you for sharing the dried pods with them.

choosing and using

What we think of as true pepper flavour and aroma actually only belongs to black pepper. White pepper was traditionally used by Europeans who didn't want black specks in their white sauces. It should always be used in moderation, as white pepper's heat can override more subtle ingredients and leave you with a musty old socks flavour.

Green peppercorns are usually included in peppermill blends. Not often seen alone, they are ideal in gravies and white sauces for poultry, red meats and seafood. Pâtés and terrines are enhanced by green peppercorns as are rich foods like duck, pork and game.

True pink peppercorns have to be rinsed thoroughly first to remove the saltiness of the brine. They are delicious crushed in a pestle and mortar with a little olive oil and even less vinegar to make a colourful and tasty salad dressing. As with green peppercorns, they shine in pâtés, terrines and rich foods.

Cubebs have a distinct fragrance and characteristic pepper-like flavour. They are at their best blended with black, white and green peppercorns in a mill, and this blend goes particularly well in casseroles and with game.

Used in many exotic Asian dishes and clear soups, long pepper is most at home with galangal, turmeric and kenchur in rich, thick curries.

In all its various guises, shapes and sizes, the pepper flavour is the very backbone of our expectations in everyday meals, whether we realise it or not. Even on airlines, this spice is supplied with every meal. Although we often take it for granted when it's there, we would miss it if it were not.

Pepper is a spice that many people associate with that little silver pepper shaker on the table, or the flamboyant waiter who takes a proprietary grasp of an ornate, phallic pepper grinder, and twists it over one's meal with an aroma-releasing flourish. For a spice that is familiar to us all by its presence on the table, pepper is used in a surprising number of spice blends. Pepper is a key component in most curry powders and it is used in baharat, berbere, stuffing mixes, barbecue spice blends, Chinese master stock, Jamaican jerk spices, garam masala, Chinese five-spice, ras el hanout, Cajun spice mixes, pickling spices and naturally peppermill blends.

Black pepper is by far the most popular. Its flavour and heat combine with nearly all culinary herbs and spices, but have a special affinity with allspice, basil, caraway, cardamom, chicory, chilli, cinnamon, cloves, coriander seed and leaf, cumin, curry leaf, fennel seed, fenugreek seed and leaves, garlic, ginger, oregano, paprika, parsley, rosemary, sage, savory, thyme and turmeric.

peppercorn mixes

Different mixes of peppercorns are not new and the majority of them are made to go into peppermills. A peppermill blend does need to be practical though, as the inclusion of dried pink (schinus) peppercorns may be fancifully attractive, but the reality is that their friable husks will tend to clog the most robust of peppermill mechanisms. So, if you want a good mill blend, mix together 5 parts of black peppercorns to 3 parts of white peppercorns and 1 part each of green peppercorns and small (less than 3 mm diameter) allspice berries.

mélange of pepper

Cooking with a mix of peppers is a different story, and we were captivated by the mélange of peppers we saw on sale in the Cavaillon markets in the south of France. Over many centuries, this part of France has been influenced by the Marseilles traders who had contact with North Africa and many spices from the Near and Far East. When we arrived home we got to work replicating this highly fragrant pepper blend, which can be made by mixing:

9 teaspoons black peppercorns
6 teaspoons white peppercorns
4 teaspoons schinus pink peppercorns
3 teaspoons dried green peppercorns
3 teaspoons cubeb pepper
3 teaspoons Sichuan pepper

This blend goes well in most slow-cooked dishes when a tablespoon is added to the dish at the beginning of cooking. We love it in a chicken casserole with red wine, and winter-warming beef and lamb stews take on a new dimension with this fragrant pepper mix, one that transports us back to the Cavaillon market experience.

Makes about 1 cup

chicken with lemon couscous

Lemon and Herb Pepper

1 teaspoon salt (or to taste)

3–4 teaspoons cracked black pepper

1 teaspoon turmeric powder

1/2 teaspoon ground ginger

2 teaspoons finely chopped fresh parsley

1/2 teaspoon dried green dill or

    1 teaspoon fresh chopped dill

2 teaspoons lemon juice

1 teaspoon lime juice

1 x size 14 or 16 chicken

6 cloves garlic, peeled

1 tablespoon olive oil

2 wedges preserved lemon

1/2 teaspoon Ras el Hanout (see pages 140–2)

1 cup quick-cook couscous

To make the Lemon and Herb Pepper, combine all the ingredients in a small bowl. If it seems too dry, add a little more lemon juice or a teaspoon of olive oil.

Preheat the oven to 180ºC. To prepare the chicken, halve 1 garlic clove and rub the cut side all over the chicken. Sprinkle on 3–4 teaspoons of the Lemon and Herb Pepper and rub it in all over the chicken. Drizzle the oil into a baking dish then add the chicken and the remaining garlic cloves. Roast for an hour, or until the chicken is cooked.

Meanwhile finely chop the preserved lemon and mix with the Ras el Hanout and the rest of the Lemon and Herb Pepper. Stir into the uncooked couscous.

When the chicken is cooked, prepare the couscous according to directions on the pack.

Serve the chicken on couscous, and spoon a little of the pan juices over.

Serves 4

asparagus and pink peppercorn soup

250 g asparagus spears

1 teaspoon salt, plus extra to season

1 teaspoon pink peppercorns, plus extra to serve

100 m light cream

1 large basil leaf

Place asparagus in a large pan and cover with water. Add salt and peppercorns and poach until just cooked. Drain and reserve 1/2 cup of the cooking water and peppercorns. Cut 4 of the nicest tips off the asparagus and set aside to use as garnish.

Tip the asparagus into a blender with the reserved water. Blend to a smooth purée then add cream and basil leaf and season with salt to taste. Serve the soup cold or warm, garnished with asparagus tips and a few lightly crushed pink peppercorns.

Serves 2

pepperberry – tasmanian

Tasmannia lanceolata

Australia's unique contribution to the world of herbs and spices packs a pretty powerful punch with more kick than a footballer. Tasmanian pepper is both a herb and a spice – that is, both the leaf and the berry are used.

A native of the eastern seaboard rainforests of Tasmania, Victoria and parts of south-eastern New South Wales, you will find this bush growing at altitudes up to 1200 m. It is not to be confused with the big *Schinus* species of pepper tree often found shading a corner of the school-yard.

Tasmanian pepper has glossy, dark, leathery, elliptical leaves, which can vary in length depending on where they grow, and range from around 2 cm in alpine areas up to 13 cm down on the lowlands.

choosing and using

Fresh, dried or powdered, the leaves, berries and fresh flower buds all have a distinct woody fragrance and flavour, albeit at varying intensities.

If you're a lover of pepper, you could get very excited about this Australian version. But watch out, as the heat has a lingering quality – building on your palate for some minutes after you taste it. You might have a moment to regret your enthusiasm before the heat begins to recede!

The dried leaves have a soft woody fragrance along with a hint of pepper and dry, cinnamon-like notes. The flavour is similarly woody until its sharp pepper taste and lingering heat become apparent.

The leaves can be dried and used in much the same way as bay leaves for a peppery flavour. You can buy powdered mountain pepperleaves from gourmet delicatessens and herb and spice specialists. A little

goes a long way, so buy only small quantities. In addition, it's not a herb that retains its flavour well once ground, even under optimum storage conditions.

The ground leaves are ideal for infusing in olive oil for dipping crusty bread or for drizzling over soup or polenta. Extra virgin olive oil infused with mountain pepperberries and whisked with just a dash of balsamic vinegar makes an unforgettable dressing for salads.

And as for pepperberries, as Ian said in *Spice Notes*, 'only the brave, foolish, or taste-bud-deficient would entertain putting ground mountain pepperberries directly onto food; they are just so hot and numbing, that when not cooked, the flavour attributes cannot be fully appreciated'.

So take a tip from us and introduce these berries into slow-cooked casseroles and hearty stews, where the flavour can be best appreciated. They are excellent with game meats and, used very, very sparingly, in marinades for red and white meat. And how much should you add? Well, Ian's rule of thumb is to use about one-tenth the quantity you would use of conventional pepper.

You can occasionally buy frozen pepperberries, but they are more readily available as whole, freeze-dried berries or as a coarse-ground, oily looking purplish-black powder.

Dorrigo pepper (*Tasmannia insipida*) is related to mountain pepper. From the botanical name it's easy to deduce that the flavour is likely to be less aggressive – insipid, in fact – but possibly making this one a better starting point for the uninitiated.

Native pepperleaf combines well with bush tomato (akudjura), basil, bay leaves, coriander leaf and seed, ginger, lemongrass, lemon myrtle, mustard seeds and wattleseed. Native pepperberry blends with black pepper, cardamom (green and brown), coriander seed, fennel seed, garlic, juniper berries, marjoram, parsley, rosemary and thyme.

growing

Tasmanian pepper is an attractive tree for a large garden, growing to about 4 or 5 m, albeit slowly. It likes a moist climate and well-drained fertile soil in a semi-shaded position with plenty of water. The new growth is a striking deep red and the tree bears creamy-yellow flowers in summer, which produce the black fruit or seed pods we know as Tasmanian pepperberries.

This rather fascinating primitive flowering plant is a dioecious species. This means that it bears male and female flowers on separate plants and if you want to harvest pepperberries you will have to grow one of each.

drying

Pick a handful of leafy stems, making sure they have lost their newborn red glow, as the young leaves won't dry successfully. They can be dried in a hanging bunch, or the leaves can be snipped off and dried on a rack.

The berries also dry successfully on a rack, and of course, once they're dry, store them in airtight, clearly labelled containers.

bushman's pepperpot

Salt and pepper are mainstay seasonings and we like to have a version of salt and pepper with a difference, to sprinkle on tomato sandwiches, salads, grills and just about anything else. We call it Bushman's Pepperpot, as we make it from all Australian-grown spices and it is a handy spice to take camping or on a picnic. The best way to make this blend is to mix the whole spices together, crush them in a pestle and mortar and then add the salt.

2 teaspoons yellow mustard seeds
2 teaspoons coriander seeds
1 teaspoon black peppercorns
1 teaspoon Tasmanian pepperberries
3 bush tomatoes
1 teaspoon salt

Crush the spices in a pestle and mortar, then add the salt. Mix thoroughly and store in an airtight container – and don't forget to take some on your next picnic. It is delicious on hard-boiled eggs as well.

Makes about 1/3 cup

mountain
pepperleaf blends

Mountain pepperleaf blends well with other Australian herbs and spices to sprinkle over meats before roasting or barbecuing.

When making a herb blend, be adventurous, experiment and choose proportions of these ground herbs and spices to please your palate. Here are two of our favourites. Use the measures we suggest as a starting point for your own culinary adventures.

Kangaroo Fillet Blend

1/2 teaspoon ground mountain pepperleaf

1 tablespoon ground coriander seed

1/2 teaspoon roasted and ground wattleseed

1/2 teaspoon akudjura

1/2 teaspoon salt

Lemon Pepper Blend

1/2 teaspoon ground mountain pepperleaf

1/2 teaspoon ground lemon myrtle leaf

1 teaspoon salt

poppy seed

blue poppy seed *Papaver somniferum*

white poppy seed *P. somniferum var. album*

There are around 50 or so annual, biennial and perennial species of the poppy genus with their cheerful cupped petals and nodding buds making them a delight in both house and garden.

The poppy seeds we traditionally use in cooking don't come from these 'garden' varieties, however, but from the opium poppy. Eating poppy seeds won't give you a mind-altering experience, as they have virtually no narcotic content; that's in the morphine-containing milky sap that oozes out of unripe seed pods ... but we won't go there!

Opium poppies are grown on large-scale plantations under strict government supervision. A poppy crop provides a number of useful products including morphine, which hasn't been successfully synthesised to date. The opium is gathered by first making careful cuts in the unripe green capsule and collecting the latex that oozes out. The plants then go on to ripen naturally and form their absolutely seed-packed pods, which are harvested just before they burst open. Each pod contains hundreds of tiny, kidney-shaped seeds; buy a kilogram and you'll end up with well over half a million seeds!

Both the blue and white seeds have a mild, nutty taste. Blue seeds are a little larger than white and also seem to be a bit oilier. The flavour of the blue poppy seed is marginally stronger which is especially noticeable after roasting. The seeds we buy for cooking are commonly 'de-natured' by heat treatment so that they can't germinate and they can be sold freely. This doesn't appear to affect their flavour.

The seeds also produce oil — one a clear cold pressed oil the French call olivette (it can be used as a substitute for olive oil); the other non-edible — an oil for artists' paints.

choosing and using

Most major supermarkets and delis will stock blue poppy seeds. For white poppy seeds you'll probably have to look in a specialty spice shop or an Indian or Middle Eastern food store. Because poppy seeds contain a fair amount of oil, it's better to buy them in small quantities; they can become rancid when they get old.

If you are using the seeds for toppings and they aren't going to be cooked, it's a good idea to lightly toast them first. Simply tossing them for a minute or two in a hot, dry pan will bring out the nutty flavour and accentuate their bursting-in-the-mouth crunchiness.

When stored in an airtight container away from light, heat and humidity, they will keep for 12–18 months. As poppy seeds have a tendency to get infested with insects, make sure the lid is on extra tightly if they are in a cupboard or pantry along with your stocks of flour and other grains. Insect infestation has nothing to do with the cleanliness of the product you buy — even silky, triple-sifted flour can somehow manifest wildlife just by sitting in the pantry.

Blue poppy seeds are used mostly in European cooking while the slightly smaller white ones are a regular feature in Indian recipes.

Both have a pleasing, nutty taste that goes well with breads, biscuits, cookies, strudels, pastry crust and cakes — in fact poppy seeds go well with carbohydrates in general, including pasta. A fiery vindaloo curry will get some of its texture from white poppy seeds, which grind to a rich, nutty paste, and have the same effect as ground almonds in making a dish richer and thicker.

Most of the poppy seeds used in Australia end up in the bottom of the bag when you buy your bread rolls, as more fall off than stay on! Get a spoon and eat up the spillage, and enjoy the pop and crunch of these little seeds.

- Noodles or pasta shapes, drained and tossed in butter or oil and blue poppy seeds, was a particular family favourite when our daughters were small.
- Add poppy seeds to dressings for salads.
- Soak white poppy seeds in warm water for 30 minutes, then crush to a paste in a mortar, as an alternative to ground almonds.

Poppy seeds combine well with allspice, cardamom, cinnamon and cassia, cloves, coriander seed, cumin seed, ginger, nutmeg and mace, sesame seeds, sumac and turmeric, but they are so rarely found in spice blends that it comes as a surprise to experience how well they complement a vindaloo curry. When one thinks of the nutty taste of both blue and white poppy seeds, it is perfectly logical to assume that they would go well with the same sorts of ingredients as sesame seeds.

vindaloo curry

Vindaloo curries are infamous for their sharpness and blistering heat, however a well-balanced vindaloo should not be a painful experience The inclusion of white poppy seeds in this traditional fare has a big impact on the flavour by bringing in an element of rich nuttiness.

We make a vindaloo using the same method as for our other curries on page 75, but using the following combination of ground spices:

6 teaspoons medium-heat chilli powder (mild or hot chilli powder may be substituted depending on your tolerance to chilli heat)
4 teaspoons white poppy seeds
3 teaspoons ground cumin
2 teaspoons mild paprika
1 teaspoon ground cassia
1 teaspoon ground ginger
$1/2$ teaspoon amchur powder
$1/2$ teaspoon coarsely ground black pepper
$1/4$ teaspoon ground cloves
pinch ground star anise

Makes about $2/3$ cup

mandarin and poppy seed puddings

The delicate mandarin flavour makes these little puddings a perfect winter dessert. We love this recipe because it's so forgiving – we've used plain flour instead of almond meal, and oranges instead of mandarins, and the result is still fabulous. A little tip … make the sauce first!

This recipe is by Richard Hauptmann, chef at the Healesville Hotel in Healesville, Victoria. It first appeared in *Delicious* magazine.

Citrus Salad Sauce

1 pink grapefruit, peeled

1 lemon, peeled

2 mandarins, peeled

150 g caster sugar

200 g mandarins

$2/3$ cup almond meal

80 g caster sugar

2 eggs, lightly beaten

1 tablespoon poppy seeds

1 teaspoon baking powder

crème fraîche or ice-cream, to serve

To make the Citrus Salad Sauce, segment the fruit over a bowl, reserving any juice. Place the sugar in a saucepan with 1 cup water and cook over a low heat, stirring until sugar has dissolved. Increase the heat to high and cook 4–5 minutes until golden caramel. Remove from heat, add $1/3$ cup reserved fruit juice and fruit segments, then allow to cool.

Preheat oven to 180°C. Grease and flour 4 small ramekin dishes. Place mandarins (skin and all) in a pot of boiling water and simmer for 30 minutes, drain and refresh. Break mandarins into segments and remove any seeds. Blend or process the fruit and skin until smooth.

Place the mandarin purée in a large bowl with almond meal, sugar, eggs, poppy seeds and baking powder and stir to combine. Fill ramekins three-quarters full with the mixture, place in oven and bake for 20 minutes. Remove puddings from oven and allow to cool slightly before turning out. Serve warm with sauce drizzled around and with a dollop of crème fraîche or a scoop of ice-cream.

Serves 4

ras el hanout

spice mix

How do you judge the credibility of a spice merchant? Easy, check out his ras el hanout. This traditional Moroccan spice mix has the reputation of being the very pinnacle of all spice blends. *Ras* was the title given to an Ethiopian king and the name ras el hanout, when loosely translated, means 'top of the shop' and it is meant to represent the very best the spice merchant has to offer. For the Moroccan *souks* (spice merchants) it is a point of honour to outdo one's competitors by providing customers with the most sought after version, his king of spices.

What makes this blend so special is the number of ingredients, sometimes over 20, and the subtle manner in which so many spices merge to form a balanced, full-bodied blend, that believe it or not does not taste like a dog's breakfast! A good ras el hanout is arguably the finest example of how well a collection of diverse spices can come together to form a complete ingredient that is immeasurably greater than any of the parts taken individually.

Ras el hanout is subtly curry-like, with a spicy yet floral fragrance and robust yet subtle flavour. The notable aspect of this blend is that although it is by no means pungent, so pervasive is its effect on food that about half the amount is required in a dish, when compared to other spice blends such as curry powders.

The first step we took in developing a ras el hanout was to identify all the traditional spices used in Morocco. The list included paprika, cumin, ginger, coriander, cassia, turmeric, fennel, allspice, green and brown cardamom, dill seeds, galangal, nutmeg, orris root, bay leaves, caraway seeds, cloves, mace, grains of paradise, cayenne pepper, black pepper, cubeb pepper, long pepper, lavender, rose buds, saffron stigmas, Spanish fly and hashish.

The next step was to bring these ingredients together in harmony, minus the Spanish fly and hashish! Other considerations were that in 21st century Western countries, the quality of spices we buy is often higher than those available from open sacks in exotic markets where the storage conditions are anything but ideal.

In Morocco, mutton tends to be served more than lamb, and its strong flavour is well served by a combination of spices that allows for this. Our ras el hanout recipe is tailored to the quality of milder flavoured lamb and beef that would normally be bought in Western countries.

Ras el hanout is extremely versatile, adding an aromatic and enticing flavour to chicken and vegetable tagines (casseroles). When sprinkled onto chicken and fish before pan-frying, grilling or baking it gives a golden colour and mild, aromatic spiciness that is quite delicious. The solution to all those recipes that blithely state 'serve with spiced couscous' is as easy as adding ½ teaspoon of ras el hanout to a cup of rice or couscous before cooking. It will give radiant colour and a lightly spiced taste that complements almost any dish.

ras el hanout

10 teaspoons mild paprika

7 teaspoons ground cumin

7 teaspoons ground ginger

4 teaspoons ground coriander seed

2 teaspoons ground cassia

2 teaspoons Alleppey turmeric powder

1½ teaspoons ground fennel seed

1¼ teaspoons ground allspice

1¼ teaspoons ground green cardamom seed

1¼ teaspoons whole dill seed

1¼ teaspoons ground galangal

1¼ teaspoons ground nutmeg

1 teaspoon orris root powder

1 teaspoon dried rose petals

½ teaspoon crushed bay leaves

½ teaspoon ground caraway seed

½ teaspoon cayenne pepper

½ teaspoon ground cloves

½ teaspoon ground mace

½ teaspoon coarsely crushed cubeb pepper

1 ground brown cardamom pod.

30 saffron stigmas

Mix all the ingredients together and store in an airtight container.

Makes about 1⅓ cups

ras el hanout chicken

This recipe is easy, once you have the ras el hanout!

2 tablespoons ras el hanout (see this page)

4 x 300 g chicken thighs, bones left in

2 x 300 g chicken breast fillets

1 tablespoon olive oil

2 small onions, peeled and quartered

4 cloves garlic, peeled and halved

3 tablespoonswater

salt to taste

2 small carrots, sliced

140 g shelled peas

12 small mushrooms, halved

Put the ras el hanout into a shallow dish and roll the chicken pieces to coat lightly. Heat the oil in a heavy-based saucepan and sauté the chicken pieces, turning until they are browned all over. Add the onions, garlic and water and reduce the heat as low as possible. Cover the pan and do not lift the lid for at least 15 minutes, by which time the chicken will have released its juices.

Season with salt if desired and add the carrots. Continue to cook very slowly until the carrots are almost tender. Stir in the remaining vegetables and add enough water or stock to cover. Return to a gentle boil, then lower the heat and simmer gently until the mushrooms and peas are cooked. Serve over plain rice or couscous.

Serves 4

saffron

Crocus sativus

This is one of the prettiest of all spices. The deep
red, trumpet-shaped stigmas are picked from
a lovely, simple little purple crocus that reaches
a full height of only about 15 cm. Blooming in
autumn for just a couple of weeks, hanging its
head demurely until the morning mist disperses,
it lifts towards the sun and opens to drink in
the warmth almost as you watch.

Also called azafran, Asian saffron, Greek saffron, Italian saffron, Persian saffron, true saffron
Flavour and aroma strongly perfumed, with an aroma of honey and tannin and a pungent bitter-honey taste
Flavour group pungent

Picking saffron is backbreaking work. With one foot on either side of the row and a bucket held between his knees, the farmer works his way along the row, picking the blooms by hand. Baskets full of the flowery harvest are loaded into the back of the family station wagon and taken home. This is when all the aunts, in-laws, grannies, retirees and children, as soon as they are old enough, gather around the family table and put their nimble fingers to work removing the three precious deep red stigmas from the centre of each bloom. The stigmas are usually dried in a sieve positioned over hot embers, but methods vary from place to place. Seeing the remnants of these lovely flowers, discarded in a ragged heap, is rather sad.

Saffron stigmas are the female organs of the flower – that's why they are gently trumpet-shaped with an opening at the wide end. Great care is taken to ensure that no pollen-bearing stamens are plucked, as they have no aroma or taste. It takes the stigmas of around 200,000 crocus flowers to get just one kilogram (about two pounds) of saffron, which explains why it's the world's most expensive spice by a long shot.

In a good year, five acres of saffron plants will yield somewhere between only 500–750 g of stigmas! There is no flavour or aroma when the stigmas are fresh because these attributes only develop when the spice is cured. Fresh saffron stigmas lose about 80 per cent of their weight in the drying process which means a region producing 10 tonnes of saffron a year has harvested at least 50 tonnes of fresh saffron.

Saffron really is just about worth its weight in gold. These days a gram of pure saffron stigma costs about the same as half a gram of gold. Because of this, you can imagine the temptation for a trader or producer to stretch the truth a little and boost the weight with just a little of something else. Saffron is often adulterated with safflower petals, coconut fibre, cornsilk and any other similar looking material that an unscrupulous trader can pass off as saffron. Even in Roman times, when saffron was frequently scattered on the floors of theatres and public halls to sweeten the air, Pliny glumly noted that it was the most frequently falsified commodity. Low-grade saffron may even have been treated with urine to give it colour, though it is most often falsified with dried calendula or marigold petals.

We had an interesting experience in India, when we purchased a pack of 'saffron', which somehow didn't seem quite right to us. We soaked it in a little water, and to our amusement, it dissolved completely, having been made of tiny threads of coloured jelly!

Festive Seafood Paella (recipe page 147)

Salad of Grilled Chicken with Black Sesame (recipe page 152)

Although most of the world's saffron comes from Iran, it has always been regarded as something particularly Spanish – ask any tourist! The Moors introduced it in the 10th century, and it is grown in the La Mancha district, famous for the Don Quixote story. At the small town of Consuegra, just south of Toledo and nestled at the foot of a high ridge dotted with those famous windmills, the Festival de la Rosa del Azafran is held over the last weekend in October. This annual event is a cross between a country fair and an agricultural show. Farmers and their families from surrounding districts come to enjoy competitive events such as saffron plucking, cooking competitions and the festival highlight – the crowning of the Dulcinea Saffron Queen. We thoroughly enjoyed being there for the festival a couple of years ago.

The atmosphere was electric as the saffron plucking heats began, reminiscent of the eisteddfods our children used to compete in. This competition is not just about speed. Contestants are also judged on accuracy in picking only the stigmas and not the bright yellow stamens, and they lose a point for each stigma left behind or each stamen picked in error. Schoolchildren competed first, the smallest being a cute little tot of four. Each child was given a plastic bag with 30 blooms (adults have 50 in theirs) and on the count of three they begin, the winner bolting to an outright lead like a bingo champion. Although it's very competitive, by the finals the lines of contestants were all smiles, jokes and laughs as fingers nimbly removed the fresh, blood-red prizes from each flower.

Feasting was just as important as saffron picking on day two. The cooking competition was a worthy prelude to the main event – the *paella gigante* cooked in a 7 m cast iron paella pan, which has to be the world's largest. From the time the fire was lit, we watched and waited for three hours, while olive oil, chicken, snails, broad beans, capsicums, tomatoes, about a kilogram of paprika, over 100 kg of rice, ten milk cans of water, and various other ingredients were added and stirred and simmered. But not a single thread of saffron was added – sadly, like most commercial paellas, yellow colouring was used instead.

choosing and using

Buying saffron is a buyer-beware endeavour. One answer lies in choosing a reputable source. But out there in the wide world, how can you tell what you're getting?

Can you see pale yellow threads amongst the red saffron? That yellow bit is the style, the section that joins the stigmas into the base of the flower, and doesn't have the colouring abilities of the stigma. So because it's inferior to pure saffron stigmas, you should be paying about 20 per cent less for it. However, the name of what you are buying can change depending on its country of origin. Saffron with the style attached is called either *mancha* (Spain and Kashmir) or *poshal* (Iran). Sometimes this type of product looks quite curly, like a little bundle of coloured steel wool.

Pure stigmas detached from the style are called *coupe* (Spain and Kashmir), *stigmata* (Greece) or *sargoal* (Iran). You should find only the occasional yellow style in this grade, which is the premium and therefore more expensive. Each stigma should be easily identifiable as a long trumpet shape.

Because of its high cost and the efficacy of a small quantity, saffron is usually sold in half or one gram packs. Store in the same way as other spices, in an airtight container away from extremes of heat, light and humidity. Do not store saffron stigmas in the refrigerator or freezer.

Powdered saffron is sometimes available, but unless you are absolutely confident as to its grade and purity (it's frequently adulterated and it may even be turmeric), we recommend grinding your own if you want saffron powder. It's easily ground: lightly toast the stigmas in a hot dry pan, then crush them in a pestle and mortar. In the spice markets of Istanbul, we were offered three different types of 'saffron' – Indian saffron, which was ground turmeric, Turkish saffron, which was dried safflower petals, and true saffron, which was in fact, saffron!

Saffron has traditionally been used mostly in those areas where it grows best – Kashmir, Iran, Spain, Italy and Greece. Therefore we find it in creamy Milanese risotto, fabulous Persian rice pilaff, sumptuous North Indian delicacies, bouillabaisse on the Mediterranean coast of France, and Spanish seafood dishes and paella. Once upon a time, there was a flourishing saffron industry in England, home to the once-famous saffron bun, but it unaccountably died out.

You need very little saffron in cooking; the key is to distribute it evenly throughout the dish, and the best way to do this is to allow the stigmas to infuse before adding them. You just add your saffron (about 10 stigmas to colour 1 cup of rice) to about 3 tablespoons of warm water or milk and let it stand for at least 15 minutes. If there's time, leave it for a full hour, and you'll be amazed at the strength of colour – like an egg yolk from a corn-fed hen. Add this vibrantly coloured water along with the stigmas to your dish.

To achieve speckled rice with some grains yellow and some white, cook the rice by the absorption method, and trickle the yellow water over the top half-way through the cooking time, leaving at least half of the surface white. The saffron water will bleed down through the rice, colouring only those grains it touches. To make all of the rice yellow, stir the infused water in at the beginning of the cooking time.

Saffron is not found in many spice blends these days and we suspect this has a lot to do with its very high cost. Saffron stigmas are generally best used in blends that will be cooked for over 30 minutes, as this gives a chance for the colour and flavour to effectively infuse. If you want to enjoy saffron's appetising dry woodiness in a quickly cooked recipe, grind your own by heating the stigmas gently in a hot pan, and then crushing them in a pestle and mortar.

Saffron combines well with all herbs and spices when it is used in moderation, so use no more than 8–12 stigmas per 500 g of proteins, vegetables or carbohydrates. The two spice blends that most famously include saffron are ras el hanout (see pages 140–2) and a paella spice mix. It is worth making your own paella spice blend as due to the high cost of saffron most commercial paella spice mixes contain artificial colours instead of the real thing – just look at the ingredient listing on the label!

paella spice mix

Our paella spice mix is a blend of paprikas, lavishly spiked with saffron and garlic, and a hint of rosemary. The Spanish smoked sweet paprika from the La Vera region of Spain, helps to re-create the smokiness traditionally developed by placing one's iron paella pan on an open wood fire. The overall effect is simply delicious. The Spanish pronounce this wonderful dish 'payeeya', but, however you say it, it's a fantastic crowd-pleaser!

6 teaspoons mild Spanish paprika

6 teaspoons sweet paprika

3 teaspoons sweet smoked paprika

2 teaspoons onion powder

1½ teaspoons garlic powder

1 teaspoon finely chopped dried rosemary

1 teaspoon coarsely ground black pepper

50 whole saffron stigmas

2 or more teaspoons of salt, to taste

Combine all the ingredients and store in an airtight container.

Makes about ⅔ cup

festive seafood paella

When feeding a crowd, if you want to spend more time with your guests and less time in the kitchen, make this fantastic, lavish paella in your biggest pan on the barbecue. It's a minimum-effort, maximum-effect, meal in one dish! We acknowledge our dear friend Margaret Fulton's original paella recipe from which this one is derived. You can change the ingredients to include your favourites – rabbit, chorizo, snails, broad beans, and so on.

4 cups chicken or fish stock

2 teaspoons Paella Spice Mix (see this page)

⅓ cup olive oil

2 half chicken breasts

2–3 cloves garlic, crushed

1 red capsicum, seeded, peeled and sliced

1½ cups rice

1 kg mixed seafood (blue swimmer crab,
    lobster tails, green king prawns,
    baby octopus, mussels and scallops)

12–15 anchovy fillets

2 tomatoes, peeled and chopped

140 g shelled peas

Make the stock using an MSG-free stock base or good-quality stock cubes with hot water. Add the Paella mix and set aside.

Heat the oil in the pan and brown the chicken on both sides – it doesn't need to be cooked through, as it will be cooked further later on. Remove and slice each fillet into 3 or 4 pieces, and set them aside.

In the same pan, fry the garlic and capsicum until soft, then add rice, stirring to coat for a couple of minutes.

Add the stock and bring to boiling point, then reduce heat and begin the decoration of the paella, which is traditionally done in a symmetrical wheel-spoke pattern. Start with the chicken pieces, laying them in equally spaced spokes, then put an anchovy fillet between each one, then add tomato pieces and peas.

Cover the pan lightly with a piece of aluminium foil, and add the seafood pieces over the next 20–25 minutes so that everything is cooked by the end of that time. Prawns, mussels and scallops need very little time, and the heat of the rice is enough to cook them. Crab claws and lobster tails can be tucked into the rice around the edges. Serve direct from the pan.

Serves 6–8

baked fish with saffron sauce

4 x 200 g pieces blue-eye cod
    (or a similar firm white fish)
½ cup good-quality fish stock
½ teaspoon saffron threads
40 g butter, diced

Preheat oven to 220ºC. Place the pieces of fish in a deep baking tray. Sprinkle with saffron, and pour the stock over. Cook for 10–12 minutes, or until the fish starts to separate into flakes. Carefully remove the fish to warmed plates.

Drain the stock into a saucepan, bring to the boil, and add the diced butter. Stir until the butter melts and the sauce thickens, then pour over fish.

Serves 4

pear and saffron relish

Thanks to Robbie Howard of Collector's Lynwood Café in New South Wales for this delicious relish that is ideal served with cheese, fruit or ham.

1 cup white wine vinegar
300 ml honey
4 cloves garlic, thinly sliced
40 g ginger, peeled and thinly sliced
pinch saffron, soaked in 1 tablespoon hot water
pinch cayenne
2 teaspoons coriander seeds, roasted and ground
1 teaspoon salt
250 g pitted prunes
850 g William pears (about 3 pears),
    peeled, cored and chopped

Place all the ingredients, except the prunes and pears, in a small saucepan (include the saffron's soaking liquid). Stir over low heat until well combined, then bring to the boil and cook for 4 minutes.

Add the prunes and pears and simmer for 30 minutes or until the fruit is very soft. Spoon hot relish into hot sterilised jars. Seal and invert for 5 minutes before storing. Unopened relish will keep in a cool, dark place for up to 6 months. Refrigerate after opening.

Makes about 3 cups

sesame seed

Sesamum indicum

At the slightest touch, sesame seeds burst forth from their sun-ripened seed pods with a dramatic explosion – not an unlikely origin for that famous phrase: 'Open sesame!'

Native to Indonesia, tropical Africa and possibly India according to some experts, the sesame plant is an annual growing to around 1–2 m tall with hairy leaves that have a surprisingly unpleasant smell and white, lilac or pink foxglove-like flowers that are borne in summer. The ripe fruit or capsules do shatter every bit as dramatically as described above when you touch them – a very good reason for harvesting the seeds before they are fully ripe.

The harvested seeds are hulled mechanically or by using chemicals that dissolve and remove the husks. However, with today's focus on natural health products, there's an increase in demand for organically grown sesame that has been hulled without using chemicals. High in protein, low in cholesterol and packed with polyunsaturated fats, sesame seeds are a nutritional goodie-bag, particularly for vegetarians.

The seeds are used in food in various ways – soup, porridge, sweetmeats, nut snacks; and sprinkled on top of cakes, bread, cookies, crackers and pastries. One of the best known products is tahini, the creamy smooth paste made from ground raw sesame seeds. It's used on its own as a spread or to make Middle Eastern dishes such as hummus, baba ganoush and halva. To make your own, purée a cup of sesame seeds with a little oil in a blender until you have the desired consistency. Tahini paste tends to settle into layers and requires stirring before use. It should be kept in a tightly sealed glass jar.

choosing and using

When you think you've got a pretty good handle on the herb and spice scene, it can be disconcerting to be asked 'black or white?' when you just want sesame seeds. **Black (or golden brown) sesame seeds** are simply white ones with their shell or outer husk still attached, making them a little tougher to bite on, and not quite as nutty in flavour as the better known white seeds. However, it's these that have the calcium, although it's not as well absorbed as calcium from milk. When choosing, be careful not to confuse them with nigella as the flavour is quite different. You'll probably have to go to a specialty spice store or Asian food shop for these, or buy online.

White sesame seeds are hulled seeds and are the most popular type to use in cooking. They are readily available in supermarkets, health food shops, spice shops and Asian food stores.

Sesame oil accounts for much of the world's production of sesame seeds, and it's especially favoured in Asian cooking.

Toasted sesame seeds are white sesame seeds that have been lightly toasted (in much the same way that nuts are roasted) to accentuate their nutty flavour.

Sesame seeds are best purchased regularly in smaller quantities and should not be kept for too long before you use them as the high oil content can lead to rancidity. Store in airtight containers away from the light.

When baked or toasted, sesame seeds acquire a delicious nutty, crunchy taste, which makes them popular on biscuits and breads and even sprinkled over ice-cream instead of chopped nuts.

Black sesame seeds are used in Japanese and Chinese recipes. They have a delicious mild nuttiness with more crunch than their white counterparts. Golden, unhulled sesame seeds garnish and flavour the traditional Turkish bread called simit that is sold by street-side vendors.

- Add toasted sesame seeds to mashed potato for a delicious nuttiness and crunch.
- Stir fry bok choy in sesame oil with pine nuts and toasted sesame seeds.
- Sprinkle sesame seeds over creamed spinach or buttered noodles.

The crunchy, nutty taste of sesame is found in surprisingly few spice blends, however those that do use it – dukkah (see this page) and za'atar (see page 162) – would have to be among the most popular with food lovers. The three forms of sesame (golden unhulled, white hulled and black) are all used in spice blends, with toasted, hulled sesame seeds being common to both dukkah and za'atar.

Sesame seeds combine well with allspice, green cardamom, cinnamon and cassia, cloves, coriander seed, cumin, ginger and galangal, nutmeg, chillies and paprika, sumac and thyme.

dukkah

Dukkah is an Egyptian specialty that has many inter-pretations, the common thread being that each blend is a combination of roasted nuts seasoned with spices. Our favourite way to use dukkah is to take Turkish bread, break off a piece and dip it in olive oil, then dip the oiled morsel of bread into the dukkah, so a generous amount sticks to it. Consume this as a tasty snack, but be prepared to have a napkin handy, and you may even have to lick your fingers.

Dukkah also makes a crunchy coating for chicken and fish when dusted on before pan-frying and it is a tasty topping for fresh salads.

3 tablespoons hazelnuts
1$\frac{1}{2}$ tablespoons pistachio nuts
3 tablespoons white hulled sesame seeds
2 tablespoons ground coriander seeds
1 tablespoon ground cumin seeds
pinch salt and ground black pepper to taste

Roast the hazelnuts and pistachio nuts, then chop them finely in a food processor.

Toast the sesame seeds in a dry pan until golden brown. The coriander and cumin seeds may be roasted whole and then ground for a more robust taste, however we find the flavour is lighter and fresher when unroasted ground coriander and cumin are used. Blend all ingredients together and store in an airtight container.

Makes about 1$\frac{1}{2}$ cups

salad of grilled chicken with black sesame

A regular customer of ours, Sean Anderson, National Food Product Manager at Eurest, gave us this recipe and we make it all the time because it is a complete meal. We can't thank him enough really, because the leftovers are just as delicious, if not more so, the next day. We save preparation time by barbecuing the chicken while we roast the pumpkin and onions. Save leftover dressing in a covered jug or jar.

1 kg pumpkin, peeled and
   chopped into 1 x 1 cm dice
1 large Spanish onion, finely sliced
3 tablespoons olive oil
1 x 250 g chicken breast
sea salt and pepper
2 x 400 g cans chickpeas,
   rinsed, drained and set aside
2 teaspoons finely chopped fresh parsley
2 teaspoons finely chopped fresh coriander leaves (cilantro)
1 teaspoon black sesame seeds

Dressing
250 ml olive oil
2 teaspoons mustard powder
$\frac{1}{2}$ cup white vinegar
3 teaspoons pomegranate molasses*
juice of $\frac{1}{2}$ lemon
2 teaspoons caster sugar

Preheat oven to 180°C. Toss the pumpkin and onion lightly in 2 tablespoons of the olive oil and place on a baking tray. Roast for about 20 minutes, or until the vegetables are just lightly browned and cooked through. Remove from the oven and set aside to cool.

Trim and remove any excess fat and skin from the chicken breast, season with salt and pepper. Heat the remaining tablespoon of olive oil in a heavy-bottomed pan and seal the chicken on both sides until lightly browned. Place the chicken on a baking tray and roast in the oven for about 8–10 minutes or until it is just cooked through. Remove the chicken from the oven, allow it to cool completely, then slice it finely on an angle, crosswise. Place the chicken slices in a bowl, cover with cling film and refrigerate until you are ready to assemble and serve the dish.

To make the dressing, whisk the olive oil, mustard powder, white vinegar, pomegranate molasses, lemon juice and sugar together thoroughly in a medium-sized bowl.

To assemble, put the pumpkin, onions and chicken slices in a large bowl with the chickpeas, herbs and black sesame seeds. Gently fold in half the dressing until all ingredients are just lightly coated.

To serve, place a couple of spoonfuls of the salad in the centre of 4 large plates. Drizzle a little of the remaining dressing around the edge of the plate and serve immediately.

Serves 4 as a main course or 8 as an accompaniment

*Note: Pomegranate molasses is a deep red, almost black, thick molasses with a rich berry-like fruitiness and citric tang. It is available from Middle Eastern and specialty food stores and does not need to be kept in the fridge after opening. However, in winter the 'liquid' can get very thick and you may have to sit the bottle in hot water to get it to pour.

shichimi togarashi

This Japanese blend is often blisteringly hot, with chillies as the main ingredient. We have developed a recipe that is still quite warm, however we took the liberty of increasing some of the other spices traditionally used, added a non-traditional (Australian native lemon myrtle), and came up with the versatile combination below.

Shichimi Togarashi is delicious on salmon and tuna, seasons tempura dishes and may be used as a condiment at the table to spice up vegetables, salads and even hot sweet corn dripping with butter.

3 tablespoons long dried chillies,
    finely chopped in a food processor
1 tablespoon white poppy seeds
1 tablespoon golden unhulled sesame seeds
1 tablespoon black sesame seeds
2 teaspoons brown mustard seeds
2 teaspoons finely chopped dried mandarin or orange peel
1 teaspoon coarsely ground Sichuan pepper
$1/2$ teaspoon ground lemon myrtle leaf
    (an ideal substitute for sansho, the leaf of the
    prickly ash (Sichuan pepper) tree
2 tablespoons salt (more or less to taste)

Combine all the ingredients and store in an airtight container.

Makes about 1$1/2$ cups

star anise

Illicium verum

Please don't confuse star anise with anise seed, and never, ever, call it 'star aniseed'. This term brings out the pedants in us, because there actually are smooth, shiny seeds within the star-shaped pod, but you don't really ever want them for flavouring!

Star anise is a dried, many-pointed seedpod from a small-to-medium evergreen tree of the magnolia family. As the name suggests, it's star-shaped, radiating about eight petal-shaped sections, each of which contains a seed. A perfect star anise also looks remarkably like a child's drawing of a daisy. It is because the rich flavour, with hints of clove and licorice, echoes the flavour of aniseed that the anise description is attached to its name – the two plants are not related, although their essential oils are of similar composition.

Native to China and Vietnam, star anise is grown almost exclusively in southern China, northern Vietnam and the Philippines. The trees take about six years to mature and fruit, and they have a productive life of up to 100 years. Although it is sometimes referred to as a fruit, we like to use the term 'seedpod', which seems more definitive.

In a process that is very similar to that used for cloves, allspice, pepper and even vanilla, the fruits are harvested before they have ripened and are dried in the sun. This is when they turn a deep reddish-brown, the woody pods harden, and their characteristic aroma and flavour fully develops.

choosing and using

Star anise can be bought whole or ground from major supermarkets and the majority of food specialty stores. The sleek, shiny brown seeds have much less flavour than the pod, so dispose of any that are loose in the bottom of the bag.

It's best to buy ground star anise in small quantities when required, as home grinders and pestles and mortars are not strong enough to grind this tough spice.

Perfect eight-segment stars are dramatic and eye-catching, however, the presence of some broken stars is not a sign of poor quality and there is no flavour difference between whole and broken star anise.

You can determine the freshness by breaking off one segment and squeezing it between your thumb and forefinger until the brittle pod snaps. Now's the time to sniff for that distinctive aroma; if you don't experience it immediately then this star is probably no longer twinkling as it should.

Optimum storage life is around three to five years if kept in an airtight container away from light and extremes of heat and humidity.

Star anise is richly pungent, therefore only small quantities are required to deliver the flavour you prefer. For example, a pinch of star anise powder is plenty to flavour a wok of stir-fried vegetables and a single star will flavour a soup or hot pot with delicious licorice aromas.

Because of its origins in China, star anise is a mainstay of the Chinese spice shelf, and its distinctive flavour is evident in Chinese five-spice. Traditionally it has been used in savoury meat dishes, and in the marinade for marbled Chinese tea eggs.

Cooks everywhere have now discovered the wonderful effect of adding the very picturesque stars to syrups for poached fruits and other desserts. Chefs have made it one of the spice stars of the third millennium, marrying it not only to fruit desserts, but also to meat courses, particularly duck.

A classic Chinese master stock always contains star anise (see page 96), and is made by slowly simmering soy sauce with sugar and a combination of spices. The stock is then used in slow-cooked beef, pork and chicken dishes as well as soups.

Star anise joins many other spices in contributing its distinctive flavour to a liqueur, in this case, anisette, which carries the dark flavour beautifully.

- To make oriental mixed vegetables, stir-fry your favourite vegetables with chopped chillies (or chilli flakes) to taste and a small amount (say ¼ teaspoon) of ground star anise and toasted sesame seeds.
- Poach pears, figs or stone fruits with a whole star anise in the syrup.
- Add a little ground star anise to South Indian curries and vegetables.
- Star anise goes well with chocolate (see our cake on page 158), so try a conservative amount in chocolate mousse and even hot cocoa.

Star anise is one of the most pungent of spices and it seems that it doesn't engender half measures in some spice blends. Occasionally it is used in subtle, fragrant proportions or more often so much is used it totally dominates the spice mix, leaving its companion spices to make a humble contribution indeed.

Star anise combines well with allspice, cardamom, chilli and paprika, cinnamon and cassia, cloves, coriander seed, cumin seed, fennel seed, ginger and galangal, nutmeg and mace, pepper and Sichuan pepper.

Star Anise Chocolate Pudding Cake (recipe page 158)

Cauliflower with Indian Spices (recipe page 171)

chinese five-spice

Chinese five-spice is almost as ubiquitous in Chinese cooking as garam masala is in Indian cooking and mixed herbs in European cooking. The sweet, pungent and highly aromatic profile of Chinese five-spice makes it an ideal accompaniment to rich, greasy meats such as pork and duck. Stir-fried vegetables are greatly enhanced by sprinkling a teaspoon or two of Chinese five-spice powder over them during cooking. With a little salt, it makes a perfect dry meat rub for chicken, duck, lamb and seafood.

6 teaspoons ground fennel seeds

4 teaspoons ground star anise

4 teaspoons ground cassia

2 teaspoons ground Sichuan pepper or black peppercorns

1 teaspoon ground cloves

Blend all the ingredients together and store in an airtight container.

Makes about $1/2$ cup

wuxi spare ribs

100 g sugar

$1/2$ cup water

$1/2$ cup dark soy sauce

$1 1/2$ teaspoons fresh ginger, peeled and grated

2 whole star anise (or 8–10 points)

6–8 pork spare ribs, not too fatty

Put the sugar in a large saucepan with the water and soy sauce and stir until completely dissolved. Add the ginger, star anise and pork spare ribs and bring to a gentle boil.

Lower the heat and simmer for an hour or more, or until the liquid has reduced and become a sticky coating on the ribs.

Finish for the last 5 minutes on the barbecue, or let them emerge magically from the kitchen to become part of the barbecue spread.

Serves 2–4

*Note: 'Wuxi' is pronounced 'Wooshi'.

star anise chocolate pudding cake

This luscious cake recipe comes from our dear friend Kerrie Cant, who cleverly combines casual work with us at Herbie's Spices, with a small catering business and a young family. This cake will be deliciously moist for 3–4 days, and freezes well.

250 g good-quality cooking chocolate

250 g butter

200 g caster sugar

6 egg yolks

100 g plain flour

1½ teaspoons ground star anise

6 egg whites, beaten until soft peaks form

Preheat oven to 200ºC and grease a 25 cm springform cake tin.

Melt chocolate and butter together in the top of a double boiler.

Cream sugar and egg yolks until pale, then fold in the chocolate-butter liquid, the flour and star anise. Gently fold in the beaten egg whites. Pour the mixture into the prepared tin and bake for 25 minutes. The cake will be wobbly, but this is okay. You might like to try this cake with more ground star anise, but we think this level is just right.

This rather dense cake requires small slices and will easily serve 12

licorice and anise – birds of a feather

Along with star anise, the spices anise and fennel contain a magic ingredient – it's the volatile oil, anethole, with refreshing top-notes that stimulate the appetite and actually disguise bitter tastes. This is what makes our taste buds samba when we chew on candy treats like licorice straps, black jellybeans and aniseed balls. Licorice root, too, gets our taste buds dancing, not only in Chinese master stock blends, but also in alcoholic drinks like Guinness beer, raki and sambuca.

sumac

Rhus coriaria

Sumac has been around since Adam was a boy. If you have ever seen a burgundy powder sprinkled over freshly sliced onions in kebab shops, you have discovered sumac. It's a spice with a refreshing fruity tang that's delicious with avocado or fish or simply anywhere you'd use lemon. In fact one can become somewhat addicted to its fruity sourness.

Also called elm leaved sumac,
Sicilian sumach, sumak
Flavour and aroma fruity, astringent
Flavour group tangy

Sumac for culinary use comes from a tree that grows throughout the Middle East and the Mediterranean, and its small red berries are partly dried before the crimson flesh is rubbed off the hard seed and ground into a coarse powder. It's a rather dense bushy shrub with attractive 'frondy' leaves almost like big curry leaves, growing to only about 3 m in height.

Having found frustratingly scant information on sumac in books, we headed off to Turkey to see it for ourselves. With our local companions, we found ourselves in central Turkey, in that amazingly barren looking, white-soiled country that exceeds all expectations by growing abundant crops of all kinds.

We pulled up near a cluster of smallish trees that looked, at first glance, rather like Australian bottle brush. They seemed to grow randomly rather than in ordered straight lines and reminded us of secondary growth on an old building site! Clusters of fruit hung like conical bunches of grapes from the branches, the unripe berries looking just like miniature kiwi-fruit. Each ripe berry glowed with an ebullient rosiness, looking for all the world as though a bright little Christmas light had been turned on inside it.

When the berries have their little lights on, the bunches are picked, dried in the sun for a couple of days, then crushed. Our companions bundled us into the car and took us off to a nearby township to find out what happened next. In a concrete-floored shed, we saw an ancient-looking stone vat with a large flat base, within which a huge stone wheel rolled round and round, crushing the sumac berries. The resulting pulp is passed through a sieve to give us the tangy, flaky condiment that has become an essential ingredient to those who have discovered it. What is left in the sieve goes back into the stone crusher for more punishment, and then back to the sieve for what becomes the second-grade sumac. The process is repeated a few times, each batch a little less exciting than the one before.

The decorative sumac tree that is found in American and English gardens is different from the edible sumac tree (although the two are related) and is definitely not to be eaten. Do not attempt to identify and gather sumac berries yourself, as there are many varieties of the *Rhus* family that are poisonous and can create severe allergic reactions in some people. Make sure you're not one of them! The edible clusters droop like bunches of grapes, while the fruits of the poisonous trees sit up like pyramid-shaped candles. Each berry is not much larger than a raisin.

choosing and using

Sumac powder is a deep burgundy colour, coarse textured and moist. Colour and texture should be good indications of quality, the darker more uniform material having less stem and pulverised seed than the lighter grades. But having said that, watch out for *amazingly* deliciously coloured dark, rich, moist sumac, because it may have oil added to buff up the gloss! Buy sumac in its powdered form from a reputable supplier.

Sumac is best stored in the same way as other spices, in airtight packs away from light and from extremes of heat and humidity. It's one of the few spices that is equally delicious uncooked.

The Romans used sumac for its tang and acidity, having not yet discovered lemons, and still today, in the Middle East and especially Lebanon, sumac is used extensively as a souring agent instead of lemon juice, tamarind or vinegar. It is rubbed on kebabs before cooking and may be used in this way with fish or chicken as well. It garnishes salads, particularly those with tomatoes, parsley and onions, and can be added to stews and vegetable and chicken casseroles.

- Sprinkle over salads, particularly avocado and tomato, and use to season meats during cooking.
- Sumac forms a tasty crust when coated onto lamb before cooking.
- A customer shared his favourite 'to die for' sumac recipe with us. Place a whole chicken in a baking tray and add enough good-quality chicken stock to a depth of about 2 cm. Sprinkle up to a tablespoon of sumac into the stock and roast the chicken. The liquid will reduce during cooking and make an unbelievably delicious sauce for the chicken. Makes your mouth water, doesn't it?
- For brunch bruschetta, heat extra-virgin olive oil in a pan, add a big handful or more of sliced Spanish onions, a big tablespoon of sumac, a good pinch of thyme and 1/2 cup of chopped sundried tomatoes. Allow to cook until the onions are tender, then serve on bruschetta.
- Sprinkle a generous amount of sumac onto halved tomatoes before slow roasting.
- Rub meats for roasting with sumac or with the crusting mix (page 124). The sumac-enriched pan drippings will make a memorable gravy!
- Use sumac as a low-salt (not salt-free) condiment.

And for something completely different: Our very dear mother uses her spectacles a little less than she should. One evening, she made a delicious dessert of passionfruit yoghurt mixed with fresh blueberries. Thinking a little nutmeg would be nice sprinkled over the top, she took a pack from the pantry and sprinkled the contents across the creamy surface. Imagine her surprise when we remarked on the wonderful innovation of sumac on yoghurt! The tangy elements of both married surprisingly well ... try it for yourself!

Sumac is a spice that is not conventionally associated with spice blends and yet its mellow fruitiness, tangy, appetite-stimulating acidity and pleasing saltiness combines well with other spices. Sumac is comfortably at home with chilli, garlic, ginger, oregano, paprika, parsley, pepper, rosemary, sesame seeds and thyme.

The blend that is best known for its inclusion of sumac is the Middle Eastern mix called za'atar (pronounced zaa-taa). Its name does create some confusion, as in many parts of the Middle East this Arabic word is also used to describe a sort of wild thyme, as well as the za'atar mix.

za'atar

Homemade za'atar is easily prepared from the following readily available ingredients, listed below. It complements carbohydrates and that is one reason why it goes so well with breads and potatoes. We like to put about a teaspoon of za'atar in mashed potato and we use it to season potato wedges. Traditional za'atar bread is easily made by brushing flat bread (such as Lebanese or pita bread) with olive oil, sprinkling it with za'atar and lightly toasting it under the griller. We have also found that za'atar is an attractive and tasty coating for whole chicken and chicken pieces, whether roasted, fried, grilled or barbecued.

3 teaspoons dried thyme

2 teaspoons dried parsley

1 teaspoon dried oregano

1$\frac{1}{2}$ teaspoons sumac

1 teaspoon toasted sesame seeds

$\frac{1}{4}$ teaspoon olive oil

pinch of salt

Crush the thyme, parsley and oregano in a pestle and mortar until they are a very coarse powder. Then add the remaining ingredients. Mix thoroughly with a spoon until all the olive oil has blended thoroughly with the herbs.

Makes about $\frac{1}{3}$ cup

warm lamb salad

2 lamb backstraps or tenderloins

2 teaspoons sumac

200 g spirali pasta, or similar

15 tiny tomatoes, halved

80 g corn kernels (canned are fine, or freshly cooked and cut from the cob)

$\frac{1}{2}$ cup torn mint leaves

1 tablespoon good olive oil

2 tablespoons hummus

extra sumac, for serving

Coat the lamb with the sumac. Cook the pasta following the directions on the pack. Meanwhile, cook the lamb quickly on a hot barbecue, approximately 2 minutes per side or longer to taste. Rest the lamb briefly while you drain the pasta.

Combine the pasta, tomatoes, corn, mint leaves and olive oil in a large bowl. Slice the lamb into thin rounds and fold through the pasta salad. Divide between two bowls, and serve topped with a dollop of hummus and a sprinkle of sumac.

Serves 2

tamarind

Tamarindus indica

The sight of this tropical evergreen tree immediately brings back a childhood in North Queensland, when there was no conception that the light brown pods lying on the road, their brittle shells cracked by the tyres of countless cars, sticky contents squashing on bare soles of feet, were actually edible.

Also called assam, Indian date
Flavour and aroma tangy, sour, slightly fruity, tingling, refreshing
Flavour group tangy

A member of the pea family, this lovely spreading shade tree bears long, knobbly, plump pods that contain around their smooth brown seeds an acidic pulp, held together by a mass of longitudinal strings and fibrous veins.

Although this enormous tree is a native of East Africa, it's also grown extensively in Asia, India and the West Indies (as well as North Queensland). India is a major exporter and here the trees grow wild, flourishing as if it were their native habitat. Today tamarind is possibly the most popular of souring agents in Indian and Asian cooking, bringing an appetising tang to curries, sour soups and sauces. Like many spices, it's multi-purpose ... over-ripe fruits are used to clean copper and brass!

These trees can grow to about 24 m, and one can't help but wonder how the pods on the high branches can be harvested. While visiting a lovely hospitable family in Mangalore in southern India, we found the answer when the foliage high above us started to quiver furiously. High up, a man was standing on one branch while holding on to another one, bouncing energetically up and down to shake the branches and dislodge the fully developed pods which fell like hail all around us. One of the women showed us how the pulp was separated from the seeds and fibre. Breaking away the brittle, thin shell, she took the mass of tamarind pulp in one hand and pressed it against a fierce-looking sickle held upturned between the soles of her feet. The seeds plopped softly into a palm frond dish and she was left with an ever-growing ball of de-seeded pulp.

The bulk of commercially produced tamarind is still hand-peeled, but we have never seen such clean pulp, free of fibre and seeds, as that done on the verandah of the Sediyapu farmhouse. After a few days the moist brown pulp oxidises and turns black, but when it's broken up in water, the resulting liquid is brown, not black.

In the Philippines, the young pods are added whole to hot, sour soups, while in Thailand, they are eaten fresh with sweet shrimp paste. The young leaves are also sour and are eaten raw in fish salad.

choosing and using
You can buy tamarind from spice shops and from Asian and Indian grocery stores either in slabs about the size of a thick block of chocolate, or in a molasses-consistency black paste. In Middle Eastern stores you'll also find a sweetened tamarind cordial.

The block style is either a product of Thailand or India, and although the products vary (Asian is cleaner-looking and very sticky), you probably won't detect a difference in the flavour.

Recipes usually call for tamarind water to be added during cooking. Think of it as another form of lemon juice and use it in roughly the same proportions. To make tamarind water, break off a walnut-sized piece from the block and put it into ½ cup of hot water, stir, leave for about 15 minutes, then strain the liquid off, squeezing the remaining pulp as dry as possible before you discard it. You can make tamarind water in bulk and freeze in ice cube trays to use as required.

Due to the high amount of acid, tamarind block is quite stable and requires no special storage conditions. Just keep it in an airtight pack to prevent it from drying out.

Tamarind concentrate is very convenient to use and you can buy it in plastic or glass jars in a variety of sizes. It is usually sharper and more acidic in flavour than the pulp. To make tamarind water from concentrate you simply dissolve 1 teaspoon of concentrate in 2 tablespoons of warm water; alternatively, you can simply add the concentrate direct to the dish.

A less common form is a powder called cream of tamarind or assam powder. It's made by mixing tamarind extract with a carrier such as dextrose.

Tamarind's main role in the kitchen is as a souring agent, so it's in the company, flavour-wise, of lemon, pomegranate, kokum (also called fish tamarind), green mango and vinegar. Lemon juice is favoured in much of Europe and America, but tamarind is the souring agent of choice in most of India and Asia.

Adding a souring agent doesn't necessarily mean that sourness or tanginess is the first taste sensation of the dish. Tamarind is used in many Indian dishes, from lentils to curries and chutneys, where it's not only the tang, but also a light fruitiness, that tamarind contributes to the overall flavour.

Tamarind has a secret life that's not so well known, because it is rich in pectin. It slips unnoticed into commercially made jams and jellies, and is an important ingredient in Worcestershire Sauce.

In Asia, tamarind is sometimes cooked with sugar to make a cordial base, which is particularly refreshing when topped up with icy-cold soda water. The same idea is popular in the Middle East – who borrowed the idea from whom is anyone's guess!

- Combine tamarind water with brown sugar and other spices such as cumin, chilli and ginger, to create a sweet-and-sour dipping sauce.
- Before baking a whole fish, take a walnut-sized piece of tamarind block and rub all over the skin. Discard the leftover tamarind.

chicken in tamarind marinade

Inspired by a Charmaine Solomon recipe for chicken in tamarind sauce. Don't be tempted to use tamarind concentrate as a shortcut for this recipe – it is too sharply flavoured. The flavour of next-day leftovers just continues to improve.

1.5 kg roasting chicken

185 g dried tamarind pulp

2 cups hot water

3 tablespoons ground coriander

2 tablespoons dark soy sauce

5 tablespoons sugar

2 teaspoons salt

Cut chicken into serving-sized portions. Soak tamarind in half the hot water and when cool enough to handle, squeeze to dissolve the pulp in the water. Strain through a fine sieve and if there is more pulp on the seeds, add the remaining hot water and continue rubbing pulp between the fingers to dissolve. Strain and discard the seeds and fibres.

Roast coriander in a dry pan over low heat, stirring constantly, until it becomes fragrant and darkens in colour. Combine with the tamarind. Add soy sauce, sugar and salt and stir well.

Put the chicken in a bowl just large enough to hold it and pour over the marinade. Leave for 4 hours, turning chicken pieces over at least twice.

Put the chicken and marinade into a non-reactive pan, and simmer on a low heat, uncovered, until tender, about 40 minutes. Lift chicken pieces from the gravy and drain thoroughly. Continue to simmer the sauce if necessary – it should be very thick and reduced. Place chicken on a serving dish, ladle the tamarind gravy over and serve with steamed rice.

Serves 4–6

turmeric

Curcuma longa

Turmeric is most familiar as the brilliant yellow spice
with a pungent aroma that stains irrevocably when
you spill it on your clothes (no we don't have
a handy hint for removing turmeric stains;
the rule is be careful).

Grown throughout tropical Asia, turmeric is closely related to ginger and galangal. The plant has bright green, lance-like leaves and forms clumps up to about a metre high. Its lumpy, orange-fleshed rhizome (commonly called fingers) has a distinctly earthy aroma and flavour and contains a powerful colouring agent called curcumin. After harvesting the rhizomes are dried and pulverised to produce the powdery spice we all know so well.

Fresh turmeric rhizome is used in some Asian recipes, however, the powder is the most common ingredient in Indian cooking. The large leaves can also be shredded finely and added to curries and other dishes or used as a garnish, and are an important ingredient in Nonya and Indonesian cooking, especially in the spicy rendang meat dishes. In Thailand, the young tender shoots are gathered during the rainy season, and boiled as a vegetable served with nam prik.

choosing and using

If you find yourself in the Spice Bazaar in Istanbul, you'll hear traders calling it Indian saffron because of its ability to colour like saffron at a fraction of the price. However, turmeric should never be used as a substitute for saffron as the flavour is completely different.

There are two types of turmeric most commonly used – Alleppey and Madras. Alleppey turmeric is produced in Kerala (India) and gets its name from the beautiful waterway-laced Alleppey district near Cochin where much of this turmeric is traded. It's a deep orange-yellow in colour and has a flavour very close to fresh turmeric root. This is the best variety to use in cooking when the true flavour of turmeric is desired. However, the texture is 'oily' due to the high curcumin content and when blending it with other spices we normally sieve it through a small strainer to prevent clumping.

Madras turmeric is grown in Tamil Nadu and traded mostly from Chennai (formerly Madras). It is a light yellow and has been the most readily available variety for cooking, probably because it colours curries, pickles and mustards without contributing too much flavour.

Always buy dried turmeric in its ground form, as the hard dried fingers are virtually impossible to pulverise at home. Store ground turmeric as you do other spices, in airtight packs protected from light and extremes of heat and humidity. Under these conditions both Alleppey and Madras varieties will keep their flavour and colour for 12 months or more.

Fresh turmeric is often available from Asian food markets and produce shops. Choose plump, firm and clean rhizomes and store them in an open container in a cupboard as you would onions or garlic. When peeling and chopping fresh turmeric, make sure you use gloves, and even then some of the oily curcumin content will transfer to your skin and give you nicotine-yellow fingers for a couple of days.

Turmeric is used extensively in Asia and the Middle East as a condiment and culinary dye. It's a major ingredient in curries and curry powders and is also added to chutneys and pickles. Keep in mind that a bright yellow curry powder will probably be both cheap and lacking in flavour because of its high proportion of turmeric.

India not only produces most of the world's crop, it also uses about 80 per cent of it. Western cuisine has never really adopted turmeric directly, but the food industry uses it in several sauces and as an edible colouring for mustards.

Once one gets over the notion of turmeric being mainly used to colour food, it's surprising how versatile its flavour becomes (especially Alleppey turmeric) in a wide variety of dishes. Chermoula depends on its warm earthiness to amalgamate spices such as cumin, paprika chilli and pepper, and we have found it goes well in stir-fries with galangal, lime leaves, chilli and Australian native lemon myrtle.

Turmeric may suffer from the ignominy of being passed off as Indian saffron and relegated in many cooks' minds to being just another colouring, however there is no substitute for the unique flavour given by a good-quality turmeric. The majority of curry powders rely on turmeric for flavour as well as colour, as does the North African chermoula spice mix. Ras el hanout even needs it. The versatility and importance of turmeric can only be guessed at when one looks at the number of spices this earthy rhizome complements.

Turmeric combines well with allspice, caraway, cardamom (green and brown), chilli, cinnamon and cassia, cloves, coriander (leaves and seeds), fennel seed, fenugreek, galangal (a member of the same family), garlic, ginger (also from the same family), kaffir lime leaves, lemongrass, lemon myrtle, mustard, nigella, paprika, parsley, tamarind and Vietnamese mint ... to mention just a few!

vegetable curry blend

This vegetable curry blend contains no chilli, so it is very mild, yet it is highly aromatic and tasty with its combination of ground and whole spices. We find it is also excellent for fish curries, as the light flavour profile does not overpower delicate seafood. We do not recommend dry-roasting this curry blend for vegetable and seafood curries. However, if you wish to make a beef or lamb curry with this mix, a light roasting before making the curry will develop a more robust flavour.

6 teaspoons ground coriander seed

2 teaspoons sweet paprika

2 teaspoons Alleppey turmeric powder

2 teaspoons cumin seeds

2 teaspoons brown mustard seeds

1 teaspoon ground cumin seeds

1 teaspoon ground fennel seeds

1 teaspoon ground cassia bark

1 teaspoon ground ginger

¼ teaspoon ajowan seeds

¼ teaspoon ground green cardamom seeds

¼ teaspoon asafoetida powder

Combine all the ingredients and store in an airtight container.

Makes about ¾ cup

dhai baingon
(eggplant with yoghurt)

On one of our Spice Discovery Tours to India, we encountered this dish in a splendid domed dining room in Jaipur. We immediately begged the recipe from the chef.

1 large eggplant, sliced

vegetable oil for frying

1 teaspoon cumin seeds

3 onions, peeled and chopped

3 tomatoes, peeled and chopped

1 teaspoon Alleppey turmeric powder

1½ teaspoons salt

2 teaspoons ground cumin

1 teaspoon ground coriander

1 teaspoon chilli powder

1 teaspoon fenugreek leaves

1 tablespoon tomato paste

1 cup water

250 ml natural yoghurt

1 tablespoon fresh chopped coriander leaves

Preheat the oven to 180°C.

Drain the eggplant in a colander for 5–10 minutes. Heat about 1 tablespoon of oil in a heavy-based pan and fry the eggplant slices in batches until lightly golden, adding more oil if necessary. Remove and set aside.

Heat another tablespoon of oil in the pan and add the whole cumin seeds. Fry for 45 seconds, then add the chopped onion and tomatoes. Cook, stirring occasionally, until onion is transparent. Add turmeric, salt, 1 teaspoon of the ground cumin, coriander, chilli powder, fenugreek leaves and tomato paste, then stir in the water. Continue cooking over moderate heat until onion and tomato are soft and most of the liquid has evaporated.

Oil the inside of a medium-sized ovenproof dish or casserole and spoon in half the onion-tomato mixture. Arrange a layer of eggplant slices on top. Cover with the remaining onion-tomato mixture and finish with more eggplant slices. Mix the yoghurt with the remaining teaspoon of ground cumin and spread over the top. Cover tightly with foil, then place in the oven until warmed through. Serve sprinkled with fresh coriander leaves.

Serves 4 as part of a meal

cauliflower with indian spices

1 teaspoon brown mustard seeds

1 teaspoon ajowan seeds

1 teaspoon Madras turmeric powder

1/2 teaspoon tamarind paste

1 tablespoon vegetable oil

1 small onion, chopped finely

2 cloves garlic, crushed

500 g cauliflower, broken into small florets

2 mild green chillies, seeded and finely chopped

2 teaspoons nigella seeds

salt

Crack the mustard seeds lightly with a pestle and mortar. Combine with the ajowan, turmeric and tamarind, then add water to make a smooth paste.

Heat the oil in a heavy-based pan or wok, and fry the onion and garlic over medium heat until soft and golden. Add the cauliflower in batches, stirring until lightly browned. Add more oil if necessary.

Remove the cauliflower and set aside.

Put the spice paste, chilli and nigella seeds into the pan, then add all the cauliflower and stir to combine. Cook over low heat, adding more water if it begins to stick on the bottom. Season with salt to taste and cook until cauliflower is tender. It should be quite dry, with nearly all of the liquid evaporated.

Serves 4 as part of a meal

*Note: For a lovely recipe using fresh turmeric, see Tony Tan's Balinese Duck Curry on page 91.

growing

You can grow turmeric successfully in temperate area gardens in a warm, sunny position in well-drained soil. Being from the tropics, turmeric likes to be watered regularly – and fertilised. Propagate by rhizome division in spring. To divide a rhizome, just break a finger with one or two buds (the daughter rhizome) from the main tuber, or you can re-use your original tuber (the mother rhizome) and even cut it in half lengthways to make two plants. Plant it in sandy potting mix in a pot or tray until they have sprouted leaves and are large enough to transplant. After about 8 months, when the lower leaves turn yellow, your crop will be ready for lifting.

whiting fillets grilled in turmeric leaves

This delicious recipe is one of Carol Selva Rajah's specialities. A delicate fish like whiting works best with this subtle spice mix. It should be cooked slowly at first to allow the spices and the turmeric leaf to impart their flavour. In Malaysia, whiting is a delicacy and the fish would be cooked whole. Carol tells us that the fish would be eaten using fingers, so the bones can easily be removed and the flesh picked out and eaten with rice and sambals.

6 turmeric leaves, the length of each whiting fillet

1 tablespoon vegetable oil

1 teaspoon turmeric powder

6 whiting fillets

8 shallots or 1 red Spanish onion, roughly chopped

3 stalks lemongrass (about 8 cm of the thick, juicy end, roughly chopped

3 cm piece of fresh ginger, peeled

1 teaspoon chilli powder, or to taste

1 teaspoon cumin powder

2 tablespoons lime juice, to taste

salt and pepper

2 kaffir lime leaves, centre stem removed and thinly sliced

1 beaten egg

2 tablespoons coconut cream

Wash the turmeric leaves, then dry them well, rub with a little oil and wrap them in foil until ready to use. Sprinkle turmeric powder over the whiting fillets and set aside until ready to cook.

Put the shallots, lemongrass and ginger in an electric blender, or use a mortar and pestle to pound them to a paste. Add the spices and the lime juice and season with salt and pepper to taste. Stir in the kaffir lime leaves and beaten egg until well combined.

Soften the turmeric leaves by plunging them briefly in hot water, then lay them out on a clean work surface. Place 1 whiting fillet and 1 tablespoon of the herb and spice mixture on the centre of each leaf and top with a little coconut cream. Overlap each edge, and fix in place with a bamboo skewer. If the turmeric leaves do not hold fast you may have to wrap the made up parcels in a piece of kitchen foil before placing them under the griller to cook.

Preheat the grill to a medium temperature. Cook the whiting fillets for 6–8 minutes, turning over as each leaf turns brown. After about 5 minutes, or when the fish smells aromatic, turn up the heat to finish cooking for a further minute or so.

Serve with rice and a sambal made from coconut cream and thinly sliced kaffir lime leaves.

Serves 6

vanilla

Vanilla planifolia, var. fragrans

When we were kids, the vanilla essence in the pantry was nothing to get excited about – it was just what you put in cakes, custards, and milk drinks as a matter of course. Since then, 'artificial' has become a dirty word, and 'real' is trendy!

Also called vanilla bean, vanilla pod,
vanilla extract, vanilla essence
Flavour and aroma rich, full, sweet, aromatic
Flavour group sweet

One of the charms of vanilla beans is the appearance of millions of the tiniest black spots imaginable throughout your sweet cooking. Like a banana, the vanilla bean carries its seeds in the middle of its entire length, so it's a simple matter to cut the bean lengthwise and scrape the sticky mass of seeds out with a spoon or a round-ended knife blade.

Vanilla is one of the world's most expensive spices (number two after saffron). It is such a valuable crop that in the past farmers had to 'brand' each bean using a cork with some pins in it to prevent 'bean rustling'! Native to Mexico and Central America, where it is still grown commercially, vanilla is a tropical, climbing orchid with a long green fleshy stem and aerial roots that parasitically cling to the tree. Its greenish-yellow flowers grow in bunches, which bloom one by one during the flowering season. They are followed by flat green pods 15 cm in length that look similar to big French beans and contain thousands of tiny black seeds.

Vanilla flowers need human intervention to be pollinated. The flower has a tough little membrane separating the stigma (the female organ) and stamen (the male organ) that can only be penetrated naturally by a tiny bee of the *Melapona* genus. This bee is native to Mexico and is, in fact, the smallest bee in the world. As there are fewer bees and more flowers these days (and as vanilla is also grown in places like Madagascar, New Guinea and India as well as Mexico), each short-lived vanilla flower is hand-pollinated. The method still in use today was devised by Edmond Albius, a former slave, way back in 1841 on Réunion. He simply lifted the membrane with a thin bamboo skewer and smeared the pollen with his thumb.

Hand-pollinating a plantation of vanilla flowers is painstaking and time-consuming to say the least. Each flower is only open for eight hours and during that time the farmer must find every open flower, push aside the membrane and touch the stigma and stamen together. (It's a bit like opening the mouth of a snapdragon.) After all this, only about 50 per cent of the flowers will go on to produce pods. You can see where the high prices come in when you think of the labour cost of all those fiddly little acts with the toothpick! If fertilisation is successful, farmers can calculate the date for harvesting as exactly nine months from pollination.

Freshly picked pods have no smell or flavour – it's the lengthy process of alternate sweating and drying that brings about the enzyme reaction which creates the wonderful creamy vanilla bean aroma we know and love. The curing process takes up to three months of sun-drying during the day, wrapping in blankets every night, and finally drying on open racks in the drying sheds. When the pods are dried, they become black and shiny, soft, flexible and moist to touch, but not too high in moisture or they will go mouldy. Their perfume is sweet and permeating, and for connoisseurs there is no substitute, especially in dishes such as French vanilla ice-cream.

You may have noticed that most vanilla beans are uniform in length and look quite straight. This is because a good farmer will go through his plantation removing curved and crooked pods, retaining the vine's energy to develop the straightest, best-looking pods which are the most sought after as gourmet grade whole beans. It takes farmers two days to pick about 300 kg of pods from one hectare; and after all that, 5 kg of his freshly harvested green pods will produce just 1 kg of shiny black vanilla beans.

For us, one of the delights of the spice business is receiving a new shipment of vanilla – the aroma is delicious! Some of our vanilla beans are organically grown in the traditional way in the highlands of Papantla, Mexico. We visited the farm, where the fourth generation of the same family carried on the business, to see first-hand the growing, harvesting and processing of this precious product, and incidentally were given a bottle of delectable vanilla liqueur that we have never found anywhere else.

We also saw the cottage industry of making the soft, flexible beans into shapes such as simple flowers and heart shapes, as well as intricate baskets and almost life-size chrysanthemums. The women of the grower's family do this painstaking craft by using one piece of vanilla bean to make a stem, and attaching shaped and cut pieces with strong black thread to serve as petals and leaves. Unfortunately, since the supply of beans has been so short, this home craft has been discontinued.

choosing and using

Vanilla beans are readily available from specialty food shops. A good bean is dark brown or black, moist to touch, as pliable as a piece of licorice and immediately fragrant. You should be able to wrap a vanilla bean tightly around your finger – if you can't, then it's too dry. This is what food and recipe writers mean by a fresh vanilla bean – it is as fresh as possible in its dried state. You can't cook with a fresh, undried bean. If someone refers to a vanilla stick, stay well away from it, because by the time a luscious, succulent, flexible bean has become a brittle stick, it is more a has-been than a vanilla bean.

Beans should be stored in an airtight pack in the coolest part of the kitchen (but not in the refrigerator) away from light. In these conditions, a bean will keep nicely for up to 18 months.

You can rinse and re-use beans two or three more times. Pat your rinsed bean dry in paper towel, then store it in the sugar canister; it scents the sugar and remains dry and clean. However, if a vanilla bean has been infused in milk for a custard, be particularly careful to rinse the milk residue from all the little wrinkles, and wrap this bean in plastic wrap and keep for just a short time in the refrigerator.

In Sri Lanka, vanilla growing is a relatively new industry. A man with a spice stall in the markets of Colombo tried to interest us in his locally grown vanilla, and we have to say it certainly looked beautiful – dark, plump and supple. However, our noses told a different story ... where was that swoon-inducing aroma? Back in Mexico, that's where! It seems to be an inferior variety being grown in Sri Lanka, perhaps also hindered by trial-and-error drying methods.

One of the most common questions we are asked is what is the difference between extract and essence? An extract is made by literally extracting the desired attributes of a substance, be it almond, coconut, vanilla or whatever. Vanilla extract is made by steeping chopped, cured vanilla beans in alcohol and water and then distilling-off much of the water. It's hard to quantify an exact comparison between whole beans and extract, because much depends on the quality of the bean. Roughly, one good bean would equal about 1 teaspoon of extract.

The plot thickens when you come to 'vanilla essence'. This may either be a distilled or concentrated vanilla bean extract or it might be something completely different that doesn't contain vanilla at all. Some of the imitations could have been synthesised from eugenol (clove oil), waste paper pulp, coal tar or 'coumarin', found in the tonka bean, whose use is forbidden in several countries. Some products muddy the waters even further by combining real extract with artificial vanillin flavour.

And on the subject of plots thickening, there's a misconception that good liquid vanilla is really thick and syrupy. Ask yourself: what makes a syrup? The answer is sugar, of course, so your thick vanilla extract or essence will be very sweet.

Vanilla is one of the most popular flavourings in the world. It all began with the Aztecs who flavoured their royal drink *xocolatl* with a mixture of cocoa beans, vanilla and honey. Cortez brought vanilla back to Spain in the 16th century, after having observed Montezuma drinking this sublime concoction. Like cocoa and coffee, it became an instant success and spread across Europe like wildfire.

The mellow fragrance of this sweetest of spices enhances almost every variety of sweet dish: puddings, cakes, custards, creams, soufflés and, of course, ice-cream. Classic examples include crème caramel, peach Melba and apple Charlotte.

- Slit the bean open and scrape out the millions of sticky seeds within and blend through ice-cream, unflavoured yoghurt or rich, thick cream.

- Store vanilla beans in sugar, (particularly caster sugar), burying the bean so that no light can reach it. After two to three weeks the sugar will be lightly scented and can be used in coffee or in dessert recipes. The bean can be removed for other uses once or twice, and returned to the sugar after being thoroughly cleaned and dried. Keep topping up the sugar, making sure it's airtight to retain the aroma.

- Vanilla complements coffee just as deliciously as cocoa! Allow one-third of a bean for four cups. Cut the bean into 5 mm pieces and pop in the plunger with the ground coffee. Pour in the very hot but not boiling water, brew, plunge and enjoy.

Sadly, when one thinks of vanilla and blends that contain it, the first thing which comes to mind is vanilla sugar, something that should be a wonderful celebration of natural vanilla, but is nearly always made using artificial vanillin powder. Make your own vanilla sugar by putting a couple of whole beans in a canister of caster sugar, and even allowing for normal top-ups, they'll give you vanilla sugar for up to a year.

The flavour of natural vanilla combines well with allspice, crystallised angelica, green cardamom, cinnamon and cassia, cloves, ginger, lavender, lemon myrtle, lemon verbena, licorice, mint, nutmeg, poppy seeds, rose petals, sesame seeds and wattleseed.

We love the flavour of vanilla with poached and stewed fruit, so we always make up a batch of this fruit infusion blend, tie it up in a muslin ball and dangle it in the pan of pears poaching in champagne or pot of stewing fruits during cooking.

vanilla chicken

Using vanilla in a savoury application is unexpected and subtle. We first tasted it at a now-disappeared Mauritian restaurant in Sydney, and encountered this vanilla sauce, created by Lawry Gordon, on the Central Coast of NSW.

Vanilla Sauce

3 finely chopped shallots

50 g unsalted butter

50 g plain flour

5 tablespoons verjuice

¾ cup chicken stock

2 vanilla beans

pinch saffron threads

1 tablespoon tomato paste

2½ tablespoons rice vinegar

100 ml cream

salt and pepper

2 whole allspice berries

4 x 300 g chicken breast fillets

salt to taste

500 g white bean or potato mash, for serving

8–12 cooked asparagus spears, for serving

Make the vanilla sauce at least an hour before cooking the chicken. Sweat the shallots with the butter and flour for a few minutes, then add the verjuice. Slowly add the stock, and simmer for 10 minutes with the vanilla beans and saffron. Remove from the heat and pass through a fine sieve into a clean pan.

Place the pan on a low heat and stir the tomato paste and rice vinegar into the sauce until thoroughly blended. Slowly add the cream, taste and season and remove from the heat.

Split the vanilla bean, scrape the seeds and return them to the sauce. Replace the scraped-out pod in the sauce and leave to infuse for 1 hour. Gently reheat before serving, and remove spent pod.

To prepare the chicken, fill a large saucepan with water, add the allspice and bring to a simmer. Add the chicken breast fillets in a single layer, making sure they are completely covered by the water, bring up to boiling point, then immediately reduce heat to a simmer. Poach gently for 12–15 minutes until the chicken is tender, moist, and just whiter than pink when cut through the thickest part. Remove, drain and set aside, discarding poaching liquid.

To serve, spoon enough vanilla sauce on to the warmed plates to cover the base. Place mashed potato or white beans in the centre of the plate and top with chicken. Drizzle extra vanilla sauce over the top, then garnish the chicken with a few asparagus spears.

Serves 4

fruit infusion blend

Like a master stock ball (see page 96), the fruit infusion ball can be stored in a jar in the refrigerator and re-used at least three times.

6 teaspoons allspice berries

1 vanilla bean, cut into 2 cm bits

2 broken cinnamon sticks

1 broken cassia stick

4 teaspoons chopped dried ginger

3 teaspoons broken dried mandarin or orange peel

5 whole cloves

Wrap the spices in a square of muslin to make an infusion ball.

Makes 1 infusion ball

wattleseed

mulga *Acacia aneura*

coastal wattle *A. sophorae*

gundabluey wattle *A. victoriae*

wirilda *A. retinodes*

golden wattle *A. pycnantha*

'Just follow the creek, keeping it on your left and when you get to Tanami Road, you'll see the road house on your left. Don't forget to refuel before heading off to Yuendumu, and give Frank my regards.'

Also called mulga, coastal wattle, gundabluey wattle, wirilda, golden wattle
Flavour and aroma richly roasted, mocha aroma, slightly bitter
Flavour group pungent

The Herbies Indigenous Spice Hunt Party, water bottles filled, anticipation and excitement welling, headed north-west from Alice Springs in a cloud of red dust to find Frank and discover wattleseeds.

Frank, a geologist, is the manager of the Yuendumu Mining Company (YMC) that became involved with wattleseed thanks to an inquiry from Iran for a tonne of viable acacia seeds. Iran had problems with sand dunes that were constantly on the move and engulfing villages in the process. They had begun to dig great swathes with D9 bulldozers, spray them with bitumen to retain moisture and plant acacia seeds. The magnificent wattle root systems would then hold the dunes. The only problem was, that by the time the YMC had identified the seed source and amassed sufficient quantities, the Iran–Iraq war broke out (March 2003) and the market for the seeds disappeared into thin air.

However, wattles not only bind the earth with their deep root systems, but certain varieties also have culinary talents, and, with plenty of edible wattleseeds on hand, Frank and the YMC tumbled headlong into the food business.

You don't go out into the bush and harvest your own wattleseeds unless you really know what you're doing, because only a small handful of the 700 plus varieties are safe to eat. One kind that is considered as a 'food wattle' is *Acacia aneura*. It has seeds with high nutritional levels, including protein, much of which is contained in the tail-like connecting tissue attached to the seed. While wattle trees grow and bear pods prolifically, the task of gathering and preparing the seeds for consumption is painstaking and labour intensive. The seed-bearing pods are harvested while they're still green and immature.

Australia's Aboriginals ate cooked green wattle pods for sustenance. Traditionally, the green pod was thrown onto an open fire, where the moisture inside created steam and cooked the pod. It might be nutritious, but there was not much flavour to get excited about.

Once the seeds are steamed, however, some of the background astringency is diluted and the seeds can be roasted in a pan over hot embers until some of the seed coat begins to crack. After this the roasted seeds are removed to cool and are sieved to separate them from the ash, an extremely dusty, sooty task. Once they're roasted, the seeds are very hard, so grinding is the only way to make them easily usable. So the cleaned, roasted seeds are milled to make 'roasted and ground' wattleseed that is ready to use in cooking.

The resulting product is a dark brown, grainy powder looking something like ground coffee, with a distinct, light coffee-like aroma and pleasing, slightly bitter, nutty, mocha taste.

choosing and using

Roasted and ground wattleseed is available from specialty spice shops, adventurous delicatessens and food outlets that sell Australian native foods. It is relatively expensive when compared to the majority of spices (about five times the price of ground nutmeg) because of the labour involved in processing. In addition it is mostly wild-crafted (gathered from its wild state) and not commercially cultivated. Buy small amounts regularly as even though the flavour profile is quite stable, it is always best if not stored for longer than two years. Keep roasted, ground wattleseed in an airtight pack, just as for other ground spices, and avoid extremes of heat, light and humidity.

This uniquely Australian spice burst on the scene in the early 1970s, featuring in a roulade of meringue filled with wattleseed-flavoured cream. This take on the Aussie icon, pavlova, was an instant hit. The dark, rich flavour of wattleseed is excellent in sweet dishes such as ice-creams, sorbets and chocolate mousse. It can also be added to yoghurt, cheesecakes and whipped cream in much the same way as we add the tiny, sticky seed mass scraped from a vanilla bean.

In these applications, roasted wattleseed grounds give their best flavour when infused with the liquid ingredients (preferably boiling or at least heated). Then you can either strain the infusion and add it to your dish, or add the liquid including wattleseed grounds for extra colour and texture. Soaking will also soften the seed particles.

- Add roasted and ground wattleseed to batter for pikelets and blinis, then top with a dollop of sour cream and a generous pile of smoked salmon.
- Include wattleseed in bread dough and damper for a true Aussie flavour.
- Use the Aussie Barbecue Spice (see page 182) to season grilled salmon or chicken.
- Add a couple of teaspoons of wattleseed to biscuit dough.

Wattleseed's roasted, nutty, coffee-like taste is not something that one would immediately associate with a spice blend, however for many of us who find the flavour of hickory smoke a touch artificial, wattleseed is an excellent substitute. Wattleseed combines well with allspice, bush tomato (akudjura), green cardamom, cinnamon and cassia, coriander seed, lemon myrtle, mountain pepperleaf and native pepperberry, pepper, thyme and vanilla.

We have found this spice complements chicken, lamb and fish particularly well, especially when a small amount is blended with sympathetic spices as in the spice mix on page 182. Sprinkle this over the food before cooking – it is particularly delicious with salmon steaks – and then pan-fry, grill or barbecue the meat. The wattleseed adds a subtle barbecued note that is far more appealing to the Australian palate than the popular American natural hickory-smoke flavour used in many seasonings and snack foods, which always seems artificial-tasting to us.

aussie barbecue spice

This Aussie barbecue spice blend is so versatile that as well as the suggestions above, it can be used to season potato wedges, and vegetables like eggplant before cooking.

4 teaspoons ground coriander seed

2 teaspoons ground akudjura

1/2 teaspoon roasted and ground wattleseed

1/4 teaspoon ground mountain pepperleaf

1/4 teaspoon ground lemon myrtle leaf

2 or more teaspoons salt, to taste

Blend well and store in an airtight container.

Makes about 1/3 cup

lemon cheesecake with a wattleseed crust

Chef Kellie-Ann Travers has created the best cheesecake in the world, and here it is.

Base

3 tablespoons wattleseed, roasted and ground

100 g melted butter

400 g Anzac biscuits, homemade are best

Filling

2 1/2 leaves gelatine, or 20 g gelatine powder

1/2 cup boiling water

175 g caster sugar

750 g cream cheese

250 g sour cream

juice and zest of 4 lemons

Preheat the oven to 160°C and lightly grease a 20 cm springform tin. Infuse the wattleseeds in the warm melted butter for at least 15 minutes. Tip into a food processor with the Anzac biscuits and blend to a crunchy paste. Press into the base of the springform tin and bake for 6 minutes. Remove from the oven and set aside

To make the filling, dissolve the gelatine in the boiling water and set aside. In an electric mixer, beat or whisk together the sugar, cream cheese and sour cream for around 10 minutes. Add the lemon juice and zest and continue whisking for a further 5 minutes. Still whisking, add the gelatine and beat until well blended. Pour onto the biscuit base and refrigerate overnight to set.

Serves 10–12

chocolate mousse with wattleseed and lemon myrtle cream

We love this classic Cordon Bleu recipe with its distinctive Australian twist.

125g dark cooking chocolate

50g unsalted butter

1/3 cup orange juice

2 tablespoons cocoa powder

1 1/2 teaspoons wattleseed

2 egg yolks

1 tablespoon Cointreau

300 ml thickened cream

3 egg whites

1 1/2 tablespoons caster sugar

1 1/2 teaspoons lemon myrtle

Place chocolate, butter and juice in a bowl and micro-wave until melted. Whisk in the cocoa and wattleseed, then the egg yolks and Cointreau. Set aside to cool.

Meanwhile, beat 100 ml of the cream in a small bowl until soft peaks form – set aside. Beat the egg whites in a clean, dry bowl until soft peaks form, then add the sugar and beat until smooth and glossy. Fold the whites into the melted chocolate mixture. Fold in the cream, and when completely mixed, transfer to a serving bowl or individual bowls, and refrigerate.

Add the lemon myrtle to the remaining cream, beat until thick, and let stand for a minimum of 3 hours to allow the flavours to infuse. Serve the cream with the mousse.

Serves 6

herb essentials

So just what are herbs? For those of us who use them regularly, we generally refer to the leaf of a plant that we use in cooking as a culinary herb and any other part of the plant that is most often dried, as a spice.

Spices can come from all sorts of parts of plants, ranging from dried, unopened flower buds in the case of cloves, to the bark of a tropical evergreen tree for cinnamon.

Sections of roots of plants, often referred to as rhizomes, give us spices like ginger, turmeric and galangal. Berries from trees, shrubs and vines are gathered and dried to create allspice, barberries and peppercorns. Even the stigma of a particular purple-flowered crocus is plucked in the case of saffron. The aromatic seeds of many herb plants are gathered and dried to give a vast array of seed spices, including fennel, dill, caraway, anise and cumin.

Many of the aromatic seeds we call spices are actually gathered from herb plants when they have finished flowering. A familiar example is coriander: the leaves are referred to as a herb, however the dried seeds are always called a spice.

So now you may ask, 'What about the stem and roots of coriander that are used in cooking, and what about onions, garlic and the delicious bulb of fennel?' These sections of vegetable material that are mostly used fresh to enhance the flavour of food, tend to be classified with herbs. Therefore when a cook is adding ingredients such as coriander leaves, lemongrass stalk, garlic and coriander roots these may all be referred to as the herbs. The cumin, pepper, chilli, galangal and ginger will probably be referred to as the spices.

fresh or dried?

An important characteristic of most spices is that they are generally used in their dried form.

Many herbs, on the other hand, tend to be used when they are fresh, because those herbs with delicate fragrances and highly volatile 'top notes' only contain their truly aromatic attributes when they are fresh.

'Fresh' is a word that is much bandied around these days and is often used in different contexts, which can be confusing. Freshness is always critical in the context of being 'ready to consume' or 'not old and tasteless'. However when we say 'fresh herbs' the term means herbs that have been freshly picked, and have not been dried, frozen or processed in any way.

In some cases the fresh item is clearly best, for instance basil, coriander, rocket and Vietnamese mint leaves are among many herbs that are significantly better when fresh. Having said this, when deciding to use a fresh or dried herb you do need to consider which is more appropriate for its particular application.

For centuries people have been drying the different varieties of herbs and spices for varying reasons, the most common being that it preserves them in a storable form for later use, when either the crop is not available or is not conveniently to hand when it is required.

With the majority of spices, the drying or curing process creates certain enzymatic reactions within the spice itself, and this in turn creates the distinctive flavour we are looking for. It is what produces the uniquely different flavours of spices such as vanilla, cloves, pepper and allspice. For example, the drying of peppercorns in the sun turns them black and forms the volatile oil piperine, which gives pepper its unique taste. Before curing, the vanilla bean is a green, tasteless, odourless bean that grows on a tropical, climbing orchid.

Another reason for drying herbs that is often overlooked, is to have them in a form that imparts the flavour most effectively into the food being cooked.

An example would be to try and make a cup of peppermint tea with fresh peppermint leaves. The result would be an infusion with very little flavour and a low level of the therapeutic volatile oils in the tea. However, the drying and processing of peppermint leaves makes them infuse readily with hot water to make an effective cup of herbal tea, with the characteristic flavour we know so well. The infusion would be comparatively bland and entirely different if made with fresh peppermint leaves.

The same principle applies to cooking with herbs such as thyme, sage, marjoram, oregano and bay leaves.

drying your own herbs

It is not difficult to dry your own herbs and it is possible to achieve a professional result when a few logical guidelines are followed.

Firstly, herbs will dry best when you pick your own fresh from the garden. Bunches that have been kept in cold storage or transported for long distances after harvesting will often develop spots of discoloration on the leaves, caused by oxidisation or partial fermenting.

Next, if picking your own, remember to gather your herbs in the morning, just after the dew has dried and before the heat of the day has reduced their pungency.

The traditional method of drying is to tie up the stems of the herbs into bunches about the size of a small feather duster. Hang these bunches in a dark, warm, dry and well-aired place for up to a week. When the leaves feel perfectly crisp and dry, strip them off the stems and store them in an airtight container. If the leaves feel at all soft or leathery, they are not dry enough and will go mouldy.

If you are very keen, it is not difficult to make drying frames about half a metre square and 10 cm deep with a fine mesh insect screen stretched across the base.

The herbs should be spread out in the frames to an approximate depth of 2 cm, and then placed in a dark, well-aired place where the air can circulate freely around them. It is important to note that the herbs will dry faster if the leaves are removed from the stems first. The leaves dry more quickly on their own because you are not trying to remove the moisture from the thicker stems at the same time.

We have actually experienced a phenomenon when perfectly dry leaves were left on the stem for a couple of days after drying. The moisture in the not-so-dry woody stems migrated back into the dry leaves and they had to be dried for a bit longer after being stripped off.

Every herb has its own structural characteristics and so each type of herb will dry a little differently to another. Leaf size, density, moisture content and a host of physical attributes will cause each individual herb to yield up its water content in different ways, so you will always need to feel for that tell-tale crunchy texture of a properly dried herb.

It is also possible to dry herbs in conventional and microwave ovens. To dry herbs in a conventional oven bring the heat to about 120ºC. Place herb leaves that have been removed from their stems in a single layer on a baking tray lined with greaseproof paper. Place them in the oven, turn off the heat and crack the door just open. After half an hour, remove the tray of herbs, reheat the oven to 120ºC and repeat the process. Keep repeating the process until the leaves are crisp and dry.

When drying herbs in a microwave oven you need to be careful not to kill the magnetron, which is something that can happen when there is not enough moisture to absorb the microwaves. Place the picked herb leaves on a sheet of paper towel in the microwave oven with a microwave-safe cup, half full of water. Zap the leaves for 20 seconds on high and then remove any dry, crisp leaves. Keep zapping in 10-second bursts until they are all dry, continually removing the dried leaves. You won't damage your oven because even when all but a few leaves have been taken out, the water in the cup will still absorb the microwaves.

When a herb is dried, most of the water content is removed leaving the dried, shrivelled leaf still containing the essential oils that give the herb its flavour. Because the dried herb is like a concentrated form of the fresh, a general rule of thumb for recipes is to use one-quarter to one-third of the dried quantity that you would have included of fresh.

storing dried herbs

Optimum storage conditions for your own dried herbs, or ones you have bought already dried, will mean that they can be kept ready to use for up to 18 months or more.

Dried herbs should be kept in airtight packaging to retain their essential oils and to prevent excessive exposure to the air that will cause the oils to oxidise more rapidly and lose their pungency.

oregano

French tarragon

winter savory

The packs must be kept away from extremes of heat, light and humidity. This is because heat will evaporate the herb's volatile components and the flavour will deteriorate.

A spice rack is attractive in one's kitchen, however unless it is used to store the herbs and spices you use regularly, light from fluorescent tubes or direct sunlight pouring through a kitchen window will bleach out colour and flavour will be lost at the same time.

Humidity is another major enemy of effective dried herb storage. A rise in humidity brings with it extra moisture, and the result of that is faster deterioration of flavour. Never store dried herbs in the refrigerator. When a pack is taken out of the cold environment, condensation will form. The condensation introduces more moisture that will shorten the storage life of dried herbs.

storing fresh herbs

Believe it or not, there are many ways you can get the most from those bunches of fresh herbs you buy, and never seem to use entirely in one hit.

Most soft-leaf herbs such as basil, chervil, coriander, dill, parsley and tarragon may be kept for up to a week in a glass of water in the refrigerator. Wash them in clean, cold water first and make sure the bottom 2.5 cm of the stems are immersed in water, then cover the foliage, snood-like, with a clean plastic bag.

Herbs with harder stems and more robust foliage, such as thyme, sage, marjoram and rosemary, may be kept in a glass of water in the kitchen and need not be refrigerated.

Whether storing in the refrigerator or not, try to remember to change the water every couple of days.

freezing fresh herbs

You can freeze many herbs when you need a longer storage period.

Hard-stemmed herbs store well when sprigs are wrapped in foil and placed in a freezer bag in the freezer.

A convenient method for freezing softer herbs is in ice-cube trays. Chop the herb finely – with a herb like coriander where we use all of the plant, chop the leaves, stems and roots – then fill sections of an ice-cube tray two-thirds full with chopped herb, just cover with water and freeze. When frozen, turn out the herb-cubes and store them in a freezer bag. You need to keep the frozen herbs in freezer bags, otherwise they may pick up unwanted aromas from other foods stored alongside them.

when to use fresh or dried herbs

There are many dishes where we would say it is preferable to use fresh herbs to get the true effect. For example in Thai cooking, fresh coriander leaves, ginger, garlic, lemongrass and lime leaves are essential for achieving the classical flavour. An Italian salad with fresh tomatoes tastes better with fresh basil, however when making a Bolognese sauce or a stew or casserole, we would always include dried herbs such as basil, oregano, thyme and bay leaves.

These dried herbs have more robust, concentrated flavours, which amalgamate and infuse more readily into the food because they are dried, allowing the essential oils to migrate easily out of the leaf structure and flavour the meal.

Should you particularly want the flavour of some fresh herbs as well, then add them about 10 to 20 minutes before the end of cooking time. This way the heat of cooking does not destroy the delicate fresh 'top notes' and you have the best of both worlds.

So keep in mind, when it comes to fresh or dried, it is simply a matter of using the most appropriate form for the particular meal or dish.

processed herbs

On your shopping expeditions you've probably seen the 'freshly prepared' herbs and spices in jars and tubes, which require refrigeration after opening. These are a good substitute for fresh herbs, however the flavour is sometimes sweet, salty and acidic, which is due to the amount of vinegar or other food acids needed to achieve preservation.

When using these products in cooking, taste them first and then adjust the amount of sweetness, saltiness or acidity in the dish you are making to allow for what you are adding with the prepared herbs.

angelica

Angelica archangelica

With its sweet and refreshing aroma, angelica was long considered something of a guardian angel against all ills. An old-time remedy for flatulence advised chewing the stems until the condition was relieved; this was probably helpful, as we now know that angelica contains pectin, an enzyme that acts on digesting food.

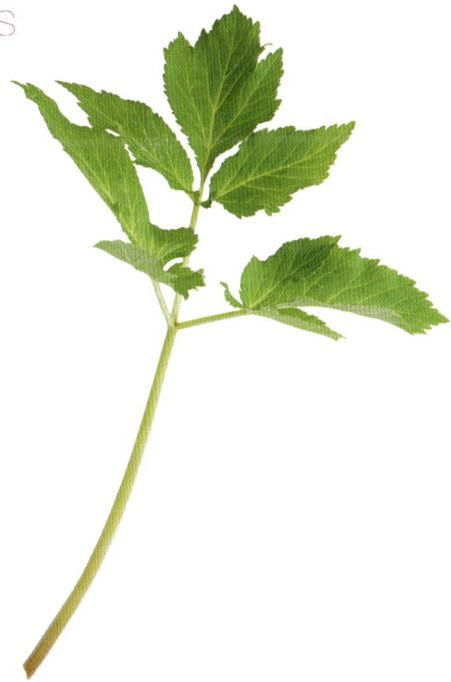

Also called garden angelica, great angelica, holy ghost, master wort
Flavour and aroma sweet, aromatic. When candied, intensely sweet
Flavour group mild

Although there's a tendency to think of angelica as an old-fashioned herb, it's cultivated commercially today because it is very much in demand for medicinal and cosmetic preparations – and for the liqueur Benedictine, which wouldn't be the same without it!

Today, we are probably most familiar with angelica in its candied or crystallised form – used for decorating desserts, cakes and cassata with those brilliant green stems – and tasting overwhelmingly of sugar because of the amount you use in crystallising.

choosing and using

Fresh angelica stems picked straight from the plant lend a distinctive sweet flavour to jams, jellies and stewed fruits – particularly those made with tart fruits like rhubarb and plums – that's not sugary at all.

If you want fresh angelica for your cooking you will probably have to grow your own, as it is not widely available. However, once you have it in your garden, you can add a few tender leaves to salads or stock, or enhance sweet infusions by adding leaves to custard or sugar syrup. It's best to pick leaves just before you need to use them to retain the flavour. Like all herbs with juicy green leaves, chop or tear them roughly and add to hot dishes at the last minute.

You can cut and use fresh angelica stems at any time, however their flavour is usually best just after flowering.

The dried leaves make an aromatic tea and are a fragrant addition to potpourri and herb pillows. For a relaxing bath, make a simple sachet by tying a few leaves – fresh or dried – in a muslin bag and letting it soak in the hot water.

growing

This delicately perfumed, fast-growing plant enjoys a shady spot in the garden and needs space, taking up about as much room as a tall, fat man when it's mature – that is, 1.8 m tall and 1 m wide. The hollow, branching stems bear a strong resemblance to celery stems, and carry bright green serrated leaves most of the year.

Angelica is a biennial, forming foliage the first summer, and round, whitish-green flower heads that bloom in late spring or early summer of the second year, when you may need to stake the plant as it gets rather top heavy. Cut the flowers (they look pretty stunning in a vase), and the leaves will grow more prolifically. And if you cut the stems back frequently, your plant may flourish for longer than the customary two years. It dies down completely in the winter but is frost-hardy.

Rosemary's Glazed Pears (recipe page 193)

Compote of Dates with Figs and Aniseed (recipe page 198)

It is best to plant seedlings or seeds in spring in a sheltered spot in the garden about 90 cm apart. Use fresh seed, as the germinating period is very short. Angelica likes moist, well-drained, rich soil in filtered sunlight. Water well. If your plant develops yellowish-green leaves, then it's probably thirsty.

You can grow angelica in a container, but keep in mind that tall, fat man and make sure the pot is large enough to contain him and that there is enough soil to prevent him from falling flat on his face! Remember also that any plant growing in a pot is like a bird in a cage – it depends on you entirely for food and water.

drying

To dry the leaves, snip them off the stems and spread them out on sheets of paper or on drying racks in a shady, warm place. When they are dry and brittle, store them in an airtight container.

Harvest the seeds just before they start to fall by snipping off the flower heads and drying them. Sift out any dried husks and stalks, then store the seeds in airtight containers. If you want them for sowing, plant them within the week as angelica seeds lose their viability fast.

rosemary's glazed pears

For a spicy change, you can try a coriander seed in each pear instead of the sugar and cinnamon mixture.

4 even-sized beurre bosc pears
1 teaspoon ground cinnamon
1 teaspoon caster sugar
butter
1 cup passionfruit pulp
4 stems candied angelica, about 2.5 cm long

Syrup
1 cup water
110 g caster sugar

Wash the pears, peel and cut out the cores from the stalk end. Mix together the cinnamon and sugar. In each hollow put a knob of butter and a little of the sugar and cinnamon mixture.

Make a syrup by boiling the water and sugar together for 10 minutes. Place the pears in a saucepan, pour over the syrup, cover and simmer gently until just tender. Ladle the syrup over the pears continually so that they become nicely glazed.

Lift the pears out carefully and place them on a serving dish. Stir the passionfruit pulp into the remaining syrup to combine, then pour the mixture over the pears and decorate each one with an angelica stem. Chill, and serve with heavy cream.

Serves 4

candied angelica

Candying angelica to decorate desserts or cakes isn't hard, but does take time.

You can reduce these amounts proportionately depending on how much stem you want to crystallise. 500 g of stem would decorate many cakes and desserts.

500 g fresh young stems of angelica

500 g caster sugar, plus extra sugar to coat

2 cups water

Cut the angelica stems into 12 cm lengths. Add enough water to cover and boil until tender. Drain and peel the stems, place them in a shallow dish and top with 500 g of sugar. Cover and set aside for two days. Transfer the stems to a saucepan, add the water and bring to the boil, stirring all the time. Reduce the heat and simmer gently until the syrup is absorbed and the stems are clear.

Place the stems on a wire rack to drain (a cake rack will do). When cool, sprinkle over plenty of sugar to coat thoroughly and leave to dry. Store the candied stems in airtight containers where they will keep well for about 6 months.

stevia – another naturally sweet alternative

Stevia (*Stevia rebaudiana*) can, literally, be called a sweet little plant as its leaves are absolutely the sweetest product in the natural world, around 30 times sweeter than cane sugar but with no kilojoules (calories). It is increasingly used as a natural alternative to artificial sweeteners since a method was found to remove the slightly bitter aftertaste from the dried leaves.

You can use stevia leaves fresh or dried. In its dry form, less than 2 tablespoons can replace 1 cup of sugar, although it's hard to be specific as actual sweetness varies from one harvest to another.

A member of the aster family, stevia bears doily-shaped flowers in the summer. It likes fairly moist conditions and can cope with any range of temperatures above freezing. It's a rather spindly-looking plant, growing 60–90 cm tall, and has pale green, narrow leaves about 2 cm long.

Growing stevia from seed, though possible, is a hit-and-miss operation, and therefore possibly destined to be disappointing. Taking cuttings from the mature part of the plant is a safer option. Allow them to take root in a pot of good sand or potting mixture before planting out. Sweet success.

anise

Pimpinella anisum

Almost everyone will know those black, marble-sized aniseed balls that are found in specialist candy stores. Today you can even buy them over the internet. The word aniseed is actually an abbreviation of anise seed. It is the seed of the anise plant rather than the leaf that we mostly use in cooking, which is why anise, with its warm liquorice flavour, is perhaps better known to most of us as a spice.

Also called sweet cumin
Flavour and aroma licorice, fresh and warm
Flavour group medium

Originally from the Middle East, word of its usefulness as an aid to digestion (thanks to a volatile oil compound it contains called anethole) and as a breath freshener spread fast from Roman times onwards. In fact the Romans were such fans of its digestive benefits that they added aniseed to their spice-filled mustaceus cake which was served at the end of over-indulgent banquets.

choosing and using

Rather resembling young coriander or salad burnet, freshly picked anise leaves bring a subtle tarragon-like tang to green salads, fruit salads, soups, stews and egg dishes. Use with discretion however, so that the flavour doesn't overpower other ingredients. Add whole anise stems to vegetable soups at the start of cooking, and when the vegetables are tender, simply discard the stems as you would a bay leaf. Or, for a fresher flavour, stir through a few chopped leaves a minute or two before cooking is completed.

Whole or ground, aniseed brings distinctive liquorice and fennel notes to many traditional cuisines.

The seeds are an essential ingredient in German baking and in rye breads from Scandinavia. Anise is widely used in Italian cooking, especially in puttanesca sauce with pasta and for rabbit dishes. You may also read that it's the ideal spice for Indian vegetable and seafood dishes. But the Indians more commonly choose its close cousin, fennel. The confusion arises because many people (including those who should know better, like fruit and vegetable retailers), still call the fresh fennel bulb 'aniseed', which it isn't.

Because it is a very small seed, you can use aniseed whole and simply sprinkle it over stewed or baked apples or pears, and over vegetables such as cabbages (cooked or raw), onions, cucumber, carrots, turnips and beetroot.

Anise is cultivated commercially for confectionery, cough lozenges, herb tea blends, a popular French cordial called anisette, and ouzo, pernod, pastis and aguardiente – a favourite aperitif in South America. Dogs are also rather partial to its flavour, which is just as well, because pet food manufacturers include it in pet foods as an aid to digestion and as a flatulence preventative.

Renowned for its freshness and fragrance, anise oil is an ingredient in perfumes, toothpastes, soaps and mouthwashes, and crushed aniseed is in demand for potpourri.

growing

A spindly plant with feathery leaves and flat, white flower heads that bloom in late summer and rise above the foliage, anise grows to about 45–50 cm. It likes a garden with plenty of sunshine, warmth and protection from prevailing winds. As the soft, fragile seedlings don't transplant well, sow the seeds where the plants are to grow. Make sure that the soil is well broken and in what is often called 'good seedbed condition', which basically means light and crumbly. Anise likes an alkaline soil, so you may need to add a little lime if the ground is very acid.

Plant seedlings or seeds in spring, about 30 cm apart. Cover the seeds with a very thin layer of soil (the old rule of thumb was always that the thickness of soil cover should equal the thickness of the seed itself). Pack it down well, and keep the ground moist, using a gentle spray nozzle so that the water pressure doesn't dislodge the covering layer of soil, until the seedlings appear. Once the seeds have begun to sprout, they only have to dry out once for them to die of thirst. It is best to water anise in the late afternoon or early evening so that you do not scorch the delicate leaves.

Anise is also very happy growing in a pot, but choose one large enough for its root system and make sure it's in a sunny spot. And remember it depends on you for water.

By late summer, the flower umbels will droop with aromatic, small, brown seeds with a distinguishing fine hair at one end. The flower head is called an umbel because it's shaped in a wide, shallow dome that is almost the shape of an umbrella. Each umbel is made up of lots of very tiny individual flowers.

drying

Cut the heavy flower heads off before they drop, preferably before the day gets too hot, but after the dew has dried off. Spread them out to dry on sheets of paper, or tie the stems in a bunch and hang in a warm, well-ventilated area with some direct sunlight. Rub the flower heads between the palms of your hands when they are crisp and dry, then sift to separate the seeds from the flowers and pieces of stem.

Store the seeds in airtight containers away from extremes of heat, light and humidity. Try not to be impatient, because if you store the seeds before they are completely dry, you'll possibly find mould developing, and all your efforts will be wasted. Make sure you label and date the pack. Seeds will last for two to three years for culinary use, but germination is more successful if you sow seeds the following season.

puttanesca sauce

Serve with penne or your favourite pasta.

4 cloves garlic

6 anchovy fillets

1/2 teaspoon brown sugar

1 x 400 g can whole tomatoes

1/3 cup red wine

1 tablespoon capers

18 black olives, pitted and chopped

1/4 cup virgin olive oil

4 whole birdseye chillies

1 tablespoon Italian herbs

1/2 teaspoon aniseed

Make a paste by crushing the garlic cloves with the anchovies in a pestle and mortar. Combine the paste with all the other ingredients in a pan and simmer gently for 30 minutes, uncovered, until the sauce has reduced and the flavours have blended and developed.

Serves 4

compote of dates with figs and aniseed

Serve a small amount of this delicious compote with cream, or enjoy with cheese, crackers and fruit.

1 cup pitted dates, halved or quartered

1 cup tenderised dried figs, cut to similar size as the dates

1 cup port

1 teaspoon aniseed

To make the compote, place all the ingredients in a small pan and bring to the boil, then remove immediately from heat and cover. Let the compote cool to room temperature before lifting the lid off the pan. By this time, most of the liquid should be absorbed. Store in the refrigerator until needed.

Makes about 2 cups

balm

Melissa officinalis

The lingering lemon scent of this member
of the mint family gave it the popular name
of lemon balm. Balm was long highly
regarded as a remedy to revive the spirits.

It was traditionally used in pickled herrings and eels in Belgium and Holland, the lemon overtones complementing the seafood. It was also used in liqueurs such as chartreuse. These days balm is considered rather old-fashioned and is sought after more for its cottage-garden appeal than its culinary use.

choosing and using

Balm's palate-pleasing, lemon-flavoured leaves deliver a distinctive tang to a green salad with a light-on-vinegar dressing or to lightly steamed vegetables. Try adding a few bruised leaves to fresh fruit salad or a compote of oranges – or use as a substitute for mint for a refreshing change. Season chicken, fish or pork with a little finely chopped balm before serving. It's traditional to add fresh sprigs to wine cups and fruit drinks, while chopped leaves are added to fruit salads, stewed fruit and fruit jellies. Infuse a sprig in custard, removing it just before you serve so that only the lemon fragrance lingers.

Balm tea is refreshing; even one leaf in the teapot with Indian tea will give a lift. The dried leaves make a fragrant addition to potpourri and herb pillows.

A small bunch, washed, wrapped in foil and stored in the refrigerator will stay fresh for a week or two. Another option is to stand the bunch in a jar of water and cover it entirely with a plastic bag, folding the open ends under the base of the jar. To keep longer than a week, chop fresh leaves finely into ice-cube trays, cover with a little water and freeze.

growing

Balm, a compact leafy plant with crinkly leaves similar to mint, grows to about 60–75 cm depending on conditions. It likes a sunny garden with moist, rich soil. Sow the seeds in spring fairly thickly, or plant seedlings close together and you will soon find you have a pleasing clump. When buying seeds or seedlings, opt for a frost-hardy variety. From late spring, out shoot long thin flower stalks covered with clusters of tiny, white, bee-attracting blooms.

This perennial has something of a spreading habit, but its thick, matted, shallow roots are not as rampant as mint. Cut it back quite hard in late autumn, and you will see plenty of new growth coming up by spring. Fungus can be a problem if conditions are too wet and shady, and keep a watch out for voracious leaf-eating grubs and insects.

The simplest way to propagate balm is by root division in spring, just as the new growth is starting. To take cuttings, wait for new tips to grow to about 7.5 cm long, and when firm enough, take a 10 cm long tip, removing all the leaves except the top two. Press the cuttings deeply into a pot of river sand or good-quality potting mix, leaving one-third of each cutting exposed.

If you are growing balm in a pot, choose one with plenty of room for its shallow, rampant root system. And remember to water regularly because, as with all shallow-rooted plants, as soon as the top layer of soil is dry, balm gets thirsty.

drying

Because balm's delicate lemon fragrance is easily destroyed on drying, fresh is best. If you really want to dry the leaves, cut the stalks back almost to ground level just as the flowers begin to appear and dry them on airy racks in a shady place. You can also tie them loosely together in bunches and hang them to dry. As soon as the leaves are crisp and dry, cut them from their stalks and store in airtight, labelled containers.

chicken salad with lemon balm and thai spices

Balm's palate-pleasing, lemon-flavoured leaves deliver a distinctive tang to this chicken salad.

500 g chicken tenderloins

1 teaspoon sesame oil

1 teaspoon thick soy sauce

3 cups baby rocket leaves

1 cup lemon balm leaves, loosely packed

1 cup coriander leaves, loosely packed

Dressing

¼ cup lime juice

2 tablespoons sesame oil

1 tablespoon fish sauce

2 tablespoons mirin or sherry

2 small red chillies, finely sliced

2 teaspoons gula melaka or brown sugar

1 clove garlic, crushed

Preheat the oven to 200°C. Mix the oil and soy sauce together and brush over the chicken pieces. Place them on an oiled baking tray and bake for about 15 minutes, or until cooked, turning once. Remove from the oven and set aside.

To make the dressing, combine all the ingredients in a jar and shake well. Place the rocket, lemon balm and coriander on serving plates, top with the chicken, and spoon dressing over.

Serves 4

swiss breakfast

⅔ cup rolled oats (not the instant ones)

200 g plain yoghurt

juice of 1 orange

1 apple (skin left on), diced

2 tablespoons raisins

2 teaspoons chopped balm

2 teaspoons finely chopped walnuts

raw sugar or honey, to taste

Combine all the ingredients in a bowl and serve with extra raw sugar or honey to taste.

Serves 1

balm for bees

Herb gardens and bee hives were traditionally linked together, and Thomas Hyll wrote in 1579 that the hives should be placed near: 'The hearbe Baulme ... and manye other sweete and wholesome floures.' Balm's association with bees goes back over 2000 years when every pantry was packed with jars of honey and hives were traditionally rubbed with sweet-smelling herbs, especially balm leaves, to prevent the bees from swarming and to encourage them to come home.

basil

sweet basil *Ocimum basilicum*

bush basil *O. minimum*

Versatile sweet basil with its heady, clove-and-anise perfume sends cooks into raptures and brings summer to mind.

Also called sweet basil, bush basil, Thai basil
Flavour and aroma less pungent in flavour than the initial aroma indicates, fresh, clove-like, slightly minty
Flavour group strong

As the taste of the fresh leaves is less pungent than the aroma, you can safely use a whole bunch in your cooking if you are so inclined. However, in its fresh state, it has quite a peppery pungency, so be judicious if you still want other flavours to shine through.

choosing and using

Basil has a special affinity with tomatoes and tomato-based dishes and is excellent with eggplant, zucchini, marrow, squash, and spinach. Added during the last 30 minutes of cooking, basil brings zest to split pea, bean or lentil soups. It is delicious with cream or cottage cheese in sandwiches, lifts crisp green salads and enhances pasta dishes. Above all, it gives pesto its unique character. Basil also complements poultry, veal, fish and shellfish and its volatile notes counteract the richness of liver and game in pâtés and terrines. In fact, as any true 'basilophile' will tell you, it can be added to just about anything! Simply steep a few fresh, washed leaves in a bottle of white wine vinegar for a few weeks and you will have tasty vinegar on hand for dressings.

Basil leaves are best when used whole or torn. Chefs say that you shouldn't cut them with a knife because this takes away some of their aroma.

When buying basil, steer clear of bunches that have black marks on the leaves or look wilted. Fresh basil will keep in the refrigerator for a couple of weeks. Simply wrap paper towelling around the base of the stems, wet it and seal the whole bunch in a plastic bag.

Leaves can be frozen too: tear them finely, mix with a little water and freeze in ice-cube trays.

To preserve basil in oil or vinegar, pick the leaves, wash and dry them and stack in a shallow container, sprinkling salt on each leaf as you go. Cover the leaves in olive oil, pop the lid on the container and store in the refrigerator for up to three months.

Varieties of basil have long been important in South-East Asian cooking – Thai cookery uses three main kinds. Probably the best known is Thai basil (*O. canum sims*) with its slender, oval, slightly hairy leaves. The leaves are eaten raw with vermicelli, chopped and served as a garnish on fish curries, added to salads or included in clear vegetable soups. Basil seeds are frequently used in drinks on the Indian subcontinent and in Sri Lanka. Known as subja, they come from a variety of wild basil and are used for their texture rather than their unforgettable taste. Once they are wet, the tiny black seeds develop a jelly-like consistency while remaining crunchy in the middle. Their most common use is in the Indian milk drink called falooda.

growing

The old favourites, sweet basil and bush basil, with their tender bright green leaves, are still the best varieties to grow for the kitchen. Sweet basil is the most popular and is a vigorous grower in the summer months. For limited space, bush basil is more compact but with the same wonderful flavour. Both produce small, white, long-stamened flowers that you have to nip in the bud ruthlessly to prevent the plants from going to seed and finishing the life cycle too soon. Nipping also encourages thicker foliage and thus more basil, a more abundant harvest and more pesto ...

This easy-to-grow, sun-loving annual thrives on heat and turns up its toes with the first wintry blasts. If your soil is sour, lime it well two weeks before planting, making sure that the bed is well broken up and as fine as possible. If the soil is heavy, a small quantity of river sand will help to make the ground more suitable, both for sowing and drainage. Plant seedlings or sow seeds directly into the garden in late spring or early summer when the weather is definitely warm as a cold change can kill the plants. Thin out sweet basil seedlings to 30 cm between plants. For bush basil, 15 cm between seedlings is plenty. Pinch out the centres to encourage branching and a sturdy, spreading, bushy habit.

Water well and keep moist (but don't drown) to ensure germination and good growth and remember that snails are very partial to young basil leaves and can devour a seedling at a single sitting. If your young plants develop horrible black spots on the leaves, it could be from water staying on the leaves overnight. To prevent this, only water the plants in the morning once they are established, and bring a pot under cover in the event of wet weather.

Pick fresh leaves throughout the summer and harvest in the early autumn before the cold weather turns the leaves limp and yellow. In hot climates where basil can grow throughout the year, the seeds will often self-sow.

Basil makes a pretty border as the plants sit so neatly in the garden. The more compact bush basil is a good choice for balcony baskets and pots. Choose an 18 cm pot; fill it with a good-quality potting mix and plant three or four seedlings. When they are established, leave the sturdiest in the pot, pick out the rest and plant them in other containers or in the garden. Remember that basil (or any other herb) is not a houseplant. It wants a warm terrace or exterior windowsill where there is sunshine and fresh air. A lack of both of these elements could lead to black, rotting stems and a very sick plant.

drying

For the fullest flavour, cut long, leafy stalks for drying, and spread them out in a shady place on wire mesh to encourage quick drying. Do not hang them in bunches, as the soft foliage will dry too slowly and may possibly spoil. Oven or microwave drying is not satisfactory as the leaves bruise easily and are liable to scorch.

perfect pesto

There's no need to introduce pesto. If you work your way through our 'dollop' suggestions on page 205, you'll soon need to whip up another batch.

4 packed cups basil leaves
8 cloves garlic
1 cup toasted pine nuts
1 cup good-quality parmesan cheese, finely grated
1 cup extra virgin olive oil
salt and pepper, to taste

Combine ingredients in a food processor adding a little of each at a time. Stop to stir once or twice. Will store in the refrigerator for up to 3 weeks.

Makes 2 cups

Chicken Salad with Lemon Balm and Thai Spices (recipe page 201)

Borage Soup (recipe page 217)

basil variations

This delicious 'variation' recipe is reproduced with kind permission from Amy Nathan, from her book *Openers*, (Chronicle Books, San Francisco, 1988).

2 tablespoons vinegar

salt to taste

4 small fresh eggs

500 g yellow wax beans,
    ends trimmed and cut lengthwise into strips

1 handful each green and opal basil leaves, mixed

¼ cup light olive oil

3 tablespoons white wine vinegar

3 bacon slices, cooked and crumbled

cracked black pepper

8 thin baguette slices, toasted lightly

1 cup Perfect Pesto (see page 204)

In a pan, bring 5 cm depth of water to a gentle boil. Add the vinegar and salt, and poach the eggs in the liquid. As yolks begin to set (about 5 minutes), transfer the eggs with a slotted spatula to a shallow pan of cool water to hold for serving.

Blanch or steam the beans for approximately 2 minutes, or until tender. Rinse under cold water and set aside. Cut half the basil leaves into thin strips and set aside, reserving some whole leaves for garnish. In a large bowl, combine the olive oil and vinegar. Toss the beans in enough dressing to coat.

Divide the beans among 4 serving plates. Sprinkle each serving with basil strips and a little bacon. Top with one poached egg, being sure to allow excess water to run off eggs before placing over the beans. Sprinkle with cracked pepper and add some whole basil leaves to each plate. Serve with baguette toasts spread with Perfect Pesto.

Serves 4 as an entrée

add a dollop of pesto to:

- a bowl of minestrone
- a crusty roll
- a bowl of pasta
- cheese and crackers
- salad dressings
- oven-dried tomatoes
- grilled chicken slices
- stuffings
- goat's cheese canapés
- rare roast beef.

what you need to know when choosing basil plants

With the immense popularity of this herb, nurserymen have had a field day producing new and fascinating varieties, such as lemon, purple, pesto, lime, ruffled, and dark opal basils.

CAMPHOR BASIL – *Ocimum kilimansharicum* – an interesting variety, but not suitable for eating.

CINNAMON BASIL – *O. basilicum 'Cinnamon'* – for novelty value, try a few leaves in fruit salad. Dry and add to potpourri.

GREEN RUFFLES BASIL – *O. basilicum 'Green ruffles'* – simply gorgeous in salads.

LEMON BASIL 'SWEET DANI'- *O. sp.* – a delightful blend of flavours. Toss some shredded leaves in a chicken salad.

LIME BASIL – *O. americanum* – add whole leaves to cool drinks, or place a few leaves on fish before wrapping in foil to barbecue.

PERENNIAL BASIL – *O. sp.* – has the benefit of lasting through the winter, but the flavour is not as good as sweet basil. Enjoy the seasonality that nature intended – basil is a summer flavour.

PURPLE RUFFLES BASIL – *O. basilicum 'Purple ruffles'* – showy in the garden. Great in salads.

RED RUBIN BASIL – *O. basilicum 'Red rubin'* – another showy-in-the-garden and great-in-salads variety.

SACRED BASIL – *O. sanctum* – this faintly lemon-scented basil has a warm aniseed aroma and a pretty mauve-pink flower. Many a Hindu home will have a pot growing by the front door. Do likewise and choose a more appropriate variety for your meals.

THAI BASIL – *O. basilicum 'Anise'* – quite different from sweet basil. Absolutely essential for authentic Thai cooking.

Note: Japanese basil is in fact a herb called shiso and is not related to European basil.

bay leaf

Lauris nobilis

The bay tree is a fairly unremarkable evergreen tree. If you saw it in an old, well-established garden, you'd probably not notice it amongst the rhododendrons and more showy specimens. But an avenue of bays can be quite stunning in its simplicity.

Also called sweet bay, poet's laurel
Flavour and aroma piney, oily, rich, resinous
Flavour group pungent

The long, narrow, dark green leaves have a dull gloss, giving a healthy tree a rather radiant look. And when you break or crush the leaves, the volatile oils give off a warmly pungent aroma with fresh camphor notes; younger leaves are lighter and less aromatic.

choosing and using

Mediterranean and Middle Eastern soups and stews, and traditional roasts just wouldn't be the same without bay's lingering, pungent flavour. Add one or two dried leaves (too much spoils the flavour) to fish, meat and poultry recipes that need long, slow cooking. Bay also has an affinity with vegetable and pasta dishes, and especially with tomatoes.

Parsimony pays when cooking with bay because the strong flavour amalgamates readily during cooking but all too easily overpowers. Bay combines well with basil, garlic, oregano, paprika, pepper, rosemary and sage and makes an appearance in herbes de Provence mixes and in pickling spices.

Dried bay leaves are better than fresh for cooking. Look for clean, dark green ones – the darker the better. Yellow leaves are poor quality and may have been exposed to light for too long. Powdered bay leaves are convenient, but buy small quantities as they lose their flavour within 12 months of grinding.

growing

Bay trees can grow to about 10 m. Trimmed into tidy balls of foliage on slender stems, the trees look very elegant in doorway tubs – those potted toffee-apple trees bracketing restaurant and corporate doorways in many American movies of the 1960s are usually bay trees. They can also be grown as a hedge, as left to themselves they send up many suckers. Although they do best with good-quality, well-drained soil, they actually come from the rocky, parched hillsides of the Mediterranean, so they are quite hardy. Bay trees are fairly slow growers, but they do shoot up if they have to compete with taller plants for the sunshine.

Propagation is best from cuttings, as there's about a 95 per cent failure rate in trying to germinate their pea-sized, nut-hard seeds. Take 15 cm long cuttings of new wood when the fresh spring leaves have just hardened. Break the cutting away from the old wood, leaving a 6 mm heel. Trim the heel carefully with a sharp knife to remove any overhanging bark. Strip the bottom leaves off the cutting, leaving about two-thirds of the stalk bare to insert into a pot of river sand or a good-quality potting mix (choose one with good water retention qualities). Just firm the cuttings down with your fingers and keep them watered. By the end of spring they should have made roots and be ready to plant out. Pots are best (for the first year at least) for slow growers like bay.

Bay blooms mid- to late-spring. The waxy cream flowers, though small, are intensely scented, nectar-filled, and much loved by bees. The flowers are followed by purple berries that have no culinary use at all. Don't be tempted to experiment – they contain laurostearine and lauric acid and are poisonous.

Bay is very susceptible to white wax scale which affects leaf growth and makes the leaves sooty and unattractive, to say the least. You can control it by spraying with white oil in hot weather or scrubbing the affected places with soapy water. A word to the wise – act as soon as you see the scale appearing, because once it reaches epidemic proportions, you'll have a hard time scrubbing the whole tree!

drying

If you have your own bay tree, you can pick mature, dark, firm leaves for drying year-round. Try to take only the stalks that are at least a year old. Never pick the most recent growth for drying. To dry leaves (and stop them from curling), cut them off the stem and spread them out in a single layer over a piece of gauze on a wire rack or insect screen. Cover with more gauze, weight with small pieces of wood to keep flat and leave to dry somewhere that's dark and well aired for about five days. Alternatively, hang leafy branches in bunches to dry. Remove the leaves from the stems when they are crisp-dry and store them in airtight containers in a cool cupboard away from light so that they will keep their colour and quality (for up to three years).

tuna and fresh fennel stew

We've adapted this recipe from one of Loukie Werle's, from her book, *The Trattoria Table* (Webber & Werle Publishing, 1994). Our version for the 'fennelophile' uses less tuna and much more fennel.

2 bulbs fennel, thinly sliced

1 onion, chopped

2 cloves garlic, finely chopped

2 tablespoons extra virgin olive oil

1 x 400 g can whole tomatoes

2 dried bay leaves

1/4 cup continental parsley

1 generous strip lemon rind

2 tablespoons freshly squeezed lemon juice

1/2 cup white wine

500 g fresh tuna, cut into bite-sized cubes

1 cup fish stock

salt and freshly ground black pepper

1/4 cup chopped fennel leaves

Combine the fennel, onion, garlic and oil in a large pan and cook over moderate heat, stirring frequently until just softened, about 5 minutes. Add the tomatoes and cook for a further 5 minutes, stirring frequently. Add the bay leaves, parsley, lemon rind and juice and the wine and simmer for about 20 minutes. Just before serving, add the tuna and simmer until cooked, about 3–4 minutes.

Transfer the tuna and vegetables to a bowl with a slotted spoon and reduce the liquid by about a third. Discard the bay leaves and lemon rind and return the tuna and vegetables to the pan. Heat through, seasoning to taste with salt and pepper. Sprinkle over the fennel leaves and serve the stew with plenty of crusty bread to mop up the sensational juices.

Serves 4

bay leaf sorbet

This aromatic sorbet is reproduced with very kind permission from *Herbes de Provence* by Anthony Gardiner (New Holland, 2002).

200 g caster sugar

juice of 1 lemon

2 cups water

4 dried bay leaves, plus extra for garnish

Combine the sugar, lemon juice and water in a saucepan. Bring to the boil, then add the bay leaves. Remove from the heat, cover with a lid and leave to infuse for at least 30 minutes. Lift out the bay leaves, and churn the mixture in an ice-cream maker for 30 minutes.

If you don't have an ice-cream machine, pour the sorbet mixture into a metal tray or bowl and freeze. Stir after about an hour, and then every half an hour after that so that the ice crystals are broken down into small particles as they form. Four stirrings should be enough.

Remove the sorbet from the freezer 10–15 minutes before serving, and decorate each serving with a fresh bay leaf.

Serves 4

bouquet garni

Bay leaves are an essential ingredient in bouquet garni – a savoury posy or bunch of herbs – where they are firmly tied together with sprigs of parsley, marjoram and thyme; sometimes a few peppercorns and a stalk of celery are added.

Drop the bouquet garni into the pot at the beginning of cooking then remove it just before serving (the herbs can look rather drab and worn when they have done their job).

When a bouquet garni is made using dried herbs, they can be crushed and stirred directly into the pot; however, traditionalists like to tie up the dried herbs in muslin, so they can easily be lifted out just before serving.

indian bay leaves

If you come across a reference to Indian bay leaves or *tejpat* in an Indian cookery book, what the writer is talking about is cinnamon leaves. The evergreen cinnamon tree is a beautiful addition to any garden in tropical or temperate areas. It's a member of the laurel family, which includes the bay laurel and the avocado. Its aromatic leaves, just like the twigs and bark, have their uses. Young cinnamon leaves are an intense red, maturing to a dark glossy green with conspicuous white veins running lengthwise down the leaf. They have a distinctive clove-like aroma and flavour, and are used fresh or dried, in Indian and Asian cooking in curries and slow-cooked pot meals. If you have a tree, select mature leaves, preferably last year's growth, snip them with secateurs and use them fresh in your cooking.

bergamot

Monarda didyma

lemon bergamot *M. citriodora*

Bergamot is the show-off of the herb garden.
Its spidery, shaggy, pompom blooms
in pinks, mauves and rich reds
dominate the herb garden
greens in early summer.

Also called bee balm, oswego tea

Flavour and aroma orange, thyme

Flavour group medium

The bees are in a frenzy of delight over this fragrant orange-scented, nectar-packed plant, so it's no wonder it is sometimes known as 'bee balm'. Honey-eating birds like it too. Bergamot is known in North America as Oswego Tea because the Oswego Indians used the leaves as an infusion.

The slightly hairy leaves are best fresh in tossed salads, fruit jellies, teas and cool summery drinks, delivering a flavour reminiscent of thyme, sage and rosemary. Bergamot also combines well with vegetables, duck, pork and veal dishes.

choosing and using

The leaves make a fragrant change from mint or basil, and the soft honeyed flowers can be gently torn and added to salads. 'Cambridge Scarlet' is the best known of the red bergamots and is the variety most often used in cooking. Pink flowering bergamot with its lemon, pepper and thyme-flavoured leaves complements meat dishes.

If you want fresh bergamot, you'll probably have to grow your own as fruit and vegetable retailers are unlikely to stock it. This is another of those 'best fresh' herbs. But you can stock up on fresh supplies year round if you freeze finely chopped leaves mixed with a little water in ice-cube trays. Or, carefully place fresh flowers in an ice-cube tray, gently cover with water and freeze.

The dried flowers and leaves make a fragrant addition to potpourri and a revitalising hot bath.

The oil of bergamot that is famous for flavouring Earl Grey tea doesn't come from this herb at all. It comes from a citrus fruit, bergamot orange (*Citrus bergamia*). In fact the herb was named after the orange because the aromas are so similar.

growing

Position! Position! Position! Bergamot needs the right spot. Its creeping, matted root system wants to be cool and moist, but the leaves and flowers like to bask in the morning sun for an hour or two. Bergamot grows to 1.2 m, making it ideal for shady background clumps in the herb garden or decorative clusters in the flowerbed. In the right position, the tubular red flowers bloom from early summer right through to autumn on their 90 cm stalks. At Somerset Cottage, there was a distant bed of bergamot set in the lawn and surrounded by leafy trees. In summer, not one member of the Hemphill family could resist its splashes of vivid red, and would often rush down to pick a flower or sip a honey-laden petal.

Plant seeds or seedlings in spring in rich, moist soil about 15 cm apart. And prepare for snails, because they are more than partial to the irresistible combination of shady moist conditions and soft young bergamot leaves. Stake the slender, rather brittle stems that shoot up in summer and mulch during hot weather. After flowering has finished, cut this perennial back to ground level. Propagate by root division year round.

drying

Harvest the leaves and flowers in late summer when the plant is in full bloom and dry as quickly as possible. Pick the leaves and blooms off the stems and spread them out on a wire rack or insect screen in a shady, airy place. As always, when drying, the words to remember are 'dark' and 'dry'. When the leaves and flowers are crisp-dry, store in airtight containers.

tomato and bergamot loaf

Serve this Hemphill family favourite from Somerset Cottage days straight from the oven with a mesclun and fresh herb salad on the side.

1½ cups canned tomatoes with liquid

2 tablespoons water or tomato juice

2 tablespoons chopped fresh bergamot leaves

½ cup lightly roasted pine nuts

½ cup finely chopped celery

1 cup grated tasty cheese

2 tablespoons virgin olive oil

1 small onion, roughly grated

1 teaspoon each salt and paprika

2 eggs, beaten

Preheat the oven to 180ºC. Break up the tomatoes and combine with the remaining ingredients. Spoon the mixture into an oiled ovenproof dish and bake for 20 minutes.

Serves 4

borage

Borago officinalis

The whiskered leaves of borage have a faint
cucumber flavour, and its leaves and flowers
impart this fresh aroma to cool drinks. You must
use the very young leaves, otherwise
the gentle whiskers are more
like two-day-old stubble!

Also called bee bread
Flavour and aroma cucumber, salt
Flavour group mild

choosing and using

Chop them very finely and mix with cottage cheese or cream cheese, and use the mixture in sandwiches and salads. The young leaves are delicious cooked in tempura batter and served Japanese-style, and the leaves and flowers are used for herbal teas. In making our Borage Soup, it is quite amazing how the cooked borage and potatoes smell like Jerusalem artichokes.

As borage is rich in mineral salts such as potassium and calcium, the finely chopped leaves make a useful seasoning in a low-sodium diet.

Borage flowers are literally the stars of the edible-flower world. The five-pointed stars of pure blue petals are ideal for crystallising to decorate cakes and desserts, and the clusters of demurely drooping flowers have long been favourite subjects for painters, ceramic artists and embroiderers. Bees love the nectar-rich blossoms, which were once floated in the stirrup cups given to the Crusaders and to the gladiators in Roman times – perhaps this was because they were traditionally thought to give courage.

Borage leaves and flowers are generally used fresh. Your best option is to grow your own if you want to enjoy this popular, self-sowing, culinary herb year round because the plant wilts so quickly after picking, making it nigh on impossible to find good-quality leaves to buy.

The flowers freeze well. Pick them when they are just fully opened and freeze whole by carefully putting them one by one in an ice-cube tray and gently covering them with water. When you want to impress your guests with your panache and originality, a flowery ice-block can be dropped into a glass of fruit juice, gin and tonic, or any other beverage.

growing

Borage grows to 1 m high and about 75 cm wide and has a thick, hollow central stalk. Because the stalk is hollow, it's not very strong, and as the plant grows, it needs a stake to help bear the weight, otherwise your borage plant will fall about all over your garden.

The stalk and the branching stems are covered with stubbly hairs. The broad fleshy leaves are hairy too, becoming pricklier as they mature, and the clustered buds are covered in a soft down. The leaves when fully grown are approximately 23 cm long and 15 cm wide. The flowers are star-shaped and a pure blue, with an occasional pale pink bloom appearing amongst the blue. There is also a rare variety with white flowers.

Borage will bloom nearly all through the year, and is continually seeding itself, so once planted, you should never be without it. It seems to do best when allowed to grow in thick clumps; the plants help to support each other and the massed effect of the downy buds and blue flowers is quite delightful. If, on the other hand, borage begins to take over the garden, it is easily thinned out and the shallow roots dislodged – even when fully grown – by pulling out the stems by hand, remembering that the stalks are prickly.

Gourmet snails find young borage plants very tempting, so be sure to protect them either with snail bait or a 'magic circle' of coiled rope or sand. Snails can't navigate these barriers. Established plants can be susceptible to a rather unsightly form of mildew, usually late in the season. At this stage it is probably better to dig the plant up and dispose of it rather than resort to chemicals.

Borage is easily grown in any light, moist, well-drained, rich soil. It is a hardy annual and continually self-sows, thriving just as well in winter in temperate zones as it does in summer. Once the plant is established it usually looks after itself and will keep coming up, often in unexpected places.

Borage seed germinates so easily that it can be sown year round in mild climates. In very cold areas, the best time for planting is in spring, when the oblong black seeds can be sown directly into the garden about 30 cm apart. Make sure that the ground has been well turned over first, so that the soil is reasonably fine. Borage likes a sunny position that is sheltered from the wind as the soft main stems are easily broken – another reason for giving it a stake for support.

Borage is quite happy in a tub, but make sure there's plenty of room for its root system and has a stake to prop it up, and remember you will need to fertilise.

drying

If you're really keen to try it, drying the leaves and flowers is possible, but it's hardly necessary with such a prolific plant. You have to be quick to prevent spoilage as the leaves wilt so quickly after picking. Pick unblemished leaves and opened flowers after the dew has gone. Take the flowers and leaves off the succulent stalks and place them on wire racks in a shady, airy place. When dry and brittle, store them separately in airtight containers.

Chamomile Cooler (recipe page 220)

Scrambled Eggs with Fines Herbes (recipe page 223)

borage soup

For that extra special touch, top each bowl of this creamy soup with a fresh borage flower before serving.

2 large potatoes, peeled and cubed

2 cups vegetable stock

a good handful young borage leaves, washed and chopped (about 1 cup)

150 ml pouring cream

$\frac{1}{2}$ teaspoon grated nutmeg

borage flowers, allow 1 per serving

Simmer the potatoes in the stock until almost tender. Add the borage leaves and continue cooking for a few minutes further until the potato is cooked. Let the soup cool a little before blending in batches in the food processor until smooth. Return the soup to the saucepan, add cream and nutmeg, and reheat before serving. Garnish each serving with a borage flower.

Serves 2

borage tempura

To make borage tempura, you need to rinse the leaves and dry them well first. Don't worry about the little whiskers, they will not be noticeable once they are cooked.

20 young borage leaves

120 g cornflour or potato flour

120 g plain flour

1$\frac{3}{4}$ cups very cold water

vegetable oil for deep-frying

Make the batter by combining the flours and cold water in a bowl and whisking until well blended. Heat the oil in a deep saucepan or deep-fryer until a blob of batter dropped in sizzles and cooks immediately.

Dip each leaf in the batter, allowing excess batter to drain off, then deep-fry until crisp and golden brown, around 50 seconds. Spread the fried leaves out on kitchen paper to absorb excess oil.

Serves 1–2

chamomile

English chamomile *Chamaemelum nobile*

syn. *anthemis nobilis*

German chamomile *Matricaria recutita*

This is the herb loved by natural blondes!
Chamomile tea is famous not only
as a calming cuppa, but as
a super highlighting rinse
for fair hair – numerous
shampoos proudly
(and loudly) proclaim
their chamomile content.

Also called English chamomile, manganilla
Flavour and aroma pungent, slightly bitter
Flavour group pungent

Perennial English (also known as Roman) chamomile is a great addition to herb and cottage gardens, with its low-growing, spreading ferny foliage and yellow-centred, white-petalled flowers like tiny daisies on long thin stems. The Spanish called this chamomile *manzanilla* (little apple) because of the apple aroma of the leaves. Although both the flowers and foliage are edible, chamomile flowers are used almost exclusively for making tea or for infusions for cosmetic use.

choosing and using

German chamomile is an annual with a more upright stance and a wonderful profusion of flowers during the summer. It is widely used in natural therapies as its highly scented dried flower heads contain an aromatic oil that has powerful antiseptic and anti-inflammatory properties.

If anyone tells you they have a yellow-petalled chamomile, they are probably referring to a daisy-like plant known as Dyer's chamomile, which should not be used as an alternative to true chamomile.

Chamomile is an excellent addition to the compost heap, so put spent chamomile tea flowers there, and even your old chamomile tea bags, as well as any unwanted foliage or plants.

growing

The spreading perennial English and annual German varieties are by far the most popular chamomiles to grow.

English chamomile (possibly called 'chamomile flowering lawn' in your local plant nursery or garden shop) has fine, feathery leaves and a creeping, matting habit, which makes a beautiful, if somewhat tousled, informal lawn. For good coverage, you'll need a minimum of about 30 plants per square metre (25 plants per square yard) and pre-ordered 'plugs' are available. In a dry season chamomile needs to be kept well watered, but it will reward you in late summer when it sends up stems of flower heads to about 30 cm. Cut the flowers to dry for herb tea, and then run the mower over the lawn with the blades set fairly high.

German chamomile thrives in a sunny, well-drained spot. It grows quickly into a bushy little plant about 45–60 cm high that has fine foliage and bears flowers profusely for quite some time throughout the warmer months.

Plant seedlings or propagate English chamomile by root division. Sow German chamomile seeds in spring. Work the soil very well before planting if it is heavy, add some sandy loam, dampen the ground, and put in the divided roots or seeds.

As the seeds are very small, you may prefer to start them off in a prepared seed box, remembering to keep the soil constantly moist (but not sodden) until the shoots begin to show. When large enough to handle, plant out the seedlings to about 15 cm apart, and keep them moist until well established. Pests and diseases tend to leave the highly aromatic chamomiles well alone.

drying

Pick the opened heads carefully with scissors on a clear day, before the sun has drawn the valuable, volatile essences from the blossoms. Spread them out on a wire sieve, or on sheets of paper, in a cool, airy place. When papery-crisp, put the fragrant heads in clean, dry airtight containers for tea or potpourri.

chamomile tea

Using fresh flowers for tea is not as successful as using dried ones. Chamomile mixes well with other herbs, in combinations such as chamomile, fennel and sage, or chamomile and mint.

To make the tea, steep 1 teaspoon of dried chamomile flowers in 1 cup of boiling water for a few minutes and then strain. Sweeten with honey or add lemon to taste.

Try a chamomile cooler by combining a stronger brew of chamomile tea (sweetened with honey to taste) with natural, sparkling mineral water. Add ice-cubes, thin slices of lemon, and float a few whole chamomile flowers on top.

making herb teas

Simply pour boiling water over fresh or dried herbs, allow the brew to infuse, then strain and serve with a slice of lemon, orange or lime for flavour and with honey or sugar to sweeten. You can make the tea directly in the cup, but a teapot is better for very aromatic herbs that have a large amount of volatile oil such as peppermint or rosemary, or for combination teas.

Serving herb tea on ice and adding long leafy stems and sparkling mineral water makes an unbeatable summer cooler.

DRIED HERB LEAVES

Allow about 1 teaspoon dried leaves per cup. Add boiling water and infuse or brew for about 3 minutes.

FRESH HERB LEAVES

Allow 2–3 teaspoons fresh leaves per cup to taste. Add boiling water and brew for 5–6 minutes.

FRESH OR DRIED FLOWERS

Allow about 2 teaspoons per cup. Add boiling water and brew for 5–6 minutes before straining and serving.

SEEDS

To bring out the full flavour of teas made with seeds, crush the seeds slightly before placing them in the teapot to release the volatile oils. Allow ½–1 teaspoon of seeds per cup. Add boiling water and let the brew draw a little longer than usual.

chervil

Anthriscus cerefolium

If plants had a gender, then pretty, lacy, delicate,
decorative chervil would surely be female!
It even blushes, as older leaves take
on a reddish glow towards the
end of summer. Although it
has the same flowering
habit as dill, caraway and
fennel, its seeds are
not used in cooking.

Also called gourmet's parsley, French parsley
Flavour and aroma mildly parsley-like, delicate and herbaceous
Flavour group mild

Chervil is one of the four fragrant herbs that make up the delicate fines herbes bouquet – the others are chives, tarragon and parsley in equal parts, and all finely chopped. Chervil's soft fresh leaves with their mild aroma, reminiscent of parsley, are an excellent garnish for light-textured foods such as eggs Benedict, herb sandwiches and salads. They are delicious too, cut finely and folded into scrambled eggs, omelettes, creamed potatoes and cream cheese, sprinkled liberally on salads or used as a filling for sandwiches.

choosing and using

Chervil complements poultry and fish and is excellent over *al dente* vegetables with melted butter and freshly ground pepper and salt. Hold back and only add chervil to the dish or pot at the last minute – it should never be cooked for more than 3–5 minutes, and never at high temperatures, or you will lose the subtlety of its delicate flavour.

Fresh chervil is sometimes available from fruit and vegetable retailers. However, if you like to use it in your cooking, you'll probably have to grow your own and pick it throughout the summer as required. For year-round fresh leaves, freeze finely chopped leaves with a little water in ice-cube trays.

Well aware of the 'don't leave home without it' rule, the Romans took this native of Eastern Europe (it supposedly originated in Siberia) with them as they colonised the Mediterranean world. It has tended to be most popular in French cuisine, but chervil soup is still traditional Holy Thursday fare in many parts of Europe.

growing

Chervil rather resembles a miniature parsley plant, although the fern-like leaves are smaller and finer, and it's a brighter green. The white flowers are so minute, it's as though nature knew that the lacy leaves alone would give this herb enough beauty. Chervil is frost-sensitive and needs a sheltered position in colder areas. On the other hand, it also dislikes hot, dry conditions, so you need to protect the plants from the summer sun, too. One solution is to plant chervil near a deciduous tree where it can have the best of both worlds – summer shade and winter sun.

Although sometimes classed as a biennial, it is best to treat chervil as an annual, sowing seeds in spring and in autumn about 30 cm apart in a well-prepared garden bed. Never start chervil in a seed box as the seedlings are *much* too delicate to transplant. Cover the seeds with soil and pat down. When the seedlings are about 5 cm high, they should be sturdy enough to thin out. Keep them watered at all times and don't forget to feed them occasionally. Or, if that all seems like too much work, just buy nicely established seedlings in little pots at your nursery.

Frequent picking encourages new growth and prevents seeding and dying off. Break the stems off carefully, taking the outside leaves first, as with parsley, so that the new centre leaves unfold and grow. Pick and use the foliage as required. If you wish chervil to self-sow, which it will do very readily, do not harvest all the plants when they are in flower; leave about one-third to go to seed.

As chervil only grows to about 30 cm, it is ideal for pots. Select one that's at least 30 cm in diameter, with about 20 cm depth for the roots. Fill it with a good-quality, porous potting mixture and scatter the seeds over the surface. Press them gently down with a flat piece of board, and lightly sprinkle with water. Keep the pot moist, and when the seedlings are big enough, thin them out.

drying

Drying fragile chervil is something of a challenge as the leaves shrivel during dehydration and lose their volatile top notes. Spread the leaves out on a wire rack in a dry, airy, dark place, as light will fade the green colour. Crumble the crisp leaves from the stems, store in airtight, labelled containers and use within three or four months.

scrambled eggs with fines herbes

Serve these creamy scrambled eggs hot from the pan on squares of toast and garnish with fresh chervil sprigs.

4 or 5 x 60 g eggs

3 tablespoons milk for each egg

salt and pepper

1 teaspoon finely chopped chervil

1 teaspoon finely chopped tarragon

1 teaspoon finely chopped parsley

1 teaspoon finely chopped chives

Fill the bottom half of a double saucepan with enough water to just touch the base of the top half of the saucepan. Bring to a gentle simmer. Break the eggs into a bowl and add the milk, salt and pepper. Whisk to combine, then add the fines herbes. Transfer the egg mixture to the top of the double saucepan, and stir frequently until the mixture begins to thicken, about 3 minutes, covering when not stirring. When the eggs thicken, replace the lid and leave to set for about 2 minutes, checking frequently.

Serves 2

chicory

Cichorium intybus

If you find the flavour of raw chicory (witloof) leaves
on the bitter side, try pouring boiling water over
them in a colander before using. Crisped
in icy water, these compact, shapely
leaves make nifty scoops for
dips and fresh salsas.

Also called witloof, witlof, Belgian endive
Flavour and aroma bitter
Flavour group medium

If you feel confused about chicory, Belgian endive, witloof (or witlof), don't worry, you are not alone. However, it's essentially one and the same plant in its various herb or vegetable guises.

In Belgium, France and Italy this species has produced a whole range of leafy vegetables (including radicchio), all of which have well-established places in those countries' cuisines.

Closely related to the lettuce family (Lactuca), chicory is delicious both raw and cooked. The young fresh leaves picked straight from the garden make a crisp, slightly bitter addition to salad greens. If you're prepared to sacrifice your chicory plant, the roots can be steamed as a vegetable, but with such an abundance of root vegetables around, it seems more sensible to hold on to your plant and enjoy the leaves.

Chicory greens are also renowned as excellent fodder for sheep, cows and horses, so the larger leaves that are not suitable for the table can be put to good use keeping your favourite animals in good nick. Otherwise, they can be added to the compost heap.

Today, although we don't necessarily know it, most of us are more familiar with 'chicory' in its commercially grown guise as the vegetable, witloof, which looks rather like an elongated lettuce heart – the whiter the better.

To achieve those tightly folded, compressed, creamy, blanched heads (chicons), young plants are forced in warm, moist dark conditions, in much the same way that fennel bulbs are grown as vegetables. Exposure to light during this process makes the leaves greener and increases their bitterness. Chefs pick the fattest, firmest and creamiest specimens.

choosing and using

Chicory is ideal for baking or braising. Try cooking whole (or halved) heads, wrapping each in a piece of ham, arranging them in a lightly buttered gratin dish in a single layer, topping the lot with a creamy bechamel sauce and baking for about 15 minutes until just bubbling and lightly golden on top.

growing

Although your greengrocer will call it witloof, you'll find at the garden shop or plant nursery that this herb is more likely to be identified as chicory.

Left alone, chicory is one of the taller herbs with broad, long lower leaves rather like spinach leaves. The higher leaves are smaller and sparser, growing on branching stems, and are not usually eaten.

Chicory is not a plant for a pot, growing to about 1.8 m in the right conditions. Above the fairly prosaic lower leaves, a flurry of thinner stems form a crown where daisy-like flowers grow in clusters, two or three along the stems, bursting open in the morning sun. The starry blooms have finely serrated, pale blue petals radiating from dark blue stamens. They are very popular with bees – but the bees have to be up early, as the flowers usually close by noon, unless the day is very dull.

This frost-hardy herb likes a sunny position with well-drained soil. Plant the seeds or seedlings in the garden in spring about 30 cm apart. Keep watered until the shoots appear, and watch out for those gourmet snails, slugs and caterpillars. Rust fungus and mildew can be a problem too.

drying

Pick chicory leaves off the stems and spread them out on a wire rack or insect screen in a cool, airy place away from the light. Crumble the crisp leaves and store in airtight, labelled containers.

Drying, roasting and grinding chicory roots is a commercial procedure that is usually carried out by manufacturers with the appropriate kiln-drying equipment.

a coffee substitute too ...

The roasted root of the chicory plant has been used as a caffeine-free coffee substitute or additive since about 1800, and it had a bit of a resurgence in the Depression and war years of the 1930s and 1940s, when it was mixed with coffee to make a coffee essence.

turning chicory into witloof

If you want to try your hand at growing your own witloof ('blanched' chicory), here's how. Dig out the roots in autumn, about six months after planting.

Cut off the foliage and stand the roots upright, close together, in a deep box or pot, with a covering of light, sandy soil to about 15 cm above the top of the roots.

Keep the plants in a moist, dark place such as a warm shed, laundry or garage. As they grow, the new young leaves will become elongated and blanched. If it's not dark enough, the foliage turns green and bitter.

As soon as the white leaves show above the soil the plants are ready for lifting. Cut the root away, leaving just enough at the base to hold the leaves together. Use as soon as possible as witloof deteriorates quickly.

witloof stuffed with pork and prawns

125 g peeled green prawns

125 g minced pork

1 spring onion, finely chopped

1/2 teaspoon chilli powder

1 clove garlic, crushed

salt and pepper to taste

1/2 teaspoon ground allspice

1 tablespoon vegetable oil

2 heads of young, crisp witloof, leaves separated

De-vein the prawns and chop them very finely. Place all the ingredients, except the witloof, in a large mixing bowl and combine thoroughly. Heat the oil in a large frying-pan or wok and stir-fry the mixture until the pork and prawns are cooked. Remove from the heat and allow to cool to room temperature.

Soak the leaves in a bowl of icy water until crisp. Drain well and carefully pat each one dry. Spoon the just cool meat mixture into the witloof boats and serve as finger-food.

Serves 3–4 as an entrée

wilted witloof with sesame oil and pine nuts

2 tablespoons pine nuts

2 heads of witloof, or about 20 chicory leaves
    from the garden

1 tablespoon sesame oil

salt to taste

Place the pine nuts in a hot, dry frying pan, and toast until they turn golden brown. Shake the pan constantly so the pine nuts colour evenly. Transfer the pine nuts to a dish and set aside.

Separate the heads of chicory into individual leaves. Heat the sesame oil in a frying pan, add the leaves and cook over a medium heat until they are just wilted. Add the pine nuts to the pan, season with a little salt and toss to combine with the chicory leaves. Serve immediately.

Serves 2

chives

onion chives *Allium schoenoprasum*

garlic chives *A. tuberosum*

Chives go with eggs the way salt goes with
pepper – it's hard to imagine one without
the other. 'Garnish with snipped chives'
has long been a culinary catch
cry, and tying tiny bundles of
French beans with a chive
'spear' is a clear indication
that you have gone to a lot of
trouble. (Do it for your in-laws.)

Witloof Stuffed with Pork and Prawns (recipe page 227)

Watercress Sandwiches (recipe page 237)

Also called rush leek, Chinese chives
Flavour and aroma fresh onion and garlic with similar aroma
Flavour group medium

Chives are the smallest members of the onion family but it's the leaf, not the bulb, that packs the punch. There are two types of chive, onion and garlic, and they are easy to tell apart. Onion chives are the tubular ones that resemble tufts of fine grass; garlic (or Chinese) chives have flat, rather blade-like leaves.

choosing and using

Because chives don't contain as much sulphur as onion, their subtle flavour is just right in many dishes where onion would overpower. Finely chopped chives go into egg dishes, cream cheese, fish and poultry dishes, savoury sauces, mayonnaise and just about every kind of salad. Try them in a creamy mushroom sauce for serving with penne or your favourite pasta.

One important tip when using chives is not to wash them until you are about to use them as moisture promotes decay. And add chives during the last 5 or so minutes of cooking as their flavour is destroyed with long heating.

Garlic chives are widely used throughout Asia in soups, noodle dishes and with seafood and pork. 'Yellow chives' have a much milder, delicate onion flavour and are obtained by growing garlic chives without sunlight.

Fresh chives are sold in bunches about 2.5 cm in diameter, often wrongly labelled – onion chives labelled as garlic and vice versa. Don't buy them if they look wilted.

If you are growing your own chives, pick off the leaves at the base with your fingers, as cutting with scissors causes them to die back slightly and leaves an unattractive brown edge. Chives will keep for about a week stored in a plastic bag in the refrigerator. Fresh chives, both onion- and garlic-flavoured, may be chopped finely, mixed with a little water, and frozen in ice-cube trays to be thawed when needed.

growing

Onion chives grow to about 30 cm and have tubular hollow leaves like drinking straws. Their charming lavender pompom flowers are actually thick knots of cylindrical petals forming round heads like clover blossoms. The flowers are edible as well, however once chives have flowered, their flavour changes. As with most herbs, the stem that will bear the flower is visibly different (thicker as a rule), so prevent flowers forming by removing the stalk as soon as it appears.

Garlic chives grow to about 60 cm and their flowers form white star-like clusters at the top of long, round strong and tough stems.

There are some important guidelines for successful chive growing. First of all, never let the clump grow too large, as the centre will die out from lack of nourishment. If the base of your clump is as wide as the open end of a teacup, it's time to dig it up and divide into four or five smaller clumps.

Chives can also die of exhaustion – they simply disappear if allowed to flower too much. So pick off flower buds as they appear (literally nipping them in the bud) and you will be rewarded with healthy plants as long as you water them well and dig a little decayed manure into the soil occasionally. For a continuous supply, pick chives about 5 cm above the ground rather than pulling them out by the roots.

You can buy chives as established plants, as seeds, or divide the roots from an older clump. They will grow year round in a sunny position, but not very vigorously in winter. Sow seeds in a seed box in spring in fairly rich well-drained soil. When the seedlings have passed the point where they look like delicate grass, plant them out in the garden, or in 15 cm diameter pots. They will be happy on a sunny exterior windowsill. Because chives form a small bulb, allow about 12 bulbs to a clump when planting, keeping the clumps 30 cm apart. In winter the tops of chives tend to wither; then they shoot again in spring making this the best time to divide the clumps – about 5 cm in diameter.

Aphids find chives totally irresistible, which is why chives are sometimes planted with roses, to act as a decoy for these pests. If you're averse to using pesticides, adjust your hose nozzle to a firm jet and blast the aphids off the chives. Mind you, it won't stop them coming back!

dried chives

Don't even to begin to give yourself the heartache of trying to dry your own chives. Drying chives in the normal way is not satisfactory as they lose their colour and flavour. The chives that one buys in bottles from the supermarket are probably onion chives and will have been freeze dried. The cell structure and colour are so delicate that once you have bought freeze-dried chives, you have to keep them in the dark (they are inordinately light sensitive) or they will fade very quickly.

summer carrot and chive salad

This summery salad has become something of a family staple. We discovered it in Jane Grigson's wonderful book, *Good Things*, first published in 1971, and we have adapted it over the years to suit our enthusiasm for chives and preference for a sharper dressing. Jane Grigson is absolutely right when she says it is the easiest dish in the world to prepare. And everyone always comes back for seconds.

6 medium-sized carrots (choose bright orange ones),
   peeled and grated
1 bunch chives, snipped (use more if you like)
2–3 tablespoons extra virgin olive oil
juice of 1 lemon
pinch sea salt
sugar to taste

Combine all the ingredients adding the salt and sugar to taste. Chill for about an hour then gently turn the mass of carrots over with a fork. If the salad seems to be swimming in liquid, drain it before serving.

Serves 4–6 as an accompaniment

fines herbes

The classic blend of delicately flavoured herbs known as fines herbes consists of onion chives, chervil, parsley and tarragon. These herbs are finely chopped and mixed together in equal quantities making a delightfully mild, savoury blend to flavour omelettes, cooked chicken and fish, salads, steamed vegetables, soups, and mornay dishes.

coriander leaf

Coriandrum sativum

Coriander (known as cilantro in the Americas), with its delicate green foliage, has an air of innocence. But don't be misled, this herb is a heartbreaker.

Also called Chinese parsley, cilantro
(perennial coriander)
Flavour and aroma lemony, appetising
Flavour group strong

We have seen people in tears as they relate the sad tale of how their healthy plant suddenly turned up its toes and died for no apparent reason. The awful truth is that this annual is the shortest-lived of all, with a hasty life cycle of grow-flower-seed-die within a short couple of months. Do you really think market gardeners would pull the plant out, roots and all, if there were a chance of a second harvest? (Does that taproot remind you of a carrot? Yes, it's a member of the same family.)

Many herbs, such as anise, caraway, dill and fennel, have, in varying degrees, the same warm, spicy, anise pungency. However, the unique flavour of fresh coriander leaves also carries hints of lemon peel and sage. From its home base in Southern Europe, the aromatic leaves and spicy mature seeds of this international traveller have made themselves indispensable.

choosing and using

If you are looking for flavour and value for money you can't go past coriander because you can eat the whole herb.

The leaves have the strongest flavour, though it is quickly diffused with cooking. They are best added at the last minute or they can become bitter. Consequently coriander is frequently used to garnish Asian and Indian stir-fries and curries, hence the nickname 'Chinese parsley', coined by those of European heritage who use the ubiquitous parsley sprig to garnish everything from eggs to sandwiches to goulash. The stems don't have as much flavour as the leaves, but finely chopped are a crispy addition to stir-fries and clear Asian soups, perhaps combined with garlic and lemongrass. The same applies to the grated roots.

Coriander is a key ingredient in curries, tagines, ceviche, gumbos, and in past times was even added to the centre of rainbow balls, to give a unique piquancy.

In Mexican food, coriander is always used fresh. The cilantro/coriander question has confused countless Australian cooks following American recipes, but the answer is easy – in American recipes, cilantro refers to the leaves, and coriander to the seed or powder; pretty much everywhere else, it's all called coriander.

Coriander leaves are widely used in Cajun cooking, where seasoning is all. Traditional Louisiana gumbos may contain any combination of okra, seafood, meat or vegetables, with seasonings of chopped fresh herbs including cilantro, garlic, parsley, bay leaves, basil, thyme or fennel – whichever the cook fancies.

South America's seafood ceviche with capsicum, Spanish onion, lemons and limes wouldn't be the same without fresh coriander. To make a good ceviche, the seafood and all the other ingredients must be absolutely fresh including citrus juice, peppers, onions, and a choice of vegetables. Finely chopped coriander is used in nearly all the recipes, sometimes with parsley as well.

If you are growing your own coriander, pick leaves fresh at any time. As with other delicate herbs, fresh leaves provide the best flavour and frequent picking will encourage growth and prevent the plant from going to seed. To freeze, wrap freshly washed sprays in foil, folding the edges in securely. They will keep for several weeks in the freezer. The ice-cube tray method isn't appropriate for coriander.

When you buy fresh coriander, make sure that you buy it in bunches with the root system intact as this will keep it fresh longer. To store, stand the bunch in a glass of water in the refrigerator. Pull a plastic bag down over the leaves and fold under the base of the glass to make its own little igloo of humidity so that the leaves don't dry out. If you discard the leaves as they turn yellow the coriander should last for a week or two.

growing

Coriander likes sun and shelter as the young plants need protection from prevailing winds to prevent them from falling over. If you don't have an obviously sheltered spot, try planting it in the garden among the other plants. Work the soil until it is fine and crumbly, adding a little lime if the ground is acid. Plant coriander seedlings (or sow the seeds) in spring or summer (and again in autumn in temperate zones) about 30 cm apart directly in the garden – it has a taproot that doesn't like being transplanted. Cover the seeds and pack the soil down well, then keep moist until the seedlings appear. Water regularly in hot, dry weather, preferably in the late afternoon or evening so as not to scorch the plants. As they grow, they may need staking.

In high summer conditions, coriander has a tendency to bolt, going to seed almost as soon as it has reached maturity. To prevent this, nip off the thick flower-bearing stems as soon as you see them, and this way you can delay the inevitable blooms for a week or two. The alternative is to allow the flowers and seeds to develop and drop, so that new plants will self-sow, giving you a continuing supply of leaves.

The mauve-tinted white blossoms appear in summer in frothy profusion, followed by fruit, which, when green and unripened, have an even stronger scent than the foliage. When the small, oval coriander seeds have hardened and ripened to a pale fawn colour, they are one of the most deliciously fragrant of all spices used in cooking.

drying

Cut leafy stalks for drying, pick off the individual leaves and spread them out in a shady place on wire mesh to encourage quick drying. Do not hang them in bunches, as the soft foliage will then dry too slowly and may possibly spoil. Oven or microwave drying is not satisfactory, as the leaves bruise easily and are liable to scorch. When crisp, crumble the leaves from the stalks and store in airtight containers.

To test the quality of dry coriander leaves, place a few on your tongue and wait for the flavour to emerge. Dried leaves can be used in stir-fries or added in the last couple of minutes of cooking time, but they are not suitable for garnishing.

To harvest the seeds, cut off all the heads when they are about to drop, and dry them, like ripe anise, on sheets of paper in a shady place, exposing them to the sun when possible. They are ready to store when the fruit falls away from the shrivelled flower heads if given a light shake. Sieve out any pieces of stalk, and pack the seeds into airtight containers.

See also pages 63–6 for coriander seed.

kate's fantastic fresh spring rolls

Like Ian, our daughter Kate has grown up surrounded by the flavour and aroma of herbs. She is now making her mark in the family business with her fresh and exciting recipes. These spring rolls can be prepared ahead of time and arranged on a platter ready to serve. Simply cover and refrigerate until you need them. Serve with sweet chilli or peanut sauce.

1 x 100 g portion of vermicelli rice noodles

1 bunch coriander

½ bunch mint

¼ iceberg lettuce, chopped

½ red capsicum, finely diced

1 Lebanese cucumber, peeled and finely diced

1 tablespoon sweet chilli sauce

1 packet rice paper squares or rounds

Soak the rice noodles in warm water until soft, then drain well. Pick the coriander and mint leaves from the stems and chop them roughly. Place all the ingredients (except the rice paper squares) in a large mixing bowl and combine thoroughly.

Soak the rice papers, one at a time, in a bowl of warm water. After 15–20 seconds they will be pliable. Carefully spread the rice papers on a damp chopping board. Place a spoonful of mixture in the lower part of the paper. Carefully fold the edges in then fold the bottom up and roll them tightly.

Makes about 20 spring rolls

coriander dipping sauce

A lovely tangy dipping sauce to serve with fresh peeled king prawns.

1 bunch coriander, leaves picked

1 bunch mint, leaves picked

1 bunch spring onions, roughly chopped

2 cm piece of fresh ginger, peeled

juice of 1 lime

250 g plain yoghurt

salt and pepper to taste

Blend the coriander, mint, spring onions and ginger in a food processor to make a smooth paste. Add the lime juice and yoghurt to the paste, and stir to combine. Season with salt and pepper to taste.

Makes about 1 cup

powder to paste

To make a quick curry paste, lightly fry some finely chopped onion and garlic in oil, add the curry powder of your choice and enough water to make a paste. For a richer and redder brew, add tomato paste to taste. And for extra flavour add chopped fresh coriander and use a little tamarind water (made by soaking a piece of tamarind pulp in water and straining). Keep refrigerated and use within 5 days.

cress

watercress *Nasturtium officinale*

curled cress and French cress *Lepidium sativatum*

American upland cress *Barbarea vulgaris*

People commonly think that the only type of cress is the watercress that grows wild in fresh flowing streams or babbling brooks. However, there are several cress varieties, all rich in iron and all from the Cruciferae family, famous for having no poisonous plants among its two thousand-odd species.

Also called garden cress, watercress, French cress, curled cress
Flavour and aroma sharp tasting while fresh and peppery
Flavour group medium

Watercress can grow in soil too, as long as it is planted in shade and kept damp. In fact it is easy to grow and its biting taste spikes summer salads, makes refreshing chilled soups and substitutes for spinach in quiches, frittatas, dips and eggs Florentine. You can get a less pungent result by combining cress with spinach in a ratio of about 1 to 4.

choosing and using

Watercress is a hardy perennial with small, round, dark green leaves and tiny white flowers and its taste is rather peppery, like nasturtium. In fact the true nasturtium with its creeping habit and show of flowers is sometimes called Indian cress.

Land cress has a similar flavour, and the best-known species are the curled, French and American upland cress.

Curled cress looks rather like curled parsley, but its leaves are fleshier and the flavour is hot and sharp. You can sprout this cress indoors on trays without soil, cutting before it matures into a fully-grown plant and serving with its lifelong chum, mustard.

French cress resembles young lettuce with undivided pale-green leaves with a frilled edge. It may not look at all like the other cresses, but its leaves have the same pepper-hot bite.

American upland cress has long leaves like a dandelion forming a full rosette of dark-green jagged leaves up to 15 cm long, with a typically hot flavour.

Fresh cress leaves are best for flavour and appearance. You can chop the leaves finely, mix them with a little water and freeze them in ice-cube trays for adding to soups and stews at the end of cooking time. Sprigs of cress may be wrapped in foil, sealed, and kept in the deep freeze for some weeks.

growing

The old suggestion that watercress needs flowing water to survive is wrong. It seems to be just as happy in the garden or in a container. But although it may not need that babbling brook, it does need fresh water (not stagnant) as well as soil for growing. So, if you don't happen to have natural spring water nearby, a shallow trough where you can change the water will do just fine. In fact, plant it in a damp, shady place, or stand a pot in a tray of water, and watch it thrive!

The first step is to sow the seeds in spring or autumn in a prepared seed box. When the seedlings are big enough to handle, transfer them to the shallow trough, half filled with loamy soil. Place the trough under a tap in semi-shade, and as the seedlings grow, gradually fill the trough with water, carefully draining it about once a week and refilling it with fresh water. The more cress is cut, the more it will branch. In summer, frequent cutting will prevent flowering and assure plenty of leafiness for harvesting.

Grow all land cresses the same way, as annuals. Sow the seeds in a semi-shady part of the garden virtually year-round, unless you are in an area that gets frosts, about 2 cm apart straight into what will be their permanent home. Apart from watering in dry weather, there is no need for any special attention. Just dig in a little fertiliser from time to time. Germination is rewardingly speedy (about a week), which is why cress is very popular with beginning gardeners. Plants should be ready for harvesting in about four weeks although they can take longer in cooler climes – like many plants, cress does not thrive in frosty conditions. Once the plants have reached 10–15 cm tall, cut them to just above ground level with a pair of scissors.

drying

Cress is a difficult herb to dry, and really, why bother when it's so readily available fresh?

For herb teas, dry watercress leaves on an airy rack, and when crisp, crumble into airtight containers.

watercress sandwiches

If you cut the bread corner-to-corner into triangles the cheese and cress mixture makes enough for 40 small sandwiches. Simply arrange on a platter and serve. Use a good grainy bread sliced as thinly as possible at your bread shop and allow one tightly packed cup of fresh watercress leaves per loaf (about 20 slices).

1 tightly packed cup of fresh watercress
    leaves, finely chopped
1 cup cheese spread (or cottage cheese,
    ricotta or cream cheese)
20 slices of a good grainy bread, sliced as thinly as possible

Mix the leaves with your preferred soft cheese. Spread the slices generously with the mixture, make into sandwiches and remove the crusts if you prefer.

sprouting

Sprouts are seeds that have been brought to life with water and allowed to develop a soft green shoot. They are very easy to grow and ready to eat within a week. And you can eat them roots and all – they are a complete, living food.

There are a couple of standard methods for sprouting and they work for cress seeds, lentils, mung beans, Chinese beans, alfalfa and mustard seeds.

One method is to take an empty jar about the size of a honey jar and a piece of thin material or a strip cut from tights or stockings. Put 2 teaspoons of cress seeds (or whatever you want to sprout) in the jar, stretch the gauzy fabric over the top and hold it in place with a rubber band. Now add a little water and let the seeds soak for a minute or so before straining. Shake the jar to make sure all the excess water is out, and lie it on its side away from direct sunshine. Water every morning and evening following the same procedure and watch your cress seeds turn into tender shoots. Tuck in when you see the first tender leaves.

Alternatively, place a layer of cotton wool or paper towel on a plate and sprinkle the seeds on top. Water and watch your seeds grow and harvest them as they sprout.

curry leaf

Murraya koenigii

Although they don't exactly taste of curry,
the neat, spicy leaves of the curry tree
bring a tantalising, fresh aroma
and flavour to curries. Rather
than echoing the flavour
of curry, they complement
it, gaining their name by
this happy association.

Also called karipattar, daun kari
Flavour and aroma citrus-like and appealing acrid,
like burnt oil, fragrance
Flavour group strong

choosing and using

The leaves are more pungent fresh than dried and it is
almost impossible to use too many in a curry or South-
East Asian dish. For maximum flavour when curry
making, gently cook the leaves in a little oil first. Whole
leaves are also perfect for pickle-making or adding to
seafood marinades. Crushed they can be added to
curry pastes and powders. To create a truly
professional presentation of an Indian dish, top it with
a little cluster of crispy, deep-fried curry leaves.

Fresh leaves will keep in a plastic bag in the
refrigerator for a week. Good-quality dried leaves are
worth searching for, but it's not impossible to dry your
own with a little care.

The curry tree is absolutely unrelated to the curry
plant (*Helichrysum angustifolium*) with its silvery-grey
foliage. Although there are those who claim its leaves
have a curry aroma and flavour, we don't consider this
to be a culinary herb at all (which is why we haven't
written about it in this book). Just for the record, it's an
oregano-sized plant suitable for garden edges.

growing

The evergreen curry tree is a native of India and Sri Lanka
and belongs to the citrus family. Its shiny, frond-like
leaves grow to 3–7 cm long and 1–2 cm wide. Although it
is a tropical plant, the curry tree does well in a sunny spot
in sub-tropical and temperate zones when well protected
from frost and wind.

Curry trees thrive in well-drained soil that's rich in
organic matter in a raised bed or large tub, but bear
in mind that it grows to about 4 m. Prune lightly in the
autumn so that the buds for new spring growth have
time to establish.

In summer, clusters of tiny white flowers are
followed by small, blue-black, edible fruits, which will
self-sow around the base of your tree if you're lucky.
Suckers or runners, spreading from the parent root
base, provide a much more satisfactory method of
propagation than planting cuttings or seeds. And it is
much quicker.

In the tropics the leaves are there for the picking
year-round, however in places where winters are
colder, your tree might lose its leaves or look rather
sick, completely contradicting the evergreen label it
adopts in the tropics.

Some trees develop miserable-looking dark spots
on the leaves, some turn completely yellow, some drop
every single leaf. Don't despair, as beautiful new
growth will gladden your heart when the days warm up.

drying

If you take care when drying the leaves, you will find that they retain more of their colour and flavour. Strip healthy green leaves from the main stem (don't take the youngest ones), and spread them out in a single layer on paper or wire gauze in a dark, airy, warm, dry place – with zero humidity if possible. When the leaves are crisp and dry, store in labelled airtight containers.

cochin-style barbecued seafood

For a moister, more succulent result, wrap the prawns and bug tails in foil before barbecuing.

2 tablespoons grated onion

6–8 curry leaves, crumbled

1 teaspoon garam masala

$1/8$ teaspoon medium chilli powder

$1/2$ teaspoon salt

8 king prawns

2 Balmain bug tails, halved

Purée the onion and curry leaves to make a paste (add a little water if it's too dry to purée), then add garam masala, chilli powder and salt. Combine with the peeled prawns and bug tails in a bowl and mix until the seafood is well coated. Let stand for 30 minutes then cook on the barbecue griddle.

Serves 2

herbie's kerala chicken stir-fry

This spicy mix is also delicious with fish fillets such as ling or fresh green prawns. In India they would use coconut oil, but we suggest you opt for a polyunsaturated vegetable oil.

1 onion, diced

1 tablespoon vegetable oil

1 tablespoon garam masala

$1/2$ teaspoon medium chilli powder, more if you prefer

20 fresh curry leaves

$1/2$ teaspoon salt

600 g fillets skinless chicken, sliced

Blend the onion, oil, garam masala, chilli powder, curry leaves and salt to make a paste. Coat the chicken slices with the mixture, cover and set aside in the refrigerator for about 30 minutes. Stir-fry until cooked and serve with steamed rice.

Serves 6

Cochin-style Barbecued Seafood (recipe page 240)

Risotto with Garlic and Fennel (recipe page 249)

dill

Anethum graveolens

Smoked salmon just wouldn't be the same
without those ever-so-feathery refreshing
dill tips, which not only garnish but add
a flavour zing as well. This frond-like herb
with its subtle anise aroma belongs
to the far-flung Apiaceae family
that also includes kissing
cousins anise, caraway,
coriander, cumin and parsley.

choosing and using

Refreshing is the word that perfectly describes dill; it's a summer thing. Finely chopped dill leaves bring their palate-pleasing liveliness to cottage or cream cheese, omelettes, white sauce, salads and dressings, cucumber, seafood, chicken, rice, egg dishes, soups, steamed vegetables and infused herb vinegars.

When you buy dill, it's pretty hard to find a bunch that is not wilting, because it's a delicate creature and doesn't like lying around in a shop. Choose the best you can find, and when you get it home, immerse the entire bunch in a bowl of water and keep it in the fridge. The leaves will crisp up in the cold water, but try to use it as soon as possible after purchasing it.

For freezing, chop the fresh leaves finely, mix with a little water, and put into ice-cube trays in the freezer. Sprays of fresh dill may be wrapped in foil, sealed, and kept in the deep freeze for some weeks.

The seeds have a more robust aroma than the tips and are used to flavour cabbage, coleslaw, sauerkraut, cucumbers, onions, chutneys and pickles, breads, sauces and root vegetables, especially in Russia, Germany and Scandinavia. Anyone over a certain age will associate dill seeds with dill water, an infusion of dill seeds, which used to be given to babies for colic. One has to wonder what babies thought of that anise flavour – no wonder they cried!

growing

Dill looks rather like fennel but has darker leaves and is smaller, growing to about 90 cm tall and 40 cm wide in a sunny spot. The slender central stems are easily flattened by wind, so grow the plants in a sheltered position in light, well-drained soil.

In temperate areas, you can do two plantings a year – one in spring, and another in autumn. As the soft, delicate seedlings do not transplant easily, sow the seeds (or plant seedlings) directly into the garden about 25 cm apart. Gently cover, firm down the soil and water well. If the soil is sour, lime it well first. An occasional feed of a good organic fertiliser will pay leafy dividends – but if you're keen on chook manure, it must be well composted and dry. To keep those feathery tips coming throughout the summer, pick leaves from the centre to delay flowering.

Dill will be happy either in the garden or in a pot, but watch out for aphids as they tend to zoom in on this little herb, and can even kill it if they are in heavy numbers. Ladybirds are a natural predator of aphids, so only spray as a final resort or you'll chase away the cure as well as the pest.

In the summer, dill bears pale yellow umbelliferous flower heads, like those of anise and fennel, made up of about 20 tiny florets that form oval, flat seeds in abundance in late summer and autumn. Dill seeds – which are actually the minute fruit divided in two – are about 4 mm long. They ripen in autumn and can be collected as soon as the first few fall.

drying

To make the most of these aromatic, anise-tasting leaves, cut the feathery fresh green tips just as the flower buds start to form. Spread them out on a piece of absorbent paper such as kitchen paper towel and place in a warm, well-aired, dark place for a few days to dry. They will feel crisp when they are dry. To retain the lovely green colour, store them in a cupboard in an airtight container rather than an open spice rack.

You can also dry dill successfully in a microwave oven. Place the tips on a piece of kitchen paper towel in the oven with half a cup of water in a microwave-safe cup and cook on high for a couple of minutes then check. Continue to cook in 30-second bursts until the leaves feel crisp and dry.

To collect and dry the seeds, snip off the heads when the flowers have finished and spread them out on a tray in the sun for a few days. When they are completely dry, the seeds shake out easily from the heads. You might like to winnow the seeds or sieve them to remove any little pieces of dry flower or stem, then store your harvest in airtight containers. If you wish to re-sow dill seed, it should be done within three years for good germinating results.

smoked salmon with capers and dill

'Refreshing' perfectly describes the flavour of dill, as well as these tasty toasts with smoked salmon or trout slices and capers.

3 slices wholemeal bread, crusts removed
2 tablespoons mayonnaise mixed with an extra teaspoon chopped dill
200 g smoked salmon slices or smoked trout, flaked
24 capers
fresh dill tips

Roll the bread slices gently with a rolling pin to flatten until they are about half their original thickness. Toast the slices until golden, and cut each into quarters – in squares or triangles. Top each piece with a dollop of mayonnaise, a generous serving of salmon, a couple of drained capers, and a sprinkle of dill tips. Serve immediately.

Makes 12

elder

Sambucus nigra

This fascinating tree was long regarded as the medicine chest of country people, and it was not only the berries and flowers that they put to use. The close-grained white wood of old trees was cut and polished and made into butchers' skewers, shoemakers' pegs, needles for weaving nets, combs, mathematical instruments, and some musical instruments. The stems, with pith removed, made whistles and popguns for country boys.

The European (black or common) elder is the one to grow in a herb garden, although you would probably need to have two or three trees to provide sufficient flowers and berries to make wine. From late summer, filmy heads of creamy-white flowers put bees in nectar-heaven. Birds have their turn for feasting in autumn, when drooping bunches of rich garnet-coloured berries cover the tree in prolific splendour.

choosing and using

The uses of the flowers and berries are legion. However, unlike the birds and the bees, we humans generally prefer our elderberries processed first! This is because when fresh they contain toxic alkaloids that will make you sick, but they are safe to eat when cooked or dried. The minute petals make infusions for cordials and teas and the fresh flowers are used for wine.

Elderberries have been used for centuries to make wine, but today they are more often used to colour conventional wines, particularly some ports produced in Portugal. Tasting rather like blackcurrants, elderberries add a distinctive sharpness to jams, jellies, fruit tarts and apple sauce. They are also used on their own to make jam, jelly, chutney and ketchup.

growing

Elder is a deciduous tree with finely serrated leaves advancing in pairs along supple, pale green stems that cling to bronze, woody branches. It grows to around 4–6 m tall, with a dense spreading habit that can quickly become an impenetrable thicket in the right growing conditions.

Elder trees are hardy and will grow almost anywhere, but they do best in rich, moist soil. If for some reason you want a grove of trees, leave at least 3–4 m between each one. However be warned, because of their suckering habit, you'll have a solid jungle rather than a grove if you're not prepared to be vigilant and act. They are fond of moisture and partial to a sunny position with semi-shade, though they will soldier on regardless if you forget to water them for a while. They should be cut back hard in winter (remember that spreading habit).

Back in the Somerset Cottage days, John reported the greatest success in propagating by taking 15 cm hardwood cuttings in late winter before the spring shoots appeared, and putting them in a container of river sand. Tip cuttings can also be struck in river sand in late spring when the new growth has firmed. When roots appear the cuttings can be planted out, or put into containers with potting mixture. It is also possible to strike cuttings of sprouting wood in early spring in the open ground. Suckers, with some root from the main plant attached, can be dug and transplanted throughout the year, unless winters are harsh, when you may lose them.

If you should decide that you no longer want your elder tree, or that you'd rather it was somewhere else in your garden, it's too bad. We tried in vain to kill an unwanted elder tree for years, first chopping it out (we thought), then burning out the stump (we thought) and finally in desperation, hitting it with Round-Up. It outlasted our days at Grose Vale. And while we have moved on, as far as we know, 15-plus years later, it's still there, growing strong.

drying

Gather the blooms when all the tiny buds on each pearly cluster are open, and do this by midday before the sun draws out too much of the flower's etheric substance.

Put the heads somewhere shady to dry – a sheet of paper in a warm dry place – and when they shrivel, and look like fine, yellowed crochet, remove them to make room for more fresh flowers. Store the dried ones whole in airtight boxes or jars, or rub them from their frail stalks first. Leave some flowers on the trees for using fresh and to ensure that there will be some fruit later.

When the shiny green berries form, watch them ripen and pick them as they begin to turn reddish purple. If it is not convenient to use the berries at once, allow them to dry, and store in airtight containers. They keep their flavour well and are used like dried currants.

elderflower fritters

8 elderflower heads

1 tablespoon orange-flower water

1 teaspoon ground cinnamon

$\frac{1}{2}$ cup light-flavoured unsaturated oil, or more if necessary

1 or 2 tablespoons caster sugar

Batter

3 tablespoons plain flour

1 tablespoon cornflour

$\frac{1}{2}$ tablespoon caster sugar

1 egg, separated

around 1 cup milk

Place the flower heads in a bowl and sprinkle with orange-flower water and cinnamon.

To make the batter, sift the flours into a large bowl and stir in the sugar. Mix the egg yolk with $\frac{1}{2}$ cup of the milk and stir into the dry ingredients. Add more milk, bit by bit, until the batter is smooth and of a thick pouring consistency. Whisk the egg white to soft peaks in a clean bowl (to make the batter as light and airy as the flowers themselves) and fold into the batter.

To make the fritters, heat the oil in a small deep saucepan. Dip the elderflowers into the batter, one at a time, and deep-fry them in the hot oil. As soon as the fritters colour, remove them from the oil. Drain on kitchen towel for a couple of minutes, then arrange on a platter, sprinkle with caster sugar and serve while hot with clotted cream.

Makes 8

fennel

Foeniculum vulgare

All things to all people – that's fennel
(also known as Florence fennel,
common fennel or sweet fennel).
You want a vegetable, a herb,
a spice, a garnish? Then
fennel's the one for you.

Also called finnichio, Florence fennel, aniseed (incorrectly), common fennel, sweet fennel
Flavour and aroma licorice, anise
Flavour group leaves: strong

The feathery, dark green leaves have an anise aroma similar to that of dill, and the prolific umbels of summery yellow flowers make way for juicy plump seeds that are delicious eaten straight from the garden. Sometimes these seeds are referred to as the fruit of the fennel, which in a way is technically correct; however, if you plant it and it grows, it's a seed.

choosing and using

The fragrant leaves have a delicate flavour and are best fresh. They are used very much the same way as their little cousin dill – in salads, sauces, with all kinds of seafood and to garnish terrines, soups and aspic. Pick a lavish bunch of fresh fennel to make an aromatic bed for baking a whole fish.

Like so many other fresh herbs, chopped fresh fennel can be made into ice-blocks for later use, and sprigs of fresh fennel can be wrapped in foil, sealed, and kept in the freezer for up to a month.

The bulb is a serious contender for the 'versatile vegetable' prize. It is delicious whatever you do with it: sliced fresh for crisp-textured salads, added to stews, simply steamed, served with a light sauce or quartered and baked Italian-style with a little nutmeg, butter and garlic and topped with sizzling freshly grated parmesan cheese.

It's a sad fact that poor old fennel doesn't get the recognition it deserves – you'll often see fennel bulbs beautifully displayed in fruit and vegetable shops and wrongly labelled 'aniseed'. Try to convince anyone to call it otherwise, and you're up against generations of habit and you'll never win.

growing

Because fennel is an annual, it will die away in winter and needs to be replanted again each year. If you have plenty of space, plant seedlings (or seeds) in late spring or early summer about 30 cm apart straight into a sunny part of the garden. A rich, well-drained soil will give the best results and you may need to fertilise occasionally. Fennel grows to about 90 cm, so it is perfectly suitable for potting – just make sure your pot is at least 30 cm deep so that there's room for the bulb. Remember to give your plant plenty of water to encourage lots of bright green foliage.

The fennel bulbs sold as vegetables have been specially treated so that they grow beyond their natural size. When the bulb is as big as a golf ball, heap some soil up around it, continually adding more as it grows, to keep the bulb covered. Remove the flower heads as they appear. When the bulbs are large enough to use, cut them away from the roots, tie them together by the foliage and hang in a dry place. Use within 10 days after cutting, otherwise you will lose the fresh, crisp texture. For using in salads, cover the bulb in a bowl of water in the fridge for a while to get maximum crispness.

drying

Don't even bother trying to dry the fragile, wispy leaves. There are too sappy and by the time they have dried, most of the flavour will be lost.

Drying the seeds is quite easy. Allow them to develop and ripen in autumn, then clip off the heads and tie them together by the stems. Hang the bunch in an airy, shady place with clean paper or cloth spread underneath to catch any seeds that fall. After a few days, hold the bunch by the stems and shake out all the seeds. Store them in an airtight container, and delight in their freshness as you use them. Try grinding a few teaspoons of them and sprinkling over tuna fillets, then brush the fish with olive oil and grill – yum!

See pages 77–81 for fennel seed.

risotto with garlic and fennel

8–10 strands saffron

2$\frac{1}{2}$ cups chicken stock, kept simmering

freshly ground black pepper

1–2 tablespoons olive oil

1 small onion, finely chopped

4–5 cloves garlic, finely chopped

1 cup arborio rice

1 bulb fennel, halved lengthways and thinly sliced

$\frac{1}{2}$ cup fresh chopped parsley

$\frac{1}{2}$ cup freshly grated parmesan

Infuse the saffron in a tablespoon of the warm stock for 10 minutes, then return it to the rest of the stock with a few good grinds of black pepper.

Heat the oil in a large, heavy-based saucepan, add the onion and cook for 60 seconds. Add the garlic and cook for another 60 seconds, then add the rice, stirring to coat each grain with oil. Add a cup of warm stock and the sliced fennel, stirring constantly until the fennel starts to wilt. When most of the liquid has been absorbed, add the remaining stock in 3 or 4 batches. Stir frequently and make sure that each batch of the stock is fully absorbed before adding the next.

You will notice the risotto change to become thick and creamy towards the end of the cooking time. At this stage, stir in the parsley and the parmesan. Taste, and season with salt and pepper if desired. Serve immediately.

Serves 3–4

kalamata olives with fennel and basil

We are most grateful to Lucio Galleto and Timothy Fisher for allowing us to include this incredibly more-ish recipe from *The Art of Food at Lucio's* (Craftsman House,1999).

250 g kalamata olives, pitted

1 fennel bulb

3 garlic cloves, peeled and slightly bruised

5 fresh basil leaves, chopped

extra virgin olive oil

Rinse the olives under running water and dry them in a salad spinner to remove all traces of water. Wash the fennel and cut it into pieces twice the size of the olives. In a large bowl, combine the olives, fennel, garlic and basil. Drizzle with olive oil and mix until all ingredients are well combined. Let stand for at least 4 hours, and remove the garlic before serving.

wild fennel

This tall-growing perennial (*F. vulgare*) does not produce the swollen stem base of the annual variety. It is looked upon as something of a weed and is usually found growing wild in low-lying places that are subject to flooding and also along roadside banks and ditches. It is often wrongly referred to as aniseed because of a similarity in flavour and appearance.

fenugreek leaf

Trigonella foenum-graecum

Fenugreek is one of the oldest cultivated plants – you can read all about it in papyri from Egyptian tombs (it was used in the embalming process).

Also called methi
Flavour and aroma grassy and leguminous
Flavour group strong

choosing and using

Fenugreek has the ability to make itself indispensable wherever it is grown. In India, the leaves are used as a vegetable known as *methi*, as a flavouring for curries, as a key ingredient in tandoori marinades and are added torn or whole to green salads served to freshen the palate (and tone up the system). Their mild flavour goes well with potatoes and spinach.

The Iranians make a delectable and one of the easiest-ever appetisers with a variety of fresh herbs – usually fenugreek, parsley, garlic chives, tarragon, coriander, mint, and watercress. All you do is wash, dry and roughly tear the herbs, crisp them in the refrigerator, and serve them on a platter with cubes of feta and flat bread.

The sharpness of fenugreek sprouts combines well with the mild grassiness of alfalfa. Add them to sandwiches and salad with a little oil and lemon dressing.

If you have fenugreek growing, freeze the fresh leaves in ice-cube trays by chopping them finely and mixing with a little water.

growing

Fenugreek is a small, slender annual from the pea family (Fabaceae, formerly Leguminosae) with aromatic light green leaves about 2 cm long. It looks rather like alfalfa. The Romans called it *foenum-graecum* (meaning Greek hay) when they brought it to Italy, because the foliage was a fodder crop used to sweeten mildewed, sour hay.

Fenugreek grows to about 60 cm and likes full sun and well-drained, rich, alkaline soil. Sow some seeds in spring, and more a few weeks later to stagger your crop. Make narrow furrows, plant your seeds or seedlings about 10 cm apart, and water well. Because it is a rather delicate annual, don't try to transplant it. Just pop it straight into its permanent spot in the garden (or into a container). Pick the leaves as soon as they are large enough to add to salads.

Small, yellowish-white flowers bloom in late summer, and are followed by typical leguminous fruits in light brown, sickle-shaped seed pods about as long as your finger, about three to five months after sowing. These contain small, furrowed, golden-brown seeds that look like little pebbles with their rather square irregular shapes. When the pods are ripe, collect them as the first few seeds fall from them.

Gyoza with Kaffir Lime Leaf (recipe page 268)

Top to bottom:
Native Pepperberries; Herbes de Provence (recipe page 271);
Mountain Pepperleaf Blends (recipe page 135);
Panch Phora (recipe page 113)

drying

Drying fenugreek leaves is not hard – pick sprays of the spindly leaf-bearing stems and spread them out in a thin layer on clean paper or cloth. Leave them in an airy, shady place until they're dry, or if the weather is humid, you can spread them on a baking tray and dry them in the oven. Heat the oven to about 50°C, then turn it off. Put the tray of leaves in and leave the oven door ajar. By the time the oven has cooled, the leaves should be dry – if not, repeat the whole process.

To dry the seeds, snip off the pods and hang them in bunches or spread them out on a tray in a warm dry place. When completely dry, shake the seeds from the pods and store them in labelled airtight containers.

See pages 80–5 for fenugreek seed.

spinach frittata with fenugreek leaves

This versatile frittata is made in minutes and is equally delicious hot or cold. Serve it with a mesclun salad.

4 eggs
2 tablespoons water
salt and pepper
pinch of chilli powder (optional)
1 cup cooked spinach leaves, roughly chopped
about 15 fresh fenugreek leaves
1 teaspoon butter

Beat the eggs and water together with the salt, pepper and chilli. Stir in the spinach and fenugreek leaves. Melt the butter in a heavy-based frying pan, tilting the pan as the butter melts to coat the surface. Pour in the egg mixture and cook over low heat, gently lifting the edges of the frittata away from the pan as they set, to allow uncooked mixture to flow down the sides. Pre-heat the grill as you continue the lifting-and-tilting action, letting the uncooked portions flow to the edges and base of the pan. When it is nearly all set, transfer the pan to the grill until the top has lightly browned and the frittata is completely cooked.

Serves 2

methi muttar
(peas with fenugreek leaves)

This recipe from Ajoy Joshi, a Sydney-based restaurateur and chef, makes use of his own special garam masala blend of whole spices, which is a little different from ours, and a reminder that it's a loose term. Keep in mind that peas cook differently depending on how young and succulent or old and tough they are, so keep checking as they cook.

'Whole' Garam Masala

¼ cup vegetable oil

5 green cardamom pods

1 brown (Indian) cardamom pod

5 cloves

1 cassia stick, about 8 cm long

1 Indian bay leaf (tejpat)

1 piece blade mace

3 large onions, chopped

1 teaspoon salt

3 tablespoons crushed ginger

2 tablespoons crushed garlic

3 green chillies, chopped finely

½ teaspoon turmeric powder

½ tablespoon ground coriander seed

½ teaspoon chilli powder

180 g tomatoes, peeled and chopped

125 ml plain yoghurt

1 kg fresh shelled green peas

2 tablespoons dried fenugreek leaves* (kasoor methi)

¼ cup chopped fresh coriander leaves

Preheat the oven to 180ºC. Heat the vegetable oil in a heavy-based, ovenproof saucepan, then add the garam masala spices and fry until they start to crackle. Add the chopped onions and salt and stir over a medium heat until the onions are golden.

Add the crushed ginger, garlic and green chillies, then the turmeric, ground coriander and chilli powder. Stir in the chopped tomatoes and cook until soft, stirring occasionally. Add the yoghurt and continue to cook until oil rises to the top – about 5 minutes.

Add the green peas to the sauce. Simmer for about 5 minutes, then cover the pan and place in the oven to cook for about 10 minutes. Test the peas to see if they are tender and give a few minutes more if necessary.

Remove from oven and sprinkle with the crushed, dried fenugreek leaves and the fresh coriander leaves. Serve with steamed rice or chapattis.

Serves 6–8 as part of a meal

*Note: If fresh fenugreek is available, wash the leaves and immerse in salted water for about 15 minutes to remove bitterness. Drain and add to the pot before placing in the oven.

garlic

Allium sativum

Garlic's culinary virtues have been indispensable
in many cuisines from East Asia to Spain for
centuries, as its unique aroma heightens
the taste and aroma of a dish.

Also called lover's treacle, poor man's treacle
Flavour and aroma sharp and acrid when raw,
sweeter when cooked
Flavour group pungent

Garlic has been known for so many thousands of years that its origins are rather obscure. It belongs to the same family (Alliaceae) as onions, chives and leeks, and the *Macquarie Dictionary* tells us the name we know it by today comes from the Middle English word garleac – 'gar' meaning a spear and 'leac' a leek.

There was a time not so very long ago when eating garlic in even minute quantities would put one at the receiving end of dark looks and 'you've had garlic!' accusations. How our cuisine has changed. So, what goes with garlic? Easier to ask today what doesn't!

choosing and using

Although the garlic-growers of California delight in putting it with jams and ice-cream, most of us would draw the line there and say you can add garlic to virtually anything that's savoury – lamb, pork, veal, beef, chicken, tomatoes, eggplant, zucchini, curries, Asian cooking, certain sauces and dressings.

For those who feel that garlic is an acquired taste and prefer only the merest whiff, rubbing the sides of a salad bowl or casserole dish with a cut clove may deliver the desired effect.

For the rest, there is aïoli ...

This thick, strong-tasting, golden mayonnaise from rural France is made with eggs, olive oil and crushed garlic and goes with just about anything. It is delicious with steamed baby new potatoes, a bowl of shelled hard-boiled eggs, globe artichokes, avocado, asparagus, fish, chicken, or simply mopped up with chunks of baguette.

When buying bulbs of fresh garlic, look for ones that are firmly held together. The cloves should be hard and not shrinking away from each other. There are various types of garlic on the market, ranging from small Asian ones to the Californian giants. Keep bulbs intact until you need to use a clove or few, and store in an open container like a wicker basket in a cool, airy place (not the refrigerator as the bulbs tend to sprout in damp conditions). So long as they have their protective husk the bulbs don't smell – that only emerges when you crush or peel the cloves.

There is also a single clove type of garlic, about the size of a golf ball, that has been grown in the high, cold areas of China for centuries. The Japanese love its extra hot and pungent flavour used raw. When cooked, the flavour is milder than our more familiar garlic and it makes a fantastic baked vegetable. It's peeled just like onion, and with the outside rather caramelised and the inside cooked to creamy perfection, it is a mouth-watering delight.

Should garlic be chopped, crushed or sliced? It's a matter of taste – encountering a slice of well-cooked garlic in a hearty beef casserole is a delight to any garlic-lover, while a fine purée of crushed garlic cloves is perfect for a curry paste.

Or you can try this: slice the top off an entire bulb of garlic, just low enough to cut the tops off the cloves, then cook in the oven or on the barbecue until the garlic flesh is soft and creamy. Squeeze the flesh out of the papery shells, and enjoy this delectable taste sensation that has none of the pungency of raw garlic.

You can buy garlic ready prepared, as peeled cloves, paste or dried. Store peeled cloves and pastes in the refrigerator once opened and dried garlic products in their airtight pack in a cupboard. Don't buy garlic powder if it looks lumpy as this may reveal telltale signs of extra moisture – meaning that it simply won't pack the necessary punch.

growing

Garlic grows to about 90 cm high and has flat, greyish leaves about 30 cm long, a bit like a nondescript lily. However there's nothing nondescript about the fabulous flower, which appears in summer. A willowy, round, flower stalk thrusts upward from the centre above the leaves and produces a typical allium pompom flower – a blossomy ball of mauve-tinted white petals sometimes used in arrangements by imaginative florists.

Spring is the best time for planting garlic. Mature bulbs are made up of tightly clustered cloves, each sheathed in a pearly, papery skin. The whole bulb is tissue-wrapped by nature in the same covering. Separate the cloves (but don't peel them) and, press them upright with the root end pointing down, in pre-dug holes 5 cm deep. The root end is the one with the tough, flat, button-sized base. Plant the cloves about 15 cm apart in a sunny spot in the garden or in a container in rich, well-dug and well-drained soil. If the soil is poor, dig in some well-decayed manure or compost. Cover the cloves with soil, and water well.

Soon the spear-like, grey-green leaves appear, followed by the flower stalks, each with a long, swelling bud at the end. As the stalks lengthen and the buds grow plumper, they eventually burst into flower. Harvesting usually takes place about six months after planting the cloves, when the flowers are fading and the leaves are yellowing and beginning to shrivel. You can plant garlic seeds, but the results are very erratic as many are infertile. In cooler districts the bulbs are likely to be smaller.

drying

Pull the whole plant out by hand after loosening the roots first. Remove the excess soil by tapping the bulbs against the spade or your boot. Trim off the roots with garden shears and leave the tops intact so that the sap will move down into the corms (bulbs). Leave the bulbs in a shady place for about a week to toughen up the skin, then cut away any foliage and store in a dry airy container such as a basket. Bulbs should keep for around four months. You can also plait several bulbs together with the remaining leaves and hang them in a dry place where air is circulating. In a moist atmosphere the bulbs will mildew.

aïoli with lemon myrtle

12 cloves garlic, peeled

1 teaspoon salt

3 egg yolks

1¾ cups extra virgin olive oil

a few drops of lemon juice

1 teaspoon dried and crushed lemon myrtle leaves

Chop the garlic cloves very finely to a thick paste consistency, then transfer to a bowl. Add the salt and the egg yolks, stirring with a wooden spoon, until well blended. At this stage, swap your wooden spoon for a wire whisk and beat in the olive oil drop by drop. As the mixture thickens, and when about half the oil has been used, pour the rest of the oil a little more quickly, in a steady stream, still beating. Finally, add the lemon juice and lemon myrtle.

If the oil separates, put a fresh egg yolk in another bowl and slowly add the curdled sauce to it, beating constantly.

Makes about 2 cups

horseradish

Armoracia rusticana

It is rather like a radish, but is hairier
and more wrinkled, has a faithful following,
and can clear your sinuses in a whiff.
It is horseradish, a member of the
sulfurous mustard and cress
family (Cruciferae).

Also called great raifort, mountain radish, red cole, Japanese horseradish (wasabi), horse root
Flavour and aroma biting, pungent, hot, sinus-clearing
Flavour group pungent

The root system of horse radish comprises a main or taproot, about 30 cm long and 1.25 cm thick, with several smaller roots branching out at various angles.

choosing and using

Like so many herbs, horseradish has been valued for so long no-one knows quite where it came from originally. But finely sliced rare roast beef cries out for it. Horseradish combined with vinegar was a favourite condiment in Germany and its reputation spread from there to England and France, where it became known as *moutarde des Allemands*. A little freshly grated horseradish adds zest to dips, sauces and dressings and is the perfect partner for beef, pork, oily fish, and poultry. It is also good added to coleslaw, or pickled beetroot.

Horseradish is best eaten cold as it loses its piquancy when cooked because its volatile oil evaporates quickly. Grating releases the volatile oil. However, only grate the outer section of the root because that packs the pungency. The inner core tends to be on the flavourless, rubbery side.

Fresh horseradish roots are not readily available unless you grow them yourself, or live in a major city with a Chinatown area, where you can find them if you're lucky. You can buy jars of horseradish relish or paste and grated fresh horseradish root these days (refrigerate after opening), but they're quite a bit milder than the freshly grated root.

Dehydrated horseradish granules or flakes are convenient to use when making sauces and dressings.

Store in airtight packs in a cupboard away from heat and light to preserve the flavour. When these are reconstituted, the chunky pieces can be a bit leathery – keep them covered with water for about 24 hours, adding more as it is absorbed. Then purée them in a blender to make a paste and store it in a covered container in the fridge until you need it.

The young leaves can be added to salads, but their flavour and texture is rather coarse, so it's no wonder that, more often than not, they're passed over in favour of more pleasing salad herbs such as salad burnet, mitsuba, chicory, purslane and sorrel.

Japanese horseradish (*wasabi*) is from a different plant (*Wasabia*) but packs an equivalent punch, and is the key to the popularity of sushi and sashimi.

growing

Perennial horseradish is easily grown in temperate zones in rich, loose, moist soil in sun or light shady conditions. 'Easy to grow' is an understatement. It is such a vigorous grower that even the most dedicated devotees should possibly think twice before planting. Its large, dark green spinach-like leaves are soft and fleshy, and constantly under attack by leaf-eating pests, particularly snails.

If you want to grow horseradish in your garden, give it plenty of room, allowing about 30 cm between plants all round. Unless you have a remote corner of your garden where your horseradish can reign supreme, it might be wise to restrict it to a large tub, planting it in a nice sandy loam. In early spring, select your taproots, cut off any side roots and plant in prepared holes about 20 cm long and 2.5 cm wide, pouring a little sand around the sides before covering with soil. Keep watered so that the roots don't become coarse.

To encourage root development, the panicles of white flowers that develop in summer are usually cut back, which is no great loss, as horseradish doesn't usually set seed. Propagate by dividing an established clump, although this is seldom necessary, because once you have it, you have it for life.

Dig up roots in autumn or as needed. You only use the small side roots in cooking, not the main taproot, which can be replanted as described above. Scrape the soil away from the side of the plant, and cut the small roots away. Every two years, pull the whole plant out, keeping the taproots for propagation. Store the side roots in dry sand or wash them well and preserve them whole or sliced in white wine vinegar.

horseradish sauce

For roast beef, pork or lamb.

200 ml sour cream

1/2 tablespoon white vinegar

1 teaspoon mustard powder

1/2 teaspoon salt

1 teaspoon sugar

2 tablespoons fresh grated horseradish or 1 tablespoon
   dried horseradish, reconstituted in warm water

Whip the cream until thickened, and stir in all the other ingredients. Let stand for at least 30 minutes before serving. Store in the refrigerator and use within 3 or 4 days.

Makes about 1 cup

apple, mint and horseradish cream

Combined with mint and apples, horseradish adds a zing to vegetables like avocado, beetroot and cucumber and also to sashimi.

2 Granny Smith or other cooking apples

2 tablespoons freshly grated horseradish

juice of 1 lemon

1 teaspoon salt

1 teaspoon sugar

2 teaspoons chopped fresh mint

200 ml sour cream

Peel and grate the apples and combine with all the other ingredients. Store in a covered container in the refrigerator and use within 3 or 4 days.

Makes about 1 cup

hyssop

Hyssopus officinalis

Go easy with this one in your cooking, though
it's a lovely plant to have in your garden.
Hyssop's leaves have a curious musky
aroma and a palate-tingling flavour
of Angostura bitters,
so judicious use is,
well, judicious.

Flavour and aroma pungent, pine and juniper notes
Flavour group pungent

Used sparingly, though, the distinctive aroma of hyssop never intrudes, but rather enhances. This herb has an intriguing, pungent, pine flavour that combines well with fatty meats like duck, pork, or goose and it can also be added to stuffings for these meats. In this way, we could consider it the herb equivalent of spicy juniper berries. Stir a few chopped leaves into a rich gravy or sprinkle into soup during the last half-hour of cooking. The delightfully scented, rich blue flowers colour a green salad. But you will have to grow your own as it's not available through fruit and vegetable retailers.

Hyssop was a holy herb used for purification rites in temples. Monastery gardens were planted with hyssop for religious, medicinal and landscaping purposes – the good monks found its bushy habit and sapphire flowers useful for outlining their cloistered, formal herb beds.

This particularly useful plant provided not only culinary delights, but also aromatic oil for perfumes and medicines for all sorts of medieval mishaps, from acne to worms. Even today, the leaves, flowers and stems are distilled to produce a fine, colourless oil used in manufacturing perfumes and liqueurs.

growing

Hyssop can be mistaken for winter savory until it flowers in late summer: both carry spires of small, lipped blooms in late summer and early autumn. However, winter savory's flowers are white, while hyssop's, which are full of nectar and loved by bees, are deep blue – except for some scarcer pink or white varieties. Like savory, hyssop draws back into itself in winter, looking squat, and its leaves dark green and unyielding. Come spring, up shoot the tender green shoots on lengthening stalks and this is when it is hard to tell them apart.

Hyssop is a densely compact perennial growing to about 60 cm, making it excellent for low hedges (remember the good monks). It is also suitable for container planting. It's easy to grow, either by root division (in spring or autumn), from cuttings (in late spring to early summer), or from seed (in the spring). When planting out, choose a sunny spot and light well-drained soil. If you're growing hyssop as a low hedge, set seedlings about 30 cm apart. It is frost-hardy and, thanks to its Mediterranean origins, happy in dry conditions. Prune stalks and stems back to the main plant in autumn, which will assure its shape and vigour for the following spring.

drying

Dried hyssop flowers are used extensively in herbal medicine, and are harvested during peak blossoming time in late summer. Cut flowering stems in the morning and hang in bunches in a dry, shady place, or spread out on sheet of paper or one drying racks. When dry and moisture-free, strip the flowers and some leaves from their stalks and store in airtight, labelled containers.

honeyed carrot straws with hyssop

2 medium carrots, cut into julienne strips

1 tablespoon water

1 teaspoon honey

1 teaspoon finely chopped hyssop

salt and pepper to taste

Place all the ingredients in a heavy-based saucepan, cover and simmer slowly for about 10 minutes, depending on the size of your carrot pieces. Serve hot.

Serves 2–3 as an accompaniment

raw cauliflower and hyssop salad

This recipe is for those weeks when cauliflower is at premium freshness.

2–3 cups cauliflower florets

1 apple, chopped into small dice

1 tablespoon finely chopped hyssop

2 teaspoons salt

500 ml plain yoghurt

1 tablespoon lemon juice

Slice the florets paper-thin lengthwise, and mix with the chopped apple in a bowl. Add the hyssop, salt, yoghurt and lemon juice, mix well and chill. A couple of fresh hyssop sprigs will add panache to the presentation.

Serves 4 as an accompaniment

kaffir lime leaf

Citrus hystrix

The fresh leaves of this delightful smelling but ferociously thorny tree are used extensively in Asian cooking – in sambals, with steamed fish, in the beef rendang of Indonesia, in laksa, green curries, soups and many dishes made with coconut cream.

Also called Indonesian lime leaves
Flavour and aroma intense lemon/lime
Flavour group medium

Kaffir lime leaves add a fresh nuance to chicken soup or any spicy fish dish. Lemon leaves, or leaves from West Indian and Tahitian limes, are sometimes substituted. For maximum freshness and flavour, the leaves are best straight from the tree. They are usually removed from a dish before serving.

The kaffir lime is a typical evergreen citrus tree with dark green, smooth leaves that are long, flat, and deliciously lime-scented. What makes them different is the unusual double leaf, which looks as though a whole new leaf has grown out of the end of the original leaf. Botanists will tell you that the original leaf is in fact just a very large nodule from which the real leaf grows, but to we lay persons, the important thing is that we get twice as much leaf! The aromatic foliage is high in volatile oils, which give the leaves their unique flavour.

choosing and using

Not only are the leaves perfect in the pot, but you can also crush a few and place them in a small glass dish as a natural room deodoriser. They emit a heavenly scent that's a cross between lemon, orange and lime, but not like any one of these on its own.

You don't have to grow your own. You can buy fresh leaves from fruit and vegetable retailers, Asian food shops and produce markets. If you do have a tree, pick your own fresh lime leaves as needed, watching out for the prickles. You can freeze fresh leaves in a plastic bag (it helps them keep their flavour) and simply add the frozen leaves straight to the dish; there's no need to thaw them first.

growing

Kaffir lime trees thrive in tropical and sub-tropical climes, and even in temperate zones in full sun in warmer areas. As the branches have large prickles, plant the trees away from where children play. You can also grow them very satisfactorily in large pots. And if your pot can be wheeled around, you can follow the sun. In summer, the white, fragrant flowers come into bloom, followed by small green limes with a rough, bumpy surface that contain very little juice.

As kaffir limes trees are grafted, buy them ready to plant from the nursery. Plant in light, deep, well-drained soil in a sunny, frost-free position. They are tropical, surface-rooting trees, and need mulching to prevent evaporation of moisture from the soil, especially in dry weather. Keep them weed free and give the tree a good soaking in dry weather, rather than watering lightly. Prune away dead wood, being careful of the long thorns.

As citrus trees are ravenous feeders, an annual application of some good fertiliser is essential in spring. Be careful cultivating near the surface so as not to injure or cut the fine, shallow roots. By fertilising and cultivating regularly as the tree grows, the roots are encouraged downwards and are in better condition to resist dry, hot weather. If your tree is in a tub, remember that it is depending on you for all its nutrients, and you will need to feed it more often.

Pests and diseases like aphids, ants, lace bug and scale can be a problem, as with all citrus. As it is the leaves you eat, opt for a minimum chemical cure, or look for a treatment formulated for vegetables. Try soapy water for the aphids, white oil for the scale and for the ants, try this tip. Wrap a band of electrical tape around the trunk of the tree and apply a weekly dose of cooking oil over the tape. The ants can't climb over it.

drying

The leaves dry well if you take a little care. You can hang them in bunches like bay leaves, and use them in varying degrees of dryness. But for best results, spread freshly picked leaves out on porous paper in a single layer in a warm, dark place where humidity is low. Store crisp, dried leaves in airtight containers away from light, extreme heat and humidity and they will last about 12 months. The dry leaves should be green, not yellow.

coconut rice

2 cups basmati rice
1 cup water
1 cup coconut milk
1 stalk lemongrass, finely chopped

Put the rice into a saucepan with the water, coconut milk and lemongrass. Cover the pan and bring to a boil over a medium heat. Once the rice is boiling, turn off the heat and allow to steam for 15 minutes.

Serves 4

beef stir-fry with kaffir lime

1 tablespoon sesame oil
300 g sirloin steak, sliced
5 red shallots, sliced
2 cloves garlic, finely chopped
2 long red chillis, sliced
3 kaffir lime leaves, sliced into julienne strips
1 cup sugar snap peas
1 tablespoon soy sauce
2 teaspoons fish sauce
2 cups Thai basil

Heat the sesame oil in a wok. Add the beef and stir-fry for 2–3 minutes. Add all the remaining ingredients, except for the Thai basil, and stir-fry for another 3–4 minutes. Turn off the heat and add the Thai basil to the wok. Stir it through until just wilted and serve immediately with coconut rice.

Serves 4

gyoza with kaffir lime leaf

The remaining wonton wrappers can be frozen and used later.

12 round wonton wrappers

3 tablespoons vegetable oil

$1/2$ cup water

Stuffing

150 g pork mince

2 kaffir lime leaves, cut into strips

1 long red chilli

1 cm fresh ginger, chopped

1 cup chopped white cabbage

1 tablespoon soy sauce

1 teaspoon sesame oil

1 teaspoon fish sauce

Dipping Sauce

2 tablespoons soy sauce

1 long red chilli, sliced, seeds intact

Place all the stuffing ingredients in a food processor and pulse until they are well combined and form a smooth paste.

Place a generous teaspoon of stuffing into the centre of each wonton wrapper. Lightly brush around the edges of each wonton wrapper with water. Bring the edges together and pinch to seal firmly, forming a crescent shape with a flat base. Once made, the gyoza can be covered and refrigerated until ready to cook.

Heat the vegetable oil in frying pan and when hot, add the gyoza, flat side down. Fry for 2–3 minutes, or until the undersides are golden-brown. Add the water and cover the pan with a lid so the gyoza can steam. Reduce the heat and cook for 3–4 minutes. When cooked, the dumpling wrappers will appear soft and translucent.

Stir together the soy sauce and sliced chilli and serve with the gyoza.

Makes 12

lavender

Lavandula angustifolia

The familiar pungency of lavender
usually reminds us of
Grandma's linen cupboard
rather than her kitchen.

Also called English lavender, French lavender, Italian or Spanish lavender, cotton lavender
Flavour and aroma camphorous, piney, floral, pungent
Flavour group pungent

A few centuries ago, sweet-scented flowers were often used in cooking. 'W. M.' (cook to Queen Henrietta Maria in 1635) had a recipe for a conserve of lavender flowers that consisted of lavender petals finely chopped then mixed with icing sugar and enough rosewater to make a thin paste. It was then spread as a fragrant icing on plain cakes and biscuits. Lavender is also used in herbes de Provence, and in the exotic Moroccan mixture, ras el hanout.

These highly perfumed plants of the labiate or mint family are found naturally in the Mediterranean region right through the Middle East and south to India; and today are grown and loved around the world. There are about 25 species and numerous hybrids and, as the common names can vary from country to country, plant nursery to plant nursery and gardening guide to gardening guide, we recommend sticking to the botanical name when talking about this herb.

L. angustifolia, the variety we call English lavender, was not actually cultivated in England until about 1568. Today, flower colours available in hybrids of this beautiful variety range from snow white, dusty pink and shades of blue, and go through the spectrum of mauves from pale lavender to deepest purple.

Other favourites are *L. dentata* (known as French lavender or fringe lavender) and *L. stoechas* (also known as French, Italian and Spanish lavender).

L. allardii (giant lavender) is a hardy and successful hybrid; it is larger than most lavenders and has the long flower spikes and smooth leaves of *L. angustifolia*, while the foliage has the indented edges of *L. dentata*.

L. angustifolia seems to be everyone's favourite and is the one that's very popular for lavender handcrafts thanks to its highly perfumed flowers and long, elegant, leafless stalk below the bloom. Make lavender vinegar by infusing whole stems with their flowers in white vinegar for several weeks. Use it for a dressing with a green leaf and flower salad featuring nasturtium petals, heartsease flowers, marigold petals and lavender.

growing

When lavenders are in a position they like, the difference in the size of the bushes and the depth of colour in the flowers is very marked.

L. angustifolia is a bushy, small shrub growing 90 cm high in the right place, with silvery, smooth, pointed leaves and highly perfumed, tiny mauve flowers at the end of long, spiky stems. Although each individual flower is indeed tiny, there are lots of them all grouped together, so that the flower head is about the diameter of a pencil, and somewhere between 2 and 4 cm long. When the bush starts blooming in summer it is a beautiful sight, especially if several plants are massed together as a hedge. This type of planting suits all the lavenders.

L. dentata is the hardiest, and in many ways the most rewarding of the varieties to grow and we have seen it reach a height of 1.5 m. The bush blooms continuously for about nine months of the year, especially if mature flower stalks are cut back regularly to where two new shoots are beginning to branch. This helps to keep the bush a good shape while preventing it from having to nourish flowers that are past their peak.

Lavender can be propagated from seed, but as many lavender plants available today are hybrids, taking cuttings is a much safer and quicker option. (If you try planting seeds from a hybrid lavender, the new plants will probably revert back to the original type.) Plant seeds in spring, preferably in seed boxes or trays made from bio-degradable egg cartons, with just a light dusting of soil patted down on top of the seeds. Tip cuttings of any variety should be taken in late spring when the soft, new leaves are firm enough not to wilt when they are put into a pot of sand.

When the seedlings are big enough, or when the cuttings have made roots, plant them out in a sunny, well-drained position. This is very important for lavender, as it will not grow sturdily nor flower well, if you plant it in a shady or damp place. When the plants have finished flowering, prune them hard, but not to ground level, and if you have an open fireplace, save the branches for the fire.

drying

The best time to pick and dry *L. angustifolia* is before the last flowers on each stalk are fully opened. This is when their oil content, and therefore their fragrance, is greatest. Pick the stems on a dry day before the heat of the sun has drawn out the volatile essence, then tie them in bunches and hang in a shady, airy place to dry. When they're really dry, strip the flowers from the stems and store them in airtight, labelled containers.

Leafy and flowering stems of *L dentata* may be cut at any time for drying, providing there is no moisture in the air and harvesting is done before midday. The benefit with *L. dentata* is that the leaves are as fragrant as the flowers, so you can achieve much more bulk by using the dried leaves as well. This lavender is better for craft than cooking. Hang the stalks in bunches in a shady, airy place to dry. When they're really dry, store the flowers and leaves in airtight, labelled containers.

herbes de provence

Add herbes de Provence to casseroles or cassoulet, allowing about 1 tablespoon per kilo of meat.

4 teaspoons dried thyme

2 teaspoons each dried marjoram and parsley

1 teaspoon dried tarragon

2/3 teaspoon dried lavender flowers

1/2 teaspoon celery seeds

1 bay leaf, crushed

Combine all the ingredients and store in an airtight container.

Makes about 1/4 cup

lavender ice-cream

2 tablespoons white dessert wine

2 tablespoons finely chopped fresh lavender leaves

500 ml thick cream

100 g caster sugar

2 egg whites

2 tablespoons fresh or dried lavender flowers

Warm the wine gently and infuse the leaves for 15–20 minutes. Strain and discard the leaves. Beat the cream until stiff and gradually mix in the wine and half the sugar. Whisk the egg whites until stiff, and whisk in the remaining sugar. Fold the meringue mixture into the cream with the lavender flowers. Spoon into a container and freeze, or use an ice-cream maker if you have one.

Serves 4

lavender potpourri

This potpourri is perfect for scented sachets or coathangers, or left in an open bowl to freshen the room. After about 6 months, gently stir through a few more drops of lavender oil with your fingers.

1 cup dried English lavender flowers

½ cup dried marjoram leaves

½ cup dried rose petals

1 tablespoon dried mint

1 tablespoon orris root powder

2 teaspoons ground coriander seed

½ teaspoon ground cloves

a few drops lavender oil

Mix the flowers and leaves together. Blend the orris root powder, coriander and cloves, then stir in the lavender oil and add to the dried ingredients. Stir well to combine.

if lavender is the queen of herbs, sweet cicely is surely the princess . . .

Sweet cicely (*Myrrhis odorata*), one of the tall, stately herbs – reaching 60–150 cm in the right position – is covered with a froth of white flower umbels in the spring, much to the delight of the bee population. This charming plant has ferny foliage with a sweet, warm, anise taste and thick, hollow and branching stems, similar to those of angelica. It has also been called fern-leaved chervil or giant sweet chervil, although it is a much bigger plant in every way than the real chervil. Most parts of sweet cicely are edible. The leaves, green seeds and stems can be chopped and used in all kinds of salads. The hollow stems may also be candied like angelica. The finely chopped leaves are excellent to use when cooking sharp fruit like rhubarb to counteract acidity, and, although not as sweet as stevia, the leaves will bring a natural sweetness to cooling summer drinks.

lemongrass

Cymbopogon citratus

Lemongrass is a great multiplier, growing
in bushy clumps about 90 cm tall that
increase in girth with each passing year.
Its long, narrow, lemon-scented
leaves bend gracefully outwards
and have a slightly sticky
texture. Watch out, the
edges are razor sharp.

Also called serai, citronella, camel's hay
Flavour and aroma lemony, grassy
Flavour group strong

Usually a pale yellowish-green, at certain times of the year the leaves are rust coloured at the tips. The bulbous lower stem is an essential ingredient in South-East Asian cooking where it is used whole or finely sliced in curries, soups, salads and Thai curry pastes.

One reason it is so popular in Asian recipes is that the stem is packed with citral, the substance found in the outer rind of lemons – lemons themselves don't grow well in the tropics. Lemongrass is delicious with steamed seafood and poultry dishes, marinades for pork, and whole fish barbecued in foil.

The leaves aren't often used in cooking, but try snipping a few fresh pieces of leaf into a pot of tea for a refreshing, lemony flavour, or adding to the water when poaching fish or chicken.

choosing and using

Lemongrass is a very fibrous plant so there are some tricks of the trade to using it. Peel away the tough, outer layers and finely slice the pale lower stem crosswise so that there are no long fibres to spoil the texture of your finished dish. The electric blender comes to the rescue if you need to pound or grind the sliced stem to make a paste. Tie a couple of complete stems into a knot, bruise lightly with a rolling pin, and drop it whole into soups or sauces, so that it is easy to lift out before serving.

If you are buying lemongrass, avoid dry stems and pick out ones that are firm and white, with the slightest hint of a greenish tinge. Excess stems can be bruised and used whole or cut into slices. Wrap in plastic and store in the freezer for up to six months. Our old friend Bernard King freezes the stalks, then uses kitchen scissors to snip lengthways at one end to make a little brush. He then uses this to brush his marinade over barbecued chicken and fish.

growing

In temperate zones, perennial lemongrass will grow easily year round. However it does not like dry conditions (remember, it is from the tropics), and flourishes best in rich, moist soil in a sheltered position in the garden where it can bask in morning sun. If your winters are cold and frosty, lift the plants in mid-autumn, pot them using a good soil mixture and keep indoors until spring, when you can plant them back into the garden.

Lemongrass grows to about a metre high. If your clump is losing its attractive, bushy appearance and becoming too spindly and straggly, cut about 15 cm off the tops of the leaves. Frequent cutting is good for the plant, so chop away and use it with gay abandon in your cooking.

In spring, the old leaves should be cut down to where the new shoots are appearing, then divide the roots by digging well down into the ground with a spade, cutting cleanly through the main bush and taking as many clumps as you can without damaging the parent plant. Put the new shoots into prepared ground immediately, firm down the soil and water well. In mild areas the clump may be cut through and divided in the same way at any time of the year. In autumn, when the grassy clump is thick and green, cut the leaves back to within a couple of inches of the base.

drying

Dry leaves by hanging them in bunches in a shady, airy place, or spreading them out on racks or on clean newspaper. As the leaves are full of etheric oils, they will dry quickly. Cut them with scissors into short lengths and put into clean, dry, airtight containers.

vietnamese chicken with lemongrass

Lemongrass lends its own special character to many dishes, however we couldn't go past one of our all-time favourites from Charmaine Solomon's *The Complete Asian Cookbook* (New Holland, 2002).

1 small roasting chicken, about 1 kg

3 or 4 stalks lemongrass

3 spring onions

1 teaspoon salt

¼ teaspoon black pepper, plus extra to taste

2 tablespoons oil

1 or 2 fresh red chillies, seeded and chopped

2 teaspoons sugar

½ cup roasted peanuts, finely chopped

2 tablespoons fish sauce

Cut chicken into small serving pieces, Chinese style, chopping through bones with a cleaver. Remove the outer leaves of lemongrass and finely slice the tender white part at the base of the stalks. Bruise with mortar and pestle. Finely slice the spring onions, including the green leaves. Mix the chicken with the salt, pepper, lemongrass and spring onions and set aside for 30 minutes.

Heat a wok, add oil and when oil is hot add chicken mixture and stir-fry for 3 minutes. Add the chillies and stir-fry on medium heat for a further 10 minutes or until the chicken no longer looks pink. Season with sugar and extra black pepper and add the peanuts. Stir well. Add the fish sauce and toss to distribute evenly, then serve with rice or noodles.

Serves 4

lemon myrtle

Backhousia citriodora

Lemon myrtle is probably the best known and most loved of the Australian native plants that have been accepted as herbs and spices.
As the name suggests, the flavour of the leaves is intensely lemony, with suggestions of lemon verbena, lime and lemongrass.

Also called sweet verbena tree
Flavour and aroma intensely lemony and fragrant
Flavour group strong

choosing and using

Like many other native herbs, the flavour of the leaves can be lost in long cooking, so it's best to use them in an infusion where they can be lifted out, like bay leaves. For example, warm the leaves with milk for a custard or ice-cream – the heat will be sufficient to release the flavour but not destroy the volatile oils responsible for the flavour.

Lemon myrtle complements chicken, vegetable and seafood stir-fries and is a good substitute for lemongrass. Try sprinkling a little on meat, chicken or fish before grilling or barbecuing. And if you have a sore throat, it makes a deliciously soothing lemony tea.

If you have a tree, pick the more intensely flavoured darker, mature leaves as you need them. You can sometimes buy fresh leaves from specialty Australian native foods suppliers; however dried whole or powdered leaves, which have a more intense flavour than the fresh, are usually readily available from gourmet herb and spice outlets. Because lemon myrtle's essential oil is so volatile, it's best to buy in small quantities – say 10 g at a time.

The history of this herb is proudly Australian, though there are now plantations in many other parts of the world, and they are growing trees for oil extraction in parts of southern Asia. Lemon myrtle's citral content – the component identified as the lemon flavour – is about 90 per cent; compared with around 80 per cent in lemongrass and only 6 per cent in lemons. So it's understandable that the food industry is interested in harvesting this intense flavour (without any citrus acidity) for food manufacture and processing in products ranging from yoghurt and ice-cream, to biscuits and breads, and sauces and syrups.

growing

Lemon myrtle reaches about 20 m in its native Queensland rainforests, and about 8 m in more southern, frost-free areas. Because of its rather shrubby shape, it makes a very ornamental native addition to the garden, and is especially useful for filling up a corner or hiding a wall.

Trees are readily available from native plant nurseries in Australia. When not influenced by us humans, they propagate from seed; but we are impatient by nature and have found that cuttings strike quite easily. Take cuttings about 20 cm long from branches with a pencil-sized diameter, trimming the leaves from the lower end. Plant the cuttings about 7.5–10 cm deep in good river sand or potting mixture in a pot with a top diameter of about 10 cm. Keep watered until you can see roots appearing in the drainage holes in the pot, then transfer to a larger pot. Let it grow on in a bucket-sized pot in a sunny spot until it's about 50 cm tall and the roots are well established.

Now's the time to plant your lemon myrtle in its permanent spot in the garden in deep rich soil. Once established, it is quite hardy and will be happy so long as it gets at least 2–3 hours sun a day.

drying

Choose mature leaves as they have more flavour than the young ones. In addition, if you pick the young leaves, the tree won't look as lovely in the garden and will have nothing left to grow to maturity. Dry the leaves on a rack in a cool, airy, dark place, and store in an airtight, labelled container for later use.

tuna steaks with lemon myrtle

This mixture of lemon myrtle and salt can also be rubbed over the skin of a chicken before roasting. When a few extra lemon myrtle leaves are stuffed into the cavity with a wedge of lemon and a couple of cloves of garlic, the smell is heavenly.

$\frac{1}{2}$ teaspoon ground dried lemon myrtle, or 2 fresh leaves, shredded finely
$\frac{1}{2}$ teaspoon flaky salt
2 pieces of boneless tuna
a good-quality olive oil spray

Mix the lemon myrtle and salt together, and rub over both sides of the tuna. Spray the tuna lightly with olive oil and leave to stand for about 10 minutes. Heat a heavy-based pan, spray with oil, and cook the tuna for 2–3 minutes on each side, or a little longer if you like your fish well done. Serve immediately.

Serves 2

lemon verbena

Aloysia triphylla (formerly *lippia citriodora*)

The fragrance of lemon verbena always reminds me of our early married years and the countless sleep pillows I made using dried lemon verbena for sweet dreams, lavender for sound sleep and rose petals to wake refreshed.

Also called lemon-scented verbena
Flavour and aroma lightly perfumed, lemon flavour with no acidity
Flavour group strong

There was a double row of these small deciduous trees growing in the Somerset Cottage herb garden, and in summer, the pale, hazy pinky-mauve flowerets clustered in scented plumes at the tips of their leafy branches.

During spring, summer, and autumn, lemon verbena is covered profusely with pointed leaves of light green, about 10 cm long, with a slightly sticky feel owing to their rich oil-bearing properties. I used to pick boxes and boxes of the long branches, preferably without flowers, and strip the leaves from them until my fingers were stained green. Their perfume is strong and easily released, even by merely brushing past the foliage, which immediately fills the air with a delicious lemony fragrance.

choosing and using

A traditional use for lemon verbena leaves was to float them in finger bowls at banquets. In a more domestic setting, however, two or three fresh lemon verbena leaves placed on top of a rice pudding or baked custard before it goes into the oven impart a delicate flavour. In the same manner, a few leaves arranged on the bottom of a buttered cake tin before the mixture is spooned in, release their aromatic oils while the cake is baking; they can be peeled off when the cake has cooled. This is particularly delicious with chocolate cakes.

Ever the experimenter, I once thought to use lemon verbena-infused rainwater for my iron, imagining the divine scent it would impart – it didn't work, proving that even with something so strongly aromatic, there are limits.

Because the dried leaves retain their flavour so effectively, lemon verbena is a must in the mix for potpourri and many fragrant gifts. The fresh leaves can also be added whole to Asian clear soups and stocks in the same way as lemon myrtle. Treat them like bay leaves and remove them after cooking. However, if you want to use fresh lemon verbena leaves, you'll probably have to grow your own tree. The leaves are rarely available fresh; and dried you are more likely to come across them inside fragrant gifts in craft shops or blended with herbal tea mixes.

growing

Plant your lemon verbena tree in a sheltered, sunny position where the soil is medium to light and well drained. During hot summers, mulch the roots with leaf mould or grass cuttings and water well; later, the roots will also need mulching to protect them from frost. When the tree is about three years old, you need to prune it, either in autumn or early winter, otherwise it will get too leggy. When it's pruned regularly, the tree will reward you by growing thicker and taller every year, to an eventual height of about 2 m.

Young trees are readily available from major garden nurseries. You can also propagate from hardwood cuttings in late winter. Divide the wood into 15 cm pieces, trim off any side shoots, and press each piece into a deep pot of river sand, leaving one-third of the wood exposed at the top, and water well. When the cuttings have made strong roots, plant them out into the garden. Tip cuttings are taken in late spring to early summer; trim the stems of foliage, allowing several leaves to remain at the top, then insert into the sand and continue in the same way as described for hardwood propagation.

For harvesting the leaves, cut the branches before midday, particularly during the vigorous growing seasons of summer and early autumn. Flowers on the boughs are an excellent addition with the leaves to potpourri.

Remember, lemon verbena is a deciduous tree, so as winter approaches the leaves will begin to turn yellow and fall, until, by mid-winter, the branches are quite bare.

drying

You can dry the leaves quickly and easily by tying cut branches together and hanging them in a cool, shady, airy place. When they're dry, strip off all the foliage and store in airtight containers. However, there are hazards in this method, as you'll also strip the skin from your fingers on the brittle leaf-stems.

By stripping the fresh green leaves from the branches before drying, you're rewarded with a luscious pile of fragrant foliage that can be spread out on sheets of newspaper, or better still, onto fly-screens raised up on a few bricks. I used to wish I could dive into them the way Scrooge McDuck dived into his money bin! The dried leaves should be dark-green, crisp and lemon scented. They should not smell musty.

fresh and zingy chicken broth

1 chicken carcass (available from poultry shops and some
    delicatessens) or 1 chicken with legs, wings and
    breast removed

1 onion, peeled and quartered

3 cm fresh ginger, peeled and finely chopped

2 cloves garlic, finely chopped

1/2 teaspoon ground nutmeg

juice and grated zest of 1 lemon

1 carrot, scraped and chopped

3 cups water

a sprig of Vietnamese mint (about 12 leaves)

a sprig of lemon verbena (about 20 fresh leaves, or
    12 dried leaves)

salt and pepper to taste

Place all the ingredients in a large saucepan and bring to the boil. Cover, reduce the heat, and simmer very gently for 45 minutes, or until the chicken flesh falls from the bones. The longer and slower the cooking, the more flavour you will extract from the chicken bones. For the last 5 minutes of the cooking time, remove the lid and increase the heat so that the stock reduces a little. Remove the carcass and bones and skim off leaves before serving the broth with its delicious vegetables and aromatics.

Serves 2–3

lovage

Levisticum officinale

Lovage looks rather like a sparse version of angelica, although it does not grow as tall or as densely and has smaller, sulphur-yellow flowers borne in delicate umbels rather than great round heads. The slim stems bear flat, serrated, dark, green leaves in threes branching out from thicker, channelled stalks.

Also called Cornish lovage, Italian lovage, old English lovage
Flavour and aroma slightly peppery, yeasty
Flavour group mild

You could almost say, in a Russian-doll kind of way, that Italian parsley is a small version of lovage, which in turn is a small version of angelica. The flavour of the leaves is a combination of celery and parsley, but predominantly celery, with an extra peppery bite. When they're young, the plants also look like a rather obscure herb called smallage, said to be the forerunner of our modern celery.

People on a salt-free diet like lovage for its spicy peppery taste, and since we opened Herbie's Spices, we've often had customers looking for this herb for medieval-style banquets.

choosing and using

The fresh leaves are really excellent in soups and stocks, and they complement omelettes, scrambled eggs and mashed potato, just chopped and sprinkled on top. Chop the leaves finely for best results, as they are a little coarse. The hollow stalks and stems can be preserved as a confection in the same way as angelica.

The popularity of peppery lovage leaves has waned since its medieval heyday, which is why you won't find it in fruit and vegetable retailers. If you want it you'll probably have to grow it. Pick and use the leaves fresh throughout the spring and summer or freeze for when you need them by the ice-cube method. Whole leaf sprays may be stored for several weeks in the freezer by sealing them in foil.

Stems can be cut and used at any time. If you're candying them like angelica stems, the flavour is best just after flowering.

growing

Like angelica, perennial lovage likes rich, moist soil and a rather shady spot to grow well. Plant seedlings or sow seeds in the spring, directly into the garden about 50 cm apart, or directly into a suitable container (but remember that lovage grows about a metre tall). If you sow seeds in a seed box, plant them out when your seedlings are about 7.5 cm high. Keep them watered well in dry weather – they don't like dry roots. The summer flowers produce oblong brownish seeds, which you can harvest for future planting just before they start to fall, by snipping off and drying the whole flower heads. Sift out any dried husks and stalks and store the seed in airtight containers.

drying

Lovage leaves are dried in the same way as parsley. Spread the leaves out on sheets of clean paper or on mesh in a shady, warm place where the air can circulate until they are dry – it should take a few days. When they are brittle, crumble them into airtight containers.

lovage, carrot and chicory salad

1 tablespoon finely chopped lovage leaves

1 large carrot, shredded into long curls using
    a potato peeler

1 firm unpeeled pear, shredded into thin strips
    using a potato peeler

12 chicory leaves, crisped in cold
    water and drained

3 tablespoons plain yoghurt

1 tablespoon mayonnaise

a squeeze of lemon juice

Toss the lovage, carrot and pear together and pile into the individual chicory leaves. Whisk the yoghurt, mayonnaise and lemon juice together and drizzle over the salad scoops.

Serves 4–6 as an accompaniment

marjoram and

marjoram, sweet marjoram *Origanum marjorana*

oregano

O. vulgare

pot marjoram, greek oregano or rigani *O. onites*

golden oregano *O. vulgare 'Aureum'*

These two perennials are so closely related and their use in the kitchen is so similar that it is useful to discuss them together.

Also called oregano: wild marjoram; marjoram:
knotted marjoram, pot marjoram
Flavour and aroma grassy, thyme-like, peppery
Flavour group strong/pungent

In addition, while fresh marjoram and oregano are delicious with salads and mild flavoured foods, both have the best taste and greatest pungency when they are dried.

Like siblings, the differences between the two are subtle when they are young, and you can tell them apart more easily once they begin to mature. Sweet marjoram is a reasonably compact, shrubby perennial growing to about 45 cm tall, with grey-green leaves that are small and soft. Its mildly savoury, almost grassy aroma is reminiscent of thyme.

Oregano is the assertive, older child; a bold, robust and densely spreading plant, thriving in most climates and growing to about 60 cm. It has rounder leaves that are covered by a down of fine hairs and a more piercing, almost peppery flavour. Both sweet marjoram and oregano have small, white flowers that form tight clusters at the tips of their stems – in Greece and Italy it is these very pungent dried flower tops that are mainly used in cooking.

choosing and using

You could safely add oregano to 90 per cent of Mediterranean recipes, as it relates perfectly to the food of that area. Therefore you'll find it in pasta and rice dishes, on pizza, in moussaka, avocado dip, tomato dishes, and with zucchini, capsicums, and eggplant. Greek oregano is usually sold in dried bunches packed in cellophane bags and is the most of pungent of all dried oregano, although the Australian-grown leaves have a similar intensity of flavour.

Oregano has even more potent qualities. It's a star on the antioxidant scene, ranking higher than even fruits and vegetables. The US Department of Agriculture says: 'Oregano has 42 times more antioxidant activity than apples, 30 times more than potatoes, 12 times more than oranges, and 4 times more than blueberries. For example 1 tablespoon of fresh oregano contains the same antioxidant activity as one medium-sized apple.' So eat up!

Dried marjoram is a classic ingredient in herb mixes such as bouquet garni and herbes de Provence. Its subtle aroma makes it an ideal companion as it helps give body and depth but never dominates. Try it on its own with lightly cooked fish and vegetables, scrambled eggs, omelettes, savoury scones, dumplings and clear soups. The fresh leaves have some of oregano's pungency, and add an assertive quality to herb sandwiches and potato salad.

Fresh marjoram and oregano are readily available from fruit and vegetable retailers and in the fresh herb section of supermarkets. Sometimes they are prepacked in airtight containers and will keep well in these in the refrigerator for a week or more. If you buy loose bunches, put the stems in a glass of water to keep them fresh. Sprays of fresh marjoram or oregano can be wrapped in foil, sealed and kept in the freezer for some weeks. Or you can chop fresh leaves finely, mix them with a little water, and put them into ice-cube trays in the freezer.

growing

In your local garden nursery, you'll find variations of oregano and marjoram available as seeds and seedlings. Oregano is usually more piercing in scent, although sometimes it's hard to tell them apart – a puny oregano may resemble a healthy marjoram.

Oregano and marjoram will grow easily from cuttings. Take new shoots about 7.5 cm long in late spring, when the young leaves have firmed enough not to wilt when placed in a pot of coarse river sand. Once they're well rooted, they can be planted out in pots, or put straight into the ground, leaving at least 30 cm between them. It's also possible to grow them from seeds, although of course it's much slower. Sow the seeds in a seed box or pot in spring and plant them out into a sunny spot in the garden in well-drained soil when the seedlings are 7.5 cm high.

Both marjoram and oregano should be harvested just before the plants are in full flower in the summer or early autumn. Both have a tendency to become woody as they get older, so to delay this as long as possible, it's a good idea to cut out the old wood at the end of winter before the new spring growth appears. You can be fairly ruthless with this and the plants will thank you with strong new growth. After about four years, the plants often become so woody that it is best to replace them.

drying

Cut the long stems, together with any flower heads, and hang them in bunches in a cool, airy place. The leaves tend to fall as they dry, so it is a good idea to enclose bunches in mosquito net, muslin, or a big paper bag with holes in it. When the leaves and flowers are crisp-dry, crumble them between your thumb and fingers to remove them from the stem. Store in airtight containers and they will keep their pungent flavour for months.

herbed roast potatoes

1 tablespoon virgin olive oil

2 large potatoes, peeled and cut into approximately
    2 cm cubes

2 good sprigs fresh marjoram, about 25 leaves,
    finely chopped

1 clove garlic, finely chopped

 salt flakes, to taste

Preheat oven to 180ºC. Spread the oil into a shallow ovenproof dish or baking tray. Using paper towel or a clean tea towel, remove excess moisture from the cubed potatoes. Spread them out in a single layer in the baking dish, sprinkle with the herbs and garlic, and bake in the hot oven for about 30 minutes. During that time, turn them once or twice so that all the edges are crisp and golden. Sprinkle with a good pinch of salt before serving.

Serves 2–3 as an accompaniment

lamb roast rub

The sumac tree produces crimson berries that are dried and pulverised to make a spicy powder. Its flavour complements tomatoes and avocado so well that we hardly ever eat them these days without sumac. In the Middle East it is widely used instead of vinegar or lemon juice as a souring agent sprinkled over kebabs just before cooking. And it is simply delicious combined with oregano on roasted meats.

1 tablespoon sweet paprika

1 teaspoon sumac

1 teaspoon dried oregano

¼ teaspoon ground black pepper

½ teaspoon salt

2 cloves garlic, peeled and crushed

Combine all the ingredients and rub well all over a leg or shoulder of lamb before roasting, for a full-bodied flavour and mouth-watering crust.

Makes enough for that lamb roast

mexican oregano

At least two different kinds of plants are known as Mexican oregano – *Poliomentha longiflora* and *Lippia graveolens*. Neither is a true oregano. Mexican oregano is essential in *pozole*, a pork and hominy stew.

five-minute pizza

2 rounds pita bread

2 tablespoons tomato paste

1 teaspoon dried oregano

1 teaspoon dried marjoram

toppings to taste – try chopped cooked chicken, ham, capsicum, mushrooms, onions, peeled prawns or whatever you fancy

grated mozzarella cheese

Preheat the grill to a moderate temperature, about 180ºC. Spread the pita breads with a generous layer of tomato paste and sprinkle over the dried herbs. Decorate the pizza base with whatever toppings you have on hand, and top with the grated cheese. Place the pizzas under the grill for 3–4 minutes, until the cheese is bubbling and browning in patches, by which time the pizza will be heated through. Serve immediately.

Makes 2

mint

spearmint or English spearmint *Mentha spicata*

common or Moroccan spearmint *M. spicata 'Moroccan'*

applemint *M. rotundifolia*

Can anyone imagine a world without mint?
A world with no mint sauce with the roast
lamb, no fresh and minty-tasting toothpaste,
no spearmint chewing gum, no after-dinner
mints, and worst of all,
no Minties for long
car trips!

Also called sage of Bethlehem
Flavour and aroma fresh, clean, bright, almost peppery
Flavour group strong

Mint crops up wherever there's an aroma issue – as breath fresheners, in toothpastes, chewing gums, mouthwashes, and even toilet cleaners. It's not a modern discovery, though – the Romans introduced the versatile mint family to Europe, where the leaves were initially used as an air freshener and insect repellent.

There are numerous varieties of mint, all with quite different flavours and scents even though they may look alike. One of the reasons for the diversity is that mints have a tendency to hybridise with each other, which is why the list of mint varieties continues to grow. Sometimes, as well as the flavour and aroma variations, there can be plain and variegated versions of the same thing.

Spearmint stands out from the crowd in the culinary department, followed closely by apple and ginger mints; their names describe the flavours and aromas.

Peppermint, which has a high menthol content and produces the true oil of peppermint, is mostly used medicinally and for herbal teas, but is not a regular in the kitchen due to a rather overpowering antiseptic character. It's useful for candy making, however.

Brush past **eau de cologne mint** in the garden and delight in the delicious fragrance that causes this decorative herb to find its way into potpourri. Its flowers are larger than most in the mint family and a deep shade of mauve, making them a pretty addition to mixed posies.

Pennyroyal with its creeping habit makes great ground cover in a shady part of the garden. While it's great as a flea-deterrent, it's definitely not for eating.

Vietnamese mint is not a mint at all, it's a Polygonum (see page 337).

It is spearmint, either fresh or dried, that gives flavour to mint sauce, as well as to mint jelly and mint julep. Chopped mint goes with hot, buttered peas the way tomato sauce goes with sausages, and gives a bright lift to new potatoes, and tomatoes too. A few fresh leaves on buttered bread with cream cheese make delicious sandwiches. Mint is a versatile herb, as much at home with ice-cream, sorbet and cheesecake as it is with roast or minced lamb and Middle Eastern salads.

choosing and using
Spearmint is an absolutely indispensable ingredient throughout the Middle East and Mediterranean, where it is used either fresh or dried. It gives its distinct aroma and taste to meat and vegetable dishes, to tabbouli, to yoghurt sauces, to soups and to salads. In Morocco, where mint is known as *naa naa*, spearmint is used to make mint tea, said to be the nation's most popular beverage. Mint is also used in tagines and kefta (ground meat grilled on skewers or made into a meatball stew). Dried or fresh leaves are used in the making of koftas and kebabs in India, as well as a cooling yoghurt raita.

Several types of mint are used in Thailand (where it is called *saranay*) and in Vietnam as a salad, a garnish and an ingredient of certain curry pastes.

Applemint, as the name suggests, has a strong scent of apples. You can mix the chopped leaves into fruit salads and fruit jellies, or include them in the batter for Asian-style deep-fried bananas.

Fresh spearmint is the one that's readily available from fruit and vegetable retailers and the fresh herb section of supermarkets. Opt for the smooth narrow-leaved English variety that has a better flavour for cooking if you have the choice. To keep it fresh, stand the bunch in a glass of water in the refrigerator. If you change the water every few days it will keep for a couple of weeks. You can freeze it using the ice-block method, and sprays of fresh mint may be wrapped in foil, sealed, and kept in the freezer for some weeks.

Spearmint butter can also be frozen and is delicious with lamb. Chop the fresh leaves, pound them into softened butter, allow to set in the refrigerator, then cut into squares and seal into small polythene bags or other suitable containers.

growing

English spearmint has elongated, smooth, bright green leaves, and the same pungent, warm flavour and aroma as its twin, common or garden or Moroccan spearmint, which has oval-shaped, crinkly, dark green leaves. Both are ideal for adding the finishing touch to the lamb roast. And both like a moist position in the garden or in a large tub under a dripping tap.

English spearmint is more difficult to grow than the crinkly-leafed variety. While the scent and flavour of English mint is clearer and stronger and its leaves have a finer texture, it is rather too susceptible to leaf-eating insects and thus something of a heartbreaker for the gardener.

Applemint grows approximately 30 cm high, with oval, wrinkled, soft leaves and small white flowers that appear in autumn. Sometimes this variety is called pineapple mint.

This perennial herb has an overactive root system, and will completely take over your garden if you let it, so it is probably better off kept in control in a tub. Unlike many herbs, mint prefers a shady damp position. The shadier and damper the better it will thrive. If you want to plant it in the garden, put it into a 25 or 30 cm plastic pot with the bottom cut out, and plant the entire pot. The pot will act as a barrier, preventing the runners spreading under the surface – at least, that's the theory – but sooner or later it will take over. Perhaps it's a good short-term method, if you're planning on selling your house within the next 12 months!

Propagate mint by root division, as even the smallest piece stuck in the ground will grow. Short stem cuttings taken after the new growth has hardened in late spring can be put straight into the ground, too, and roots will quickly form. It will grow from seed, but it's really never necessary to use this method.

Mint thrives in rich, moist soil, in semi-shade, but will also grow in poor, sandy soil if the ground is fertilised from time to time. Cut plants back to ground level in winter.

If your mint is attacked by rust, there's nothing for it but to dig out the plants, dispose of them and start afresh with new stock in a different part of the garden, or clean out the container and completely change the soil.

drying

Mint is easily dried. Cut the leafy stems just before they come into full flower and hang them in bunches in a dry, airy place. Make sure that when the crisp, dried leaves are stripped from their stalks they are kept in airtight containers, as this herb does not keep its full aroma and flavour if exposed to the air for long.

It's possible to dry mint in the microwave by placing the leaves in a single layer on a sheet of paper towel and 'cooking' on high for 20-second bursts, checking for crispness after each burst. As the leaves become dry to the touch, remove them, zapping only the remaining leaves until they too are dry. Stand a half a cup of water in your microwave with the leaves to prevent damaging the magnetron.

cool, refreshing minty drinks

Mint is a great flavour to add to summer coolers and frappés combining well with all sorts of fruits and vegetables including berries, melons, pineapple, apples and pears. To make a minty watermelon and blueberry cooler, blend about 400 g peeled and chopped seedless watermelon with ¼ cup of blueberries, some ice-cubes and 2 or 3 mint leaves (more if you love the tang) until smooth. Serve with extra ice.

warm minted lamb and tomato salad

Inspired by Fiona Hammond's recipe for Lebanese Rolls with Minted Lamb and Tomato (*Good Food*, Text Publishing, 1998), this salad makes a refreshing light meal year round. The lamb fillets can be grilled or barbecued – we usually barbecue them. You can make it meatier or mintier, depending on the flavour you favour.

2 lamb fillets, each about 200 g

extra virgin olive oil

1 bunch fresh mint (the smooth narrow-leaved variety), leaves picked off the stems (use 2 if you really love that minty flavour)

1 punnet ripe baby tomatoes, halved

1 Lebanese cucumber, sliced

juice of 1 lemon

salt and ground black pepper to taste

To Serve

hummus

black olives

pita bread

Brush the lamb fillets with olive oil and cook them on the barbecue or under a preheated grill for about 3–4 minutes a side, or longer if you like your lamb well done. Remove from the heat, wrap each fillet separately in foil and set them aside to rest for 10–15 minutes. This is very important as it makes the fillets easier to slice thinly across the grain. After resting, slice each lamb fillet and place in a serving bowl with the torn mint leaves, tomato halves and cucumber slices. Toss the salad with a little lemon juice and salt and pepper to taste. Serve with hummus, black olives and pita bread.

Serves 4

mitsuba

Cryptotaenia japonica

One of Japan's most widely used herbs, mitsuba, brings a tasty, aromatic flavour, not dissimilar to parsley, to clear soups, tempura, simmered dishes (nabemono) and steamed egg dishes such as the delicate custard known as chawan mushi. Traditionally it has always been grown as an early spring herb, but these days you can find it all year round in Japanese stores in the refrigerator section.

Also called Japanese parsley, Japanese trefoil, trefoil

Flavour and aroma parsley-like, tasty

Flavour group medium

choosing and using

Mitsuba is usually lightly blanched or added fresh at the last minute to retain its flavour. The fresh leaves and blanched leaf stalks are also eaten in salads and sandwiches. Mitsuba is popular in Japan as a garnish: sometimes a few stems are tied into a knot close to the leaves, and the long ends trimmed off with a knife.

growing

Mitsuba has slim, sappy, dark green stems with three slightly serrated leaves on each. Its tiny star-shaped flowers quickly turn to seed. Related to the parsley family, it is also known as Japanese parsley, Japanese trefoil, trefoil and honewort.

Mitsuba is one of the few culinary herbs that thrives in both sunny and shady spots. In the right conditions, it grows to about 90 cm in an upright, dense, spreading mound. For best results, plant seeds or seedlings in the spring in moist, rich soil in the garden. Keep watered and feed occasionally. For a continuous supply of fresh, young leaves, sow every six weeks thinning out seedlings to about 25 cm apart.

Propagate by seed or root division.

mitsuba and tofu in clear soup

With thanks to food writer and chef, Hideo Dekura. Enjoy this very simple, very beautiful and very Japanese recipe. Serve with a deep bow.

4 squares of momen-dofu (hard tofu), each around
    3 x 3 cm

8 mitsuba stems with leaves (use 4 leaves for
    making the stock)

Snapper Stock

300 g snapper bones or head

1 teaspoon sea salt

6 cups water

4 mitsuba leaves, torn in half

1 tablespoon Japanese soy sauce

1 tablespoon mirin

50 g fresh ginger, grated and squeezed to
    make ginger juice

To make clear snapper stock, sprinkle the snapper all over with salt and refrigerate for 20 minutes. Bring water to the boil in a large pan and add the fish and 4 of the mitsuba leaves, torn in half. Simmer gently for 30 minutes then strain through a fine sieve into another pot to make clear stock. Discard the bones.

Add soy sauce and mirin to the snapper stock and simmer for around 5 minutes. Remove from the heat and add the ginger juice.

Heat the tofu pieces gently in warm water. Place one in each serving bowl and pour over the clear soup. Garnish each bowl with the remaining mitsuba leaves.

Serves 4

mustard greens

black mustard *Brassica nigra*

brown or Indian mustard *B. juncea*

white or yellow mustard *B. alba*

Mustard has been around
since Adam was a boy –
or at least, since Alexander
the Great was a boy.

Also called mizuna
Flavour and aroma pungent, peppery, strong and biting
Flavour group hot

In ancient times, 'eat your greens' meant tucking into mustard leaves and if you were feeling poorly, your physician might very well prescribe a dose of mustard seeds. Moving forward a couple of millennia, they are still very much around.

Mustard seeds that are sprouted with cress in punnets for making mustard and cress sandwiches are the same ripened seeds that are collected for grinding to make the smooth or grainy mustards that add bite to beef. There are three types – black, brown and yellow (or white) – but the most popular for mustard greens and sprouts are the black and brown varieties.

choosing and using

Bright green mustard leaves have a pungent, peppery flavour and can be steamed, sautéed or simmered or added to salads where they make a sharp, tangy contrast to other salad greens.

Our ancestors may have been partial to the strong, biting flavour of the steamed leaves on their own, but for a piquant taste with wider appeal add a few leaves at the last minute when cooking spinach. You can also throw in a few leaves when you're making any kind of vegetable stock or soup. If you are growing your own mustard greens, simply pick the leaves as required.

To add a touch of colour to salads, opt for the variety known as 'Red Giant' with its reddish purple leaf that you can pick year round.

The Japanese mizuna (*B. juncea 'Japonica'*) has elegant, slender leaves, lazily serrated, with a sweet, fresh flavour – absolutely perfect for salads.

growing

Black mustard is a tall, upright annual growing to 2–3 m with branching stalks that bear smooth, bright green, pointed leaves with notched edges.

Brown mustard grows to about the same height, though its large oval leaves are not as pungent. They bear small yellow flowers, bunched tightly together, throughout summer, and it's from these that the seed-bearing pods evolve.

Yellow or white mustard seeds grow the same way, but the leaves are less inspiring for culinary use.

Mustard germinates quickly and has green shoots within a week of sowing. Sow seeds in the spring, 30 cm apart in a sunny, open position. To grow enough to harvest your own seed crop, just scatter the seeds over your garden plot. You'll need to plant a few crops throughout the year if you want leaves to pick year round.

Mustard is often planted for its alkaline properties, which will counteract too much acid in the soil. The crop is also good for ground that has been damaged after too much mineral fertiliser, but continual planting depletes the soil. If you're addicted to those tasty leaves, move your crop around to rest the soil.

drying seeds

For harvesting the seeds, wait for the pods to swell, then pick them and allow them to dry out. Remove the seeds, and if necessary dry them further before storing in clean, dry, airtight, labelled containers.

sprouting

The important rule for sprouting is to not allow the seeds to dry out, while at the same time, not drowning them. You can grow mustard and cress on wet blotting paper, or in a glass jar with a piece of gauze, stocking or light fabric stretched across the opening and held in place by a strong rubber band. Run some water into the jar, swill around to wet the seeds, then drain it off, placing the jar on its side. Repeat this twice a day as the seeds sprout, and when the jar is full of delicious, succulent, living morsels, empty it out and start again.

summer salad greens with creamy mustard dressing

2 cups mixed salad greens, including oakleaf lettuce, sorrel, mizuna, young mustard greens, cress, rocket, salad burnet, chives, basil and chervil
160 ml plain yoghurt
1½ tablespoons white wine vinegar
2 teaspoons grainy French mustard

Rinse the salad greens and pat dry in a clean tea towel. Arrange on a platter, with the lettuce on the base and the smaller herbs on the top. Whisk the yoghurt, vinegar and mustard together, and drizzle over the salad just before serving.

Serves 2 as an accompaniment

myrtle

Myrtus communis

This true myrtle is no relation to crepe myrtle or lemon myrtle. It is a dense, evergreen shrub whose small, glossy, oval leaves have a sweet, spicy orange fragrance. For centuries, shepherds in Mediterranean countries have made fires from myrtle wood to flavour roasted meats and game birds.

Also called sweet myrtle, Corsican pepper
Flavour and aroma leaves bitter and astringent,
berries have juniper and rosemary notes, flowers
resinous and sweet
Flavour group strong

If you have myrtle growing in your garden, try placing a handful of fresh, young leaves under pork or lamb for the last 10 minutes of cooking time in the oven or on the barbecue. Or stuff a few fresh leaves inside roast pork while the meat rests before your carve it. Dried, the fragrant leaves and flowers are popular for making potpourri, sweet bags and herb pillows.

Top green salads or fruit salads with myrtle buds or the starry white flowers, or use them as a garnish for desserts, although you need to remove the bitter green part first. Season meats with ground dried berries for a delicate, peppery flavour.

growing

Myrtle is an erect, evergreen shrub usually growing to 3 m, but sometimes taller. It can be used for hedges or container plants, and because trimming keeps the plants compact, they can be clipped into formal ball or pyramid shapes, if you're so inclined. From late spring the shrubs are a swoon-inducing haze of fragrance: tiny five-petalled white flowers, almost hidden by prominent gold stamens, burst into flower from tightly folded white buds in a day. In late summer when the petals have dropped, the fruit begins to form, and gradually turns blue-black with a delicate whitish waxy bloom.

Myrtle thrives in a sheltered position in full sun or semi-shade with well-drained, medium-rich soil. Although it's hardy, it appreciates a dose of fertiliser occasionally, and a drink in dry weather.

To propagate, divide woody cuttings into 12–15 cm pieces, trim off any side shoots, and press each piece into a deep pot of river sand, leaving one-third of the wood exposed at the top. Keep well watered. When the cuttings have made strong roots, they can be planted out. You can take tip cuttings, late in summer, in the same way as for hardwood propagation. If you want to start from scratch, sow seeds in the spring in prepared trays. When the seedlings are sturdy and have a good root system, plant them out in the garden as single specimens, group them together as a hedge, or plant them in tubs.

drying

Cut flowering stems in the morning and hang in bunches in a dry, shady place, or spread them out on a sheet of paper or on drying racks. When moisture-free, strip the flowers and leaves from their stalks and store in airtight, labelled containers.

Pick the berries when they appear and air-dry on a gauze rack or on sheets of paper in a warm, dark place. When completely dry, store in an airtight, labelled jar. Grind in a peppermill, or crush in a mortar and pestle just before using.

pandan leaf

Pandanus amaryllifolius

Colour is one of the key attributes that the pandan brings to a dish, as well as its subtly sweet flavour. It always reminds us of our time living in Singapore, when we discovered that a bright grass-green pandan cake – a sponge topped with green, jelly-like icing – would be just the thing for our daughter Sophie's birthday cake. She had other ideas!

Warm Minted Lamb and Tomato Salad (recipe page 292)

Mitsuba and Tofu in Clear Soup (recipe page 294)

Also called rampe, screwpine, pandanus leaf, kenera
Flavour and aroma sweetly grassy, fragrant
and agreeable
Flavour group sweet

The leaves used in cooking come from the fragrant screw pine tree, which is a palm-like evergreen. It looks like something you'd see in a B-grade sci-fi movie, with masses of stilt-like aerial roots supporting stiff branches. The leaves are spirally arranged, rather resembling the blades on palm fronds.

Tiny, fragrant, white flowers are followed by huge fruit heads up to 30 cm in diameter that look rather like green pineapples and are in fact aggregations of berries.

The tough, fibrous leaves have been put to good use wherever the screw pine grows: they've been used for house thatching, woven into sails, and made into clothing, floor mats, and baskets. The grass skirts worn by Pacific Island women are often made from split, bleached pandan leaves. The fruit is edible but only after being cooked to neutralise the noxious qualities.

choosing and using

In cooking, the fresh whole pandan leaves are either crushed or boiled to extract the flavour and colour. Strips of fresh leaf flavour rice while it is cooking and are sometimes woven into baskets for serving glutinous rice or canapés – the ultimate dinner party tour de force. You can bruise a few fresh leaves, tie them in a knot, and add them to soups or curries during cooking, much as you can with lemongrass.

A rather eye-catching barbecue finger-food can be made by marinating bite-sized pieces of boneless chicken in some Asian spices then wrapping them in a piece of pandan leaf. Secure the parcel with a toothpick and barbecue – your guests can unwrap their own morsels, and they'll think you're wonderful.

The male flower cluster has a strong perfume that verges on the sickly-sweet. It is available as an essence or concentrate called Kewra essence – sometimes called the 'vanilla of the East' – that is added very sparingly to certain Indian sweets. On festive occasions, essences of rose and pandan deliciously flavour the spicy rice dish, biryani.

Store fresh pandan leaves (available from Asian grocery stores) whole in a plastic bag in the freezer. Carefully dried leaves (to retain the colour) are either chopped into pieces large enough to remove after cooking or powdered finely so that the texture is no longer fibrous. Sometimes you can buy the bright green spice powder from specialty shops. Dried pandan leaf is sometimes sold as *rampé* (Sri Lanka), or *daun pandan* (Malaysia and Indonesia). Store in a cool, dark place to retain colour and flavour.

growing

The screw pine grows to about 15 m in tropical and sub-tropical climates in coastal and swampy areas from Madagascar, across South-East Asia, throughout the Pacific Islands and in tropical Australia. Because the trees tend to lean at an angle, they often look windswept and somewhat shorter than they really are.

Screw pines make a decorative (and practical) addition to a seaside garden. Plant them in warm, damp areas in full sun or part shade in moist, well-drained soil. When it's young, a pandan makes an attractive houseplant, all you have to do is give it plenty of water and remove any dead or damaged leaves. As a houseplant, you can help it to survive winter in less tropical areas. Propagate from seed soaked for 24 hours before planting or by detaching root suckers.

drying

Once you have your pandan tree growing, you can just pick the leaves as you require them. Drying them is tricky because you don't want to lose the colour and flavour. Use the usual drying method, spreading out on mesh or paper, but make sure the area is completely dark. The cavity of a roof is ideal, as is the cupboard that houses your hot water system. Once they are perfectly dry, store the leaf pieces in a dark, airtight container. To make use of the green colouring, put some dried leaves in the blender and process until you have a fine powder.

coconut rice cooked in pandan leaves (nasi lemak in pandan leaves)

This rice dish is a favourite of chef and food writer, Carol Selva Rajah, and is a lovely accompaniment to her Whiting Fillets Grilled in Turmeric Leaves (see page 172). The coconut rice will be aromatic and lightly flavoured with pandan. Carol recommends cooking it in the microwave.

2 cups long-grain jasmine rice

2 fresh green pandan leaves, washed

3 cups water

1 cup light coconut cream

salt to taste

Wash the rice in a basin of water, rubbing the grains lightly between the palms of your hands. It is important to rinse the rice in many changes of water to remove the starch then drain it thoroughly.

Holding the washed pandan leaves, in one hand, run a fork from top to bottom so that the leaves shred all the way down. Add the shredded pandan leaves to the rice – tied neatly into a knot if you like – where their juice and flavour will be released during cooking.

Combine the water and the coconut cream in a deep ceramic (microwave-safe) bowl, stirring well, then add the rice and pandan leaves and a little salt to taste if you wish. Microwave on high for about 35 minutes or until all the water is absorbed, then stir with a fork. Remove the pandan leaves before serving.

Alternatively, place the rice and other ingredients in a rice cooker and follow the cooking instructions.

Serves 6

pandan-flavoured coconut pancakes (kueh dadar)

Carol Selva Rajah tells us that traditionally these pancakes were served as long, cigar-shaped rolls tied with a pandan leaf bow and served warm with green tea or fresh lemon tea.

Filling

150 g grated palm sugar

pinch of salt

¾ cup water

1 pandan leaf

1 cup desiccated coconut or fresh coconut

1 lime rind, cut into very fine julienne strips

Coconut Pancakes

3 pandan leaves shredded with a fork (see instructions in
    recipe opposite)

150 g plain flour, sieved

pinch of salt

1 cup coconut milk

½ cup water

1 egg

butter or oil for frying

Garnish

coconut cream

To make the filling, place the sugar, salt, water and pandan leaf in a heavy saucepan and cook slowly, stirring constantly until the sugar dissolves. Add the coconut and stir over a low heat until the mixture is sticky. Remove the pandan leaf, then add the lime rind and set aside to cool while you make the pancakes.

To make the pancakes, pound the shredded pandan leaves with a tablespoon of water in a mortar and pestle, strain the green juice and set aside. Place the flour and salt in a large mixing bowl. Stir together the coconut milk and water then whisk it into the dry ingredients, together with the egg, to form a smooth, lump-free batter. Stir in the pandan juice, to colour the batter green.

Melt a knob of butter or oil in a hot frying pan. Add 2 tablespoons of batter and swirl around the pan to form a pancake. Flatten with a spatula and cook until the pancake firms and the edges start to brown. Flip the pancake over and cook the other side for around 30 seconds, or until golden brown. Transfer to a warm oven while you make the remaining pancakes.

When serving these pancakes as a dessert you have two options. Either you can fold the pancakes into quarters with a tablespoon of filling in the centre. Or, if you want to be traditional, make up long cigar-shaped portions of the filling to be inserted in the centre of each green pancake and rolled up tightly. Tie each pancake roll with a pandan leaf bow and serve with coconut cream.

Makes 8 pancakes

parsley

curled parsley *Petroselinum crispum*

Italian or continental parsley *P. crispum neapolitanum*

If you are looking for a herb to grow under
a dripping tap or in a damp corner of the
garden then you can't go past parsley.

Also called flat-leaf parsley, Hamburg parsley
Flavour and aroma fresh, agreeable, mildly minty. Continental parsley has slight celery hints
Flavour group mild

The most common ones are the curled varieties that are perfect for garnishing and the flatter, darker Italian or continental parsley with its more concentrated flavour.

There are about 30 varieties of curled parsley, all with bright green, tightly curled leaves. Some, like the triple-curled and moss-curled varieties, are more crinkled and tightly curled than others. *P. crispum*, the one we are all most familiar with, is widely used for garnishing because of its decorative leaves. Italian parsley has deeply cut and serrated leaves like the tops of celery or lovage, is widely used in Middle Eastern and Mediterranean food, has a more concentrated flavour, and grows in large prolific clumps.

Parsley's taste could be described as fresh and crisp and perhaps a little earthy. It is also unassertive which makes it a perfect partner in mixtures with other herbs such as fines herbes (with chervil, chives and tarragon), or in a bouquet garni (with a bay leaf and a spray each of thyme and marjoram). Anyone who has grown parsley will know how prolific a healthy clump can be, so will understand why it's used by the cupful in some recipes ... it's because it's THERE!

choosing and using

Parsley leaves are at home with many savoury foods – in fact there is not one savoury dish that comes to mind that would be spoilt by the addition of parsley. Old-fashioned and very traditional, parsley jelly can be served with all white meats, particularly fish and chicken. Crisp-fried curly sprays of parsley are delicious with fish. Finely chopped Italian flat-leaf parsley stalks and leaves are the main ingredients in tabbouli, along with plenty of fresh mint. Italian parsley is indispensable in Middle Eastern cooking in tagines, combined at times with coriander and in chermoula – a marinade of herbs, oil, spices and lemon juice – served with meat or fish.

If you buy fresh parsley, look for bunches with firm stems and upright, springy leaves. Store in a glass of water covered loosely with plastic wrap. For freezing, chop fresh leaves finely, mix with a little water, and put them into ice-cube trays in the freezer. Sprays of fresh parsley may be wrapped in foil and frozen.

growing

When you're choosing a spot to plant parsley, remember it can thrive in areas that don't have the best drainage, and the moist soil will in fact delay the 'going to seed' cycle. Plant parsley in the garden in full sun or semi-shade, or in a pot on a sunny exterior windowsill or balcony. Just remember not to let the soil dry out. The main rule is to plant parsley in its permanent position, as its long taproot does not like to be disturbed.

Curled parsley can be tricky to grow from seed – there used to be a saying that parsley seeds go to the devil and back three times before they come up. They sometimes take two weeks to germinate, and during this time the bed *must never* be allowed to dry out, or the seeds will stop germinating altogether and you'll have to start all over again. Covering the seeds with up to 12 mm of soil will help retain moisture in the ground for a longer period.

For Italian parsley, sow seed any time of year except mid-winter, directly into the garden where the plants are to grow, thinning out later to approximately 7.5 cm between plants. Italian parsley is easy to grow. Three to four days after sowing, the seeds will usually germinate, provided that they are very lightly covered with soil to not more than 6 mm in depth, and kept moist.

Parsley plants will live for two years, especially if you cut the long flower stalks as they appear to keep them from going to seed during the first year. However, the second year's growth is never as good, and we prefer to sow seed each year to ensure strong and healthy plants.

drying

Parsley can be cut for drying at any time. It will keep its green colour and flavour if it's dried quickly in a warm oven preheated to 120°C. After turning the oven off, spread out the parsley heads, which have been snipped from the stalks, on a large tray or baking dish, and leave in the oven for 15 minutes, turning several times until crisp-dry. Store them in airtight containers away from the light.

penne with a sauce of parsley, prosciutto and pine nuts

Parsley is the perfect partner for pine nuts and prosciutto in this fresh-flavoured sauce to serve with penne or your favourite pasta shapes.

½ cup parsley leaves, loosely packed

juice of 1 lemon

2 tablespoons grated parmesan cheese

2 tablespoons roasted pine nuts

½ cup virgin olive oil

salt to taste

10–12 slices prosciutto

500 g penne pasta

100 g bocconcini, cut into small cubes

Combine parsley, lemon juice, parmesan and pine nuts in a blender and process with the motor running. Gradually add the olive oil until a thick creamy pesto is formed. Add salt to taste.

Brush the prosciutto with a little extra oil and cook under a preheated grill until crisp. Set aside to cool, then break into pieces.

Cook the pasta in a large saucepan of boiling salted water until *al dente*, then drain through a colander and return to the pan. Stir in the parsley pesto and mix well. Toss over low heat until well combined. Spoon into warmed bowls and serve topped with the bocconcini and prosciutto pieces.

Serves 4

pennywort

Centella cordifolia

Indian pennywort *C. asiatica* syn. *hydrocotyle asiatica*

Believe it or not, pennywort actually did exist before the current affairs television shows got hold of it in the late 1990s and dubbed it the 'arthritis herb'.

Also called arthritis herb, swamp pennywort
Flavour and aroma slightly bitter
Flavour group medium

It's a cheery little plant, easy to get along with and always happy, as long as you remember that its other name is swamp pennywort, for obvious reasons. Growing only 12–15 cm high, it has leaves shaped like a rather rounded fan, or like a penny with a cut towards the centre. While thinking of pennies and cents, and the Latin name *Centella*, the leaves range from about the size of a two-cent coin to about the size of a penny.

Pennywort is not really what we could classify as a culinary herb. In Africa, the dried and powdered leaves are used as a kind of snuff. For many centuries, it has been used in India and Asia as a medicine for all sorts of things, which we won't delve into here. However, it's worth mentioning that there is anecdotal evidence that three leaves a day have been know to ease the pain of arthritis – but bear in mind that the scientific evidence to back it up is still lacking.

choosing and using

You can pick the leaves and eat them directly from the plant, or tuck them into a salad or herb sandwich. To disguise the flavour (not really necessary, but some people are fussy), sandwich the leaf between two small slices of cheese.

Drying is not recommended for pennywort.

growing

This herb has a delightful trailing habit that makes it a natural for a hanging pot. Leaf stems sprout at intervals from the thin, prostrate stems, and at each leaf point, roots will sprout if there is ground available for them. Therefore it will happily run all over your garden if you let it – which is a good reason to keep it in a pot.

Once you have obtained a root from a friend, a nursery or someone's garden, this little plant will be unstoppable. Just cover the root with moist potting mix, keep it watered, and it will grow. Frequent picking will keep the plant nicely dense – less frequent picking and inadequate water will lead to long, straggly strands.

A pot is recommended because of its spreading habit – we met a man who had filled an old cast-iron bathtub with soil and had a bath full of pennywort!

purslane

Portulaca oleracea

Edible green purslane is a sappy, succulent herb from the Portulaca family. Gardeners like its red stems and stalks in herbaceous borders, especially when combined with the contrasting golden-leaved *P. sativa*. The latter is also edible, but is not as hardy as the green variety.

Also called poor man's spinach, portulaca, pigweed, green purslane

Flavour and aroma zesty and lemony

Flavour group mild

In the past, older shoots were cooked as a 'pot herb' (herbs used like vegetables for the flavour and nourishment in their leaves, roots and stems), and the pickled stems spiced up winter salads. But for many years, purslane seemed to fall out of favour, and lost its place in herb books. However, its culinary and nutritional benefits have recently been rediscovered – it is loaded with omega-3 fatty acids and is rich in antioxidants and our trendy young chefs just love it! The smooth, small, juicy leaves have a refreshing, zesty lemon tang and make a pleasant surprise to crunch on in a mixture of salad greens. With rich food, purslane's astringent properties help cleanse the palate.

Purslane is found on just about every continent. It's one of the world's most common useful wild plants (or weeds, depending on your point-of-view). Like okra, it contains mucilage, making it useful to thicken soups such as the French *potage bonne femme*. The green purslane most commonly used is thought to have come from the Middle East where you will find it in the salad *fatoush* and the cooling Armenian cucumber and yoghurt salad.

In Australia, early settlers tucked into cooked purslane as a substitute for spinach – hence the term 'poor man's spinach'. Try it with a little nutmeg grated on top. Sometimes thick stems of mature plants are sliced and pickled for the winter store cupboard. In Asia, the juicy stems and leaves with their ever-so-slight glutinous mouth-feel are dipped in fish sauce and eaten raw and added to stir-fries.

choosing and using

Purslane doesn't keep well, so it's best to buy and use it on the same day. Choose fresh-looking bunches, cut off the roots and stand the stems in a glass or stainless steel container. Avoid aluminium containers – the oxalic acid in purslane reacts with alloys in the same way that spinach does. Blanch for a few minutes in a stainless steel saucepan, rinse thoroughly and leave to cool to reduce the jelly-like texture before using.

Purslane is eaten fresh and does not dry well. If you are growing it, gather 5–7.5 cm leafy stems as you need them for making salads. When it's starting to look a bit hen-pecked, cut the plant low and after a short time it will produce a fresh crop of foliage. After repeating once more, the original plant will be depleted and the new crop of purslane, having been sown earlier, should be ready to pick.

growing

The juicy leaves are attached to short stems growing from a round, succulent, red stalk and the whole plant has a prostrate, sprawling habit. Tiny yellow flowers cluster on the branches in mid-summer, opening only at noon. Each bloom is followed by a seed case packed with thousands of tiny black seeds. Dig some compost or rich loam into light, well-drained soil and sow seeds from late spring to early autumn in a sunny position 15–20 cm apart.

Keep the weeds away, water it well and the leafy stems will be ready to pick in four to six weeks. Gather purslane before it flowers, then after one or two pickings cut it back and it will shoot again. Successive seed sowing every two to three weeks is recommended so that new plants come on when the first ones have finished.

purslane with a neopolitan flavour

This makes a good brunch served on sourdough toast for those 'home alone' times.

1 bunch purslane (about 30 stalks)

1 tablespoon virgin olive oil

1 small onion, finely chopped

1 clove garlic, crushed or finely chopped

2 rashers bacon, rind and fat trimmed, finely chopped

2 tomatoes, peeled and chopped, seeds included

salt to taste

freshly ground black pepper to taste

Rinse the purslane and roughly chop into thirds; set aside. Heat the oil in a heavy-based pan and add the onion, garlic and bacon. Cook until the onion is transparent, then stir in the tomatoes. Cook a further 2–3 minutes, adding salt and pepper to taste. Add the purslane and stir through. Cover the pan and simmer for about 5 minutes, stirring occasionally.

Serves 1

rocket

Eruca sativa

salad rocket *E. sativa*

Salad rocket with its unique peppery flavour
is the essential ingredient at any number
of good sidewalk cafes.

Top to bottom:
Rocket Pesto (recipe page 314);
Apple, Mint and Horseradish Cream
(recipe page 261);
Aïoli with Lemon Myrtle (recipe page 258)

Goat's Cheese Soufflés (recipe page 336)

Also called arugula, ruchetta, Roman rocket, roquette

Flavour and aroma peppery, cress-like, tangy

Flavour group medium

It's found layered with roasted vegetables in magnificent doorstep-sized sandwiches; lurking under stacks of char-grilled chicken and eggplant; in, on and under hand-made pasta; and it constitutes the bulk of green mesclun salads in place of 'old-fashioned' lettuce.

Salad rocket is a branched plant with spear-shaped, torn-looking leaves with a mustardy, almost cress-like, tang. Culpeper called it 'rocket cress' or 'garden cress'. It is a great 'grow and pick' plant that you can harvest throughout the summery months, leaf by leaf.

It is sometimes confused with sweet rocket, *Hesperis matronali*, because they are part of the same big Brassicaceae family and both are referred to as rocket. Don't be misled by that adjective 'sweet', however, which refers to its fragrant single or double white, purple, or variegated flowers that perfume the air on warm evenings. The leaves of sweet rocket are too acrid for eating.

When you're buying salad rocket, look for firm, fresh, green leaves. If the leaves have a sickly, yellowish hue, you'd be better off going without. Store as you would lettuce, in a plastic bag in the crisper in the refrigerator. Rocket will only keep for a day or two, so it is best to buy it the day you want to use it. Rinse it well under running water, as the leaves tend to collect dirt as they grow. Drain well and gently pat dry with a clean tea towel.

growing

Salad rocket is often seen growing wild, but the cultivated herb has larger, milder tasting foliage and grows to around 90 cm. For crisp salad leaves, grow rocket fast. To do this, the plants will need a fair bit of 'tender loving care' to become established. The key ingredients for speed growing are rich soil that can absorb moisture, regular watering, a good liquid fertiliser and at least six hours of sun a day. A good way to check whether your rocket needs more water is to push your finger into the soil around the base of the plant; if it's not moist then water it.

Plant seedlings or sow seed in the spring directly into the garden. Seeds take about three to four days to germinate and the rocket should be ready for picking in about six to eight weeks. The very young leaves are a long oval shape, so be careful not to mistake them for weeds. The ragged serrations only develop as the plant matures.

Rocket flowers in mid- to late summer, and the small blooms are creamy yellow, or pale white with purple streaks. To collect the seeds for planting next season, allow them to ripen when the petals have fallen, then cut the stalks and place them, seed-heads first, into a paper bag so that the seeds will be collected as they fall.

When the leaves of the salad rocket are big enough, around 10 cm, begin to pick them from the outside of the plant. Young leaves are particularly tender. Gather leaves repeatedly until the plant begins to flower. Rocket is not a herb for drying and storing.

rocket pesto

1 bunch rocket

2 cloves garlic, chopped

$1/2$ cup raw macadamia nuts

$1/4$ cup grated parmesan cheese

2 tablespoons extra virgin olive oil

a squeeze of lemon juice

salt and freshly ground black pepper to taste

Combine the rocket, garlic, macadamia nuts and grated parmesan in a blender and process. Add the olive oil a tablespoon at a time, blending well after each addition, and finish with a squeeze of lemon juice. Scoop the mixture into a bowl and stir until smooth, adding salt and pepper to taste.

Makes about 1 cup

snowpea, rocket, capsicum, avocado and basil salad

Select the smallest, sweetest snowpeas and fresh, young rocket leaves for this combination of flavour, colour and texture suggested by food writer, Lisa Lintner, who effortlessly transforms the simple into the sensational.

2 large red capsicum

300 g snowpeas

1 bunch rocket or 2 cups rocket leaves, washed

1 large ripe avocado

2–3 basil leaves

Dressing

2 tablespoons balsamic vinegar

$1/3$ cup extra virgin olive oil

1 clove garlic, finely chopped

10 basil leaves, finely sliced

salt and freshly ground black pepper to taste

Halve the capsicum and remove all the seeds and the white ribs. Brush the halves with a little olive oil, place them on a foil-lined tray under a hot grill until the skins have blackened, then put the capsicums in a sturdy paper or plastic bag and set aside until they are cool enough to handle, 10–15 minutes. Remove the skins and slice the halves lengthwise into 1 cm wide strips.

String and blanch the snowpeas in boiling water, then drain and refresh in ice water.

Cut the avocado lengthwise into half, then gently twist to separate. Remove the seed, peel off the skin and slice the flesh into thin wedges.

To make the dressing, combine all the ingredients in a lidded jar and shake well to combine. Taste for seasoning and adjust if necessary. Arrange all the ingredients attractively on a large platter, sprinkle over the dressing, top with 2–3 extra whole basil leaves and serve.

Serves 6–8 as an accompaniment

rosemary

upright *Rosmarinus officinalis*

prostrate *R. prostratus*

A sprig of rosemary will enhance just about anything – even memory, if the saying 'rosemary for remembrance' is to be believed.

Also called old man, compass plant
Flavour and aroma astringent, a touch of camphor, pungent, peppery, appetising
Flavour group pungent

Every year as Anzac Day approaches, rosemary bushes around Australia and New Zealand are trimmed to provide sprigs for adorning lapels on this special day of remembrance.

A lamb roast simply isn't complete without sprigs of rosemary and slivers of garlic stuffed into slits on the outside and, if you really want to go to town, liberally dusted with sumac and sweet paprika before roasting.

Hardy, sun-loving, perennial rosemary is one of the most pungent herbs of all. There are two main varieties, both with delicate blue flowers and long, narrow leaves that are dark green on top and silver-striped underneath. Upright rosemary's leaves grow to over 2.5 cm long, and have the better flavour. The leaves of low-growing or prostrate rosemary are smaller and narrower. But no matter which variety you opt for, the warmly vital, freshly resinous taste and aroma adds a delicious, savoury tang to all types of meats and most vegetables.

choosing and using

Although it is famously paired with lamb, rosemary can be used in pâtés, sauces for pasta, with eggplant, zucchini, lima beans ... basically, the rule is: 'Think Mediterranean, think rosemary!'

Years ago at Somerset Cottage we made rosemary scones for visitors (you simply stir a tablespoon of finely chopped leaves into a plain scone mixture before adding the liquid). The flavour was subtle and piquant, and when served hot from the oven and freshly buttered, they disappeared like – well – like hot scones!

If you pick more rosemary than you need, or have leftover stems from a bought bunch, fear not, it keeps well for a week or so in a jug of (regularly changed) water. The ice-cube trick works well too, or sprays of fresh rosemary may be wrapped in foil and frozen for some weeks – but if you have a growing rosemary plant, why bother freezing it?

There's a real technique to stripping fresh rosemary leaves from the stem. Always hold the stem by the bottom in one hand and with the thumb and forefinger of the other pluck off each leaf in an upward motion. That impulsive downward action will tear off some of the coarse outer stem bark, which doesn't add anything to a dish.

growing

Rosemary thrives in a Mediterranean-style climate, which means dry conditions, hot dry summers, a small amount of rain and in a spot that is sheltered from wind. Plant in a sunny, well-drained spot in sandy or alkaline soil and hold back on the watering. It loves tubs.

Upright rosemary with its stiff, bushy habit grows to about 1.5 m and is ideal for hedges. Trim frequently to encourage growth and prune after flowering. Prostrate rosemary is rather more ornamental than culinary, making a thick, matted ground cover, or hanging fetchingly over the edge of retaining walls. It is excellent in rockeries and also in tubs, where it will spill toward the ground in a most attractive way. We have seen prostrate rosemary planted on a sloping bank sweeping down to a swimming pool, where the blue of the flowers and the blue water seemed to reflect one another. Both varieties start blooming in the autumn and continue on through the winter until spring.

Rosemary is fairly easy to grow from 15 cm tip cuttings. For best results, take cuttings late in winter and plant them in a pot of clean river sand or potting mixture. A dip in rooting powder is helpful, too. Once the roots have formed, you can transplant it to the garden or a larger pot. You can also grow upright rosemary from seed (in the spring is best) in a prepared seed box, planting out when the seedlings are about 7.5 cm high, and leaving about 60 cm between plants.

The prostrate variety can only be propagated by cuttings or by layering, which is an easy process described in the 'Growing herbs' section. If you're a more haphazard gardener, the same result can be achieved by putting half a brick or a rock onto the stem to keep it pressed against the garden soil. When the layered branch has developed a good root system, just cut it away from the parent bush and plant out in a sunny position.

drying

Cut the branches before the plant begins flowering (when the flavour is at its best), shaping the bush at the same time. Then hang in bunches in a shady, airy place, with cloth or newspaper underneath to catch the falling leaves. Strip the dry leaves from the stalks, crumbling them into small pieces. Stored in airtight containers, the flavour will remain strong over a long period. Dried rosemary can also be added to potpourri for scenting clothes and deterring moths.

rosemary scones

I have made so many thousands of scones over the years, that I usually make them by 'feel' rather than by following a recipe. Just for the record, here's my recipe for rosemary scones measured out. However, 'feel' is very important when making scones and you may need a little more flour or a little less milk to achieve the correct 'firm but moist' consistency.

150 g self-raising flour
70 g butter
pinch of salt
2 teaspoons chopped fresh rosemary (about 2 sprigs)
$1/3$ cup whole milk

Preheat the oven to 200ºC. Process the flour, butter and salt in a food processor, or rub with your fingertips until you achieve the consistency of breadcrumbs. Stir in the chopped rosemary, and gradually add the milk, to achieve a firm but moist consistency. (You may not need the entire $1/3$ cup, or you may need a little more – it depends on the flour.)

Sprinkle a little extra flour onto the workbench, turn the scone mixture out, and lightly pat out to a thickness of about 2 cm. Cut into squares or circles about 3 or 4 cm in diameter, and place on a flour-dusted oven tray. Bake for about 10 minutes, until the scones have risen and the tops are lightly browned. They should separate easily into top and bottom halves with gentle finger pressure; you should never cut scones. Serve them warm with a small dab of butter melting into each half.

Makes about 10 scones

sage

Salvia officinalis

fruit salad sage *S. dorisiana*

pineapple sage *S. elegans*

Sage one of those 'a little goes a long way' herbs with a flavour that rarely diminishes over long cooking times.

Also called garden sage, true sage
Flavour and aroma pungent, fresh and head-clearing, balsamic
Flavour group pungent

The silvery grey of the leaves and the bluish-mauve flowers, make common sage (*S. officinalis*) a welcome variation amongst the greens of most other herbs in the garden. When the leaves are young, they are soft, downy and pale green, but like Dickens' Miss Haversham; as they mature the colour fades, and the original softness becomes a rough-textured leaf surface, rather like a cat's tongue. Sage flowers are like miniature snap dragons, and you'll probably see bees paying great attention to these sweet morsels. In this hardy perennial's native home, Dalmatia, the honey from sage flowers is renowned.

As poor Jemima Puddleduck found to her peril, sage and onions makes the ideal stuffing for roast duck, as well as for other rich, fatty foods such as pork, chicken and oily fish. And as a bonus, its 'grease-cutting' qualities will aid digestion, or so they say.

choosing and using

Think of sage when you think 'big' flavours like full-bodied pea, bean and vegetable soups; hearty winter stews; dumplings; meat loaf and roast meats. Like most herbs, you can also add a judicious amount of chopped sage to vegetable and egg dishes. It is a traditional ingredient in mixed herbs, along with thyme and marjoram, and is currently fashionable deep-fried and served as a garnish.

We always include a small amount of sage when we make herb sandwiches, making sure the sage is about 10 per cent of the quantity of milder herbs like parsley, chives and chervil.

Fresh sage is readily available from fruit and vegetable retailers. Avoid bunches that look wilted unless you're really desperate. Stand the stems in a glass of water, changing the water every second day, and enjoy fresh sage for a week or so. You can also buy dried sage leaves crushed or powdered. The crushed leaves are the most flavoursome.

The Salvia family to which sage belongs includes some 900 species of annuals, perennials and soft-wooded shrubs, but the herb sage, *S. officinalis*, is the one with the real culinary qualities. Fruit salad sage has edible pink flowers that make a delicious addition to cordial, salads and fruit salads. Pineapple sage has edible red flowers that bloom prolifically from early summer through autumn; pick them off the stem and suck the delicious nectar straight from the flower.

growing

This hardy, erect perennial grows to about 90 cm with a base that becomes rather woody after a couple of years. As a rule of thumb, plants with woody stems and slightly greyish coloured leaves, such as sage, thyme, rosemary and oregano, like reasonably dry conditions, and they don't like to have wet feet. So pick a very sunny, slightly elevated (if possible) spot for your sage in sandy, well-drained soil. Sow the seed in spring (in mild climates you can sow in autumn as well) directly into the garden or in a prepared seed box if you prefer. Plant your seedlings out when they are about 10 cm tall, leaving 60 cm between each.

Although the seedlings need care and water, let the mature plants enjoy dry spells as nature intended. Sage will also grow from cuttings or layering – have a look at Ian's section on growing for more details (see 'Growing herbs' page 340).

As your plant ages, prune out the dead twigs so that it doesn't get too woody, too soon. Pruning every week in the summer may be a good idea, but ultimately it depends on how vigorously the plant is growing.

Because sage is a perennial, it is always available for picking. Like other herbs, the ice-cube method works if you want to do it.

drying

Harvest sage for drying just before the plant flowers. Either tie loosely bundled long sprays together and hang them in a cool, dark, airy place, or lay the branches out on racks to dry in a warm position, but never in direct sunlight. Once dried, pull off all the leaves and store them in airtight containers immediately.

It is unwise to leave the bundles, attractive though they are, to gather dust. Rubbed sage leaves will never feel as crisp as many other dried herbs due to their high oil content and the downy structure of the leaf. Dried sage makes one of the tastier herbal teas.

french-style stuffed pumpkin

½ cup fresh white breadcrumbs

1 whole pumpkin, about 20–25 cm in diameter

1 tablespoon butter

1 large onion, very finely chopped

pinch of salt

pinch of pepper

pinch of nutmeg

1½ teaspoons fresh sage, chopped

½ cup gruyère cheese, grated

500 ml pouring cream

Preheat oven to 120ºC. Spread the breadcrumbs out on an oven tray and place in the oven for about 15 minutes to dry out. Meanwhile, cut the top off the pumpkin, and scoop out all the seeds and fibrous strands. Place the cleaned pumpkin in an oiled baking dish and set aside. Increase oven heat to 200ºC.

Melt the butter in a pan and sauté the onion over medium heat until transparent. Add the dried breadcrumbs and seasonings, including the sage. Cook for another minute or so, then remove from the heat. Stir in the cheese, then spoon the mixture into the pumpkin cavity. Pour in enough cream to come to within a centimetre of the top. Fit the lid back on to the pumpkin.

Bake for about 1½ hours until the outside of the pumpkin is beginning to soften. Reduce heat to about 160ºC, and continue baking for another 30 minutes until the flesh is tender. If the pumpkin looks as though the outside is burning, wrap it lightly in foil. Present the whole pumpkin at the table, then remove the lid and spoon out the filling.

Serves 4–6

salad burnet

Sanguisorba minor

Salad burnet is a fresh-is-best herb, just as its name implies, and by rights it should be as popular as other salad herbs such as rocket and chicory.

Also called lesser burnet, garden burnet
Flavour and aroma fresh cucumber and herbaceous notes
Flavour group mild

choosing and using

Add whole sprays of this cool, light, refreshing, soft herb to a tossed green salad, or float individual leaves in fruit punches and drinks. Chop the small, serrated, cucumber-flavoured leaves into cream cheese to make a dip; or use the whole leaves in sandwiches with cottage or ricotta cheese, or as a garnish for any dish that needs a touch of green. It is a tasty topping for scrambled eggs, particularly when mixed with a few sprigs of chervil, if you have some on hand.

Sometimes you can buy bunches of salad burnet from fruit and vegetable retailers. When available, buy the day you plan to use it, as it is rather prone to wilting. Wash salad burnet and store it in the crisper drawer of your refrigerator, as you would lettuce.

If you are growing your own, pick leaves just before you need them. To freeze for drinks, pull small leaves from the stalks and put them whole into ice-cube trays. Top up with water and freeze. Salad burnet doesn't dry well, and loses its appeal when dried.

growing

This delicate perennial grows to about 30 cm. It has a weeping, fern-like appearance and was often used as a border plant in traditional knot gardens. Its leaves are small, round, serrated and spaced about 2.5 cm apart in pairs of 10 or 12 on each side of a slender stem. As the stems become long and heavy, they fall outward from the centre, so the more you pick it from the outside edge, the better. In summer, reddish pink, berry-like flowers appear on long stalks that shoot up from the centre.

Sow seeds (or plant seedlings) in the spring in their permanent position as salad burnet does not like being moved. Keep the ground moist while the seeds are germinating, then, when the seedlings are about 7.5 cm high, thin them out to 30 cm apart. As salad burnet is a soft salad herb and wilts quickly in hot, dry weather, keep it well watered at this time. It has no particular soil requirements, is very hardy, and will grow strongly all through most winters.

Salad burnet scatters many seeds that germinate easily, so it is advisable to cut the flower heads off as the stalks begin to lengthen, or it will take over the garden.

pear salad with salad burnet and borage flowers

This recipe is perfect for single servings or arranged on a platter where people can help themselves.

2 ripe, firm pears (Packham or beurre bosc)
10 sprigs salad burnet
12 fresh borage flowers
a good-quality vinaigrette, for dressing

Peel and core the pears and slice them lengthwise into long, slender wedges. Pick the leaves from 2 of the sprigs of salad burnet. Arrange the remaining salad burnet sprigs on a serving platter and place the pear slices on top. Sprinkle over the borage flowers and the picked salad burnet leaves, sprinkle with dressing and serve.

Serves 4

savory

winter savory *Satureja montana*

summer savory *S. hortensis*

Fresh or dried, summer and winter savory both add an appetising, peppery bite that doesn't overpower.

Also called bean herb (Bohnen-Kraut)
Flavour and aroma piquant and peppery
Flavour group pungent

It's good to have both types growing: summer for its fragrant, piquant, distinctive taste; winter for its compact, hardy nature and glossy green leaves.

Opt for savory whenever a peppery piquancy is called for. Beans, peas and lentils, however you prepare them, benefit from the savory touch and in fact its popular German name, 'Bohnen-kraut', means 'bean herb'. Savory is delicate enough to complement egg dishes and robust enough to hold up in slow-cooked casseroles, stews and hotpots. Mix fresh or dried savory with breadcrumbs to coat fish, pork, and veal fillets; add it to meat loaf and meat balls; or sprinkle over poultry or pork before roasting. A classic fines herbes blend will often include savory.

Fresh summer savory is available in season from specialty produce suppliers and keeps well provided you stand it in a glass of water in the refrigerator. If you change the water every day or so, it should last for a week or more. Its soft foliage may be frozen in ice blocks at any time or wrapped in foil and frozen. Winter savory freezes well, too. Wrap sprays of soft new growth in foil and freeze. It will keep well for several weeks this way.

Dried summer savory, which includes the flower tops, can be bought year round and needs to be kept in a cool, dark place.

growing

Summer savory is a small, slender, herbaceous plant with hairy branching stems that tend to snap easily. Often it will have a rather top-heavy, sprawling growing habit, as the soft stems struggle to carry the prolific burden of soft, greeny-bronze leaves. These small, oval leaves have a stronger flavour than winter savory.

Winter savory has tiny, lipped white flowers and a rather stiff appearance that makes it ideal for borders of low hedging.

There is also a decorative, prostrate variety of winter savory, *S. repandens*, which spreads in dense, cushiony mounds, and is useful for filling pockets in paved paths and patios. It's a great choice for hanging baskets, as the tiny branches will tumble enticingly over the rim.

Annual summer savory grows to about 45 cm high and likes a sunny, well-drained spot. Plant seedlings in the spring or sow seeds by scattering them over finely dug soil in the garden where the plants are to remain. You can plant summer savory in containers if you prefer. Successive sowings may be started in spring and carried on into mid-summer, each crop being harvested just as the flowers begin to appear. When about 5 cm high, thin out the seedlings leaving approximately 15 cm between plants. Summer savory bears small pink, white or lavender flowers in late summer, which are often harvested with the leaves.

Honeybees swarm around savory when it is in bloom and it was traditionally grown near beehives. An old-time cure for a bee sting was to remove the sting and rub the spot with fresh savory leaves.

Winter savory can also be grown from seed in the same way. Alternatively, take small tip cuttings of new growth in late spring when the leaves have hardened, then put them in a pot of wet river sand until roots have formed. When you transfer them to the garden, allow 30 cm between plants. Winter savory makes a good low hedge, but you'll need to group the plants closer together, about 20 cm apart, to achieve this.

drying

Both summer and winter savory can be dried with good results by hanging them in bunches in an airy place just before flowering. When the leaves are crisp-dry, they are easily separated from the stalks by running the thumb and forefinger up and down the stems. Stored in airtight containers, the flavour will remain strong for a long time.

Summer savory's stronger flavour makes it more satisfactory for drying and most commercial growers prefer it for this reason.

broad beans with summer savory

Savory brings a distinctive peppery piquancy to this dish without overpowering the broad beans.

2 cups shelled fresh broad beans

4 sprigs summer savory

1 tablespoon butter

Place the beans and half the savory in a saucepan of salted, boiling water, and cook until just tender. Drain, discarding the savory. Return the drained beans to the pan with the butter and the remaining savory, stripped from the stems. Shake the pan over heat while the butter melts, toss well and serve immediately.

Serves 4 as an accompaniment

sorrel

French sorrel *Rumex scutatus*

French sorrel is a leafy perennial that grows in thick clumps like spinach. Its broad, mostly smooth, oval leaves are approximately 15 cm long and 7.5 cm wide, and are joined to reddish stems, rather resembling thin rhubarb.

Also called round-leaved sorrel
Flavour and aroma tangy, astringent, appetising and acidic
Flavour group medium

It has a lively, tangy flavour that really brightens up a green salad and the leaves are the perfect shape for laying lengthwise in a baguette with tuna and salad.

In times past, sorrel was prepared and eaten just like spinach, often with the addition of well-beaten eggs and butter, or cream and a little flour, to bind it and mellow the sharp flavour. As sorrel has a different consistency from spinach, it softens and melts faster; you can simply blanch it or cook it very quickly in butter without any water at all and then chop or sieve it to make a purée.

choosing and using

There are several varieties of sorrel, mostly rather sour and acidic. The milder French sorrel with its refreshing, lemony sharpness is the one cultivated for culinary use. However, it contains oxalic acid and should be eaten in moderation as a side act rather than centre stage. Always use stainless steel utensils when cutting and cooking sorrel as iron or aluminium will react and cause unpleasant flavours.

The tang of torn, fresh sorrel leaves can almost make a salad dressing superfluous. They give a pleasant appetising bite to scrambled eggs, and add flavour to lentil, bean or country-style soups. But sorrel is probably best known today when made into a sauce and served as a heavenly accompaniment for fish, veal, lamb, pork or poultry, drizzled over hot boiled potatoes, or used as a filling for omelettes. You can even top a supermarket-bought quiche with home-made sorrel sauce to turn it into something really special.

You can buy sorrel in bunches from specialty fruit and vegetable markets and store it in the vegetable crisper of the refrigerator for up to a week. If you are growing sorrel in the garden, a few plants will provide tangy leaves for salads all year round. It is rarely processed and doesn't keep its flavour well when dried.

The fresh leaves are available throughout the year in moderate climates. Whole, washed young sorrel leaves may be carefully wrapped in foil, sealed down with the fingers at the edges, and frozen for some weeks.

Sorrel, long a valued pot herb, would have been gathered wherever it was found growing wild, to be taken home and put into bubbling stews, or mixed with other green leaves, for salads. It has a reputation for sharpening the appetite and English diarist, John Evelyn (1620–1706), commented on its addition to salads, saying that it 'imparts a grateful quickness to the rest as supplying the want of oranges and lemons'.

growing

Sorrel is an easy, undemanding plant to grow, and it saddens me that whenever we stocked it in our herb nursery, we eventually had to plant it out into our own garden because no one wanted it. It grows prolifically in temperate areas in full sun or part shade in moderately fertile, well-drained soil with occasional applications of manure and a drink in dry weather. The small, greenish flowers appear in summer, near the top, and on either side, of long, rhubarb-like stalks. And never forget that snails and caterpillars are the worst enemies of succulent-leafed sorrel and are completely undeterred by the oxalic acid content. In fact they seem to thrive on it!

Propagation is by seed or by root division of the clumps in the autumn; but broken pieces of taproot will also shoot, which is worth remembering if you are tossing old plants onto the compost. Plant seedlings or sow seed in a prepared box in the spring. When seedlings are big enough to handle, plant them out, leaving 15 cm between each one. Alternatively, sow seed directly into the ground where the plants are to grow, thinning out to 15 cm apart when they are about 5 cm high. In summer, as soon as the flower stalks begin to rise, they should be cut off at the base to prevent the plant from going to seed. If this is done, sorrel will continue to flourish for many years.

sorrel sauce

Serve this lemony sauce with pan-fried ocean trout fillets, or allow it to cool and serve it as a dressing with salads and cold meats. Add an egg yolk along with the cream to make a richer sauce.

1 tablespoon butter

50–60 g young sorrel leaves, washed and
    chopped (about 50 leaves)

1 tablespoon flour

1 cup chicken stock

1–2 tablespoons cream

Melt the butter in a saucepan and gently cook the sorrel until soft. Blend in the flour and gradually add the chicken stock, stirring well until smooth; the sauce should have the consistency of thickened cream. Remove the pan from the heat and immediately beat in the cream. Don't blend the finished sauce to a smooth purée as the finely chopped sorrel gives the sauce a more interesting texture. This sauce can be frozen for up to 4 weeks.

Makes about 2 cups

tarragon

French tarragon *Artemisia dracunculus*

Beware inferior imitators! French tarragon, with its unique, tart flavour and spicy anise aroma, is one of the most sought after culinary herbs.

Also called true tarragon
Flavour and aroma tart, licorice, anise aroma
Flavour group strong

The leaves are long and narrow and grow on either side of thin, wiry stalks that, together with the main stems, twist and fall in a tangled way. The mature plant is quite thick and bushy, about 90 cm high and wide.

A member of the Asteraceae family, French tarragon is the only one that has culinary uses. Other Artemisias such as wormwood and southernwood, while still recognised as herbs, are much too bitter to eat, while Russian tarragon (*A. dracunculoides*), is flavourless and an unworthy substitute.

choosing and using

French tarragon is one of the four essential ingredients in the fines herbes mixture (the others being chives, chervil and parsley in equal quantities). The warming, aromatic fragrance of tarragon complements fish and shellfish, and it is an excellent herb to use with chicken, turkey, game, veal, kidneys, egg dishes, and in chicken or fish soup – French-style, of course!

Tarragon gives an air of elegance to all sorts of dressings and sauces, and to a green salad. Eggs Benedict just wouldn't be the same without it. Tarragon steeped in white vinegar could almost be rated 'the original and best' of all herb vinegars, and it is a useful ingredient for making your own mustard.

Fresh French tarragon stems will last for a few days in water, provided that it is changed every day. Be cautious buying it fresh – if there's no distinct anise aroma or tangy taste it's probably Russian or Mexican. Bright, hardy-looking yellow flowers are a dead giveaway of the Mexican variety, so leave well alone if you see them. If you want to freeze tarragon for future use, strip the fresh leaves from their stalks, chop them finely, mix with a little water, and put them into ice-cube trays in the freezer. Sprays of tarragon may be wrapped in foil and frozen for some weeks.

Alternatively, for making sauces, or using instead of sauces, finely chopped fresh tarragon can be mixed with softened butter. Once the butter has chilled, it can be cut into pieces to be wrapped separately in plastic wrap.

Mexican tarragon (*Tagetes lucida*) isn't an *Artemisia* at all. It is a cousin of those most familiar of summer annuals, the marigold, and is an altogether sturdier looking plant than true tarragon. Its firm, dark green leaves have a spicy anise aroma and flavour similar to French tarragon, which makes it a kind of a substitute. The Aztecs used it to flavour *choclatl*, their cocoa-based drink. Sadly, many fruit and vegetable retailers sell bunches of this plant under the guise of tarragon, and some inexperienced cooks are unaware that it is not the true French variety.

growing

With typically Gallic temperament, French tarragon can choose to disappear for no good reason, as many disappointed gardeners will attest. Perennial French tarragon likes well-drained soil and a sunny position. Although it doesn't mind slightly dry conditions, you will need to water it during a long dry spell. In late summer it produces small, tight, yellowish buds, but as they rarely open into full bloom, they do not set seed. If you're lucky enough to have it survive in your garden, it needs to be replanted every third year as the fragrance and flavour deteriorate over time.

Propagating by cuttings is probably the best way to obtain new plants.

The true French tarragon is notoriously difficult to find in nurseries, so if you have one, your friends and acquaintances will be delighted if you share yours with them. Take 15 cm tip cuttings in late spring when the new, soft leaves have become fairly firm. Insert the cuttings, which have had the lower leaves carefully removed, in a pot of coarse river sand, leaving approximately 5 cm of cuttings above the sand. By mid-summer the roots should have become established enough for planting out in the garden – about 30 cm apart. It also grows well in a pot in a sunny spot.

You can propagate by root division although this will not yield as many plants. Tarragon dies away to ground level in winter (except in very warm climates). The new shoots that appear early in the spring form a creeping root system and this is the time to strike. Sever 5 cm long pieces of the main root, together with a new shoot, and plant 30 cm apart. Within about two months these root cuttings will be roughly 45 cm high. In very cold climates, it is a good idea to keep the roots covered in winter with grass clippings or straw.

drying

As tarragon withers away in winter, it is important to preserve the leaves when they are in abundance. Harvest as the flower buds appear until late autumn, just before the leaves begin to turn yellow. Hang the leafy stalks in bunches, or spread them out on wire racks for quicker drying, in a warm, dry, airy place. When dry, strip the leaves by running your thumb and forefinger down the stem and store them in airtight, labelled containers away from the light.

eggs benedict

Not traditional eggs Benedict, in that it uses a béarnaise sauce instead of the traditional hollandaise. Purists may wish to omit the tarragon from the recipe for béarnaise.

4 bacon rashers, rinds removed

4 eggs

2 English muffins, split into halves

Béarnaise Sauce (see recipe on page 332)

French tarragon leaves for garnish

Grill or panfry the bacon until crisp, then set aside in a warm place. Poach the 4 eggs, and toast the muffin halves lightly.

To serve, place one muffin half on each plate, top with bacon and an egg, and pour the sauce over. Garnish with fresh tarragon and serve immediately.

Serves 4

béarnaise sauce

2 eggs, separated

90 g butter

1 tablespoon lemon juice

1 tablespoon fresh French tarragon

Separate the eggs and put the yolks in a blender. Whisk the egg whites to soft peaks. Melt the butter and lemon juice until just boiling. Switch on the blender and slowly pour the hot butter mixture onto the yolks; the mixture will thicken as the hot liquid cooks the yolks. Remove from the blender and stir in the chopped tarragon and whisked egg whites. This can be done slightly in advance and kept warm in a thermos.

Makes ½ cup

tarragon salsa

1 slice day-old bread, crusts removed

1 tablespoon tarragon vinegar

¼ cup tarragon leaves

¼ cup Italian parsley leaves

¼ cup virgin olive oil

1 clove garlic, crushed

salt and pepper

chilli powder (optional)

Place all the ingredients except salt, pepper and chilli in a food processor and process until finely chopped and blended. If necessary, add a little water to make the salsa a moister consistency. Add seasoning to taste and a pinch of chilli powder if desired. Store any unused salsa in a sealed container in the fridge for up to two weeks.

Makes about 1 cup

chicken breast fillet with tarragon salsa

2 tomatoes, peeled and seeded

1 large zucchini

4 medium-sized mushrooms, wiped

3 tablespoons virgin olive oil

1 onion, finely chopped

1 teaspoon sweet smoked paprika

salt and pepper

4 small chicken breast fillets, tenderloin removed

Tarragon Salsa (see this page)

Chop the tomatoes, zucchini, and mushrooms into small dice and set aside. Heat a little of the olive oil in a frying-pan, add the onion and sauté until just tender. Add the diced vegetables to the pan with the paprika and continue to cook until the zucchini has just become translucent but is still holding its shape. Add salt and pepper to taste. Meanwhile, brush the chicken lightly with oil and cook on a hot barbecue or grill.

Serve the chicken on a bed of the tomato mixture, topped with tarragon salsa.

Serves 4

thyme

garden thyme *Thymus vulgaris*

lemon thyme *T. citriodorus*

Got plenty of thyme on your hands?
Tired old puns aside, there
are countless varieties of
thyme, most of them more
decorative than culinary.

Also called common thyme
Flavour and aroma pungent, warming, slightly medicinal
Flavour group pungent

Ornamental varieties such as Westmoreland, golden, variegated lemon, and pretty, grey 'silver posy' thymes may be used in emergencies, but their flavour is not as pungent, nor as true. There are also a number of creeping, mat-like varieties, but they have such interwoven, tiny branches that the tedious job of trying to disentangle a sufficient quantity for cooking is simply not worthwhile.

choosing and using

Good old garden thyme and lemon thyme have the most value in the kitchen. With very small greyish-green leaves on wispy thin stems, garden thyme has a big, generous flavour that enhances many dishes and is an essential ingredient in many herb blends, such as mixed herbs (with sage and marjoram) and bouquet garni (with parsley, marjoram and a bay leaf).

Its savoury, pungent flavour is indispensable in almost any savoury food. You name it; you can put thyme with it. A short list of special marriages partners thyme with minced beef in all its forms, with Mediterranean-style vegetables, roast potatoes, and marinated olives.

In the Middle East the word *za'atar* refers to thyme, and is also the name of a mixed herb blend consisting of dried thyme, sesame seeds, sumac (or sumach) and salt. We saw a scrubby little hardy plant growing on a harshly bare hillside in Turkey, which was identified as *za'atar*. It did look a little like our domesticated thyme and definitely had a thyme-like flavour.

Lemon thyme has slightly larger, softer and greener leaves, and an unmistakable lemony fragrance overlaying the typical thyme scent is released when they are crushed. The mild flavour is particularly in demand with fish and chicken, omelettes, asparagus and all kinds of food where a hint of lemon is appropriate. It is sometimes used as an extra ingredient in a fines herbes blend, with chervil, chives, parsley and tarragon.

Fresh thyme can generally be bought in small bunches from produce markets or fruit and vegetable retailers, and the bunch will keep for over a week in the refrigerator. If thyme is kept too moist it will blacken and lose its flavour.

As thyme's foliage is so tiny, we think it an unnecessarily laborious job to strip the stalks for freezing a few leaves in ice-cube trays, particularly when this herb dries so well. You can freeze whole sprays of thyme if you really want to.

Dried thyme leaves should be grey-green and free from any bits of stem as these don't soften in cooking.

growing

Garden thyme is a tough little survivor – those grey-green leaves tell you that, as do the hard, woody stems at the base of this bushy 30 cm high plant. Like a small, noisy dog in next-door's yard, thyme delivers lots of punch for its size, and it's not to be ignored. The flowers are pinkish white and appear in spring in whorls at the tips of the branches. Lemon thyme has slightly larger and greener leaves and the spring-blooming flowers are deep pink. It has a spreading type of habit and only grows to about 5 cm high.

Garden thyme has extremely small seeds. Sow them in spring into a prepared seed box, or scatter straight into finely dug soil, keep moist, and thin out later to about 15 cm between plants. Propagating by root division is easy and can be done in spring. Alternatively, take tip cuttings approximately 10 cm long in late spring, inserting them into a pot of river sand, and keeping them watered. This method ensures good root systems very quickly. Once it's established, garden thyme will grow better and have more flavour in dry conditions than if you pamper and fertilise it. Cut the bushes back hard at the end of flowering and renew them every two years or so.

Propagating lemon thyme from seed is not recommended, as the seedlings may not be as fragrant as the parent plant. For this reason, the seed is not readily available, and propagation is either by tip cuttings or root division. For healthy plants, cut them back after flowering has finished and start again with fresh plants every two or three years.

drying

The taste and aroma of garden and lemon thymes are much more penetrating when they're dried. Harvest the leafy branches just before they start to flower for fullest flavour, and gather them on a dry day before midday. Hang little bunches in a shady, airy place, and when crisp-dry, strip off the leaves and seal in airtight containers.

choosing the right thyme . . .

Thyme is another of those herbs like basil where, thanks to its popularity, nurserymen have had a field day. There are over 100 varieties (and many cultivars); new ones seem to be 'discovered' every year. Many are decorative, aromatic plants that are ideal for rockeries or ground covers with their tiny, entangled, dense foliage. Others are mainly a source for essential oil.

As common names seem to vary from place to place – and garden shop to garden shop – make sure you know the botanical name too. Other culinary thymes you may find in your local garden shop include:

CARAWAY THYME – *T. herba-barona*
– a tough, frost-hardy ground cover that combines well with meaty dishes

LARGER WILD THYME OR
BROAD-LEAVED THYME – *T. pulegoides*
– can be used instead of common thyme in cooking

PIZZA THYME – *T. nummularius*
– a dense ground cover combining oregano and thyme flavours that's popular with pasta and tomato dishes

WILD (OR CREEPING) THYME – *T. serpyllum*
– another thyme that can be used instead of *T. vulgaris*

goat's cheese soufflés

We have Anneka Manning to thank very much for these sensational soufflés with good old garden thyme, from her book, *More Good Food* (Text Publishing, 2000). You can prepare the soufflés in advance and keep them in the refrigerator for up to 2 hours before baking. However, they will need about 5 minutes more in the oven if you make them this way.

a little melted butter

½ cup polenta for coating

80 g butter

75 g plain flour

2 cups milk

150 g soft goat's cheese, crumbled

1 teaspoon finely chopped fresh thyme leaves

4 egg yolks

salt and ground black pepper

6 egg whites at room temperature

Preheat the oven to 180°C. Brush the inside of 8 x 150 ml soufflé dishes with melted butter then coat with polenta, shaking out any excess. Place the dishes in a large ovenproof dish or roasting pan.

Melt the butter in a medium saucepan over medium heat. Add the flour and use a wooden spoon to stir until the mixture is smooth and beginning to bubble. Cook for 1 minute, stirring often. Remove from the heat and gradually add the milk, stirring until smooth and combined. Return to the heat and boil for 2 minutes, stirring constantly.

Remove from heat and stir in the goat's cheese and thyme. Spoon the mixture into a large bowl and set aside for 10 minutes to cool.

Add the egg yolks to the goat's cheese mixture and stir well to combine. Season to taste with salt and freshly ground black pepper.

Put the egg whites in a large bowl and whisk with an electric beater or balloon whisk until peaks form. Fold a large spoonful of egg whites into the goat's cheese mixture and stir until well combined. Gently fold in the remaining egg whites until just combined.

Divide the mixture between the prepared soufflé dishes. Add enough boiling water to the ovenproof dish or roasting pan to reach halfway up the sides of the soufflé dishes. Bake in a preheated oven for 25 minutes or until puffed up and golden.

Serves 8

vietnamese mint

Polygonum odoratum

Vietnamese mint is a bit of a phoney –
it really isn't a mint at all,
in spite of its peppery
mint flavour. It's actually
a *Polygonum*, which
literally translates to
'many knees'.

If you look at the purplish stems this makes sense, as there are little knee-like joints all along them, and roots can form at any of these spots.

The smooth leaves have an elegant spearmint shape, tapering to a long point, and on the dark green background there is a smaller darker shadow, as though someone has retraced the shape with a soft crayon. In open, sunny positions, this herbaceous perennial grows to 80 cm high, and is topped with dense clusters of tiny white or pink blossoms.

Vietnamese mint's common name of 'knotweed' is an apt description of its swollen, jointed stems. There are over 200 species of Polygonum, most of them purely decorative.

choosing and using

Vietnamese mint is absolutely vital in the Malaysian/ Singaporean laksa, and is an intrinsic part of most South-East Asian cuisine. In Thailand the shoots and leaves are eaten raw with *nam prik* or added to curries, while in Vietnamese cooking, they're used in salads or served with spring rolls. Finely shredded, the leaves make an excellent garnish.

You can buy Vietnamese mint in bunches from Asian specialty stores and some fruit and vegetable retailers. It will keep well for a couple of days in a glass of water in the refrigerator.

Pick and use fresh leaves as required. Vietnamese mint doesn't dry well, shrivelling down to nothing and losing its characteristic flavour.

growing

Vietnamese mint can be grown easily (almost too easily) in the garden or in a pot on the windowsill. Growing your own is a surefire way of ensuring consistent supply for most of the year, as it tends to be both prolific and rampant in the right conditions. In fact, if you place a few stems in a glass of water they will sprout roots within a few days. Plant the sprouted stems in a pot and let them establish until roots show from the drainage holes of the pot, then plant them out into the garden or a larger pot.

vietnamese mint
and prawn salad

1/2 bunch Vietnamese mint, leaves picked

1/2 bunch coriander, leaves picked

1 punnet cherry tomatoes, halved

2 shallots, peeled and finely sliced

1 Lebanese cucumber, halved, seeds scooped out and sliced

2 teaspoons fish sauce

2 teaspoons sesame oil

juice of 1 lime

1 long red chilli, finely chopped, seeds removed

2 teaspoons palm sugar

20 medium king prawns, cooked and peeled

Place the Vietnamese mint and coriander leaves in a large mixing bowl with the tomatoes, shallots and cucumber.

To make the dressing, combine the fish sauce, sesame oil, lime juice, chilli and sugar in a mortar and pestle and mix well.

Spoon half the dressing onto the salad ingredients, and toss very gently. Divide the salad between four plates, top each serving with a few prawns and sprinkle over the remaining dressing.

Serves 4 as an entrée

growing herbs

Tremendous satisfaction can be achieved by growing your own herbs and the wonderful thing about them is that they can occupy as much or as little space as you like.

Most herbs will grow as well in tubs and pots as they do in the garden, and a basic understanding of their requirements is all you need to grow them successfully.

Because the main objective when growing herbs is to have them on hand for everyday use in the kitchen, it is advisable to grow them in a spot that is close by. The ultimate 'kitchen garden', be it in the yard near the back door, in pots on a balcony or even in a window box in an apartment, is one that is accessible and enjoyed.

Herbs are pretty robust and have simple needs. After all, they have been around for millennia and have the ability to survive and prosper without our intervention. There are a few basic rules you need to follow to keep your herbs happy. Firstly herbs, like us, need sunshine and fresh air. We have rarely seen herbs grow well indoors so put them in a suitable position outside.

annuals and perennials

Many people have told us over the years that they have a completely 'brown thumb' and lament with comments such as 'I always kill my herbs, I don't know why I bother!'

What a lot of people are not aware of is the fact that a number of the herbs will only live for one season, and then die as part of their natural life cycle. These herbs are called *annuals* and a few which prosper for two years are called *biennials*. Herbs that do not die off after a season are called perennials, and the majority of *perennials* are reasonably robust looking shrubs.

Some annuals, such as coriander and basil, can't wait to grow up and bolt out in front of their peers to blossom early, flower prolifically, go to seed and then die. This seemingly inevitable fate can be arrested, although not indefinitely postponed. We suggest nipping these hormone-charged adolescents in the bud. Pick off the flower buds as soon as they appear. This will prevent them from flowering, then going to seed and finishing their life cycle.

Perennials are much easier to manage; however, they also need some care. Herbs such as thyme, sage, oregano and rosemary may become straggly and woody if they are not regularly harvested or pruned. At the end of summer, up to half of the foliage can be pruned from a perennial herb. This is the time to shape the plant, and rather than throwing the prunings away, dry the leaves to keep you going through winter when new growth will be slower to emerge.

soil and growing conditions

Herbs are relatively undemanding, which is an endearing quality when one considers how much they give back to us in flavour, aroma and efficacy. Nearly all herbs like friable, well-drained soil that has been conditioned with good compost.

Don't bombard herbs with fertilisers and expensive nutrients; they won't appreciate them. It is fascinating to observe how many herbs, when grown in relatively poor soil on rocky Turkish hillsides, will have a stronger flavour than their lush, pampered city-living counterparts. It is a bit like those home-grown tomatoes that never look as good as the ones bought in the supermarket. But in reality, the flavour of these seemingly meagre offerings is far superior to the highly fertilised, over-watered and mass-produced product.

To grow herbs in pots, tubs and hanging baskets there are just a few practical pointers for success.

- Make sure the container is big enough for the root system of the herb you are planting. As a basic rule of thumb, for shrubs, the depth of the pot should equal the height of the plant. So if you are planting common garden thyme that will grow to about 20 cm high, make sure the receptacle is at least 20 cm deep. For shrubs such as bay trees, the depth of the pot can be approximately one-third of the height the tree will grow to.
- Always use a good-quality potting mix, as proper potting mixes have been blended to have the optimum balance between water retention and good drainage.
- Put some pieces of broken pot or flat rocks in the bottom of the pot so it drains effectively and the soil is not washed out through the holes in the base.
- Place the pot in conditions that resemble the recommendations for the particular herb. Although most herbs need to be grown outdoors, their preferences range from semi-shade and well-sheltered to full sun and exposed to the elements.
- Most importantly, don't forget to water your pots. A herb in the garden will send its roots looking for moisture if you neglect it, and may just survive. A herb in a pot however is entirely dependent upon you to keep it watered. If the pot dries out completely, the roots have nowhere to go to look for moisture and the plant will die.

insects

Many common insects have inordinately good taste and will love your herbs as much as you do. The trouble is they may get to them first – even at 'snail's' pace.

Using insecticides is not a good idea for culinary herbs because residues may be left which could be harmful to your health. Vigilance and the use of natural insect repellents can be just as effective and is safe. One of our family favourites is a garlic spray that Mum used to make and the recipe for it is very easy.

garlic spray

3 large garlic heads, unpeeled

6 tablespoons medicinal paraffin oil

1 tablespoon oil-based soap, grated

2 cups hot water

To make the garlic solution, roughly chop the garlic and put it in a blender with the paraffin oil. Blend together then scrape the resulting pulp into a bowl, cover and leave for 48 hours. Stir grated soap into hot water and stir until melted. Mix the soap and water into the garlic mixture. When cool, strain the solution into screw-top jars and store in the refrigerator.

To spray the herbs, add 2 tablespoons of garlic solution to 2 litres of water.

Remember to repeat spraying after rain, as the previous dose will be washed off.

propagating herbs

You can buy herb plants from a variety of retailers. Nurseries and garden centres tend to stock the most complete ranges of herbs, while supermarkets and greengrocers will often sell them as well. Ask the assistant if the herbs have been 'outside hardened' as it is common for some mass producers to put plants on sale that have come straight to the megastore from an igloo (a kind of hothouse shaped like, well, an igloo) or glasshouse. These protected hothouse specimens can suffer from shock when exposed to the real world and once again you will erroneously blame your 'brown thumb'.

Once you have some herbs growing, a lot of satisfaction can be gained by propagating your own.

There are four main types of propagation: root division, taking cuttings, layering and sowing seeds.

root division

Herbs like mint and pennyroyal will spread and grow into sizeable clumps, so one way to keep them healthy and to propagate more plants is to divide them up. This is easily achieved by digging up the clump, carefully separating say a 20 cm root system into 5 smaller clumps of 4–5 cm and simply replanting.

cuttings

Growing plants from cuttings is an ancient form of propagation, which involves taking a piece of plant material and growing roots on it. Cuttings are most appropriate for firm-stemmed herbs like rosemary and the process is quite straightforward.

When taking cuttings (striking) from a parent plant, always keep them in water or wrapped in a damp cloth until ready to put into sand. Be sure they do not wilt. Use coarse river sand firmly packed into a pot for striking cuttings, never use beach sand as it is too fine and more than likely has residues of salt in it.

Take tip cuttings of reasonably firm growth about 10 cm long, cutting the stem just below a leaf node with a sharp knife or secateurs. Remove the leaves from the lower 4 cm that will be put into the sand and leave at least a third of the foliage on the top. When preparing cuttings, always pull off leaves with an upward pull, or use secateurs, to avoid tearing the bark on the cutting.

Never push cuttings into the sand, as this will damage the end and hinder the chances of making a successful strike. Always make a hole first using a skewer or pencil that is slightly thicker than the cutting. Moisten the ends of the cuttings and dip the bottom 1 cm into a suitable cutting powder (available from nurseries). Shake off excess powder and insert the lower third of the cutting into the hole in the sand. Try to cover at least two leaf nodes (the part where you carefully pulled the leaf off) and press the sand firmly around the cutting. Flood with water and be sure to keep cuttings moist *at all times*.

Place the pot (which may have many cuttings in it as long as they are about 2 cm apart) in a semi-shady spot, so the sun's rays do not dry out the sand too quickly or burn the cuttings.

After several weeks, depending upon the weather, the cuttings will have formed roots and can be separated and placed into separate pots to become established before re-planting into larger pots or out in the garden.

layering

Propagation by layering works on the same principle as taking cuttings, however you don't cut the stem off the host plant until it has formed roots.

Layering works best for plants that send out horizontal stems, or ones that can be easily bent down to ground level.

Select a length of stem and bend it down towards the ground. Trim off the leaves 5 cm on each side of the part that is touching the ground in exactly the same way as you would for a cutting.

Moisten a couple of leaf nodes, dust them with cutting powder and then bury them up to 2 cm below the surface. It is a good idea to push a little hoop of wire over the stem and into the ground to stop the stem from springing back out of the ground when you turn your back.

Keep the area well watered and again, in several weeks you can pull up the layered stem, cut it off the plant and it can be grown from its own, newly developed root system.

seeds

When sowing seeds always keep the seedbed moist at all times, as drying out, even for a short period, may cause germination to cease. A pot about 20 cm in diameter or a shallow trough filled with a 50/50 mix of river sand and soil is ideal.

Put the container on a level surface, as accidental over-watering or heavy rain can wash all the seeds to one end.

Tamp the sand-and-soil mix down flat with a small piece of wood and make furrows in the surface about 4 mm deep.

Sprinkle the seeds into the furrow; ideally there should be a few millimetres space between each seed.

Cover the seeds, making sure there are no lumps in the covering sand-and-soil mix.

Tamp the surface down again and give the whole surface a good soaking watering, but do it gently so the seeds are not disturbed or washed away.

When the seedlings are about 5 cm high, carefully remove them from the seedbed and re-pot into individual pots before replanting in larger pots or in the garden when appropriate.

lemon verbena

salad burnet

English spearmint

references

Gernot Katzner Spice Pages, www.ang.kfunigraz.ac.at/~katzner/index.html

Grieve, M., *A Modern Herbal Vol. 1 & 2*, Hafner Publishing Co., New York, 1959

Hemphill, Ian, *Spice Notes*, Macmillan, Sydney, 2000; second edition 2006

Hemphill, Ian, *Spice Travels*, Macmillan, Sydney, 2002

Hemphill, John and Rosemary, *Herbs, Their Cultivation and Usage*, Lansdowne, Sydney, 1993; revised edition 2005

Hemphill, John and Rosemary, *What Herb Is That?* Lansdowne, Sydney, 1995

Hemphill, Rosemary, *Fragrance & Flavour* (revised edition), Hardie Grant Books, Melbourne, 2002

Purseglove, J.W., Brown E.G., Green C.L. and Robbins S.R.J., *Spices (Tropical Agriculture Series)* Vol. 1 & 2, Longman Group Limited, London, 1981

Rosengarten, Jr. F., *The Book of Spices*, Jove Publications, New York, 1973

Solomon, C., *Encyclopedia of Asian Food*, Hamlyn Australia, Kew, 1996

Spices Board India (Ministry of Commerce Govt. of India), *Indian Spices — A Catalogue*, Cochin, 1992

Stobart, T., *Herbs, Spices and Flavourings*, Grub Street, London, 1998

Stuart, M., *The Encyclopedia of Herbs and Herbalism*, Paul Hamlyn, Sydney, 1979

Von Welanetz, D. & P., *The Von Welanetz Guide to Ethnic Ingredients*, J.P. Tarcher Inc., Los Angeles, 1982

acknowledgements

Our loving thanks and gratitude to John and Rosemary Hemphill for generously sharing information from their many books, particularly *What Herb Is That?* And to our dear family for their unfailing support in everything we undertake, especially Kate, who has created several recipes and given helpful comments on the manuscript.

Among the people who have been so helpful over the years we would like to particularly thank Dr P.S.S Thampi, Director of Publicity, Spices Board of India. Others to whom we are indebted are the Gaya family in Papantla, Mexico for introducing us to vanilla in its native habitat; Craig Semple and his associate Yomi who arranged for us to meet the sumac producers in Nizip; and the delightful Dzoanh and his wife Oanh who showed us the cassia forests of Hhe Dua.

Because we are spice merchants and not chefs, we asked friends and colleagues who are food writers and chefs to allow us to use their recipes which we feel best illustrate the uses of the spices and herbs. Our grateful thanks to the following writers and of course to their publishers: Sean Anderson, Mark Best, Kerrie Cant, Hideo Dekura, Margaret Fulton, Lucio Galleto and Timothy Fisher, Anthony Gardiner, Richard Hauptman, Robbie Howard, Ajoy Joshi, Jennice and Raymond Kersh, Lisa Lintner, Anneka Manning, Amy Nathan, Charmaine Solomon, Carol Selva Rajah, Tony Tan, Gretta Anna Teplitzky, Kellie Ann Travers and Sophia Young.

Many thanks to Greg Elms for the beautiful photography, Sara Backhouse for the food styling and Minimax for the generous loan of props. And a very big thank you to the creative Hardie Grant team who turned our manuscript into such a beautiful book: Foong Ling Kong, Lucy Malouf, senior editor Jasmin Chua, designer Ellie Exarchos and our publisher, Mary Small.

Our staff, both at the factory and shop, have been wonderful. If they hadn't been so reliable, we would never have had the time to work on this book.

Huge, huge thanks go to our slave-driving friend Philippa Sandall, who has researched, kept tabs on where were up to, pushed when necessary, and always been her wonderful positive self.

index